CRUSADER WARFARE

Crusader Warfare

VOLUME I

Byzantium, Europe and the Struggle for the Holy Land 1050–1300 AD

David Nicolle

hambledon continuum

Hambledon Continuum is an imprint of Continuum Books
Continuum UK, The Tower Building, 11 York Road, London SE1 7NX
Continuum US, 80 Maiden Lane, Suite 704, New York, NY 10038

www.continuumbooks.com

First published 2007

British Library Cataloguing-in-Publication Data
A catalogue record for this book is available from the British Library.

ISBN 978 1 84725 030 8

Typeset by Egan Reid, Auckland, New Zealand
Printed and bound by MPG Books Ltd, Cornwall, Great Britain

Contents

Illustrations

Between pages 178 and 179

For Prof. Vassilios Christides,

for opening so many new windows onto what was really happening during these centuries.

Introduction

To a large extent the current interest in the Crusades reflects the perceived threat of a so-called 'clash of civilisations'. While warnings of such a supposed clash in our own times are based upon a misunderstanding of the natures of both 'Western' and 'Islamic' civilisations, some commentators have looked to the medieval Crusades as an earlier example of such a confrontation. In reality they were no such thing. Instead the Crusades resulted from a remarkable variety of political, economic, cultural and religious factors. The Crusades, even excluding the Northern or Baltic Crusades, also involved an extraordinary array of Christian states, ruling dynasties, ethnic or linguistic groups and the fighting forces associated with these disparate participants.

This book focusses on what might be called the Mediterranean Crusades which are assumed to include crusading campaigns and associated military activities in the Balkans, the Black Sea, along the Atlantic coasts of the Iberian peninsula and north-west Africa. It will not, however, deal with those internal crusades of medieval Latin or Catholic Christendom such as the Albigensian Crusade or the Papal Crusades within Italy, except where the forces involved throw light upon the broader Mediterranean Crusades.

Strictly speaking the states created as a result of the First Crusade in greater Syria, of the Third Crusade in Cyprus, of the Fourth Crusade around the Aegean and southern Balkans, should be referred to as Latin rather than Crusader States because the Western Europeans or 'Franks' who settled in these areas cannot really be described as Crusaders.[1] Instead they became residents who fought to defend or expand their territories while also joining forces with newly arrived Crusader armies from Europe. Only in the latter cases did they once again become, to some extent, Crusaders. On the other hand the Latin States on the Middle Eastern mainland, most particularly the Kingdom of Jerusalem, became what could be described as a huge religious relic to be defended, and its defenders were partially motivated by those same factors which caused their western cousins to go on Crusade in the first place.

Although this book does not look at the Baltic Crusades, the decision to leave these campaigns aside was an arbitrary and potentially even misleading one. Latin or Catholic Europe certainly had an 'eastern front'. Initially this ran from the Adriatic Sea across the northern Balkans and east-central Europe to the Baltic Sea, with a further but by no means isolated 'front' in northern Scandinavia. Medieval Europeans, and certainly the knightly class which came to bear the brunt of Crusading warfare, would have seen all these fronts as part of Latin Christendom's struggle against outsiders. The latter ranged from infidels to schismatics, pagans and other 'enemies of God'. The decision to exclude Crusading or Christian frontier warfare north of the Carpathian Mountains does not reflect any real military or even political factors on the Latin side of the 'front'. It is based solely upon which enemies were to be included and which excluded. As a result, Mongols are to some extent 'in' but Orthodox Christian Russians are 'out', despite the fact that Orthodox Byzantines, Bulgarians, Serbs and other Balkan peoples are 'in'.

On the other hand, this study attempts to leap beyond the Islamic World to look at Christian armies whose actions or mere existence in sub-Saharan Africa had a bearing upon military, political and economic relations between Christendom and Islam within the Mediterranean world.

The Byzantine Empire, with other non-Latin but Christian states and their armies, have their own section within this book. Not only were they occasional, and in the case of the Byzantine Empire frequent, victims of Western Crusader aggression, but their armies were to a large extent based upon military traditions which differed from those of Western or even Central Europe. Although there was also considerable and increasing overlap or similarity, these variations remained significant. Furthermore, such differences can only be properly understood if the different military heritage of these cultures is recognised.

Of course the phenomenon of the Crusades cannot be understood without looking at prior events. These were not only the conquest of most of the eastern and middle eastern Islamic world by the Seljuk Turks and the Byzantine loss of Anatolia to these same Turks, but also the rise of Italian naval power in the Mediterranean, the establishment of a warlike Norman state in southern Italy and its conquest of Islamic-ruled Sicily and, of course, the early phases of what became known as the Christian Reconquista in the Iberian peninsula.

There were, of course, major variations between the military forces and potentials of those regions which would be involved in what can be called Crusading warfare from the 11th to early 14th centuries, not to mention those peripheral areas which were drawn into these conflicts. Nothing could be more inaccurate or misleading than to see all 'Crusaders' as alike. Similarly, what could be called the pre-existing military-political status quo in these widespread regions varied enormously, as did the socio-economic foundations, wealth and international connections of such regions.

As already stated, the military and economic expansion of Western Christendom had begun well before the First Crusade, and the Muslims were only one of its victims. In some areas, notably southern Italy and the Balkans, Orthodox fellow-

Christians were already on the receiving end of Latin Christian expansionism, as were the remaining pagan peoples of eastern and north-eastern Europe.

Elsewhere non-Muslims, most notably Christians of various churches regarded as heretical by Latin Western European churchmen, formed substantial and economically powerful minorities. The fact that they continued to exist, and indeed to flourish, says much for the tolerance or cultural self-confidence of the Islamic ruling communities. This would, however, change during the course of the Crusades and associated Christian assaults upon the Islamic world.

All these factors formed the general background of the Crusades. Then came the event which served as the immediate catalyst. The Seljuk Turkish conquest of the Middle East during the second half of the 11th century altered a long-established yet fluid status quo and caused a major disruption of international trade. This was followed by a prolonged and widespread Western European assault upon the Islamic Mediterranean, justified and to some extent motivated by religion. Such an assault eventually led to a Western European, or more particularly Italian, domination of Mediterranean maritime trade. The relative importance of secular, economic and political motivation and that of religious enthusiasm remains a matter of debate. It probably always will, and to a large extent such an argument sheds more light on the values of its own time and place than it does upon the personal priorities of those who went on Crusade.

Another factor which is too often ignored is that of relative population sizes and densities. All sides tended to proclaim that their enemies greatly outnumbered themselves, not only on the battlefield but in general. The foe tended to be numberless as well as nameless, and as early Western historians have largely relied upon European sources they have too often assumed that Islamic armies were huge, and that the defeat or even annihilation of a Muslim fighting force was of little significance to an Islamic society whose manpower resources were so great – and so fanatical – that armies could be easily replaced. In reality there tended to be more fanaticism on the Latin Christian side while the numerical population advantage may also have been with the Europeans. In the 10th century, France and the Low Countries had about six million people, Italy around five million, Germany and Scandinavia some four million, the British Isles two million, Poland and Hungary perhaps one million each. Furthermore, most of these figures would triple by the late 13th century.

Not only were the populations of the Christian states of Western and Central Europe almost uniformaly Latin Catholic and Christian but the military aristocracy of Latin Europe was expanding rapidly. It was also taking advantage of the economic expansion which characterised Europe to reproduce at a surprising rate. One might even say that the knights of Western and Central Europe formed the 'seething mass'; not the Saracens, the Turks or the Moors. Add to this the fact that in many significant regions the military élites were actually expanding faster than the similarly expanding economy could comfortably maintain, then Latin Europe had suitable and motivated manpower for a period of aggressive expansion. Meanwhile, what remained of Byzantine territory in Greece and the Balkans had an estimated population of around five million, with another four million being temporarily regained for Byzantium in western and coastal Anatolia.[2]

Similarities between the religious motivations of the Christian Crusade and of the Islamic Jihad are astonishing, yet this was probably not a result of mutual influence. Instead it seems more likely that both emerged from common ancient roots which included both Old Testament Judaic, Romano-Byzantine and early Christian concepts of religiously justified warfare. It is also interesting to note that religious authorities such as the Pope tended to be more keen on major battles to 'settle' the rivalry between these two faiths than were most of the rulers, commanders or soldiers immediately involved.[3] Indeed, the shock expressed by Western chroniclers at a supposed alliance between the Byzantine Empire and Saladin at the time of the Third Crusade sounds very hollow, given the efforts which several Latin Christian states put into maintaining good commercial relations with their Islamic partners. On the other hand such relationships highlighted the major role of realpolitik during the Crusades. The Sultan of Egypt-Syria and the Byzantine Emperor of Constantinople faced common foes or rivals in the eastern Mediterranean, and within a few years the next Crusade – the Fourth – would be diverted from its intended target, Saladin's successor, against the ruler of the Byzantine Empire.

While the religious and political realities of the Crusades were more complex than is generally realised, the military realities of Crusading warfare have been even more obscured by myth and misconception. There is still a widespread tendency to see the history of warfare in terms of major battles and to regard campaigns of devastation or raiding as somehow second-rate, inferior or lacking in strategy. Where the medieval period is concerned, this approach is wholly wrong. Although medieval commanders tended to avoid full-scale battles for a variety of reasons – not merely the uncertainty of their outcome or fear of irreversible defeat – there were many occasions when a commander felt confident or desperate enough to risk everything. In fact set-piece battles were just one of several aspects of medieval warfare, as were sieges and campaigns of devastation, each to be employed when the circumstances seemed correct. Meanwhile the taking of fortified places remained central to medieval strategy, especially during the Crusades and related conflicts.

Another enduring myth is that knightly cavalry dominated early and high medieval European warfare; similarly that offence dominated defence until a revival of effective infantry in the later medieval period led to a period during which defence tended to have supremacy over attack. More recently historians of medieval warfare have highlighted the fact that military success, especially in battle, usually resulted from an effective combination of horse and foot, just as it did throughout pre-20th century history. Furthermore the clear tactical if not strategic limitations of infantry during this particular period, at least in some parts of Europe and the Islamic world, did not reflect some supposed 'age of cavalry' but more an 'age of bad infantry'. Even this is an oversimplification, as the evidence shows that highly effective foot soldiers were characteristic of a great many periods and places. Similarly, developments such as the adoption of stirrups during the early medieval period, improvements in weapons such as composite bows and crossbows, and highly visible but sometimes rather superficial changes in armour, had only marginal influence upon the balance of power between men on horses and men on foot.[4] Changes in this balance were almost always the result of political, social or economic rather than technological factors.

Before leaving this question of cavalry-versus-infantry and the widespread assumptions about their relative marching capabilities, it is worth noting that even in modern conflicts such as those in Afghanistan, the endurance of a peasant army has proved much greater than that of Westerners, especially over long distances. Furthermore it has long been clear that men can march for much longer without prolonged rests than can horses. They are also better able to cope with difficult terrain or to make use of short cuts which are too steep, boggy, rocky or lacking in grazing for horses. Even where conditions seem to favour horsemen the records show that, at the end of a full day's march, infantry often reached camp only an hour after the cavalry. Furthermore, foot soldiers could settle to eat or rest almost immediately, whereas the cavalryman still had to unsaddle, feed and water his mount before looking after himself.[5]

Then there is the matter of discipline, command and control. All too often historians still tend to assume that these were virtually lacking in medieval warfare. However, the evidence shows that on all sides of Crusading warfare, there were armies which showed considerable discipline, organisation and training. There were also plenty of rabbles. At the same time the most successful commanders of this period tended to be those who understood the limitations, not only of their troops but of their own ability to control such armies. These limitations themselves reflected inadequate systems of communication and transport rather than inadequate skill, knowledge or experience on the part of both leaders and men. Even the sometimes seemingly irrational behaviour of those involved might only appear irrational from a modern standpoint. Stephen Morillo has noted the importance of other cultural imperatives which were entirely understandable within their own cultural contexts, especially where medieval military commanders were concerned: '*... their rational concerns often included notions of personal honour, prestige, religious imperatives, superstition, and so on that we do not readily recognize as relevant to strategy, especially in the context of* *statecraft.*'[6] This was, however, written prior to some recent irrational examples of modern warfare, especially in the Middle East.

Questions of transport and communications will be looked at in greater detail later. However, the Mediterranean imposed certain basic parameters on all who used it. Almost all sailing was undertaken during those months from spring to autumn when the seas were 'open' – in other words not during the winter when the weather permitted only the most urgent of voyages. Furthermore, navigation in the Mediterranean and its connected inland seas was largely by using islands and peninsulas as stepping stones. The main sailing routes tended to follow the coasts while open water was normally only crossed when there was no alternative and where the distances involved were relatively small. These features were most obvious along the east–west sealanes, but were also true of those running north–south. Only when this is fully understood can the vital strategic significance of major eastern Mediterranean islands such as Crete, Rhodes and Cyprus be appreciated.

1

Western Europe and the Crusader States

THE MILITARY TECHNOLOGICAL BACKGROUND

Only an economically expanding, relatively rich and socially diverse Europe could have sustained the Crusading movement for as long as it did. Before the catastrophic plague known as the Black Death struck in the mid-14th century, Europe was enjoying one of the most notable economic, population and cultural flowerings in its history.

Although the First Crusade did not take place until the very last years of the 11th century, the era of aggressive Western European, Latin Catholic Christian expansion started half a century earlier. The last mainland fragments of the Latin or so-called Crusader States in the Middle East were lost in the final decade of the 13th century, yet military efforts by Latin Christians to confront Islam in the eastern Mediterranean region would continue for many more years. A similar and more successful military campaign was maintained in the Baltic region, in the so-called Northern Crusades, and all such efforts were dependent upon support from the heartlands of Western European civilisation.

To take just one of Western Christendom's expanding frontiers as an example, what became known as the Reconquista really got under way in the Iberian peninsula during the 11th century. Here the seemingly poor and rather backward Christian states of northern Spain could draw upon the financial, moral and often physical resources of the rest of Europe, north of the Pyrenees. To their south lay the richer, more sophisticated, more populous Islamic province of al-Andalus, but this was now politically fragmented and culturally unprepared to face a serious military assault from the north. Acute political fragmentation was, in fact, characteristic of most of the 11th century Islamic world, but only in al-Andalus did Muslims as yet face such a growing and determined threat.

The following century would witness what has become known as Europe's Twelfth Century Renaissance. In addition to an astonishing flowering of art, architecture and literature, the 12th and 13th centuries were characterised by a new attitude towards technology. This more positive view of 'the mechanical arts' was, in part, a result of trading and cultural contacts with the Islamic world where such an attitude had always existed. Religion remained at the very core of both Christian and Islamic medieval civilisations, but now educated Western Europeans gradually came to believe that the application of practical knowledge could help rather than hinder man's search for salvation. This was clearly seen in the *Didascalicon* written by Hugh of St Victor early in the 12th century, not long after the First Crusade. In it the author included a section which listed and named various types of arms and armour. Though old-fashioned in content and far from representing the cutting edge of 12th century Western European military technology, it did betray a new scholarly attitude towards such things.[1] Even the Second Lateran Council's ban on the use of bows and crossbows against fellow Christians, because they were too 'murderous', had a practical aspect. Whereas they were feared as a threat to the European social order, they were recognised as being highly effective weapons and could therefore be used against 'infidels' and other enemies of the Latin Church.

Latin Europe was far from being uniform in terms of military power or potential. France and its cultural colony, England, have been seen as military archetypes for the Christian side of Crusader warfare. France, if not England and the rest of the British Isles, certainly lay at the very heart of the movement. Yet the apparently precocious development of sophisticated military organisation and tactics in an area such as mid-11th century Anjou may reflect the greater abundance of information about this specific region rather than Anjou's superiority over other parts of France. Nevertheless it is worth noting the down-to-earth, practical rather than overtly chivalric attitude towards warfare in Anjou during the second half of the 11th century; similarly the important role played by trained and effective foot soldiers. This was, of course, precisely the period when the mailed knight with his lance, long shield, heavy sword and supposedly heavy horse is widely thought to have been almost the only effective fighting man in Western Europe.

In this context it is perhaps worth noting that laws restricting the use or carrying of weapons by lower social classes in France did not come into effect until the second half of the 12th century. Local armed men drawn from a wider group than merely the rising class of *milites*, knights or professional fighting men, had long been necessary for the maintenance of local law and order. They clearly played a major role in the Peace movements which became a feature of many parts of southern France. These were virtually swept away by the imposition of royal power in the wake of the 13th century Albigensian Crusade. How far such legal and structural changes to the rights of ordinary men to bear arms in France had an effect on recruitment for, or participation in, the later Crusades is unclear. What is certain is that the Crusading armies which travelled from Europe to the Middle East became ever more professional, while participation by enthusiastic amateurs declined numerically and in military significance.

In military terms The Empire, which consisted of Germany and some neighbouring territories plus a large part of Italy, was organised in a somewhat different fashion to France or Plantagenet England (see below). However, the armies of

The Empire had similar military or technological backgrounds. One has to look slightly further east, to Hungary, to find a truly different military heritage; one that was different enough to cause problems of cooperation and understanding even when facing a common foe. Yet even here, on one of the least recognised 'fronts' of Crusader warfare, the military systems common throughout most of Western Europe were already gaining ground.

Throughout most of the 10th century, Magyar Hungarian military systems and equipment were based upon what has been called the nomad tradition, a tradition common among peoples of the north Eurasian forests like the Magyars themselves as well as the Turco-Mongol peoples of the steppes further south. While the Hungarian army which defeated a significant German invasion in 1030 was still largely traditional, from the late 10th century onwards Hungarian military culture gradually became more like that of their Central and East European neighbours. So it is interesting to note the disappearance of 'eastern' style tanged arrowheads from the graves of even nomadic or semi-settled communities within Hungary and their replacement by 'western' style socket arrowheads in the 12th and 13th centuries.[2]

Thoughout the rest of the 11th century, these new-style Hungarian forces were largely concentrated in the northern frontier regions facing The Empire, Poland and Kievan Russia which continued to pose the most immediate threat. Hungary seems to have been less concerned about the south,[3] and it was around the same time as the defeat of the German invasion in 1030 that the Hungarian Kingdom finally took effective control of the south-eastern provinces of the Carpathian basin. Here, in Transylvania, the local largely non-Magyar peoples had been in closer cultural contact with Byzantium than with Western Europe.[4] Along this frontier Hungary faced not only the Byzantine Empire but also the largely Turkish, supposedly tribal and still to some extent nomadic peoples of the western reaches of the Eurasian steppes. Here Hungary would soon be involved in campaigns which had much in common with the wider Crusading movement, yet local forces remained remarkably traditional and very different from those of the rest of Central and Western Europe. It would also be here, and across the Carpathian Mountains in Wallachia and Moldavia, that the German Crusading Military Order would, briefly, be invited to bolster and extend Hungarian control in the early 13th century.[5]

Italy was again different, though the north and centre of the country shared essentially the same military-technological heritage as France and Germany. It is also important to realise that Italy played a far more important role in the Crusades than is generally recognised, even though this participation was largely outside those numbered Crusades which tend to dominate histories of Crusading warfare. Italy's contribution largely reflected its very different political, economic and social situation. For a start, Italy was more urbanised than the rest of Europe and during the 11th century most Italian cities were dominated by bishops, though forming part of broader states such as The Empire. Such urban bishops, being secular as well as spiritual leaders, had military forces consisting of *primi milites* or *milites majores* who were more or less comparable to the later knights, with men of lower status also being obliged to serve. As a consequence of the larger populations characteristic of northern and central Italian cities, major battles tended to involve larger armies than elsewhere in Europe. Substantial numbers of fighting men, either professionals or well-trained part-timers, were similarly available for service elsewhere, should they wish to volunteer for a Crusade or a warlike naval trading expedition.

There were several reasons behind the success of Italian urban communal armies during the 12th and 13th centuries. These included wealth, weapons production, discipline and highly developed political or diplomatic skills. The armies in question were characterised by closer and more effective cooperation between cavalry and infantry, which itself reflected intense urban patriotism, than what could currently be seen beyond the Alps. While northern Italy may thus have led the way in a revival of effective infantry forces within Europe, the widespread belief that Italy also led the way in the use of crossbows is probably misleading. In fact the first clear reference to the use of large numbers of crossbows in warfare in northern Italy was during the 1140s, in Piacenza and Genoa. Instead there is strong evidence that such weapons were already in common use in other parts of Mediterranean Western Europe, not to mention the Islamic world.

Enthusiasm for aggression against the Islamic coasts of the Mediterranean, or what might be called a proto-Crusading mentality, was widespread in several parts of 11th century Italy. It was not, however, universal or evenly spread. Pisa and Genoa were notably keen on 'holy war' before the First Crusade, and Muslims were widely seen as 'enemies of God' whose slaughter should be celebrated.[6] Pisa led the way, but much of the wealth of later 11th century Genoa came from raiding and piracy against Islamic Sicily and North Africa.[7] Venice and Amalfi were less aggressive, Amalfi in particular focussing on its long established and largely peaceful trading connections with Egypt and North Africa.

In some military and cultural respects the expanding Christian states of the Iberian peninsula were similar to the Latin States that would be established in the Middle East in the wake of the First Crusade. In both regions the Christians initially sought to expand their territory at the expense of their Muslim neighbours, but whereas the Latin States soon stalled, the Christian states of what are now Spain and Portugal continued to grow, albeit in fits and starts, until the fall of Granada in 1492 marked the completion of their 'Reconquista'. There were even similarities in the geographical and ecological circumstances in which their campaigns were fought. For centuries Arab literature had drawn poetic parallels between the lands and delights of al-Sham and al-Andalus, Syria and Iberia. Here, at opposite ends of the Mediterranean Sea, pastoralism had been as important as agriculture and in both lands this had a profound effect upon warfare.

The main animals raised on the upland plains of the Iberian peninsula were sheep, cattle and horses while the main crops grown in the watered valleys and irrigated areas around towns were cereals and vines. However, the Muslims' greater reliance on agriculture, as well as their highly developed and extensive irrigation systems, made them more vulnerable to the economic raiding warfare characteristic of this period.[8] Much has been made of the medieval Spaniards' supposed 'frontier mentality', especially by American historians, yet this can be overstated. Nor was an expansionist and aggressive mentality confined to the Iberian Christians. It was also seen in eastern Germany, Scandinavia, amongst the Anglo-Norman settlers in Ireland and amongst many peoples within the medieval Islamic world. Furthermore the supposed freedom enjoyed by those Christian settlers who moved into the Douro valley after the Muslims fell back was short lived and was lost during the 11th century.

The Christian states of northern Iberia received little outside help after the mid-12th century, and largely conducted their Reconquista using their own military resources. Here, even more obviously than elsewhere, major battles were almost always the culmination of several other events. Nevertheless, by the late 12th century, there seems to have been a widespread assumption on the northern side of the religious frontier that a complete Christian 'reconquest' of the Iberian peninsula was inevitable. By the 13th century it was clear that many Spaniards and Portuguese hoped, perhaps even expected, to extend their 'reconquests' to the Atlantic coast of Morocco. By the end of the medieval period some religious thinkers envisaged the possibility of an Iberian Crusade marching the length of North Africa to 'liberate' Jerusalem.

Meanwhile the Christian regions of northern Iberia retained many military differences that they had inherited from earlier centuries. Asturias and Galicia had in effect been cut off from the rest of Christian Western Europe since the 8th century and some historians maintain that they preserved Visigothic military features. In reality, however, these were more likely to have reflected a strong Arab-Andalusian Islamic military influence and a relative lack of corresponding French influence. A southern French influence was soon apparent in León and Castile, being even stronger in Navarre, Aragon and above all Catalonia. Meanwhile the separate political identity of newly emerged Portugal would not be accepted by its Spanish neighbours for many decades while its military traditions remained very close to those of Islamic al-Andalus until the reforms of the 14th century.

Competition and occasional warfare between these Christian states sometimes served the interests of the Islamic states in their own struggle to survive. For example, Castile lent military help to neighbouring Muslims in order to stop further Aragonese expansion after the latter captured Huesca in 1096 – the same year that the first armies of the First Crusade set out for the Holy Land. The more accommodating attitude of Iberian Christianity towards Islam resulted in what came to be known as *convivencia*, the ability of different religious communities to live side-by-side with some degree of toleration. The depth as well as the limitations of *convivencia* are seen in the fate of a Christian who converted to Islam in the Kingdom of Aragon in 1269, long after the area in question had been conquered by Christian arms. This man was disinherited but otherwise seems to have been left to live his new life in peace.[9]

A different geo-political and military situation existed in another of Latin Christendom's frontier zones, namely southern Italy. This had enjoyed an economic and cultural boom during the 9th and 10th centuries, being divided between several Byzantine coastal enclaves or provinces like Greek-speaking Calabria, the Lombard Duchies of the interior and Islamic-ruled Sicily, plus some short-lived Islamic outposts on the mainland. During the 11th century, Byzantine cultural domination of the southern Italian mainland almost led to a political takeover, with a substantial influx of soldiers and Greek settlers changing the character of largely Lombardic areas like Apulia. As a result the strong Byzantine flavour of Apulia was a recent phenomenon when the Normans arrived only a few years later. This probably accounted for the ease with which the local people collaborated with the Norman newcomers and rapidly accepted them as rulers. Meanwhile Byzantine efforts to reconquer Sicily had failed dismally. It is also important to note that the second half of the 11th century was a particularly violent and destructive period, drawing in Norman, Imperial German and Imperial Byzantine armies. The Arab-Islamic attacks of the 9th century had caused much less damage.[10]

The Norman conquest of Islamic-ruled Sicily is sometimes seen as a local version of the Iberian Reconquista but it is probably more correct to regard it as a proto-Crusade. This campaign was much more rapid than the Reconquista and it eventually brought into the orbit of Latin Catholic Christendom a region whose cultural and religious heritage had previously looked eastward and southward rather than northward. Sicily remained the powerhouse of a new Norman kingdom which included virtually the whole of the southern Italian mainland. This Norman 'kingdom in the sun' would make a major contribution to the First Crusade but would play a very minor military role in subsequent Crusades. This probably reflected the Norman rulers' desire not to alienate their large Islamic population in Sicily, a population whose military role continued long after the fall of the Norman kingdom itself.

Militarily significant as these Sicilian Muslims might have been, Sicily would eventually witness massive immigration from the north under Norman, Hohenstauffen and Angevin rule. As a result an island which had previously been largely Greek-speaking Orthodox Christian or Arabic-speaking Muslim became largely Latin Christian and Italian-speaking. While the Greeks were gradually though not entirely absorbed, the Muslims either converted to Christianity or migrated to North Africa or into the rugged interior of Sicily itself. Their first major rebellions against persecution came in the 1190s and were not finally crushed until the 1240s. The remnants then joined other ex-Sicilian Muslims who had been forcibly transferred to new Islamic colonies on the mainland at Lucera in Apulia and Girifalco in Calabria. During the 12th century the Norman rulers had attempted to extend their conquests to Islamic North Africa, but by the end of the Crusader period all that remained of these ambitious campaigns were the islands of Pantaleria and Lampedusa which, like Sicily, became Italian-speaking, and Malta and Gozo which retain their Maltese-Arabic dialect to this day. Islamic communities survived on each of these islands for many years before eventually converting to Christianity.

The military and technological background or context in which the First Crusade operated, and in which the Latin States of the Middle East were established, was remarkably complex (see chapter 2 on Byzantium and the Orthodox Christian States, and volume II on the Islamic World). The Byzantine Empire, though defeated and suffering massive territorial losses in the aftermath of the battle of Manzikert (1071), had been the regional great power before that battle. Many fortifications had been built or greatly strengthened in north-western Syria by the Byzantines during the 10th century apogee of their military revival. The Citadel of Antioch was just one example while the inner fortifications at Sahyun, the Saone of the Crusaders, was another.

The First Crusade itself was a campaign unlike any other, including all subsequent Crusades. It has been well described by Jonathan Riley-Smith as an army, or perhaps a number of armies, on pilgrimage and it drew upon the tradition of large group pilgrimages which had characterised the 11th century.[11] The size of the First Crusade, even when the unsuccessful advance parties led by Peter the Hermit and others were excluded, was astonishing and overwhelmed the first Islamic forces which attempted to bar its progress. During the siege of Nicaea in 1097, for example, there were probably from 4,200 to 4,500 cavalry and some 30,000 infantry, excluding any Byzantine support. Thereafter casualties and desertion were massive while losses in horses were even worse. Yet even at the final siege of Jerusalem in 1099 the Crusader force was still around 1,200 to 1,300 knights – many now lacking horses – out of a total force of perhaps 12,000 men.[12] It was almost certainly these numbers, plus religious frenzy, which enabled this First Crusade to achieve such staggering success, especially in siege warfare, under what might otherwise have been considered impossible circumstances.

To what extent those First Crusaders, their commanders and siege engineers learned to improve their skills and techniques during a long march from

Constantinople to Jerusalem remains a matter of debate. Most of the participants returned home once Jerusalem had been conquered. Nevertheless, those who remained, plus the small numbers who travelled east to join them during the early decades of the 12th century, went on to control up to three-fifths of the land and population of the cultivable parts of al-Sham or greater Syria.

Here they established four so-called Crusader or Latin States: the County of Edessa, the Principality of Antioch, the County of Tripoli and the Kingdom of Jerusalem. Each state faced different military problems and had different strategic priorities. The northern tier, consisting of Edessa and Antioch, were so close to Anatolia that they could not avoid becoming embroiled in the quarrels of the Byzantine Empire, the Cilician Armenians, the Seljuk and the Danishmandid Turks. Edessa also had a militarily open frontier to the east which lacked strong natural defences. Beyond lay the populous Islamic land of the Jazira (Mesopotamia) from which the first effective Islamic military responses to the Crusader conquests would shortly be launched.

The first seven or eight decades of the 12th century would be the high point of success as far as the Latin States were concerned. Yet the seeds of their failure had already been sown. Because of the military, political and social traditions which the Crusaders brought with them from Western Europe, these settler states needed land to maintain their feudal military structures. For long-term survival they either had to win land by crushing the neighbouring inland Islamic political and urban centres, or they had to evolve into an urban coastal military system dependent upon trade for the money with which to maintain armies. However, these Latin States lacked the manpower for the former option and were culturally unprepared for the latter option, at least until the later 13th century when it was already too late. Similarly the Crusaders' failure to expand meant that the states they created had to maintain large armies to defend their extensive and sometimes highly vulnerable frontiers. Only where these frontiers reached the edges of real deserts could they be regarded as stable. Such desert frontiers were few and were soon lost.

Then there was the persistent question of military manpower, numbers and identity. The majority of early Crusader settlers are believed to have married local women, presumably Christians or enslaved Muslims. The result was a second generation who were in many ways Middle Eastern in outlook and way of life, while still being separated from the indigenous population by religion and what might be called their élite caste. These were the so-called *poulains* who were so unfairly despised by newcomers from Europe, and to an even more unjustifiable extent by latter-day military historians.

In its effort to strengthen its position, the Principality of Antioch tried to establish a dynastic union with neighbouring Cicilian Armenia, but failed. The same motivation lay behind the Latin States' broader efforts to forge ties with the Byzantine Empire from 1150 to 1175, especially as the power and unity of regional Islamic states grew. During the 1180s they tried to attach themselves to powerful rulers in Western Europe. The Military Orders were another potential if partial solution to the problem of military manpower.

Given such an awareness of their own vulnerable position, it is hardly surprising that the rulers of the Latin States soon learned to avoid staking everything on full-scale battles, at least without the participation of substantial Crusades from the west. That was why Hattin, in 1187, was so unusual and why its outcome proved so catastrophic. The army assembled by the Latin States, almost entirely from the Kingdom of Jerusalem and the County of Tripoli, is believed to have numbered as many as 1,200 knights including those of the Military Orders. In addition there were around 1,800 mounted sergeants and 17,000 foot soldiers, mostly professional mercenaries. It was defeated, indeed utterly destroyed, by Saladin's army which numbered roughly the same.

Thereafter it was clear that the truncated Latin States, having survived this catastrophe, could not undertake major field operations on their own. Then came the dismal failure of the Fifth Crusade in Egypt, which in turn convinced the Papacy that future Crusades would need the full involvement of the German Empire. Eventually, of course, it became clear that the entire Crusading enterprise in the Middle East was doomed to failure, but such an acceptance still lay in the future.

The strategic situation faced by the remnants of the Latin States in the 13th century was different than that faced in the 12th, but only in degree, not in essentials. After 1187 the Latin-held enclaves became increasingly dependent upon food either imported from Europe or purchased from their Muslim neighbours. Eventually this dependence became absolute, and even live meat was to be imported,[13] along with virtually every other necessity including military equipment. Meanwhile the gradual adoption of many Byzantine and Middle Eastern modes of everyday life still did not extend to military matters except in a few details. Siege warfare dominated Crusader campaigns around the eastern Mediterranean in the 13th century, with the Latin States resisting Ayyubid or Mamluk sieges while the arrival of the occasional Crusade enabled the Christians to briefly take the offensive and besiege some Islamic strongpoint.

Although the Military Orders tended to favour the aggressive attitudes of Crusader newcomers rather than the caution of an established local Latin aristocracy, their own rivalries could mean that the Templars and Hospitallers made competing alliances with similarly competing Islamic rulers. By the late 13th century the Templars had also become an integral part of the Angevin power structure around the Mediterranean, not only in southern Italy and the Latin States of Greece but in what remained of the Latin States of the Middle East. Until the Sicilian Vespers uprising in 1282 undermined Angevin power in the Mediterranean, such an alliance made good sense though it did involve both Templars and Angevins in the convoluted politics of the Latin east. The Sicilian Vespers and the subsequent war with Aragon also meant that Charles of Anjou, ruler of southern Italy, could no longer spare troops to maintain Angevin control in the nominal Kingdom of Jerusalem. This in turn now consisted of little more than a narrow coastal strip with Acre as its main city. Four years later King Henry II of Cyprus seized control of Acre and effectively ended the period of good relations which Charles of Anjou had studiously cultivated with the surrounding Mamluk Sultanate of Egypt and Syria.

Nominal political authority was one thing, real power was another, and in many respects real power in the Latin coastal enclaves now lay with Italian merchant colonies from Genoa and Venice. Unfortunately these two hugely powerful maritime states were bitter rivals, whose antagonism offered tempting opportunities for outside interference by both Islamic, Byzantine and Western European states. Historians have too often dismissed the actions of these Italian maritime merchant republics as merely self-serving. They were certainly concerned about trade but, like virtually all other Christian powers that involved themselves in Crusading warfare in the later 13th century, their motives were mixed and complex. Nor were their efforts necessarily helpful. Indeed, the big effort made by Genoa to bolster the remaining Latin enclaves in the eastern Mediterranean in the 1280s probably stirred up more problems than it solved.

The end came in 1291, when the remnants of the Latin States fell, or submitted, to the Mamluk Sultan; all except the tiny offshore island of Ruad which endured for several more years. Almost until the very end, it seemed that these remaining enclaves were so confident of their economic importance that they really did not believe the Mamluks wanted to get rid of them.[14]

The Latin States established around the Aegean in the wake of the Fourth Crusade in 1204 suffered an even more acute shortage of troops than did those in the Middle East. The Latin 'Empire of Constantinople' was soon too poor to hire mercenaries, and none of these newly established states attracted many settlers from Latin Western or Central Europe. It had taken a full, though diverted, Crusade to seize the Byzantine capital of Constantinople (Istanbul) yet Greece is believed to have been conquered by a hundred or so Crusader knights and four to five hundred mounted sergeants. Not surprisingly the conquest took over forty years, despite weak and fragmented local opposition resulting in a significant degree of political, military and even cultural accommodation with the local Byzantine élite of *archontes*. This was in stark contrast to the situation in those Islamic regions conquered during and immediately after the First Crusade where the existing Islamic military élites had been wiped out or expelled.

Although the numbers of settlers and military manpower attracted to the Latin States of the Aegean was very limited, there was some outside interest in this area. Apart from the Pope, the only other major Western ruler to take serious steps to resist a Byzantine reconquest was Charles of Anjou and his Angevin successors who, as rulers of southern Italy, had their own ambitions in and around Greece. The Venetians and Genoese were also deeply interested in events, but from a strictly commercial point of view. Venice has been widely blamed as having been responsible for the diversion of the Fourth Crusade and the 'Great Betrayal' which was the Latin conquest of Constantinople. Venice certainly benefited handsomely, but focussed its efforts on taking control of significant islands and latterly several coastal enclaves to control or defend its maritime trade routes to and from the Aegean. Unlike the Latin Crusader conquest of Greece, the Venetian conquest of Crete was rapid, despite facing strong resistance. Thereafter it was maintained by armed force.

Genoa had been a strong ally or at least an entrenched commercial partner of the Byzantine Empire at the time of the Fourth Crusade. Only in the second half of the 13th and early 14th centuries, and as an ally of the Byzantine revival, did Genoa acquire its own series of colonial enclaves and islands in the Aegean and Black Seas. These were rarely conquests. Instead the Genoese were usually invited to garrison and defend outposts which the Byzantines themselves felt unable to hold. In contrast to Venetian practice, Genoese authority was maintained by good relations between the resident Genoese authorities, or *mahonesi*, the indigenous local inhabitants and neighbouring mainland powers. Genoese power was, of course, entirely maritime.[15]

RECRUITMENT AND ORGANISATION

The first and most important point to make is the huge variation seen in recruitment and organisation as aspects of Crusader warfare, not only between regions but over time. Furthermore, the use of the term 'poor' to describe participants in any Crusade, even the First, can be very misleading. None were really poor, especially amongst the knights, and those described as such were merely poorer than the élite or the leadership. Furthermore, the concept of hordes of peasants marching east in a state of religious hysteria is another myth. There certainly was hysteria, but it tended to be occasional, limited and associated with specific events along the way rather than at the initiation of the Crusading project. Another general factor which impinged upon recruitment and the availability of fighting men once the Latin States had been established was that of disease. In fact there was a tendency for Crusaders and other settlers from the West to die early. This failure of acclimatisation means that there are no records of a Crusader settler living over the age of eighty, whereas it was common for their Muslim and indeed indigenous Christian neighbours to do so.

It was above all the shortage of militarily useful Christian settlers, even in the early and mid-12th centuries especially in the frontier zones of the Latin States, which encouraged the Latin Kings of Jerusalem to give lands and castles to the Military Orders. This phenomenon became increasingly common and would also be seen on other warlike frontiers of Western Christendom in the Iberian peninsula, Hungary and the Baltic. The Kingdom of Jerusalem, and by extension the other Latin States in the Middle East, made constant efforts to confirm a traditional or territorial feudal structure, but again lack of manpower made this impossible. Instead a sort of colonial feudalism emerged in which rulers had to rely on standing armies of paid mercenaries, the Military Orders and a system of money fiefs in which a knightly military class was maintained by other sources of revenue. Consequently the great majority of the Latin aristocracy no longer formed part of the rural community, as they did in most parts of Western Europe, but became an urban and increasingly a coastal military élite whose closest parallels could be found in Italy rather than France.

Other frontier regions of Western Christendom developed militarily in different ways. For example, the ruling and military élites of the Latin States of the Aegean were even more varied than those of the Latin Middle East. Sardinia is rarely mentioned in this context, yet it was in many respects another Mediterranean frontier zone. Here a politically dominant Italian community was largely confined to the towns while indigenous Sards inhabited the rural regions and mountainous interior. Christianity in Sardinia also moved from the Orthodox Greek rite to the Latin Catholic during the 12th and 13th centuries while Sards would play a brief but distinctive military role beyond their own island.

Variety was again characteristic of the expanding Christian-ruled regions of the Iberian peninsula. Here there had traditionally been less social distinction between cavalry and infantry than there was north of the Pyrenees. Some of the Pyrenean mountain and foothill regions from which the Christian so-called Reconquista was launched had never really been feudalised at all. Although they were dominated by a baronial military class, the rest of their fighting forces consisted of mercenaries and urban militias.[16] As an example of the changing circumstances within just one of these Spanish kingdoms, Aragon expanded from the mountains into the fertile and densely populated Ebro valley. Here, in what became the Vieja Extremadura or Old Frontier, most of the Islamic ruling class left whereas the Muslim lower classes remained. Muslims were largely expelled from the fortified cities, which were repopulated by colonists drawn from many regions. The next major Aragonese expansion into the New Frontier would incorporate a rugged, mountainous and often arid land which was now organised into military zones. These would be colonised by virtually autonomous communities of warlike peasants from whom light cavalry as well as infantry could be drawn. Much of the existing Islamic population also remained, this being even more typical of Valencia in the deep south which was conquered during the 13th century.[17]

Military recruitment was as varied as were political and social structures. Even within the First Crusade there were clear differences between contingents, with crossbowmen and skilled engineers being more characteristic of southern armies like the Provençals commanded by Raymond of Toulouse than of northern armies such as that of Godfrey de Bouillon.[18] Further variety and indeed useful local experience might have been provided by volunteers the First Crusade picked up along its way, especially those soldiers who had recently been in Byzantine service. They included men like Hugh Bunel who joined the army during the final siege of Jerusalem having been in the Middle East for two years after murdering a woman in France.[19] Many of the Turks captured during the Crusaders' earlier victory at Dorylaeum converted to Christianity, perhaps in return for their lives, and one such may have been 'Bohemond a Turk' whom Raymond of Toulouse sent as a messenger and spy to the Fatimid army outside Ascalon in 1099. His Christian name of Bohemond certainly suggests that he had been captured by the Crusaders rather than having transferred from Byzantine service.[20]

Many Muslims taken prisoner in the early 12th century converted to Christianity and are likely to have formed the bulk of the first *turcopoles* in the armies of the Latin States. By this means they not only saved their lives but presumably earned their freedom, just as the slave-recruited *ghulams* or *mamluks* on the Islamic side of the frontier were freed on completion of their military training (see volume II). The only other examples of theoretically unfree troops being involved on the Crusades were the German *ministeriales* who were a special group whose unfree status was already something of a myth.

Women of the Western European aristocracies played a significant role as promoters and sometimes as financiers of various Crusades. Only rarely were they recorded as obstacles to their husbands' participation. The evidence also indicates that when women accompanied these military expeditions or armed pilgrimages, they tended to be a stabilising moral influence rather than, as some clerical chroniclers and modern authors have suggested, being sources of trouble.[21] Women from various strata of society were active in logistical support, sometimes as porters and even when necessary helping mount guard around a camp. Futhermore they seemed to have had the primary responsibility in tending the wounded, and probably also in laying out the dead. In all these roles their participation was remarkably similar to that of Muslim women on the other side of the fence.

Once the Latin States had been established in the Middle East, the theoretically feudal structure of society meant that all able-bodied citizens could be summoned in time of need when the king's *ban* was broadcast throughout the kingdom, whether they were landholders or not. In reality the knights were called first, with those of sergeant rank acting as a reserve.[22] Men were also liable for service until the age of sixty. It has been suggested that some of the earliest *turcopoles* within these armies were associated with the mixed Turkish–Greek population of Bythnia in north-western Anatolia through which the First Crusade had marched.[23] Nevertheless, the fact that Middle Eastern *turcopoles* were almost invariably executed as apostates if recaptured by Muslims strongly suggests that they were converts, forcible or otherwise, from Islam to Christianity. Furthermore most of their names, where known, are not of Orthodox or Middle Eastern Christian origin but are Latin European, presumably having been given to them on their conversion rather than as children brought up in oriental Christianity. The only substantial exceptions are found later in Crusader-ruled Cyprus where many *turcopoles* may well have been Syrian Christians.[24] By the mid-13th century the *turcopoles* of the mainland Latin States were sometimes called *barkil* in Arabic sources.[25]

Most of the professional soldiers enlisted by the Middle Eastern Latin States were probably recruited locally, from amongst Latin settlers including recently arrived European mercenaries and knightly Crusaders who had chosen to remain. Such paid soldiers suffered penalties if they deserted before the completion of their contracts, with harsh punishment for sergeants while those of knightly status suffered humiliation rather than physical mutilation.[26] The promise of rich fiefs in Egypt had been used to encourage resident knights of the Latin States to take part in the first expeditions against Egypt during the 12th century, but after these suffered a series of setbacks it became much more difficult to raise troops for Egyptian campaigns. This again forced the Kings of Jerusalem to rely ever more on mercenaries.

A great deal is known about the feudal structure and obligations of the 12th century Kingdom of Jerusalem. Yet this may not paint a very accurate picture, as it represents an ideal rather than the reality of mustering an army, especially as the Kingdom's financial, political and military problems increased. Nevertheless, according to law the king's feudal vassals owed military service for up to a year within the Kingdom, even when the ruler was not personally leading the army. The actual length of time demanded on a specific occasion may have been decided at the *Haute Cour* (the High Court of the kingdom) as the campaign was being organised, and payment was only made for additional time under arms, even to those knights or sergeants who had money fiefs.[27] The question of what exactly counted as service inside or outside the kingdom was, and still is, a matter of debate and also changed over time. Even in the early days Egypt was agreed to be 'outside' whereas the situation along the open frontiers of northern Syria was less clear. Even as early as the 1110s the Principality of Antioch was sometimes thought to lie within the Byzantine sphere of influence, and was thus clearly 'outside' the Kingdom of Jerusalem.

Although the status of the Counties of Edessa and Tripoli as vassals of Jerusalem was hardly doubted in the early days, in practice this became less clear later and eventually anything beyond Beirut was effectively 'outside' the Kingdom.[28] In later years the allegiance of the other Latin States to the Kingdom of Jerusalem rarely translated into reality. On the other hand, by 1131 Fatimid Egyptian-held Ascalon and the independent emirate of Damascus were regarded as future parts of the Kingdom and were thus perhaps 'inside'.[29]

Even when a campaign clearly took place within the Kingdom, there could be a serious shortage of knights. Yet it has been suggested that King Baldwin's making of squires into knights in 1101 may have meant that they were issued with knightly arms, armour and warhorse rather than having their legal status raised within the feudal hierarchy.[30] In addition to mercenaries hired individually or for a specific period, there was the remarkable French Regiment. This formed a permanent professional force during the second half of the 13th century, comparable in some respects to those provided by the Military Orders. Its history began in 1254 when King Louis IX of France left one hundred knights, plus crossbowmen, infantry and mounted sergeants, in the Kingdom of Jerusalem when he went home. The numbers of men and other forms of support from France varied over the next decades, but this French Regiment remained as a readily available field force to the very end. Its commanders included some remarkable men, the first being Geoffrey de Sergines who became *Senechal* of the Kingdom, as did some of his successors including Jean de Grailly, the last commander of the French Regiment during the final defence of Acre in 1291.[31]

In addition to military units under the immediate command of the king or his most senior officials there were militias maintained by the Italian merchant communes. These were particularly important in the 13th century, though their primary loyalties would have been to their home city. The best known and largest were those of Venice, Genoa and, at an earlier date, Pisa. However, there were others, including that of Ancona whose commune in Acre was obliged to supply fifty fully armoured soldiers to help defend the city in return for its legally recognised privileges in the late 1250s.[32]

Then there were the military obligations of local or indigenous Christian communities. There had in fact been a substantial migration of Syrian and Orthodox Christians from Madaba and other regions east of the river Jordan to Latin-ruled Palestine in the early 12th century. Attracted by the offer of privileges in Jerusalem, they also feared being a suspect Christian minority in what had suddenly become a frontier zone between the Latin Kingdom of Jerusalem and its Islamic neighbours.[33] Syrian Christians rarely appear as distinct military formations in the Latin States, though the garrison of the cave-fortress of Habis Jaldak ('Ayn Habis) was at one time commanded by such a Syrian Christian.

Some indigenous Palestinian Christians were also raised to knighthood in the early 12th century, including resident Armenians.

Armenian siege engineers were similarly recruited and it is clear that, of all the indigenous Middle Eastern Christian communities, the Armenians played the most significant military role in the Latin States. Not suprisingly, they were prominent in the northernmost states of Edessa and Antioch. The Maronite Christians of what is now the mountainous northern Lebanon were important, usually as infantry archers, in the County of Tripoli. Though not specifically bound by feudal allegiance to any Latin rulers, they generally recognised some degree of overlordship by the Lord of Jubayl on the neighbouring coast. The great Latin Crusader chronicler, William of Tyre, described them as: *'a stalwart race, valiant fighters, and of great service to the Christians in the difficult engagements which they so frequently had with the enemy'*.[34] Further north, in the Principality of Antioch, the recorded names of some knights suggest that they were of Greek origin.[35] To the east, in the ephemeral County of Edessa, the many Armenian feudal lordships which formed part of this state in the first decade or so of its existence had all disappeared bar one by the 1120s. This survivor, the northern mountain lordship of Gargar, survived until the fall of the County of Edessa.[36] On the other hand the Armenian urban burgess or merchant class always formed a vital source of militiamen and sergeants for Latin Edessa. In rural areas an indigenous and usually Arabic-speaking *ra'is* or headman was reponsible for maintaining order in a group of two or three villages, but there is no evidence that he or his assistants had any additional military role. In the south of the Kingdom of Jerusalem, the Latin authorities often managed to maintain such good relations with the local Arab bedouin that the bedu were occasionally suspected of being pro-Christian by their fellow Muslims.

The Military Orders would, of course, become the most important permanent military forces available for the defence of the Latin States. The Hospitallers had existed, in a rudimentary form, in Jerusalem even before the First Crusade but had been an entirely charitable and medical organisation. Following the establishment of the Latin Kingdom of Jerusalem, the militarisation of the Order of Hospitallers initially seems to have involved the hiring of military personnel. But by the 1130s some of the brethren had military obligations and within three more decades the Hospitallers were certainly involved in military matters.[37] Although the military element of the Hospitallers was small in these early days, it eventually became dominant, with the Order's charitable medical work taking second place, though never being abandoned. The Templars were a new Order and were military from the start, eventually forming a true regiment of up to three hundred fully trained, well-equipped and dedicated – indeed often fanatical – cavalry. The surviving version of the *Old French Rule* of the Order of Templars dates from the 13th century, but much of what it contains is believed to have been written in the mid-12th and is a remarkable military text. Unlike so much military writing from the medieval period, the *Old French Rule* is based upon the reality, rather than the abstract and often archaic theory, of warfare. Nor is it simply a drill manual, like many medieval Islamic and Byzantine military treatises.[38]

Recruitment into all the Crusading Military Orders changed over the years, and a *novitiate* comparable to that of ordinary monastic orders was attempted in the early days. During the 12th century, however, the *novitiate* system which accepted boys at a young age was replaced by a minumum age of entry. This would have meant that most education and military training was completed before joining a Military Order. Military training continued, of course, but other forms of education would have been at best rudimentary. This was presumably why members of the Military Orders regarded themselves as relatively uneducated when compared to the regular clergy. As these Military Orders developed into pan-European organisations with increasing land-holdings and increasing wealth, it appears that fit men of military age would be sent to serve in the Latin States while older brethren remained in the European priories in vital support or administrative roles. As the Orders became increasingly powerful they became increasingly aware of the need to maintain a good public image, not only for political and financial reasons but to continue getting recruits and public support. By the second half of the 13th century the Hospitallers, Templars and to some extent the more localised Teutonic or Iberian Orders had evolved into astonishing multi-national organisations, transferring men, ships, goods and capital across huge distances and frontiers. In some respects they were comparable to modern international corporations, and provoked some of the same resentments. One of the smallest Orders might have provoked some fear, but hardly resentment. This was the distinctive Order of St Lazarus for lepers, which seems to have drawn its recruits from existing members of other Orders, most notably the Templars.[39]

The Kingdom of Cyprus differed in many respects from the other Latin or Crusader States in the Middle East. For a start, it had been seized from the fellow-Christian Byzantine Empire rather than from Muslim 'infidels', and the indigenous population was overwhelmingly Greek-speaking Orthodox Christians. Cypriot forces were deeply involved in the civil wars which wracked the Kingdom of Jerusalem in the 1270s, but otherwise their role in the mainland Latin States was small. These military forces consisted of enfiefed knights, almost entirely of European family origins in the early days, plus urban militias from the Latin and Greek merchant class whose obligations were largely limited to the defence of their own city walls, while non-noble mounted sergeants formed the bulk of the army. In the late 13th and 14th centuries, however, the Cypriot army included an increasing number of men of mixed origins, still often referred to as *poulains*, as well as Armenians, Syrians and other Christian refugees from the mainland, plus *turcopoles* who may have included a few forcibly converted Muslims.[40] It was also during this later period that the Cypriots began to take a more prominent role, especially at sea and in some significant coastal raids.

The Latin Empire of Constantinople and the Latin States of Greece also consisted of territory taken by force of arms from the fellow-Christian Byzantine Empire. Most of the European knights and sergeants who conquered southern Greece in the early 13th century came from Champagne and Burgundy in France, though there were also many Flemings and Provençals. They brought with them shared values concerning the structure of society and the bonds which held it together. These were feudal, in other words based upon personal ties of obligation and loyalty rather than abstract concepts of statehood. Within a few decades, however, such attitudes were modified to suit the new conditions that the vastly outnumbered conquerors faced within Greece. Some of the existing Byzantine administrative and, to a lesser extent, military structures were adapted to help the Latins survive in a state of almost constant, though usually low-level, warfare with the steadily reviving Byzantine successor states. On the other hand there was very little intermarriage between Latins and Greeks, especially in the higher ranks of society where the ruling élite largely lived in isolation while desperately attempting to maintain contact with Western European culture.[41]

The military strain upon this quasi-feudal, colonial society was illustrated by the fact that, whereas the normal maximum feudal service expected in Europe was forty days, in the Latin Morea (southern Greece) it was, legally, four months plus a further four months' castle guard duty.[42] A man who lost his land to the enemy was excused military service for two years and two days, or until his fief had been regained.[43] Under such seemingly desperate circumstances the Military Orders might have been expected to play a major role. Yet their involvement in the Latin States of the Aegean was as yet quite small. The Templars may have played a little-recorded part in the initial conquest of Greece, perhaps involving brethren from southern Italy.[44] A year after the Fourth Crusade conquered Constantinople, the first Latin Emperor, Baldwin, granted the Hospitallers large estates in the Peloponnese in the hope the Order would help defend it against Byzantine reconquest. In fact the Hospitallers took little interest in the Aegean until after the final loss of the Latin States on the Middle Eastern mainland. They then conquered Rhodes and established their own state in the early 14th century.

It was clearly difficult for the Latin Aegean States to recruit local troops, as the great majority were adherents of the same Orthodox Christian Church as the Byzantine armies which were, at this stage, the Latin States' most significant foes. Most of the locals were also Greeks, like the rulers and indeed much of the military forces of the revived Byzantine states. The Latin conquerors of

Constantinople might briefly have found useful allies in a substantial Armenian community then inhabiting the Asiatic coast of the Dardanelles, having been settled there over a century earlier by the Byzantine Empire, probably as a military colony. These Armenians cooperated with the Latins immediately after the conquest of Constantinople, perhaps aware of the traditionally good military relations between Latin Crusaders and Armenians in the Middle East. After the failure of the Latins to conquer Byzantine Anatolia, many Armenians with their families and their waggons seem to have accompanied the Latins back to Thrace, on the European side of the Straits. But here they were abandoned after the army of the Latin Empire of Constantinople was defeated by the Bulgarians near Edirne in 1205, and were virtually wiped out.[45]

A few years later Greek *archontes* were mentioned in the Latin Duchy of Athens and Thebes, though not in the Principality of Achaea. Their role is not entirely clear, but by the mid-13th century such Greek-speaking Orthodox Christian *archontes* did have some limited military role.

It was said that a Latin victory over the Byzantines in 1262 resulted from taking local military advice, and that the Latin lord of Karytaina consequently decided to make some of his senior Greek soldiers into knights, and that their families inherited such a status while remaining Orthodox Christians. There are likely to have been several such cases in the later 13th century. Nevertheless most *archontes* were still not knights and were still arrayed with the squires and sergeants during a later conflict with Epirus in 1304.[46] Other *archontes* joined the Latin Catholic Church, almost certainly for reasons of social advancement, though paradoxically many more Latins would eventually become Orthodox.

Further north, Serbs and Bulgars supported Charles of Anjou against Byzantium in 1270, while many Slavs settled in southern Italy during the late 13th and 14th centuries, to the extent that part of Naples came to be known as the Bulgarian Quarter.[47] Albanians would, however, be more important in military terms for both the Latin States in Greece and for Angevin southern Italian 'Crusading' efforts to dominate the southern Balkans. During the later 13th century the Angevin authorities in Albania recruited local troops and, after a setback in 1281, also Greek mercenaries.[48] Three years earlier Charles of Anjou, King of Naples, had also become Prince of Achaea in southern Greece. There he found Kipchaq and other Turkish mercenaries already in service. These he retained, though he did not recruit more.[49]

The Italian mercantile colonies raised troops in different ways. The bulk of Genoese colonial settlers were apparently retired oarsmen and sailors, poor men who may have hoped to prosper in these economically vibrant outposts[50] and who, given the more relaxed attitudes of the Genoese in relation to local populations, may have married local women. The Venetians, in contrast, made strenuous efforts to stop intermarriage between Latins and Greeks in their largest

Aegean colony of Crete. Nevertheless it did occur, especially amongst the poorer people. In fact the resulting *vasmuli* or *gasmouli* became a significant group in Crete, being involved in an unsuccessful uprising in 1274[51] and later reappearing as a potent element in various Aegean fleets, most notably that of a revived Byzantine Empire. Much of the previous Byzantine administrative and perhaps military élite of *archontes* seems to have left the towns of northern Crete which became the centres of Venetian rule. Instead they moved south into the rural and mountainous regions, perhaps never wholly accepting Venetian occupation.

The changing patterns of military recruitment in southern Italy and Sicily closely reflected changes in political authority. Before Norman 'proto-Crusaders' appeared on the scene, the military systems of the existing Lombard principalities were built around a ruler's *famuli* or palace retainers, largely consisting of his relatives or closest servants but also including slaves, semi-free, freed and free-born men. Sometimes they were referred to as *satellites* or *milites* and included the ruler's *socii* or closest 'companions in arms'.[52] Parallels can clearly be found between this system and those of the early Lombard Kingdom of Italy, the Carolingian military systems developed by Charlemagne and his successors, and with Byzantine practice. There are also remarkable similarities with some parts of the Islamic Mediterranean world, except in a shortage of cavalry which is said to have been characteristic of the 11th century Lombard Principalities of southern Italy.

Many of the men recruited by castle-owners to garrison the fortifications of pre-Norman southern Italy were of servile or unfree origins and in some regions it was probably normal for citizens to defend their own city walls. The Church also played some military role but did not apparently have formal feudal obligations. Furthermore, the Church's increased involvement in warfare during the turbulent 11th century came to an abrupt though not complete halt when the Norman states of southern Italy were unified by King Roger II.[53]

Military recruitment and obligations in the Byzantine provinces of southern Italy differed again. Here the local *theme* armies had been disbanded around 1040 and defence was left to imperial units sent from Constantinople supported by local urban militas. Unfortunately for the Byzantine central authorities, the loyalty of these militias became increasingly localised and eventually most joined the Norman newcomers in driving out the remaining Byzantine garrisons.[54]

There has been much debate about how Norman the 'Norman' invasion of southern Italy really was. Bretons, Flemings, Poitevins and some Angevins were involved, though Normans took the primary role, while adventurers from the central regions of France and from Burgundy seem to have been more attracted to the Iberian 'front'.[55] Even in the mid-11th century, however, the Norman leader was recruiting local Calabrians, Slavs and maybe even Greeks for his invasion of Islamic Sicily.[56] On the Italian mainland, once the new state had been created, Normans and Lombards remained separate military élites for many years, despite intermarriage and the fact that Normans held the real power. The resulting military system was complex. It involved non-feudal urban militias and semi-feudal cavalry. Cavalry militias of knightly status, including that from the area of Monte Cassino, mostly seem to have been maintained on or by church estates. In terms of equipment and military styles the Lombard aristocracy had adopted Norman forms, which were in any case little different from those of the Lombards, while there was still a significant role for lightly equipped cavalry and almost unarmoured infantry.

Most of the marine troops of the Norman Kingdom are likely to have come from urban middle-class militias of the coastal cities. The coasts, of course, also provided sailors and oarsmen. Generally speaking the mainland towns enjoyed greater freedom than did those of Norman-ruled Sicily, especially those upon which the rulers had to rely for ships and crews. The Normans clearly treated their towns with respect. For example, Naples had its own class of *milites* or élite soldiers before the Norman takeover in 1130, and ten years later the king enfeoffed them with the status of knights. Similar communal military structures existed on the Adriatic coast, with the city of Bari having its own 'burgess knights'.[57] Even so the increasing centralisation of the Norman state led to growing recruitment of, and reliance upon, paid mercenary soldiers. This was especially noticeable in ex-Byzantine and ex-Islamic provinces.

Under Norman rule, the previously Islamic-ruled island of Sicily enjoyed a golden age of culture, power, prestige and perhaps prosperity. It is worth noting that while many Muslims fled the new regime, many indigenous Arabic-speaking North African Christians in turn fled Muwahid (Almohade) persecution to settle in Norman Sicily.[58] Some may have served their new rulers militarily, but by far the most significant Arab troops in the Norman kingdom were Sicilian Muslims. Though Arabised, they were by no means all of strictly Arab origins (see volume II), and King Roger I began recruiting these ex-foes, particularly those with skill as siege engineers, at a very early date.

The Muslim population of Sicily was concentrated in the west of the island and remained largely unchanged under the first Norman rulers, as did its military organisation. This community included rural peasantry, now reduced to the status of essentially unfree villeins, plus urban artisans, merchants and others and that part of the existing Islamic aristocracy which had remained in Sicily. The latter came to terms with its conquerors and thereafter raised and led contingents whose seemingly 'feudal' military obligations were actually service in return for a lack of religious persecution.

The fact that the Sicilian Islamic hierarchy was akin to that of the Normans, not least in its traditional Arab concepts of personal honour and fidelity, made co-existence and cooperation on the battlefield much easier.[59] Still organised in the previous Arab-Islamic *jund* system of military-territorial divisions, these Muslim troops, infantry and cavalry, would play a high profile role in the armies of the Norman Kingdom of Sicily and Italy for generations. The best of them formed one of the ruler's two guard units which was commanded by a Muslim.[60] The other guard unit consisted of Normans. At the close of the Norman period in 1194, the Queen of Sicily raised a large army which again included many such 'Saracens'. Although it was defeated, this remarkably loyal but, in cultural terms, isolated and vulnerable Islamic community continued to provide soldiers to subsequent ruling dynasties, first French and then German, for more than a hundred years.

The fleets of the Norman Kingdom were largely manned by Italians and Greeks rather than Muslims. During the reign of King Roger, most of the senior naval officers appear to have been Greeks, but in wider terms the Normans of the south relied on Italian sailors and marines from the urban coastal militias to a greater degree than is generally recognised. They also recruited professional sailors and soldiers from Pisa and Genoa, using them not only at sea but to garrison important ports.[61]

Although the Norman conquerors of southern Italy and Sicily were closer to being 'Crusaders' in the normal sense of the term, their successors continued to be involved in wars inspired in part by religion but largely by economic and political ambitions. These were directed against both the Byzantine and the Islamic worlds. Their Sicilian Muslim troops were, however, used against Christian rather than Islamic rivals.

Although an Islamic aristocracy survived in western Sicily until at least the mid-13th century under Hohenstauffen German Imperial rule, it was the military colony established by the Emperor Frederick II around Lucera on the Italian mainland that attracted most attention. It consisted of families forcibly transferred from Italy and settled not simply as soldiers but also as peasant farmers and craftsmen with the primary purpose of providing the ruler with an effective and reliable military force. Once again its loyalty was to be guaranteed by a promise of freedom to remain Muslim and not to be pressured to convert to Christianity.

Within such promises lay the implied threat that if the community did not remain loyal and militarily effective, the ruler's religious protection would be removed. Consequently Lucera became an island of Islam, speaking both Arabic and Italian. The city of Lucera revived with its fortifications greatly strengthened while the community was governed by its own *qa'id* or governor assisted by religious and legal *shaykhs* and *faqihs*. Muslim peasants tilled the fields and maintained a stud which bred horses for the Emperor. There was also an Imperial 'harem' which was, in reality, a textile factory rather than a place of sensual pleasure. Most important of all, Lucera provided Emperor Frederick II with a real, trained and professional standing army which no other Western European ruler could claim at that time.[62] It was so effective that Frederick sometimes added to his 'Saracen' army by recruiting soldiers directly from Tunisia.[63]

These Saracens of Lucera put up a fierce resistance to Charles of Anjou's conquest of southern Italy in 1268–9, and after his victory Charles crushed the community. Many of its men were forcibly resettled around Naples where the peasants were reduced to slavery, though the soldiers retained some rights. A vital strategic alliance between Charles of Anjou and the Islamic ruler of Tunis helped protect the remaining Muslims of Italy. More important, however, was the vital role played by these so-called 'Saracens of Lucera' as archers, javelin-men and crossbowmen, both on foot and as mounted infantry or cavalry. Those on horseback were, in fact, paid twice as much as those on foot. All were still on call during the bitter war between Angevins and Aragonese at the end of the 13th century.

Then, in August 1300, these islands of Arab-Islamic culture were finally destroyed, the great majority of their people being obliged to convert to Christianity or leave the country. Some Muslim peasants do seem to have survived in parts of Apulia for several decades, but as serfs rather than soldiers.[64] The tiny island of Pantellaria came under Charles of Anjou's rule in 1270 and its Muslim population was granted religious toleration, for a while.[65] Earlier in the 13th century it appears that some of the Maltese sailors serving Count Henry of Malta in his wide-ranging piratical campaigns were also still Muslim.[66]

Recruitment patterns in central and northern Italy naturally had an impact upon Crusader and other contingents raised in these regions. Here there were greater differences between rural and urban forces than in almost any other part of Europe. For example, feudal militias formed the bulk of the armies of Matilda of Tuscany and the Emperor Henry in the late 11th and early 12th centuries. Meanwhile urban infantry and cavalry militias of 'free men' were already vital to local defence.[67] A few rural but non-noble families whose status had been inherited since Carolingian times still owed military service as 'free infantry' during the 11th to 13th centuries, but they were few.[68] In rural areas a levy of *pedites* or those on foot included non-combatants of servile origin, and largely consisted of men from 'houses' or extended families in the retinues of the minor aristocracy.

The normal role of such *pedites* was to defend the baggage and herds, erect camps, erect and operate siege machines. Those who fought on foot were usually free men but included both conscripts and mercenaries, archers and *guastatori* or 'ravagers' whose task was to inflict as much economic damage on enemy territory as possible. For free men military service and the bearing of arms was clearly a mark of privilege, at least until the later 13th century, whereas for those of servile status it was just another form of forced labour.[69]

The urban situation in Italy was characterised by an excess of young males who were, as so often in history, a significant source of trouble, and in some places there might have been a ratio of three men to every two women. Furthermore the urban population of Italy tended to be young, resulting in large numbers of unmarried young men and a growing class of poor.[70] Another aspect of Italian military recruitment which surprised some outside observers was the status given to men of relatively humble origins. As the mid-12th century German observer Otto of Freising noted, the 'girdle of knighthood' was given to young men of '*inferior station and even some workers of the vile mechanical arts*' – in other words, to men from what would today be called the middle class. At the same time Otto was torn between scorn for these ignoble knights and respect for their military capabilities.[71] In addition to knights of seemingly lowly family origin, non-noble 'bourgeois' cavalry were already a feature of Italian urban communal forces, these men being fully equipped by the standards of the day because their cities tended to be richer than those north of the Alps. Nevertheless the majority of non-knightly militiamen still served on foot.

During the 13th century the records show that, in a city like Florence, ordinary citizens with more than a minumum of wealth, in other words those not counted as 'poor', were expected to serve in the militia from the age of fifteen to seventy. They were usually organised into groups or units of around fifty men. In late 13th century northern Italy, pride in such military service may already have been in decline, with poor men known as *sodoiers* taking the place of richer citizens in return for payment.[72] The primary responsibility of these urban militias was to defend their own city walls, though they could also serve in field armies. Although the legal basis of the cavalry service owed by a city's minor aristocracy and its *contado* or immediate surroundings remained essentially feudal, there was already a growing reliance on mercenaries. The records of Verona, for example, first mentioned recruiting such professionals in 1227 and 1230.[73]

Though initially recorded outside Italy, infantry crossbowmen soon became a typical feature of Italian communal armies in the later 12th and 13th centuries. Even so the bulk of militia foot soldiers remained archers armed with hand-bows until the status of such archers declined to that of mere 'devastators' with little role in set-piece warfare. The Genoese would become the most famous Italian mercenary crossbowmen, especially in the service of foreign rulers like the king of 14th century France. This seems to have been a result of the very fragmented and almost privatised nature of authority in Genoa and Genoese society, added to the fact that so many well-trained crossbowmen were available. Some came from Genoa itself, though the majority seemed to have been attracted to the city because of its self-perpetuating reputation as a military recruitment centre.

Here, in the words of an expert on the subject: '*Political refugees or war-merchants frequently offered capital, ships and sailors, as well as trained units of crossbowmen for service in international conflicts.'*[74] A surviving Genoese contract dated 13 April 1257 records how the crossbowman, or perhaps master crossbowman, L. Giordano recruited another crossbowman named Giovanni for twenty-nine weeks and that 'Ughetto the crossbowman' would take the place of the late Aimerico di Barbagelata.[75] Another fascinating light on military recruitment is found in the work of Giovanni da Nono who, though writing in 1318, recorded a situation which was probably just as common in the late 13th century. He told of how two impoverished Italian knights, Bartolomeo and Tebaldo da Caldenacia, lost their lands and so had to run a tavern in a suburb of Padua. Unfortunately they allowed credit to all customers and so made no profits and would, in fact, have been outlawed for debt but for the influence of a certain Guglielmo Lemici. Finally they turned for help to a kinswoman, Adelmota Maltraversi, who gave them horses and military equipment. Though Bartolomeo and Tebaldo left without thanking her, they did take service with an unnamed Count in Croatia or Dalmatia where they eventually earned enough to settle their debts.[76]

The armies of the German Emperor which fought in Italy had similarities with German forces involved in the Crusades, though most of the infantry came from Italian cities under Imperial rule. In 1238 the Emperor Frederick II recruited from particularly far afield for one such campaign in Lombardy, drawing in men from Byzantine territory and possibly from Islamic lands. His highly effective siege train was commanded by a Spanish engineer named Calamandrinus (perhaps a converted Muslim) who was renowned for his battering rams. Unfortunately for the Emperor, the enemy city of Brescia captured Calamandrinus and persuaded him to work for them instead.[77]

The indigenous people of the island of Sardinia maintained a fierce military reputation and a distinct identity throughout much of this period. There was, for example, a Sard contingent in the Pisan fleet which attacked Islamic Majorca and Ibiza in 1113–15. During the 12th century the Sards also seem to have had a habit of enslaving each other during local conflicts on the island, the victims then being sold in Genoa.[78]

During the early phases of the Iberian Reconquista, *milites* or low-status knights of the Midi in southern France played a prominent role, just as they did on the First Crusade. Colonists among the advancing Christians were drawn from many areas inside and outside Iberia, including *Mozarabs* or Arabised Christians from Muslim-ruled al-Andalus.[79] Such frontier communities naturally had substantial military obligations. However, since as far back as the 9th century the most distinctive aspect of military recruitment in the Iberian Reconquista was the very prominent role played by urban militias, both cavalry and infantry, noble and non-noble. Similarly, obligation to serve on horseback resulted from wealth rather than aristocratic birth in the 11th to 13th century Christian kingdoms of northern Iberia.

Forms of obligation included *fonsado* which seems to have meant service in a major expedition, and *cabalgada* or an offensive raid led by the king or a senior member of the aristocracy, most of those involved being cavalry. This would appear to have been much the same as *hueste*, a term first recorded in 1210 and almost certainly from the French feudal term *ost*, which meant a significant royal campaign by *caballeros* cavalry and *peones* infantry. From the late 11th century the term *apellido* indicated defensive action by a town's militia and other locally available forces, perhaps an ad hoc military arrangement, while *fonsadera* was at first a fine imposed for non-attendance which later evolved into a form of payment instead of personal military service.[80] Other military obligations involved participation in a siege, *anubda* or *arróbda*, frontier guard duties and garrisoning fortifications.[81]

Each Iberian Christian state had a slightly different recruitment system. For example, in mid-13th century Aragon the king relied on regional Catalan feudal and coastal urban forces to conquer Majorca, whereas rural militias from the mountainous interior of Aragon itself were most active in the conquest of Valencia. Despite this conquest of Valencia, many castles remained in the hands of a local Islamic military élite until the final quarter of the 13th century, this community now owing allegiance to its new Christian ruler.[82] Indeed Muslims made up perhaps half of the armies of Aragon during the second half of the 13th century. Organised either as separate Islamic units or forming parts of mixed Muslim–Christian militias, their infantry crossbowmen and spear-armed light cavalry proved their worth in the defeat of a French invasion of Aragon in 1285.[83] The most famous Aragonese troops of this period were the relatively lightly-equipped and fast moving *almugavars*, whose tactics were clearly of Moorish Islamic origin. Some if not most of the *almugavars* themselves were either still Muslim or were recent converts from Islam. Indeed, the loyalty and reliability of overtly Muslim mercenaries from Valencia to the crown of Aragon was such that the king used them against dissident baronial rebels.

Navarrese armies tended to consist largely of infantry because the larger part of this kingdom consisted of mountainous terrain where earlier traditions of warfare and recruitment continued to be relevant. Conquests by Castile and León, in contrast, broke through onto the high plains of central Iberia at an early date. Even in the late 11th century the militias of Castilian towns were divided between higher-status and invariably mounted *caballerias* and lower-status *peonias* who included both foot soldiers and horsemen. The latter came to be known as *caballeros villanos*, middle-class cavalry who were first recorded in 11th century León and shortly afterwards in Castile. In both these countries 12th and 13th century frontier warfare involved an élite of *talayeros* or *atalayeros* scouts. Their name came from the Arabic word for guard, and they were usually either selected by a commander or elected by the men.[84] Following the massive

Christian conquests of the 12th and 13th centuries, Castile acquired a substantial Islamic population, some of those living in cities being allowed equal status and a continuing military obligation. In 13th century Avila, for example, the *Mauri Pacis* 'captured in battle' provided seventy cavalry and five hundred infantry.[85] *Almogávares* were recorded in recently conquered Cordova in 1236 as being amongst the earliest inhabitants after the Castilian conquest. Whether they were recent converts, indigenous Muslims or settlers from further north is unknown but they clearly fought in Islamic style on foot and horseback.[86]

Military recruitment and organisation in León was generally similar to that of neighbouring Castile, except that urban militias played a less prominent role in the 13th century. In contrast the expanding but rather isolated state of Portugal to the west remained remarkably traditional in its military systems. Most of the Portuguese expansion southwards was undertaken by part-time rural militias carrying out raids before returning home to attend to their crops. After such persistent raiding had weakened neighbouring Islamic territory, the rulers of Portugal led larger, more carefully planned expeditions to impose Christian rule.[87]

The more northerly European states did not have frontiers with the Islamic world, but their forces played an often dominant role in the main Crusading expeditions preached by the Papacy. Consequently their methods of recruitment and organisation had a direct bearing upon Crusader warfare. In these respects France and England were essentially the same, the Norman and then Plantagenet ruling dynasties of England being French in culture, military traditions and as yet largely in speech. In both kingdoms the rulers made increasing use of mercenaries, initially in mid-11th century France but even more prominently in the 12th century Plantagenet 'empire' which included England, most of Wales, part of Ireland, the western half of France and claimed suzerainty over Scotland.[88] These professionals included various military specialists such as garrison troops, siege artillerymen, military engineers, archers, fire troops, foragers, light cavalrymen skilled in reconnaissance, patrolling, escorting and guarding foragers.[89]

As already stated, The Empire (later known as the Holy Roman Empire) based upon Germany differed from France. Here the most distinctive group of full-time soldiers were *ministeriales*. Though steadily rising in prestige and military importance, they remained legally unfree 'serfs'. During the 11th and first half of the 12th centuries even their horses could be requisitioned by their lord, just like a peasant's animals, yet the *ministeriales* were already excused the 'degrading' forced labour demanded of other 'unfree' men. Their wives and daughters were expected to prepare or mend the clothes and other items needed by the *ministeriales*, while these families were rewarded not in cash but in food from their lord's larder.[90] Such *ministeriales* played a significant part in German contributions to various Crusades, but by the mid-13th century German Imperial armies had become more professional. Feudal levies such as the *ministeriales* now became secondary to mercenaries hired and paid by the Emperor, including Germans, Italians, Sicilians and the 'Saracens of Lucera' already mentioned.

A German military aristocracy began to settle in some parts of Hungary during the mid-11th century, encouraged to do so by Hungarian rulers who believed they could help modernise or Westernise the kingdom. However, there was also an intermittent but substantial inflow of largely Turkish refugees from the steppe regions east of the Carpathian mountains. These mainly tribal groups represented the defeated élites of various semi-nomadic states or tribal groups which had been conquered during the traditional westward flow of peoples out of Inner Asia across the Eurasian steppes. They would include Pechenegs, Iasians and Kipchaqs, the latter being in flight from Genghis Khan's Mongol hordes.[91] Many of these Kipchaqs were still pagan and tribally organised when they were allowed to settle in clearly defined regions of the Hungarian kingdom in the mid-13th century. There they provided an immediately available fighting force of light cavalry using horse-archery tactics similar to those of the Hungarians themselves a few centuries earlier.[92]

FINANCES, PAYMENT AND MILITARY ORGANISATION

Money provided the sinews of war in the Middle Ages, as it did in ancient and modern times. Going on Crusade was an expensive business and the idea of the poor knight or younger son trekking east in search of his fortune is largely a myth. In fact the concept of the 'poor knight' was itself relative. The truly poor could not afford the arms, armour and horses needed for knightly warfare, and so a 'poor' knight was merely poorer than most members of the knightly class. He was certainly richer than most, though not all, peasants and even most urban artisans. In the very early Crusading period there is evidence of some participants relying on charity to be able to take part, but this became almost unknown in later expeditions.[93]

Where professional soldiers and other skilled specialists were concerned, rates of payment could be good. Engineers had particularly high status in medieval Western European armies but were almost always in short supply. On the other hand, surviving evidence concerning pay for men involved in later or merely proposed Crusades, including fleets, shows less differentiation between those of low and high status than might be expected. In one early 14th century Crusading proposal, knights would only receive four times as much as ordinary oarsmen.[94] Other evidence shows that the financial rewards offered to senior commanders could be enormous. The costs faced by those trying to raise a Crusading contingent could be daunting, even for a rich state like France. Here, in the mid-12th century, the king had to undertake prolonged negotiations with the church before its financial support was agreed. Furthermore, it was apparently commonplace for individual participants to raise the money they needed by mortgaging property to whatever organisation had money to lend.[95]

For the Latin States of the Middle East the problems could be much greater as their rulers were increasingly short of cash. Yet, by imposing tribute upon Fatimid Egypt in 1164, the Kingdom of Jerusalem briefly enjoyed a substantial source of money to pay its army and and provender to feed its horses, though this did not last long. During the 12th century Jerusalem already imposed special taxes on its own population for specific campaigns such as offensives against Egypt or defensive operations against Saladin. It is also important to stress that, although most of the money fiefs in the Latin States were urban, some involved rural sources of revenue and it is possible that they were normally more valuable than an ordinary territorial fief.

The Latin States of the Aegean tended to be even poorer and in 1233–4 the Latin Emperor of Constantinople found himself unable to pay his mercenaries, most of whom then promptly abandoned his service.[96] There was money around, however. For example, at the start of the 14th century the Catalan Grand Company was a mercenary army which either offered its services, lived by extortion or seized territory on its own behalf as occasion demanded. In this remarkable force a fully equipped knight was paid four ounces of gold, a light cavalryman two ounces and an infantryman one.[97]

Money payment was already important in 11th century southern Italy. Here a Norman knight of the new ruling élite inherited the feudal military duties of his Lombard predecessors but, as elsewhere, expected to be paid in cash after serving for the agreed number of days. Almost two centuries later, the only unpaid soldiers in this region may have been some of the so-called Saracens of Lucera who served in return for religious toleration, government protection against persecution, and the land on which they lived almost as serfs.[98] The abundant surviving records of Venice in northern Italy provide remarkably detailed information about payment in Venetian war-fleets. In 1224, for example, an armed oarsman received three *lire* or pounds, as did a sailor on a war-galley or *galleon* (merchant ship). A crossbowman aboard a *galleon* received just over four, a crossbowman on a fighting-galley five and a half, while the captain of such a galley was paid over thirty-three and a half pounds.[99]

In the Iberian peninsula nobles and knights owed their military service in return for land or cash, while people who owed infantry service were still expected to pay taxes. If they were rich enough they could become *caballeros villanos* 'villain-knights' and would no longer have to pay taxes as long as they passed muster at their city's biannual military parade where everyone's military equipment was checked. Whereas the original method of rewarding military service in Aragon had reflected the essentially defensive nature of campaigning, a sudden expansion out of the Pyrenean valleys in the 11th century enabled the ruler to reward his followers with conquered land. Nevertheless the remarkably numerous *cavalleriae* or holders of knight's fiefs in 12th century Aragon remained economically precarious and were rarely rich by those standards seen north of the Pyrenees.

Here in France financial information is particularly abundant from the reign of Philip Augustus. In the early 13th century, for example, the *milites* knights were paid seven *sous* a day, mounted sergeants from three to four *sous* a day, and mounted crossbowmen five *sous* a day, whereas infantry crossbowmen received only eighteen *deniers*, one *sous* equalling twelve *deniers*. Crossbowmen, whether mounted or on foot, were still few, and most foot soldiers were rated as infantry sergeants, being paid only nine *deniers* daily.[100] It is interesting to note that amongst the largely non-combatant but specialised workers in the army of King Philip Augustus, siege miners were paid eighteen *deniers* daily, while the *pionarii* pioneers, *macones* macons and *fabri* labourers who repaired castles received fifteen *deniers* daily.[101] Clearly the mere fact of bearing arms as a soldier did not make a man one of the élite. The same state of affairs was seen in 13th century England with the knights being paid the most. Royal sergeants and crossbowmen were divided into those mounted and those on foot, with infantry sergeants being paid least of all.[102] Rewards were similar in Imperial Germany, but here there are also interesting references to unfree *ministerial* 'serf knights' pledging their *allodial*, freehold, woodland in return for cash towards the cost of going on Crusade.[103]

There were obviously changes in the military organisation of Western Europe and the various Latin States from the 11th to early 14th centuries, but many such changes reflected social, economic and political rather than strictly military developments. Among the most noticeable concerned non-noble personnel such as squires. It is, for example, worth noting that in many parts of Western Europe distinctions between the roles of *scutiferi*, *servientes*, *armigeri*, *valetti* and others became clearer in the late 11th and 12th centuries, but then largely disappeared by the middle of the 13th century. Though care of the horses remained the primary duty of such a squire, by the end of that century most *armigeri* had become well-paid and fully armoured cavalrymen though their status remained lower than that of knights.[104]

The Crusades reflected these and other such developments. However, whereas the early expeditions and above all the First Crusade were organised like a microcosm of Western society in general, later Crusades were specialised military expeditions by military forces that reflected Western armies rather than Western societies. Returning to the First Crusade, it was based upon the extended household and dependency relationships of the senior military aristocracy and urban élites. The only non-noble rural elements to take part were men with disposable assets; in other words money. Consequently the contingents of this First Crusade were structured around the great lords and their attendant knights.

Once the Latin States had been established in the Middle East, Western archetypes remained the basis for their military organisation. The King of Jerusalem was, in practice, first amongst equals even in war and though theoretically he was head of the army, in practice he had to consult various leading men before a campaign or even before a battle. Occasionally this led to confusion or resentment, and as a consequence the Pope sometimes declared a churchman such as a Legate to be the overall leader of a particular expedition, especially when substantial newly arrived Crusader forces were involved.[105]

On a day-to-day or more practical level, there was supposed to be a clear chain of command and a differentiation of responsibilities. In the Kingdom of Jerusalem the main military officials were the *Connetable* and *Senechal.* The latter, sometimes called the *Dapifer Regis*, was largely concerned with ceremonial affairs and matters of justice. He was further responsible for the inspection of castles, their provisions and the changing of their garrisons but he could not change *châtelains*, or castle commanders, who were appointed by the king. Nor did he command a *bataille* division of the army, but he was himself usually within the king's division. The *Connetable* or *regni constabularius* was chief of the army after the ruler himself, with particular responsibility for the knights. He also commanded the army if the ruler was absent. He organised recruitment, sorted the *batailles* or military formations, gave them their duties and also checked on the readiness of knights, squires and sergeants.[106] Next came the *Marechal* or *regius marescalus* who, as second in command beneath the *Connetable*, served as the latter's most immediate assistant. Furthermore, he was responsible for recruiting knights, squires and *turcopoles*, held reviews to check their equipment, maintained discipline, paid mercenaries and generally organised the supply, maintenance and distribution of military material including horses, mules and other animals.[107] The *Grand Turcoplier* had a more limited and specific role as commander of *turcopoles* under the *Marechal.*[108]

Essentially the same military structure and officials were seen in the armies of the other Latin States, and to some extent in subordinate armies like that of Tyre which formed part of the Kingdom of Jerusalem. One difference was that there were two *marechals* in Antioch, where the *baillis* or senior local authorities were also under the command of the royal *Senechal* unless they were themselves part of the royal household.[109] In the very exposed frontier County of Edessa the basic feudal structure was again the same as that seen in Western Europe but appears to have been more rigid and more directly concerned with military service. The castles of senior barons were, for example, under the everyday command of *châtelains* whose importance varied according to that of the castle in question. *Châtelains* similarly commanded urban citadels and their garrisons.[110]

The numbers of people involved in any particular event during the medieval period, military or otherwise, are always a problem for the historian. Only very rarely are figures found in contemporary written sources reliable. It has been estimated that no more than three hundred knights and an unknown number of foot soldiers remained to defend newly conquered Jerusalem, Ramlah and Haifa after most participants in the First Crusade returned home to Europe.[111] Yet within a few decades the numbers of troops that each of the feudatories of the Kingdom were expected to provide is clearly recorded. Whether these figures were achieved is another matter. They ranged from the five hundred sergeants owed by the Patriarch of Jerusalem, to the twenty-five owed by the small domain of Le Petit Gerin. The number of knights owed was, of course, smaller but again reflected the size or value of a fief, ranging from one hundred owed by places like the barony of Jaffa, to the single knight to be maintained by the 'wife of Govert Vernier'.[112] The numbers of mercenaries were similarly specific, ranging from five hundred *armigeri* paid by the Patriarch of Jerusalem, to the twenty-five mercenaries to be supplied by Leyrim.[113] Writing in the mid-13th century, Jean d'Ibelin recorded that, almost a century earlier during the reign of King Baldwin IV (1174–85), the entire military strength of the Kingdom of Jerusalem had stood at 577 knights, 5,025 sergeants plus unspecified numbers of mercenaries and the Military Orders. According to the 13th century *Gestes des Chiprois* this strength was officially still 568 knights and 4,075 sergeants, but these figures only included those owing regular feudal service. As yet there were no officially recognised or structured communal militias other than those of the Italian merchant communities in coastal towns.[114]

Totals for the other Latin States are little more than estimates. In 1102 the County of Tripoli reportedly had some three hundred knights, this reducing to two hundred knights and around two thousand infantry in 1115, but going back up to a total of three thousand in 1116. It was clearly usual for there to be around ten foot soldiers for every knight.[115] Antioch could field similar numbers, but almost nothing is known of the military strength of the short-lived County of Edessa.

Not surprisingly, the military structure and administration of the Military Orders had parallels with that of secular realms. A Hospitaller *marshal* or *marechal* was first mentioned in the 1160s but may have existed earlier, and thereafter soon appeared in action as a military leader.[116] A Hospitaller *Commander of Knights* was not recorded until 1220 but was then appointed when the *marshal* or his lieutenants were not available to lead the brother knights. Once the Hospitaller system of ranks was fully developed, it seems clear that brother knights and brother sergeants differed in status rather than role. They had virtually the same equipment except that, from at least the early 13th century, a brother knight had four horses whereas a brother sergeant was permitted only two or three. It is certainly wrong to describe such sergeants of the Military Orders as light cavalry, though some details of their arms and armour might suggest that they were better able to fight on foot as well as on horseback than were brother knights.[117] In addition to these military brethren, the Hospitallers, like other Military Orders, attracted temporary adherents who did not take the Order's vows but fought alongside them for a while. The Order also employed mercenaries, the most important of which were the *turcopoles* who were commanded by a senior officer called the *Turcopolier*. He, however, only seems to have been appointed when required. Nearby Latin settlements which fell within territory owned by the Hospitallers may also have provided feudal contingents, though there is only limited evidence for this in the Latin States of the Middle East. In Spain and Portugal it is much clearer that local Christian frontier settlements supported Hospitaller garrisons militarily.[118]

Even as early as 1168 the Hospitallers could offer five hundred knights, not all of them perhaps brethren, and five hundred *turcopoles* for a proposed invasion of Egypt. During the second half of the 12th century the Order also started to build up a *palatinate* or virtually autonomous principality in the north-east of the County of Tripoli. Significantly, this was the only substantial area outside the currently 'neutral' Principality of Antioch that Saladin failed to retake after his victory at the battle of Hattin in 1187. Throughout much of the following century it served as a major offensive base-area and the visiting King Andrew II of Hungary called this Hospitaller fiefdom the *'key to the Christian lands'*.[119]

In 1203 the castles of Margat (Marqab) and Crac des Chevaliers, the most important Hospitaller strongholds within this *palatinate*, could themselves muster an army of four hundred cavalry and eleven hundred infantrymen plus *turcopoles* for a major raid against Islamic Ba'rin.[120] Just over sixty years later, when the remnants of the Latin States were tottering to their fall, the Hospitallers are still said to have had a garrison of six hundred cavalry in Margat. There were over four hundred or so more men at Arsuf when it fell to the Mamluks. Yet a letter from the Hospitaller Master in 1268 complained that there were only three hundred brethren in the whole of Syria. Clearly brethren of the Order formed only a small part of the Hospitallers' total military strength, as indicated by other sources which state that of the two thousand men in Crac des Chevaliers in 1211, only a handful were Hospitaller brethren.[121] All these characteristics were similarly applicable to the other great Military Order in the Latin Middle East. For example, the Templars had earlier garrisoned Gaza with merely eighty men; this figure perhaps meaning brethren supported by an undisclosed number of other troops.[122]

The administration of the Latin Kingdom of Cyprus, including its military structures, was again based on those of Western Europe,[123] though with some small or superficial Byzantine influence. During the early days of Latin Cyprus the army of Guy de Lusignan included three hundred enfiefed knights,[124] but the strength of the Kingdom during the 13th century usually enabled over two hundred Cypriot knights to be available for service elsewhere. Otherwise the island's defensive military potential was built around five fortified towns, Nicosia, Famagusta, Limassol, Paphos and Cerines, the first two of which were governed autonomously by their own city councils under royal *baillis* while defence of the others was the responsibility of royal *châtelains*.[125]

Residual Byzantine influence was more obvious in the Latin States of the Aegean, especially in the Duchy of Athens, though there was little evidence of the *pronoia* system of non-hereditary fiefs which were becoming a feature of the Byzantine successor states.[126] Other evidence shows that the size of Latin baronies in Crusader Greece was very varied, the smallest incorporating only four fiefs capable of maintaining a knight and twelve for squires or sergeants.[127] On the other hand, the militarily very exposed conditions of these Latin States meant that feudal military obligations were strictly enforced. In some other respects there were major military differences between the Duchy of Athens and the Principality of Achaia further south. In Athens the ruling Burgundian duke was the Great Lord who stood above all except one of the baronial families. In Achaia the prince was first amongst equals, which might have been why there were so many baronial Crusader castles in southern Greece and so few in Attica or Boetia to the north.[128] Where the numbers of available troops are concerned, some rather suspect sources stated that the the Latin Prince of Achaia had a force of eight thousand cavalry in 1258 but that in the early 14th century such forces included only five or six hundred knights.[129]

Information for the period of Angevin southern Italian domination of Latin Greece is sometimes more detailed, though also more prosaic. For example, the military administration of 1278 was very different from that seen earlier. What were now merely overseas provinces of a sprawling Angevin empire were governed by a *bailli* and a *vicar* sent from Italy, the two roles sometimes being invested in the same man. They had complete control over the main castles and garrisons.[130] The Angevin possessions in Albania were more difficult to maintain and often included no more than a few coastal enclaves. Yet they were considered very important, and before the main clash between Charles of Anjou, king of southern Italy and Sicily, and Michael VIII Palaeologus, Emperor of a revived and seemingly vigorous Byzantine Empire, Charles strengthened his main garrisons in Albania. This he did by sending two hundred archers to Durazzo (Durrës) in 1272 when the Angevin army in Albania was commanded by a *Maréchal d'Albanie*.[131] Other troops, including 'Saracens of Lucera', mercenary crossbowmen and cavalry followed over the next few years, usually in groups of one hundred, and their payment was duly recorded in the remarkably detailed Angevin archives of Naples. Meanwhile Byzantine pressure on Durrës increased.[132]

After the Fourth Crusade the new Venetian lords of Crete and the central Aegean islands used normal European feudal terminology where their military structures were concerned, but they also retained some of the powerful state rights that had characterised previous Byzantine rule. In fact this administration was not really feudal since the supreme authority of the Venetian Senate was firmly maintained by military force. Those who helped the Cretan resistance risked savage punishment.[133] On the ground the organisation of Venetian-ruled Crete mirrored that of Venice itself, being divided into six regions and two hundred or so fiefs. Most of the new colonists came from Venice and held land in return for feudal military service. Most of these fiefs were inhabited by unfree agricultural serfs, the majority of whom were said to be of Arab rather than Greek origin. This little-known community, which presumably originated during the Arab-Islamic occupation of Crete in the 9th and 10th centuries, could also be mustered for military service. Cretan Greeks do not seem to have been conscripted until much later, when Venetian Crete faced a growing Ottoman Turkish threat.[134]

Genoese overseas possessions in the Aegean and Black Seas were more like a commonwealth of autonomous outposts, several of which were still either technically Byzantine or recognised Byzantine suzerainty. This again reflected the fragmented nature of authority in their home city of Genoa which was dominated by several almost independent leading families.[135] There was, however, an overarching structure, especially where military matters were concerned. This seems to have changed after the fall of Acre in 1291, and, whereas the Genoese colonies around the Aegean and Black Seas had previously been administered as one, they were now divided into two distinct groups.[136]

The military and civilian administration of the Norman Kingdom in southern Italy inherited several different traditions. As a result, Lombard influence was strong in most of the mainland provinces, including ex-Byzantine Apulia, whereas Byzantine influence was dominant in Calabria in the deep south. Across the straits in Sicily, Islamic administrative structures largely survived the Norman conquest. Looking at these regions in greater detail, it is clear that the local *gastaldates* of the mainland provinces were already highly developed administrative units whose borders remained, and in many cases still do to this day.[137] The Normans then imposed a new layer of feudalism on these *gastaldates*, resulting in the three classic layers of military aristocracy: the counts centred upon the towns, the barons centred upon their castles, and the *milites* or knights with their fiefs. In the early years of Norman rule, before the unification of the kingdom, there had normally been two *Master Captains* and *Master Constables* at the same time, having both military and civilian roles. They controlled the district *constables* and commanded the army in the field.[138]

In Sicily many of the former Arab-Islamic *'iqta* fiefs were preserved as Norman feudal fiefs. However, there is still debate about the primary source of Islamic administrative and cultural influence within the remarkable Norman Kingdom of Sicily. Some scholars maintain that it was inherited from the previous Kalbite *emirate* of Sicily and reflected continuing contact with North Africa. Others point to remarkable similarities between the Norman administrative reforms after 1130 and the administration of 12th century Fatimid Egypt, also noting the exceptionally good relations between the Norman Kingdom and the Fatimid Caliphate at that time.[139] Many aspects of surviving Siculo-Norman art would also strengthen the case for Fatimid influence.

Military organisation in the rest of Italy varied between urban and rural. This was particularly true of militias. In rural regions the command structure of feudal armies was in the hands of the aristocracy, being given to men of sufficient age and experience as was the case in the rest of Western Europe.[140] Nevertheless, even here there were changes in attitudes and the use of terminology. For example, in the 11th century most of the Italian aristocracy lived in the countryside, in castles defended by *milites* knights who formed a lord's *masnata* and had their own small fiefs. By the late 13th century the word *masnadieri* or member of a *masnata* generally meant a simple soldier, a ruffian or even an assassin.[141]

The migration of the aristocracy to the cities was a major feature of medieval Italian history. Urban knights had been integrated into communal structures since at least the 10th century and Italian cities had largely dominated the neighbouring aristocracies. During the 11th and 12th centuries the increasingly powerful and autonomous urban communes were essentially the creation of the urban patrician or aristocratic class which dominated their military life. A system of powerful extended families continued to provide mutual security and commercial support within the cities throughout the 13th century, whatever the nature of political power at government level. Such families often had their own main fortified house or indeed small fortress within the city. Aristocracies also led the naval expansion of Pisa and Genoa,[142] such expeditions being largely financed as well as commanded by the nobility who consequently shared the profits. In fact aristocratic power in the cities of central and northern Italy only really declined in the 13th century. On land urban communal armies were usually commanded by members of a city's aristocracy, but this was not directly linked to their status but instead reflected their greater reputation or experience in military affairs. Nevertheless by the 12th and 13th centuries major strategic and even tactical decisions were often made by the city council. Meanwhile military command was increasingly given to a 'foreigner', meaning an aristocrat from another part of Italy or a noted mercenary captain. This, it was found, overrode the political factionalism so characteristic of city life.[143] On a more basic level, the archives show that in many parts of 13th century Italy, communal crossbowmen were usually organised into *decine* or units of ten, though in Florence they formed *venticinquine* or units of twenty-five.[144]

In Iberia the term *mesnada* was, of course, from the same origin as *masnata* in Italy or *mesnie* in France. All are generally thought to stem from the Latin *mansio*, originally meaning a stopping place but coming to mean a house in the low Latin of the early medieval period. However, it is also possible that there was a link with the Arabic word *masnad*, *masnada* meaning a support or position of honour. In the early Christian states of northern Spain the *mesnadas* were the professional guard units of rulers or senior magnates.[145] In Aragon the loyalty of *cavalleriae* who held knight's fiefs was essentially based upon personal fidelity rather than feudal obligation, and concepts of vassalage between various strata of military society only became important with an increase in French influence in the 13th century. Even in the mid-13th century it is still difficult to define quite how the Muslim cavalry élite of now Christian Aragonese-ruled Valencia fitted into the new feudal hierarchy. They were not knights, but were generally known simply as *cavalleros* or cavalry.[146]

In neighbouring Castille and León the traditional *Masnadas Reales* remained the king's own immediately available military force during the first half of the 13th century, serving as a bodyguard of close companions on campaign.[147] Lower down the military hierarchy there had already been changes where non-noble cavalry were concerned, some fiefs or *benefices* being hereditary while others were not. In 12th century León a transitional form meant that if a man died in action his heirs kept his horse and military equipment, but if he died in bed these must be returned to the king who had given them in the first place.[148]

The urban militias of Castile and León were largely based upon the *collación* or quarter of a town. The people of each *collación* elected an *alcalde* who was responsible for administrative aspects of the militia, the command structure being separate. On campaign the militias of each *collación* probably joined to form a single unit, or were expected to serve in rotation.[149] There seems to have been a tendency for the southern towns of Castile to be allowed greater military autonomy than the northern cities in the mid-13th century. Yet the famous late 13th century *Siete Partidas* treatise on government and warfare credited to King Alfonso El Sabio, 'The Wise', does not reflect such regional distinctions. In fact the only real separation was between cavalry and infantry, with the *almocadén* infantry commander being distinct from the *adalid* cavalry commander.[150]

The old-fashioned and rather isolated character of Portuguese military administration before the reforms of the 14th century was seen in the name, *Alferes Mor*, which was given to the head of the Portuguese army, beneath the ruler himself. Portugal's military structures, like many other aspects of Portuguese society, remained under stronger Islamic-Moorish influence throughout the 11th to 13th centuries than in neighbouring Spain, with an aristocracy of *ricos-homens* at the head of the *ingenui* ancient senior families of free status. Beneath them were the *infanções* or *cavaleiros* knights, and the *escudeiros* squires. In this context it is worth noting that Portugal, though expanding at the expense of neighbouring small Islamic statelets known as the *ta'ifas*, was nevertheless under strong cultural influence from these same *ta'ifas* during both the first, second, perhaps also the third and final, *ta'ifa* periods (see volume II). Furthermore the easternmost *ta'ifas* of eastern Andalus who were Portugal's southern neighbours were characterised by a particularly strong adherence to indigenous Andalusian rather than newer North African military traditions.[151]

The military administrative structures of the rest of Western and Central Europe were more uniform than were their military recruitment systems. It was these structures, most notably those of France,[152] that provided the pattern which the Latin States of the Middle East and Aegean sought to follow. They were themselves, however, evolving and changing to accommodate new weapons, new troops and new tactics. For example, the first recorded *Grand Master of Crossbowmen* in France was Thibaud de Montléar who was arrested by the *Parlement* of Paris in 1230.[153] The armies involved could, of course, be much larger than those in the Latin States or indeed those which formed most Crusading expeditions after the First Crusade. On the other hand such armies were not always that big. The Emperor of Germany was normally only able to muster around 12,000 men, and at most 15,000, which would seem small in relation to the vast territories which owed him nominal allegiance.[154]

Again, the situation in Hungary remained rather different, despite the fact that the Hungarian royal household had been restructured along normal Western European military lines since the late 12th century. Over the next hundred years French chivalric ideas and to a lesser extent military structures spread across most of the huge Kingdom of Hungary.[155] Earlier traditions survived in Transylvania, in the east of the kingdom. In the early days of Hungarian history this region had being dominated by the *Gyula*, an almost independent prince who was second in rank to the ruler himself. Subsequently its wild and rather isolated character meant that Transylvania continued to be under a militarily powerful and almost autonomous *Vojvod* military governor.

FLAGS, INSIGNIA AND MUSIC

In the early Middle Ages there had been a reasonably clear distinction between clerical and secular banners in the Christian armies of Western Europe, even when both were carried into battle. This distinction then began to blur and during the 11th century there was a growing fashion for putting images of warrior saints, particularly St Michael, on all sorts of flags while clerics also began blessing the knights' swords and banners. These changes in behaviour reflected the Church's own shifting opinions concerning warfare, especially that directed against non-

Christians or heretics.[156] Popes not only offered religious indulgences to those taking part in military expeditions of which the Papacy approved, but gave Papal banners as a mark of such approval and as signs of divine support.

Another and separate line of development was the appearance of true heraldic armorials or motifs in the mid-12th century. This really began when local lords placed their own motifs or devices on shields, helmets, saddles, pennons and eventually entire horse-covering *caparisons*. Known as *connaissances*, they developed into the system of heraldry so typical of the later medieval period. The tendency for the men of one *conrois* cavalry unit, or the followers of one lord, to use the same colours to identify or recognise each other may have been slightly earlier and may sometimes have included the use of the same simple proto-heraldic patterns on shields, helmets, other items of equipment, lance pennons and clothing.

Small pennons, or *gonfanons*, normally appear to have been nailed rather than tied to a spear-shaft at this time. By the late 12th century such unit-recognition *gonfanons* may have been replaced by a single larger flag placed in the hands of a standard-bearer. Certainly Middle Eastern sources make it clear that having even a small flag on the end of a lance made it more difficult to use the weapon. While there may have been some eastern influence upon the adoption of banners to which men of a particular unit could rally, there was certainly Islamic influence in the development of true European heraldry. For example, several tinctures or colours as well as patterns had names of Arab or Persian origin.[157]

The size and positioning of banners became important and potentially divisive, as when the followers of King Richard of England threw down the Duke of Austria's flag from the wall of conquered Acre because, as a mere duke, they did not consider him to be of the same rank as the kings of England and France. For the Duke of Austria's followers, of course, he was the representative of the Emperor and was therefore of at least the same standing as mere kings. The raising or acceptance of a banner by an individual or an entire city was a significant sign of allegiance or ownership, and became even more important during the 13th century. Within parts of Latin Europe and the Latin Crusader States the size and shape of flags also became theoretically linked to the size of a feudal landholding or an individual's ranking in the aristocratic hierarchy. What would set fully developed European heraldry apart from most other systems of insignia, however, was the inheritance of a device or coat-of-arms by successive generations. Similarly, certain heraldic colours and patterns came to be associated with a specific geographical location, though this would only become commonplace during the 13th century. By then it was also normal for mercenaries to carry the arms of their leader on their shields.[158]

Efforts to use moderation in dress and the decoration of military equipment as a visible sign of high morals and good intentions were another feature which distinguished some Crusader armies from the normal military and aristocratic values of their time.[159] In virtually all other respects, however, Crusader armies and the Latin States used the same system of flags, banners and heraldry as seen in Europe. Occasionally the best information about such matters is found in the writings of their enemies. For example, the Arab chronicler Baha al-Din was present during the Third Crusade's siege of Acre. There he described the Crusader's main banner: *'on a staff as tall as a minaret, was set up on a cart drawn by mules. It had a white ground with red spots. The top of the staff was surmounted by a cross'*.[160] This would seem to have been the banner of the Kingdom of Jerusalem set up on an Italian-style *carroccio*.

The Rules of the Military Orders included regulations dealing with associated matters. For example, the Templars' *Old French Rule* permitted higher ranks down to the *commanders of houses* and the *commanders of knights* to carry banners to show their status and as rallying points. Clothing would prove to be quite a problem for the Hospitallers. At first they had to wear essentially the same dress as other non-military monks, but soon complained that the monastic *cappa clausa* hampered their hands and arms when they fought, so a *bull* or law was issued in 1248 which permitted them to *'wear wide surcoats bearing upon the breast the sign of the cross.'* Another *bull* in 1259 allowed Hospitaller brother knights and sergeants to be distinguished by wearing different coloured *'jupons and other military surcoats'*.[161] However, this may have undermined morale and was rescinded just under twenty years later.[162] The Military Orders were clearly not immune from the perhaps natural tendency of soldiers to like finery and decorated weapons; a Hospitaller legal document of 1303 forbade the brethren in Cyprus to use finely decorated saddles and swords garnished with silver.[163]

No such inhibitions were seen in Western Europe, but there were some variations between countries. For example, the placing of large banners in carts to make a *carroccio* or mobile rallying point became particularly, though not exclusively, characteristic of Italian communal urban armies. The first was mentioned in Milan in 1039.[164] These banner-waggons were not rolled out for minor expeditions and, as was clear in late 13th century Perugia, the blessing and use of the city's *carroccio* indicated that this was a serious affair.[165] Military and ceremonial music was another feature of Italy, though the prominent use of drums to announce a high Byzantine official in Ancona in the 12th century might itself have reflected eastern influence.[166]

In Iberia the blessing of *concejo* standards before a campaign may have been even more usual than it was in other parts of Europe, in which case this habit is likely to have reflected a comparably close link between military banners and mosques in the Islamic south of the peninsula (see volume II). The abundant information about the significance of flags and heraldry in France tends to be more secular. According to the chronicler William of Poitiers writing a quarter of a century after the event, when Count Geoffrey Martel of Anjou sought combat with William of Normandy on a specified day in 1049, he arranged for the colour of his horse, his 'arms' and the figure on his shield to be known to his opponent. William of Normandy replied with a description of his own appearance.[167] One of the earliest *chansons de geste* or French epic poems, the *Charroi de Nîmes*, describes how soldiers had the same coloured pennons on lances so that they could identify each other when infiltrating an enemy stronghold.[168] The same is seen in the similarly dated *Roman de Troie*:

Armes fresches et rondes
Heaumes, haubers, escuz et seles
Totes d'un teint d'une color
Qu'ensi plaisit à lor seigneur
Por ço qu'il s'entreconeusent.[169]

A decade or so later the poem *Ile et Galeran* by Gautier d'Arras was more specific in describing how thirty knights all bore the *lioncel* 'lioncub' motif of their lord.[170] It was during this same period that the *fleur de lys* was adopted as the royal symbol of France, though it only became fully established as such in the early 13th century.

It has been suggested that the link between a specific banner and a geographical province was seen earlier in The Empire than in France, but otherwise heraldry and insignia developed along much the same lines throughout Europe. On the other hand the apparent use of a banner waggon by the Hungarians in the mid-12th century is more surprising. According to Nicetas Choniates' description of the major battle against a Byzantine army near the fortress of Semlin north of Belgrade, the Hungarians formed their array with an ox-drawn *carroccio* in the centre.[171] It is unlikely that this reflected Italian influence and it is more likely that the Hungarians were still using waggons as a form of field fortification as their ancestors had done, but had also attached one or more banners as rallying points. Indeed it is possible that the medieval Italian *carroccio* itself owed something to outside influence.

MOTIVATION AND MORALE

The historical facts do not support the still widespread belief that many men went on Crusade primarily in the hope of material gain or to carve out fiefs for themselves in the East. A few amongst the senior leadership may have dreamed of new realms and greater status, but for the great majority of participants Crusading was very expensive as well as very dangerous. To 'take the cross' involved serious sacrifices, and members of the lesser nobility, as well as ordinary knights, often had to pool their resources before they could set out. They also needed to be relatively young and fit if they were to have any realistic hope of surviving what was clearly going to be an extremely arduous adventure.[172]

Rather than material gain or even the lure of adventure, the primary motivating force for the overwhelming majority of Crusaders was religious enthusiasm, often spilling over into sheer fanaticism. This came to be expressed in terms that the warrior élite of Latin Europe could easily understand; namely vengeance for the perceived injuries inflicted upon Christianity and upon Christ, their supreme lord, by the Muslim 'infidels'. Whereas there had previously been little interest in or hostility to the Islamic world, the preaching of the First Crusade resulted in the spreading of the most extreme horror stories about Muslims, many of which were believed.[173] At the same time Muslims were portrayed as cowards who fought from a distance with bows and arrows because they had so little blood in their veins, this being caused by the great heat and dryness of their countries.[174] Yet even before the First Crusade, there had been a sudden increase in the savagery of Christian warfare against neighbouring Muslims, the most dramatic example being in the mass slaughter of women and children following the conquest of Barbastro in northern Spain in 1064.[175] This sent shockwaves across the Islamic world, but even so the behaviour of the First Crusade came as an unpleasant surprise to the Islamic peoples of the Middle East.

Though there is limited evidence of conversion by force during the First Crusade, only a few prisoners were taken. Meanwhile priests reportedly baptised dying Muslims on the battlefield. The main exception was at Ma'arat al-Nu'man in northern Syria, where the Crusader assault stirred up dormant but fierce tensions between local Christians and Muslims.[176] Some idea of the largely religious motivation of those who went to serve in the Crusader States even as late as the mid-13th century is reflected in a poem by Rutebeuf about Geoffrey de Sergines, the most famous commander of the French Regiment in the Kingdom of Jerusalem:

He held his liege lord so dear
That he went with him to avenge
God's shame, beyond the sea.[177]

In fact the Holy Land had become a huge religious relic in the minds of most Latin Christians, and the Christian inhabitants of this territory were expected to defend it.[178] A more obvious relic was, of course, the fragment of the True Cross on which Christ supposedly died, and which was the most prized religious possession in the 12th century Kingdom of Jerusalem. It was used to inspire the enthusiasm of the army and would be taken on most defensive campaigns, consequently being lost to Saladin at the catastrophic battle of Hattin. Despite the remarkable religious and cultural toleration which characterised Norman rule in southern Italy, many of the changes in Sicily during this period resulted from external colonisation, particularly by Lombard military settlers who were inspired by a similar spirit to that behind the Crusades. The result was many localised anti-Muslim pogroms despite the fact that Muslims and Jews were protected by their Norman rulers. Perhaps this was why many converts from Islam to Christianity turned first to the local Greek Orthodox Church rather than to the Latin Catholic Church of their oppressors. Much of the Sicilian Islamic aristocracy converted in order to maintain their status under the new regime, though this also resulted in social tensions within the Islamic community as well as individual soul searching. Nevertheless, there seems to have been less resistance to conversion in Sicily than there was in Spain and Portugal, perhaps because so many leading families were already in the service of the state as soldiers or administrators. Indeed families of Arab-Islamic origin remained important under subsequent ruling dynasties and could still be identified in the 14th century.[179]

Meanwhile, in the Iberian peninsula it became normal policy for the conquering Christians to slaughter Islamic religious leaders and teachers, and to burn down mosques. Otherwise the conquered Muslim population were left in place, though much of their political and military leadership migrated into remaining Islamic territory.[180] The last Christian state in Iberia to be affected by what could be called a Crusading mentality was Portugal where it did not appear until well into the 12th century. Even in countries geographically far removed from Crusader warfare, it was accepted that the military had a clear role to play in the struggle between Christianity and 'evil'. The 20th century English legal historian Holdsworth described the idealised role of each member of medieval English society as: '*The hermit in his cell, the monk in his cloister, the knight in his lord's household, all served [militare], they belonged to their distinct militia, but for each the struggle could be hard and long*'.[181]

The Church's Crusade propaganda was enthusiastically accepted by the German knightly class, though in a way which also enhanced their own prestige as defenders of the faith. This was particularly welcomed by the legally unfree but increasingly well-respected class of *ministerial* knights like the poet Hartmann von Aue. His writings did much to link the profession of arms to a common ideology of ethical obligation.[182] In more immediately practical terms, the Albigensian Crusade enabled Papal legates to take control of the existing southern French 'peace of god' military structures, originally established to maintain local law and order but now used against Cathar heretics.[183]

The position of the Military Orders was central to these changes in Church and other attitudes towards war and violence. In the 12th century there were many within the Church who doubted the validity of these new orders because they shed human blood. On the other hand the Military Orders, especially the Templars, enjoyed considerable support from Europe's rulers. Their effectiveness was also recognised by their Islamic foes; so much so that the death of the Hospitaller *castellan* of Crac des Chevaliers in 1170 was widely welcomed because, in the words of the chronicler Ibn al-Athir, he had: '*through his bravery, occupied an eminent position and who was like a bone in the throat of the Muslims*'.[184] Al-Harawi, in his military treatise for Saladin's successors, maintained that the Military Orders were tough, dedicated and truly religious, unlike the Christian clergy who, he believed, tended to be weak and disloyal. In fact, al-Harawi advised Saladin to be harsh to such men when they were captured,[185] and members of the Military Orders were often, though not invariably, executed.

By the 13th century almost all in the Latin Catholic Church accepted the role of the Military Orders, and in the second decade of the 13th century Jaques de Vitry, Bishop of Acre, wrote of them; '*The brothers of a military order have been assigned the task of defending the church of Christ with the material sword, especially against those who are not Christians, namely the Saracens in Syria, the Moors in Spain and the pagans in Prussia, Livonia and Cumania, but also at the command of their superior against schismatics in Greece and against heretics wherever they exist in the universal church*'.[186]

The rising status and popularity of most such Orders led to tighter entry qualifications. From the start, only free men could join, though some freed serfs were accepted. During the 13th century social differentiations between brother knights and brother sergeants became increasingly clear, though even brother knights were mostly drawn from the lesser rather than the greater aristocracy of Europe.[187] The words of the Emperor Rudolf of Hapsburg, in his confirmation of Hospitaller rights and privileges in 1274, indicate the high military and thus social status a member of the Military Orders could enjoy: '*Spurning wordly conflict, they fearlessly march against the forces of the pagan pestilence, staining the standards of Christian victory and the banners of their own knighthood in the blood of the glorious martyr. They fight valiantly against the barbarian nations, and do not fear to give themselves up to a worthy death*'.[188] Others clearly now regarded these Military Orders as the best part of a Church which many maintained was in disarray.

Yet the prestige of most Military Orders had slumped by the start of the 14th century. Perhaps this was primarily a reflection of their failure to preserve what remained of the Latin States in the Middle East, and above all the Kingdom of Jerusalem itself. Criticism of the Templars and Hospitallers for their wealth, bureaucracy, perceived arrogance and tendency to interfere in the political affairs of European states had been growing for some time.[189] Most of these criticisms were largely unfair but there is no doubt that they were in danger of becoming scapegoats for the failure of the Crusading enterprise as a whole. The Templars and Hospitallers had been given remarkable freedom of action within the Latin States, especially in the County of Tripoli and Principality of

Antioch where they could almost wage war as they wished and were not obliged to maintain the truces negotiated by secular rulers. They were not so free in the Kingdom of Jerusalem, but even here there were occasions when their mutual rivalries meant that, as in 1239, the Templars pursued a policy favouring good relations with the Ayyubid ruler of Damascus while the Templars pursued a policy favouring the rival Ayyubid ruler of Cairo. Even in the Iberian peninsula there were several instances where the Hospitallers and other Military Orders persuaded Christian rulers to allow them to keep any territory they conquered from the neighbouring Muslims in return for agreeing to defend one frontier castle.[190]

Where individual secular motivation was concerned, there were clear differences between social groups. Nevertheless the still widespread belief that the knightly élite of medieval Western Europe fought primarily for glory and personal honour is wrong. The evidence shows that they, like their commanders and lower-status troops, primarily fought to win and used whatever tactics or strategies were believed best to achieve that end.[191] It would be equally wrong to accept the old idea that the Latin settler aristocracy of the so-called Crusader States had grown feeble and degenerate by the later 12th century. Many were impoverished by the loss of their lands to Islamic reconquest and many families had no choice but to become an urban-based élite. Yet they continued to fight hard and well in defence of the dwindling Latin enclaves.[192]

These settler aristocracies in the Middle East and Aegean area tried to maintain the values and lifestyles of a chivalric culture that saw France as its fountainhead and heartland. Yet the courtly way of life which became central to this concept of chivalry had developed first in Occitan-speaking southern France and only later spread to northern France which was the political centre of the country. The warlike and glory-seeking aspects of chivalry had their roots in early medieval Germanic warrior ideals. Paradoxically, by the 13th and 14th centuries the fully developed concept of Chivalry was regarded as a 'Roman' institution with its supposed roots in the discipline of ancient Roman armies. Once the ideals of Chivalry had been accepted across virtually all of Latin Catholic Europe, the knightly class tended to stick to its rules because they wanted to maintain their own reputation, self-worth, pride and honour. Mercenaries and lower-status soldiers were often less inclined to do so, though even amongst these troops there was a tendency to 'ape their betters' as a means of improving their own status. The result was a generally, though not universally, accepted code of behaviour which showed the right way to do things, even when it came to the distribution of booty.[193] The values of chivalry underpinned the *chansons de geste* epic poems which were so popular amongst the European aristocracy at this time, and we known that several senior men took prized copies of such *chansons de geste* with them to the Middle East during the 13th century.[194]

Crusading had an important place in this idealised code of behaviour. The ascending scale of chivalrous activities which deserved praise and honour for young men of the knightly class, as described in Geoffrey de Charny's mid-14th century *Book of Chivalry*, may also have been true of the 13th and perhaps even the 12th century. Lowest in this list was jousting, followed by *mêlée* in a tournament, wars for one's country and, at the top, wars overseas especially Crusades.[195] One well-documented example of how participation in a Crusade could bring prestige to an aristocratic family that had previously not ranked highly was that of the Ferrers, the Earls of Derby in England during the late 12th and early 13th centuries.[196] On the other hand the local responsibilities of some senior aristocracies could stop them taking part even when they wished to do so. An example of this was Gilbert de Clare who had planned to accompany Prince Edward of England on his Crusade in 1271. In the event the need to secure his territorial and political interests at home proved too difficult and so he stayed at home.[197]

Although the ideals of chivalry were accepted, to a greater or lesser degree, by military élites throughout Latin Europe, there was also a pecking order of military reputations between nations or peoples. At the top were the northern French whose status was generally accepted by others. They in turn often looked down upon their neighbours, even when fighting side-by-side on Crusade, and in the Latin States there were often also tensions between newly arrived Crusaders and local forces.

The aristocratic cavalry similarly tended to despise their own infantry, and even in Italy the use of any form of missile weapons, bow or crossbow, was generally seen as a 'lower class' of warfare. This was despite the growing reputation of Italian mercenary crossbowmen. In Chretien de Troyes' epic poem *Perceval* there is an interesting verse in which the carrying of two javelins was criticised for making a man look 'too wild'.[198] In most respects England was almost identical to France in the military attitudes and motivations of different sections of society,[199] but in those countries where the cult of chivalry was only skin-deep one can sometimes find evidence of different motivation amongst non-noble troops. In Spain, for example, many epic poems seem to have been written for a broader readership than merely the knightly élite. They are also imbued with what might be called a non-feudal 'clan spirit' which some historians have ascribed to a survival of early medieval Visigothic, Germanic social ideals.[200] In reality it seems much more likely that they reflect comparable social organisation on the Islamic Andalusian side of the religious frontier.

Attitudes amongst the non-noble sections of society towards military service in 11th and 12th century Italy had also changed since Carolingian times. Militia duty had then been regarded as an unwelcome burden, but in the rival Italian feudal militias of Matilda of Tuscany and the Emperor Henry such duties came to be seen as a source of honour and prestige. The same period did, however, see a significant rise in very localised, city-based patriotisms.[201] It was a phenomenon which would dominate Italian military history for the rest of the medieval period and beyond.

A decline in the morale and status of the knightly class towards the end of the Crusading period has probably been greatly exaggerated. Nevertheless, Crusader defeats continued to be widely blamed on the pride, arrogance and overconfidence – in other words on the 'sins' of the Crusaders.[202] There was also a tendency amongst traditional moralists, especially in France, to complain that standards had declined, that '*The good vavasseurs who once gave good counsel are now dead*', and that knights had lost their strength to crossbowmen, miners and engineers drawn from lower social ranks.[203]

Morale within the shrinking Latin States of the Middle East does seem to have been in decline, and for good reason. Fear of anti-Latin uprisings, especially by the Islamic peasantry, increased during the 13th century[204] as many knights, sergeants and even soldiers of Syrian Christian origin left the Latin east to settle in the new Aegean Latin States established in the wake of the Fourth Crusade.[205] There was further emigration by much of the aristocracy and wealthier merchant families of Acre shortly before the final siege and collapse in 1291.[206] Two years earlier there had been a strong movement in Tripoli for the city to be placed under the protection of the neighbouring Mamluk Sultanate to avoid it becoming a Genoese commercial base. This was thwarted by the Templars and Tripoli fell to Mamluk assault the same year. Nevertheless, the most dramatic decline in the reputation and status of the Western European knightly class as soldiers did not occur until well into the 14th century.

The morale and motivation of Muslim troops in the service of non-Islamic rulers poses several obvious but difficult questions. Those in the Iberian peninsula might reasonably have hoped that, if they hung on long enough, Islamic armies from the south might one day return to re-establish their lost Islamic states. The almost entirely isolated colony of ex-Sicilian Muslims and their descendants at Lucera, on the Italian mainland, were in a different situation. They fought for their rulers in order to survive. By the 1270s many are likely to have spoken Italian rather that Arabic, and several of their leaders had Christian names though apparently remaining Muslim. For example, a certain Richard of Lucera was promoted to the status of *miles* or knight in 1272 and was in charge of the colony at the time of the Angevin conquest. His sons Hajjaj and 'Ali, however, had Islamic names,[207] while an unrelated man named Giovanni Saraceno (John the Saracen) was nominated custodian of the port of Manfredonia in 1293. It has also been suggested that these so-called Saracens of Lucera continued to use composite bows as a form of cultural and even religious identification within the doomed military colony.

Modern notions of secular patriotism and loyalty to a state were of much less importance during the medieval period, yet in some specific parts of Europe they could already be seen. This was particularly true in the economically and socio-politically advanced city-states of Italy. Even as early as the mid-12th century it is possible that the Genoese maritime crusade against Islamic al-Andalus in 1146–8 was motivated by concerns of state as well as religion and economic gain. Though seemingly a failure, this campaign succeeded in proclaiming to the rest of Europe that the often criticised Genoese were good Christians committed to the Crusader cause.[208] On the other hand not everyone wanted to take part and in May 1147, as a huge Genoese fleet was preparing to depart for its assault on Almeria, the city consuls had to issue special orders against those who were trying to evade service by leaving the city.[209]

For King Philip Augustus of France, the domestic as well as international importance of taking part in, or indeed leading, a major Crusade was considerable. It might have been even more important for rulers like the Emperors of Germany whose political position was weaker than that of the rulers of France or England.[210] In Germany, of course, Crusading warfare could mean campaigning quite close to home, not only in the Baltic or Northern Crusades but against invading Mongols in neighbouring Hungary and Poland during the mid-13th century. In fact the Crusade against the Mongols proclaimed in 1241 had a good response in Germany, among both nobles and non-nobles, resulting in a substantial but not very effective effort to help the Hungarians.[211] As far as the Hungarians themselves were concerned, Crusading warfare could involve taking part in expeditions far away in the eastern Mediterranean, but also in defending or extending their own eastern and southern frontiers. Here the majority of their enemies were fellow-Christians: Serbs and Bulgarians and in the earlier days also Byzantines of the Orthodox rather than Catholic Church. Even the Turkish Kipchaqs of the steppe regions beyond the Carpathian Mountains were in the process of converting to Christianity when their state was swept away by the Mongols.

BOOTY, MASSACRE, CAPTIVITY AND THE LAWS OF WAR

The slaughter of a non-Christian population at Barbastro in 1064 may have been the first such massacre in the history of what became the Crusades, but it was not the last. The first large-scale victims of the First Crusade were not Muslims but Jews, as the earliest contingents of the expedition travelled through Germany. Then came the slaughter of Muslims and Jews following the First Crusade's conquest of Jerusalem. This horrified and puzzled the neighbouring peoples because on the many occasions when Jerusalem had fallen to siege during previous inter-Islamic conflicts, the physical and human cost had been minimal.[212] Unfortunately torture and mutilation became a feature of the early decades of Crusader warfare in the Middle East,[213] and Tancred of Antioch's blinding of a Kurdish prisoner's right eye so that he could no longer look around his shield was just one well-recorded example.[214]

Muslim prisoners of war were always enslaved in the Latin States unless they were senior enough to be worth a substantial ransom, but they could be freed if they converted to Christianity. It was then possible for such converts to rise to quite high position in the Latin administration.[215] Latin behaviour continued to puzzle the Muslims; indeed surviving correspondence between Saladin and Popes Alexander II and Lucius III complained that prisoner exchanges were unbalanced because the Kings of Jerusalem seemed unwilling to release prisoners in their hands. Here there were clearly different priorities, with Christians wanting to retain captured or enslaved Muslim peasants while the Muslims wanted to retain captive knights and noblemen.[216] Military Orders such as the Hospitallers kept very large numbers of slaves in the Middle East, not only for exchange or ransom but as workers.[217] Even this seems to have been preferable to capture by the Mongols and in 1260 large numbers of Muslims from Damascus had fled into Latin territory to surrender.[218] Even though enslaved prisoners could purchase their freedom, it is worth drawing attention to a Hospitaller decree of 1262 which insisted that the price must be enough to purchase two or three replacements.[219]

In the Aegean region the Crusaders' most immediate enemies were fellow Christians, and would remain so until the Turkish-Islamic states of Anatolia reached the Aegean coast. This does not seem to have hindered the slave-trade and in 1246 the Pope complained that Italian ships were taking Christian Greeks, Bulgarians, Ruthenians and Vlachs into slavery, pretending that they were Muslim captives from the Latin States.[220]

The situation was again different within the Iberian peninsula where centuries of close, if not always friendly, contact between the Christian states of the north and the Islamic regions of al-Andalus in the south had led to the development of relatively humane methods of dealing with prisoners, and indeed spoils. On the Christian side, men taking part in a major *hueste* campaign were expected to elect an official known as the *quadrillero* to divide the spoils fairly and free of pressure.[221] As early as the 1130s there were established systems or rules for the ransoming of captives, these being written into the *fueros* or laws of Spanish frontier towns. They dealt not only with regaining their own people but with the release or exchange of captured Muslims, captured livestock and other booty. It was clearly considered important to obtain fair prices for such winnings, and there were comparable systems on the Islamic side of the border. The families of those captured were expected to contribute towards their redemption but the laws allowed this to be reduced if sons or daughters stood as sureties or even as substitute prisoners.

In fact some Iberian frontier towns seem to have specialised in this trade in prisoners, livestock and other captured goods during the 12th century. Merchants who traded across the frontier were sometimes given responsibility for negotiations but it was more usual for each town to have its own officials to do this. Such *exeas* carried ransoms and escorted captives home, being allowed to keep a fifth of the proceeds.[222] All the Military Orders that operated in Spain and Portugal, except for that of Alcantara, had their own ransoming hospices,[223] while a special order of friars, the Mercedarians or Order of St Mary of Mercy, was established in Barcelona in the early 13th century, specialising in ransoming Christian captives from the Moors.[224]

As far as Crusaders themselves were concerned, the morality of being held captive by infidels and paying ransoms for release seems to have been an open question at the time of the First Crusade. Indeed it was only after the failure of the Second Crusade that being taken alive by the enemy became widely acceptable.[225] Thereafter the Latin States soon adopted the long-established Islamic principle of arranging truces so that prisoners could be exchanged. The results were sometimes complex. For example, Prince Hugh II of Galilee was taken prisoner by Saladin at Marj Ayun in 1179 when still a child, and was ransomed two years later. He escaped from the disastrous battle of Hattin and in 1188 led a raid from Tyre which seized Arsuf, releasing fifty Christian captives and capturing the Muslim garrison. Their commander proved to be the same man who had captured Hugh nine years before. This *amir* was himself later exchanged for Marquis William of Monferrat, the father of Conrad of Monferrat, who had been taken prisoner at Hattin.[226]

In 1269 Eschiva d'Ibelin, known as the Lady of Beirut, agreed a treaty with the Mamluk Sultan Baybars I which concerned compensation for losses inflicted if the two sides were not actually at war. In it the parties agreed to release a prisoner of equal status to the individual who had been killed, the grades being those of knight, *turcopole* which was here translated into Arabic as *barkil*, foot soldier and peasant.

The Latin States soon learned to value ransom money rather than simply exchanging captives. Such a ransom remained the responsibility of a knight's own family until late in the 12th century when other financial support systems evolved, similar in some respects to those already existing in Iberia.[227] Sophisticated as these various methods of release became, they did not help everybody, especially not prisoners of lower status or little wealth. Indeed the fate of Christians captured during previous failed Crusader expeditions and still held in Cairo in 1239 weighed heavily upon the local troops of the Latin States, causing resentment amongst newly arrived Crusaders from Western Europe who neither knew these prisoners nor, apparently, cared much for their fate.

Did Laws of War really exist in Western European societies at this time, and, if they did, how much relevance did they have to the actual conduct of warfare? These are questions which still confront historians, and are particularly difficult where Crusading warfare against non-Christians, schismatics or heretics is concerned. A leading specialist in this area has maintained that rudimentary Laws of War did emerge in embryonic form within the Latin States as a result of interaction between the military customs or habits brought from Europe by the Crusaders and the comparable military laws or traditions of behaviour of their Islamic foes. This was apparent not only in an increasing moral sensitivity on the part of the Latins but in their coming to terms with more advanced prisoner exchange or ransoming systems long practised in the Middle East.[228]

In terms of more abstract or theoretical legal concerns, there were comparable developments within Western Europe. Here the legal scholar Gratian, writing his *Decretum* in 12th century Bologna, was one of the first Christian lawyers to distinguish between Just War to protect the state or other secular interests, and Holy War to protect the Church and Christianity as a whole. Meanwhile the Islamic world was theoretically a theocracy, so an injury to the state could be interpreted as an injury to God. On the Christian side of the conflict between Christian and Islamic states, the ideals of Just War and Holy War gradually came together, resulting in a Crusade philosophy which had many similarities with the Islamic concept of *Jihad*.[229] Nevertheless, differences between Just War and Holy War remained. The former was seen as being fought between two otherwise equal Christian forces of which one stood 'condemned' because of an injury to the other. Such war was 'allowed' by God, whereas Holy War was meant to 'further God's intentions' in the world. As such it became a moral imperative for Christians rather than being merely permitted.[230]

STRATEGY

In medieval Western Europe most of the 'science of war' took place before a battle rather than during it. This was as true of the 12th and 13th centuries as it was of the earlier and later Middle Ages. It is also essential to understand that the role of fortification was primarily to protect people rather than territory. Furthermore, many castles and in some cases even fortified towns or cities were more significant as bases of aggression than bastions of defence. Then there was the question of the varied strategic manoeuvrability and speed of medieval European armies. This could be remarkably fast, given the very poor communications and roads of the time. For example, in France in the 1170s a force of Brabançon mercenary foot soldiers marched 220 kilometres in seven days, then seized the town of Dol and defeated an opposing force of Breton cavalry.[231] Battles themselves may have been becoming more bitter, or at least resulted in increasing casualties. The appalling losses suffered by French cavalry at the hand of English armies on foot during the Hundred Years War might have been several generations in the future, but in Tuscany, in the second half of the 13th century, local conflicts were already becoming longer and more expensive in both blood and treasure. Meanwhile fortifications were being considerably strengthened.[232] In many aspects of strategy and tactics, where Italy led, most of the rest of Western Europe followed.

The Latin or Crusader States of the Middle East were in a very different strategic situation. Here, most particularly in Lebanon and the fertile western regions of Syria, the mountainous topography meant that the road system largely consisted of north–south routes, with very few east–west connections. This would have an impact upon every campaign from the First Crusade onwards. It was especially significant during Saladin's campaign of 1188 in the aftermath of his great victory at Hattin the previous year. On this occasion Saladin's army had to operate along the main coastal road in its attempt to reconquer the Latin-held coastal cities, while the Sultan's main urban bases were inland on the other side of a rugged mountain range.[233]

The mountains became little more than hills further south, and thus formed less of a strategic barrier between the coast, the interior and the desert beyond. One such upland area was the Golan Heights between Mount Hermon, Damascus, the Jordan and Yarmuk rivers. This became a virtually demilitarised area in the early 12th century because neither the Latin Kingdom of Jerusalem nor the Islamic rulers of Damascus were strong enough to dominate it. Nevertheless it does seem that the early Latin Kingdom, like its fellows further north, was still pushing for natural frontiers. Here in southern Syria and what is now Jordan the rivers and hills were too insignificant to provide such defensible borders, and the traditonal frontier formed by the desert to the east remained beyond the Crusaders' reach. In the event the revenues of the Golan Heights were shared between Jerusalem and Damascus. To the south the Latin Kingdom managed to dominate the fertile uplands of north-western Jordan whereas the Muslims maintained that the agreed demilitarised zone should extend as far as the Balqa region around Amman. Nor was competition just a matter of territorial prestige, for these regions had for centuries been a major zone of trade and exchange between the settled peasant populations of Greater Syria and the nomadic peoples of Arabia.

Such frontiers would better be described as zones rather than lines on the ground, and within these zones each side operated within generally accepted rules. The line of the Jordan had been left largely unfortified by the Crusaders but the Latin Kingdom's decision to build a new castle above a strategic crossing of the river Jordan at Jacob's Ford broke these conventions and posed a significant threat to Damascus. Furthermore, it was erected on an Islamic sacred site. As a result Saladin's reaction was prompt and ruthless, destroying the unfinished castle, slaughtering both the defenders and a large numbers of building personnel who had been working there.[234]

Most of the other frontiers of the Kingdom of Jerusalem varied according to changes in the regional balance of power. Each side tended to erect 'anti-castle' castles, this process effectively beginning when the Crusaders built small forts to blockade isolated or vulnerable Islamic cities, most notably around Fatimid-held Ascalon in southern Palestine in the 1150s.[235] Further east a line of Crusader castles erected along the frontiers of Oultrejourdain from al-Salt to Aqaba were mostly simple structures (the magnificent fortresses at Karak and Shawbak visited by today's tourists largely date from after the Islamic reconquest). Their strategic function was not to protect some ill-defined and largely non-existent frontier, but to serve as shelters in the *razzia* or raiding warfare which characterised this semi-desert area. They also protected harvests and conserved water supplies. If attackers could be denied access to food and water in such harsh terrain they would, of course, be placed at a serious disadvantage.[236]

After the loss of Jerusalem in 1187, the only other significant inland city held by the Latin States in the Middle East was Antioch. Its defence posed different and more difficult strategic problems compared to the other Latin-held cities, all of which lay on or very close to the coast and could therefore be supported from the sea. As a result Antioch was soon almost isolated. It also lost much of its commercial wealth when trade between the inland Islamic cities and the Mediterranean was redirected via the ports of Ayas or Corycos in Cilician (Lesser) Armenia or through Latakia which had been retaken by Saladin in 1188. The Mongols allowed the Prince of Antioch to regain Latakia, but within a few years Antioch itself fell to the Mamluks, despite the fact that the city's ancient and impressive fortifications had been maintained in good repair.

By then the Latin States had long accepted the need for a cautious strategy when dealing with their Islamic neighbours. This was certainly not a result of their 'going soft', as so many medieval chroniclers and modern historians have maintained. It resulted from experience of warfare against Islamic states and an entirely realistic grasp of the limitations of their own military potential. Despite the Military Orders' often belligerent reputation, there is strong evidence that their commanders on the ground in both the Middle East and the Iberian peninsula were more knowledgeable in their military assessment than other Crusader commanders. Consequently they were sometimes more cautious than their younger brother knights wished. Examples of such careful appraisals of enemy potential can be seen in the advice not to attack Islamic armies in the hills given by the Prior of the Hospitallers in Aragon; similarly in the advice given by both Templar and Hospitaller commanders to King Richard not to press his winter advance on Jerusalem during the Third Crusade.[237]

The Crusaders' offensive strategy was clearest during the first half of the 12th century when the newly established Latin States still had hopes of dominating the Middle East. The remarkable cave fortress at 'Ayn Habis made use of an extensive existing Byzantine *lavra* or cliff-face hermitage and was intended as a base from which a Latin garrison could dominate the Muslim peasantry and bedouin of the Yarmuk basin in what is now northern Jordan and southern Syria. There were other as yet unidentified Crusader cave-outposts in this area, and only a few kilometres further south a Latin garrison briefly occupied Jerash where they converted the ruins of an ancient Roman temple into a fortress.

The already mentioned Latin castles in southern Jordan were more significant as offensive bases than as defensive outposts. From here even small Latin garrisons could threaten and impose tolls upon the vital north–south road between Syria and the Islamic holy cities in Arabia. Another series of somewhat feebly fortified outposts faced Fatimid-held Sinai, but from well inside present-day Palestine-Israel.[238] Clearly the Crusaders were not capable of really controlling desert terrain, and would never be able to do so. They sometimes imposed tribute on the bedouin of such regions, but generally speaking the surrounding Islamic states were much more successful in this respect.

The most isolated of such Latin Crusader outposts was the so-called 'castle of Aqaba'. Archaeology has shown this to have been on tiny Jazirat Fara'un (Pharoah's Island) off the Sinai coast a few kilometres south of Aqaba, despite the fact that there were ruins of a substantial Umayyad period fortified town at Aqaba itself. That the Crusaders chose to build their fort on a little rocky islet shows that even here, in the Gulf of Aqaba and Red Sea, they felt more secure when surrounded by water than they did on the mainland. Most of what can now be seen at Jazirat Fara'un was, however, built by Saladin after he drove out the Latins.

Reynaud de Châtillon was the Crusader leader who had the most imaginative strategic vision in these southern regions. This was probably based on an over-optimistic interpretation of what was possible, yet it was Reynaud who recognised the need to strengthen the position of the Kingdom of Jerusalem following Saladin's retaking of Aqaba-Jazirat Fara'un. As lord of Oultrejourdain he purchased a spy service amongst the bedouin which proved so effective that Saladin had to root it out and expel politically unreliable tribes. Reynaud also made his fiefdom of Oultrejordain into a springboard for raids into the true desert, attempting to control the oases and thus the strategic roads linking Syria, Egypt and the Hijaz in Arabia. In 1182, helped by some bedouin, he penetrated as far as Taima in a raid which seemed to threaten the Islamic holy cities of Medina and Mecca themselves. Reynaud de Châtillon also claimed suzerainty over the great Christian Monastery of St. Catherine in Sinai, though this was never effective, while his remarkable naval raids into the Red Sea may have been intended as preliminary moves in a campaign to dominate Red Sea trade.[239] If successful, this would have had a devastating impact upon the Egyptian economy, and thus on its military potential. However, all these ambitious efforts came to an end with the Kingdom of Jerusalem's catastrophic defeat at the battle of Hattin in 1187 and Saladin's execution of Reynaud.

After that disaster, the Latin States in the Middle East only took part in substantial offensives when a major Crusade had arrived from Europe, and in these cases a lack of Middle Eastern experience on the part of the newcomers and their commanders almost invariably led to defeat. Even the Third Crusade was only a partial success. This was despite Saladin facing the combined Crusading expeditions of the Kingdom of France, the Plantagenet Empire in the British Isles and France, and the German Empire which were the three strongest states in Western Europe.

After a bitter siege the Third Crusade retook Acre, after which King Richard of England led Crusader forces down the coast of Palestine before turning inland towards Jerusalem. During that famous coastal march, which also involved the battle of Arsuf, Richard was as cautious as he had habitually been in his European campaigns, and certainly did not seek battle with Saladin. In this his strategy was fully within existing Western military philosophy which recognised that damaging the enemy was more sensible than risking defeat in an all-out confrontation.[240] Richard and most of his local advisors were similarly cautious in their subsequent advance towards Jerusalem. Their painfully slow progress was caused not only by appalling winter cold and rain, but by the need to restore all fortifications along their route as a defence against Saladin's more mobile forces interrupting Crusader supply lines. In the event the advance failed because these supply lines remained too vulnerable.[241] Thereafter the final phases of the Third Crusade spluttered on until a compromise truce was agreed. In strategic terms Saladin had won, though both sides were by now militarily, morally and economically almost exhausted.

Subsequent Crusades in the Middle East were even less successful, though a substantial effort in 1227–8 managed to re-establish Latin control over the southern Lebanese coast, thus maintaining the strategic landlink between the Kingdom of Jerusalem and the County of Tripoli. The Crusade of the Emperor Frederick II also regained Jerusalem for the Latin Kingdom by diplomatic means, much to the disgust of many in Europe who thought such a 'victory' shameful. Frederick II's Crusade was not, of course, only diplomatic. It had several military consequences, not least the construction of strong citadels at Jaffa, Caesarea and Sidon. These may have been intended as launchpads for future campaigns of reconquest or simply as secure coastal bases for future Crusades.[242] A final effort in 1239–41 inflicted a severe defeat on the Ayyubid army of Egypt at Gaza and left the Kingdom of Jerusalem larger than at any time since 1187, but this revival proved short-lived.

Campaigns by forces resident in the Latin States of the Middle East were now little more than raids either in response to enemy attacks or intended to intimidate neighbouring Islamic centres. In 1233, for example, the Hospitaller garrisons of Crac des Chevaliers and Margat raised a force of one hundred knights, three hundred mounted sergeants and over five hundred infantry sergeants, to which the Templars added further troops. This substantial force then attacked the city of Hama. Nine years later a Templar force from Jaffa managed to sack Nablus, slaughtering many of its inhabitants including local Christians and burning the main mosque, but beyond such small-scale operations Latin forces could do little without substantial external support.

Attempts in 1261 to take advantage of the chaos caused by the Mongol invasion of Syria failed. Yet there were those, especially in the Military Orders, who still drew up plans for highly ambitious, full-scale Crusades. One such blueprint was presented by the Hospitallers to the Pope a year or so before the final fall of Acre. It envisaged a Crusading army of a thousand knights, four thousand crossbowmen and a fleet of sixty galleys to be based in Rhodes and Cyprus. From there the Christians would hope to impose a naval blockade of the Mamluk Sultanate in Syria and Egypt, and to raid the Mamluk coastline.[243] A remarkable intelligence report called the *Devise des Chemins de Babiloine* may have been drawn up for the Hospitallers as part of a proposed Crusade. It includes information on distances and roads as well as the current military strength of the Mamluk Sultanate. Being so detailed and accurate, this *Devise des Chemins de Babiloine* is likely to have been based on Mamluk documents obtained by Hospitaller agents on the mainland.

The geography of the Latin States offered defensive advantages as well as posing problems. If Saladin attacked from the direction of Damascus, for example, his approach was reasonably predictable. Consequently Latin defensive forces usually mustered at Safuriya, where there was water and from which they could move against the enemy whatever route he took. It would also be wrong to believe that the Latins lacked an overall defensive strategy, though it would be equally misleading to see Crusader castles as being part of some integrated defensive system. Some were close enough to offer mutual support, but their primary military role was as bases from which to harry an invader or launch counter-attacks. They also served as refuges from such invaders and as symbols of Latin Crusader rule. The major urban citadels had similar functions, especially as most cities had quite weak circuit defences until well into the 13th century.

The people could find shelter in citadels and castles, but enemy raiders could still wreak huge economic damage which was, of course, the primary purpose of most such campaigns. In all these roles the fortifications proved reasonably successful until Syria and Egypt were reunited under Mamluk rule in the second half of the 13th century. This unification, added to declining support from Western Europe for the Latin States, meant that the Mamluk Sultans could pick off castles and fortified cities one by one.[244] The Latin States' only response was to maintain very large garrisons in the main fortified coastal cities, and it was the failure of these that finally marked the end of the Latin States in the Middle East.

The overall strategy of the Latin States in the Aegean area is harder to identify and there may not, of course, have been any real overall strategy. The role of fortifications is also not entirely clear, and seems to have changed over time. Only a handful of castles were built during the course of the Crusader conquest of Greece and there was no effort to construct any during failed Crusader attempts to conquer Byzantine Anatolia or Thrace.[245] On the other hand, some castles in the Peloponnese seem to have been carefully located to defend both ends of a number of strategic passes. They could thus block routes taken by local tribal raiders and later by Byzantine regional forces or, perhaps more significantly, block the retreat of such raiders once they had been slowed down by booty. This network of fortified outposts may have owed much to the strategic vision of William II de Villehardouin, the greatest of the Latin Princes of Achaia (1245–78).[246]

Even so there appear to have been minimal attempts to defend the Latin castles of Greece when they were threatened. It has even been suggested that many of them served more like prizes to be won or lost as a result of military events elsewhere, than as strongpoints to be defended.[247] In many cases such fortifications were simply abandoned or handed over by the losing side. As a result warfare in the Aegean and Greek Crusader States largely consisted of raiding by land and sea, skirmishing, a few quite small battles, even rarer major battles, and occasional sieges. The simple isolated towers which dot parts of east-central Greece and almost certainly date from the time of the Latin States mostly fit into an agricultural context and are believed to have been passive refuges[248] for the lower-ranking local Latin élite. Perhaps they also provided shelter for local peasants and in a few cases their livestock.

Similar towers dot the large neighbouring island of Evoia which, then known as Negroponte, formed part of the Venetian colonial empire. Elsewhere the Venetians built a chain of isolated forts and rather old-fashioned fortresses along their main trade routes. The Genoese adopted a different strategy, obtaining commercial bases through negotiation with local rulers who needed their support, their fleets or their money. Generally speaking the Genoese looked for places where existing harbours were easy to defend, either because they were separated from the main inland power centres by rugged coastal hills, were on islands, or already had strong fortifications. Where necessary, of course, the Genoese either strengthened these still further or built new defences.[249]

The strategies adopted by the Christian kingdoms of Iberia were varied and flexible. Certainly the Christians did not push their Reconquista all the time, but were content to hold and consolidate newly won territory for many years before a period of weakness or fragmentation amongst their Islamic neighbours enabled then to renew the attack. It seems that there was a clear appreciation of their own limited human resources, with a consequent concern to keep casualties to a minimum. These medieval states had little in common with modern societies which seem able, and often willing, to endure huge human losses.[250]

Just as in the Middle East, the geography of the Iberian peninsula had a profound impact upon how campaigns were conducted and the routes they followed. From the late 10th well into the 11th century the central Sierra mountain ranges formed a frontier and the main zone of conflict between Christian and Islamic states. Here infantry warfare predominated, with the role of cavalry largely being confined to long distance raiding. In the latter case substantial infantry forces were rarely involved unless a major battle was expected. Instead they remained behind to defend Christian towns against counter-attacks.[251] The little town of Cuenca may have been typical. Here detailed information from the surviving archives shows that half of the urban militia army, known as the *azaga*, was used to protect a base-camp while the rest, called the *algara*, actually carried out the raids. This system worked well for many years but failed against the Muwahhidun in the second half of the 12th century because the new Islamic rulers of al-Andalus adopted an aggressive policy which obliged towns like Cuenca to maintain defensive garrisons closer to the frontier. Troops were also needed to protect Christian colonists in areas already taken from the Muslims. This was a role that the Military Orders were eager to undertake.[252]

By then a further series of Christian assaults had pushed south of the Sierras and out of the Pyrenean foothills into the broad plains of the Tagus and Ebro basins, increasing the importance of substantial cavalry forces. Even so climatic factors continued to govern strategy, with most major campaigns being conducted in the dry summer and autumn, though smaller raids could be carried out at other times. Mountains, plateaux and rivers as well as the locations of towns, castles and roads all had significant impact, but it was the road system which really channelled Christian expansion from the 11th century onwards. This followed not only the ancient Roman routes but also many more recently developed Islamic ones. Bridges were vital for both commerce and warfare, and were well maintained. They, like the main ferry-points, formed strategic nodes and were usually defended by castles or fortified towns.[253]

Because the routes available for raiding and major campaigns were so clearly defined, fortifications of all sizes and types continued to play a major strategic role throughout the 12th and 13th centuries, not only in what became Spain but also in Portugal.[254] This was similarly true in defence against counter-assaults by opposing Islamic armies which tended to have superior mobility and speed. The fortified cities served as bases for aggression and defence, yet they were even more significant as targets of enemy attack whereas most rural castles were mere bases. As a result Iberian cities tended to be strongly fortified and their fortifications well maintained. Nevertheless many also had unprotected suburbs beyond their walls. These had to be abandoned if the city came under serious siege, yet the main defences were usually strong enough, and their milita defenders usually numerous enough, so that they could not be taken by assault. There were exceptions, but when a city did fall it tended to be after years of raiding and ravaging of the surrounding agricultural areas, the blocking of trade and food supplies, then finally a close siege.[255]

In other respects warfare in some parts of Iberia was unlike that seen elsewhere in Europe, or indeed in most of the Middle East with the possible exception of Anatolia. The high central plains of Spain were a sheep ranching area during the Middle Ages, and only later did the introduction of windmills from the Islamic world encourage the growing of cereals. As a result, capturing the opposition's flocks formed a major aspect of low-intensity border raiding.[256] In fact one might almost say that large-scale rustling was invented around 12th century Toledo.[257]

Massive migrations of flocks from summer pastures in the Sierras to winter pastures further south in regions such as La Mancha necessitated well-organised armed escorts. The oldest description comes from the *Fuero de Cuenca* or town law of Cuenca, dating from 1189–90. This declared that each December the flocks and herds be placed under an *esculca* guard consisting of one *caballero* horseman for each herd of cattle, and one for every three flocks of sheep. The *esculqueros* then elected an *alcalde* to lead them, and all returned north in mid-March.[258] A few years later the archives indicate that some ranching towns to the west of Cuenca were using a similar system, with their herds of pigs being guarded by a *rafala* military escort consisting of mounted *rafaleros.*[259]

Naval power played a significant role in Aragonese expansion down the Mediterranean coast of Spain, but it also became increasingly significant along Iberia's Atlantic coast. For example, a largely English fleet, on its way to join the Second Crusade in the Middle East, contributed to the success of the Portuguese conquest of Lisbon. What is less well known is the importance of Castilian naval power in the conquest of Seville a hundred and one years later. This maritime involvement is even more remarkable bearing in mind that the main Castilian ports were still far to the north, on the Cantabrian coast, so this was a real Atlantic military enterprise rather than merely an extension of Mediterranean naval power.[260]

TACTICS

At the start of the Crusader period, there was considerable variation in the tactical traditions of different parts of Western Europe. In France and Germany these were rooted in the Carolingian period, with an emphasis on mixed cavalry and infantry forces. All-cavalry engagements were rare and remained so. In England there was still strong influence from the infantry traditions of the Anglo-Saxon period to which the conquering Normans added their own highly successful and essentially French reliance on mutual support between cavalry and infantry. This was essentially the same in Italy. In the Iberian peninsula, however, warfare was, until well into the 11th century, largely based upon more complex Arab-Islamic tactical traditions. This resulted in considerable reliance upon light cavalry and an often tiny élite of armoured horsemen, while infantry had a largely separate though vital role.[261]

The tactics used by the First Crusade, and which continued to dominate warfare in the Latin States well into the 12th century, gave a vital battlefield role to non-knightly foot soldiers. Despite the distorted image provided by most contemporary souces with their deep prejudice in favour of the knightly class, knightly cavalry were not the only competent troops available. These sources also reflect a knightly prejudice against missile weapons, though the reality on the ground shows that this attitude did not prevent the Latin élite from employing archers and crossbowmen in their own wars against the Muslims. Nor were they averse to taking up such weapons themselves, either from choice or from necessity having lost their horses in battle.[262]

Close cooperation and coordination between cavalry and infantry became a feature of Crusader warfare, and probably was from the very beginning, especially on so-called 'fighting marches' through hostile territory.[263] This did not mean that existing social or class hostility disappeared, and there were many cases when Latin knightly cavalry escaped by abandoning their infantry. Furthermore, their Islamic opponents soon recognised this tendency and took full advantage of it in battle.[264] Several defeats resulted from the enemy managing to separate Latin horse and foot, as when the Crusaders ignored the advice of an experienced Armenian ally, to be outmanoeuvred and defeated by Nur al-Din's army in 1164.[265]

Close study of the surviving sources shows that there was a considerable degree of military specialisation, even amongst mounted troops in these Latin and Crusader armies. During the early 12th century, squires were still of lowly status, pillaging the dead, acting as foragers but also fighting alongside the sergeants during sieges. In the *Old French Rule* of the Templars they are supposed to ride behind the knights in line-of-battle with spare horses. They carried the knights' weapons until these were needed, then they withdrew to be placed under the command of the *gonfanonier*. A second squire might, however, follow close behind his knight into battle with a spare horse. During the 12th century, at least in those areas dominated by French culture, the squires were not intended to fight in open battle and to use such men as a rearguard to cover the knights' retreat was regarded as cowardly. Later it would become quite acceptable and before long the squires fought as second-line cavalry.[266]

Being the most disciplined and reliable cavalry available, the Military Orders tended to be used as van- or rearguards, though not invariably so, and in Iberia such troops often formed the nucleus of offensive expeditions.[267] The French Regiment left in the Holy Land by King Louis IX, and maintained at French expense, was as skilled and almost as dedicated as the Military Orders themselves. Its most famous commander, Olivier de Termes, had learned the skills of guerrilla and ambush warfare in southern France during the Albigensian Crusade. He subsequently served as a mid-ranking military commander for the French king and took part in King Louis' Crusade in 1249. After fighting at Damietta as a leader of the Occitan or southern French crossbowmen he became commander of the French Regiment in the Kingdom of Jerusalem where he successfully led a mixed force of cavalry and infantry. During this remarkable military career Olivier de Termes was renowned for clever but cautious tactics, for his concern for the wellbeing of his men and for his willingness to retreat when necessary.[268]

Military historians have traditionally had an unfortunate habit of trying to impose a simplistic and too often rigid typology on the supposedly characteristic 'battle arrays' of different peoples and periods. This tendency was itself rooted in medieval if not earlier scholarship in Europe, the Islamic world, China and indeed practically everywhere that took a literary interest in such matters.[269] Written descriptions of battle are more reliable, though even these are open to different interpretations and their writers were often prone to wisdom-after-the-event. A use of the feigned retreat in Western Europe before Western commanders supposedly learned such tactics from more sophisticated eastern foes during the Crusades is just one case in point. Historians still disagree about whether or not Duke William of Normandy and his Breton allies used it at the battle of Hastings in 1066. Yet it had already been explicitly employed by an Angevin army against the Bretons in 1027.

By the 13th century several very different battlefield tactics were available to Western commanders. For example, in southern France in 1213 Count Raymond VI of Toulouse wanted to build a fortified siege-camp and starve Simon de Montfort's army into submission in the nearby town of Muret, but King Peter of Aragon wanted an open battle. The latter was the policy adopted, resulting in Peter's disastrous defeat.[270] The battle of Muret was also characterised by the use of difficult local terrain, on this occasion a ditch, in an effort to protect the flank of a fixed position.[271]

Before battle was joined, Western European armies did not always adopt the same formation, though certain arrays do seem to have been preferred. For example, outside Antioch on 28 June 1098, the army of the First Crusade advanced against a numerically superior Islamic force, with the infantry marching ahead of the cavalry. The same was seen at the Field of Blood in 1119, though with an entirely different outcome. This may have been the Latin army's array as it advanced against Fatimid forces encamped outside Ascalon in 1099, though other information states that the Crusaders approached their enemy in nine squadrons or in three ranks of three squadrons. If this was intended to be a precaution against attack from any direction, it was astonishingly similar to the symmetrical nine-part array attributed to the Turkish armies of Central Asia by a 13th century Perso-Indian military theoretician and also used by the Chinese against nomadic Inner Asian enemies (see volume II). A Latin force seems to have employed the same array, but with *pedites* infantry in the centre, against the army of Il-Ghazi in 1118. Yet, wherever this formation is recorded it only seems to have been suitable in broad open terrain where there were few if any natural obstacles and where opposing armies had almost complete freedom of manoeuvre.[272]

On other occasions the Crusaders attempted the sort of complex battlefield manoeuvring that was more typical of Byzantine or Islamic forces, though normally with less success. Near Harran this resulted in a notable defeat in 1104. Here a Latin force consisted of the armies of the County of Edessa and the Principality of Antioch, with the Edessans on the left and the troops of Antioch over a kilometre away on the right, behind a hill. The plan was for the army of Edessa to engage the enemy until the latter tired, whereupon the army of Antioch would emerge from hiding to surround the foe. However, the Muslims used their well-known tactic of feigned flight, drawing the Edessans too far from the men of Antioch for the latter to intervene when the Muslims turned upon their pursuers. It also appears that some troops from Antioch engaged the enemy too early and thus gave away their position. When the troops of Edessa were defeated, the army of Antioch panicked and fled but was ambushed and crushed on its way home.[273] It was clearly one thing to learn ambitious tactics from one's enemies; quite another to have the capability of carrying them out successfully. Was it bitter experience of attempting over-ambitious tactics that led the Crusader army of the Third Crusade to revert to a simple traditional array when it advanced against Saladin's position during the siege of Acre? On this occasion the personal observation of those present on the Islamic side confirms that their foes came towards them at a slow pace with the foot soldiers in front of the horsemen.

Western warfare was nevertheless changing, though perhaps in terms of bitterness and savagery rather than tactics. As the Barone de' Mangiadori, a veteran Florentine commander, reportedly said to his troops before the battle of Campaldino in 1289: '*Wars in Tuscany up until now have been won by short and sharp assaults which did not last long, and few men have been killed in them. This is all changed now. The side which stands fast is the side which shall win*.'[274]

At the same time there seems to have been a growing interest in what might be called the science of tactics. Perhaps this again reflected closer contact with the Byzantine and Islamic worlds as well as the first stirrings of the European Renaissance. The works of the Late Roman military theoretician Vegetius had been known amongst a small number of educated men and rulers since the fall of the Western half of the Roman Empire. An early example of a revival of interest in such texts was the *Secunda Partida* or second section of the *Siete Partidas* attributed to the Castilian King Alfonso the Learned (1252–84) which included a digest of Vegetius. Another simplified and updated abbreviation of Vegetius was written by the late 13th or early 14th century Florentine, Bono Giamboni. In it he largely used modern military terminology, particularly for heavy cavalry equipment, though he also wrote about both heavy and light infantry as well as the crossbowmen who did not exist as such in the days of Vegetius.[275] Whether such knowledge had any practical application remains a matter of debate.[276]

Tactical communications remained a severe problem for all military commanders before the invention of radio. In medieval Western European forces, banners had several functions and were so important that the fall of the main flag or its bearer could signal defeat, or at least be interpreted as doing so. This is clear in the works of a 12th century Norman writer where, apart from the moral impact of the flag falling, its disappearance removed the army's main rallying point.[277] In the Iberian peninsula, 13th century sources record that enemy flags were often a specific target in battle, with rewards being offered for their capture,[278] and this was almost certainly true of other periods and places. In fact the Templars' *Old French Rule* laid great emphasis upon ensuring the safety of the Order's main banner, which was the responsibility of the Marshal and his retinue. The Commander of Knights was also ordered to have a furled spare banner available in case that of the Marshal should fall. The Rule insisted that standard bearers were never allowed to strike a blow with their banner, however desperate the situation, with severe punishment if they did so because using the flagpole as a weapon would mean lowering the banner or at least making it appear to totter. It was, meanwhile, to the Marshal's banner that any Templar should rally if unable to return to his own unit, and if this was not possible he should make his way to any Christian flag.[279]

Military service in the Middle Ages involved, as always, more marching and endurance than it did actual fighting. Whereas the armies of the Latin States tended to be quite small, several of the larger Crusader contingents were huge. That of the Emperor Frederick Barbarossa was said to have a line-of-march three days long while crossing Europe. In other words it took three days for the entire force to pass a given point.[280] On other occasions marching and fighting went hand in hand. This was the famous but widely misunderstood 'Crusader fighting march'. At one time the Byzantines were thought to have taught the Westerners such techniques of maintaining cohesion and fighting off enemy attacks while marching through hostile territory. More recently it has been suggested that, while the Western Europeans did learn, they also taught, and that the 'moving fortress' formation used by the Byzantine Emperor Alexios Comnenos in the early 12th century owed something to the tactics of the First Crusade during its extraordinary journey through Seljuk Turkish territory in Anatolia. It also seems clear that the armies of the Latin States established in the Middle East were more skilled in such 'fighting march' manoeuvres than were newcomers from the West.[281]

In reality it is most likely that all the forces involved not only learned from each other, but refined their own techniques in the light of experience. Furthermore, a variety of sophisticated arrays had been included in Islamic military manuals since at least the 9th century (see volume II). Whether Byzantines or Muslims had been the leading teachers, and whoever the learners were during those earlier years, there can be little doubt that, by the 11th to 13th centuries, several variations of 'fighting march' tactics were available in the Middle East and Europe.

Once again the surviving rules of the Military Orders provide further details. The Templars' *Old French Rule* stated that when the line of march was being organised, the knights went ahead of the squires, with the baggage bringing up the rear.[282] A Hospitaller statute drawn up in Acre in 1264 decreed that when the brethren were arranging their *chevaucher* or order of march prior to making a raid, *'they shall truss up behind them all their armour that they carry for their bodies, except their chapel de fer (*war hats*) and jambiers de fer (*leg armour*)'*,[283] which they would presumably be wearing. The Templars' *Old French Rule* furthermore insisted that, once on the march, any person seeking to change his position must do so downwind from the column to avoid sending dust into his comrades' eyes.[284]

It is again often assumed that the Western Europeans were rather unsophisticated when it came to field fortifications or fortified encampments, at least compared to the Byzantines. Yet there are sometimes surprising examples of the same clever, indeed devious, battlefield traps being set in very different parts of Europe and beyond. In 991 the Bretons used almost exactly the same system of hidden pits to overthrow an Angevin cavalry charge in north-western France[285] as Muslim raiders had used against Lombards in southern Italy about a century earlier. The Magyar Hungarians used baggage waggons as field fortifications in the 12th century,[286] as their semi-nomadic Magyar ancestors had done two hundred years earlier and the Huns had done well before that. Whether there was any link between that military tradition and the use of small and specialised waggons called *panthera* or *plaustrella* for the same purpose by communal armies in northern Italy in the 12th and early 13th centuries is unknown.[287] There is no evidence that the Military Orders normally, or ever, used the same tactic, but the Templars' *Old French Rule* sheds other light on the defence of a camp. If the alarm was raised and the camp attacked, those nearest the trouble were to take up shield and spear and help repel the enemy. Meanwhile others, further from the scene of action, should gather at the chapel-tent to await the Master's orders.[288]

Medieval Western European warriors, including those who went on Crusade, did not fight simply as individuals, despite another widespread myth that, especially where the knightly élite were concerned, individual glory and reputation were the primary motivating factors. These men were trained to fight as teams in military units or formations, and this was as true of cavalry as it was of infantry. Such formations were similarly trained to carry out various different tactics, some of which were more characteristic of some regions than of others. In the Iberian peninsula, for example, the tactic of repeated charge and withdrawal was used by Christian armies just as it was by Muslim Andalusians or Moors. While the former knew it as *torno fuya*, the latter called it *karr wa farr*,[289] and it had at least one of its roots in Late Roman *cursores et defensores* cavalry practice. This was a style of cavalry warfare that presupposed that the enemy was virtually static and included the infantry which were its most vulnerable target.

Torno fuya seemingly dominated cavalry tactics in 11th and perhaps early 12th century Iberia, but became just one of several tactics in the later 12th and 13th centuries when the supposedly more typical and heavier cavalry 'shock charge' spread from neighbouring France. Even so, Catalan and Aragonese light cavalry were still capable of defeating heavier French cavalry invaders during the 13th century,[290] the Iberian horsemen probably using repeated charge and withdrawal harrassment where the rugged terrain gave them an advantage. Light cavalry tactics could also be found in some other, usually isolated or marginal regions where earlier military traditions had survived. These included the Breton cavalry's continued use of javelins and attack–withdraw tactics into the 12th century, and the Irish use of the same tactics at least as late as the 14th century.

By then, of course, the fully armoured shock charge had become by far the most important cavalry battlefield tactic throughout most of the rest of Western Europe. In some places it seems to have become the only cavalry tactic available in open battle, with disastrous consequences for the French aristocracy during the first phases of the Hundred Years War. The cavalry shock charge was, in effect, a projectile to be launched against an enemy and was only really effective if the enemy was static. It also had to make contact and the enemy had to be broken, usually as a result of his morale failing. Since horses, however well trained, will not normally crash directly into an obstacle, the impact of such a shock charge was primarily psychological or culminated in a pushing match between men and horses.

These factors explain why the *conrois* was so important. It was a very closely packed but not very large cavalry formation, several of which appear to have formed a *bataille* or division on the field of battle.[291] Sometimes consisting of a single line of men riding literally stirrup-to-stirrup, the *conrois* could also be *seréement*, indicating that it included more than one serried rank.[292] The size of such a formation varied, but it has been suggested that twenty to twenty-four horsemen in two or three ranks could eventually be seen as normal.[293] The space between the ranks, and between more than one *conrois*, might also have been quite close when advancing against an enemy. Not only terrifying to look at, this *conrois* was extremely difficult to break apart. The primary purpose of a shock charge by such *conrois* was to break through the enemy's line, then turn to attack him from the rear. They also tried to make flank attacks, especially against infantry formations, which could not change position or front as rapidly as could men on horseback.[294]

The main advantage of a properly trained *conrois* was its compact mass, teamwork and discipline. The fact that in Western European warfare during this period the *conrois* normally used the *couched* lance as its initial striking weapon may have been of secondary importance.[295] An emphasis on mutual support and discipline is clear in the Templars' *Old French Rule* which ordered that no one should leave the ranks once these had been drawn up, except to test his horse and saddle or to help a straggler threatened by the enemy. Even then he must immediately return to his original position.[296] Great efforts were also made to keep the knights close together around their unit flag during the charge because horses naturally tended to spread out when moving at any speed. In a resulting *mêlée*, brother knights were not allowed to withdraw, even if wounded, unless given permission to do so.[297]

Teamwork and close cooperation between horsemen was important not only for its tactical success but for morale, and indeed for the overall ethos of 'chivalry'. This is seen in a highly detailed account of a relatively minor skirmish when a Crusader supply column was ambushed near Ramla on 17 June 1192, during the Third Crusade. The fighting soon collapsed into a general *mêlée* in which men were thrown from their horses but managed to remount, as described by one who was either there or listened to those who were: *'As often as the Turks felled one to the ground, our men closed around him and, raising him up, helped him to remount his horse, each assisting one another'.*[298] On this occasion the Muslims launched their ambush from the cover of bushes and trees. It is clear that 12th century Western European knights were trained to do exactly the same, and the word *enbuschement* or ambush originally meant precisely that.[299] Ambush tactics would remain a central feature of European cavalry warfare, not least in late 13th century Italy where élite cavalry units were often used to hit or harrass the enemy's line-of-march.[300]

During the early Crusader period squires took little or no direct part in the fighting. Mounted sergeants, however, were expected to do so, though normally as second-line cavalry. Once again the Templars' *Old French Rule* is very specific, stating that it was the duty of sergeants to keep the enemy at bay in case the knights suffered a reverse, enabling the latter to reform, perhaps while the squires brought fresh horses.[301] Sometimes the sergeants were specifically drawn up under the command of the *turcopolier*; on other occasions they followed knights closely in case they needed support or rescue. When actually involved in combat, such armoured sergeants fought in the same manner as the knights, but, unlike the latter, sergeants were allowed to retire without permission if wounded or defeated.[302] Meanwhile some of the squires were themselves organised into squadrons by the Order's *gonfanonier*, and should advance behind the knights with spare mounts, other squires following the *gonfanonier*'s banner from a greater distance at a walk with the palfreys, which were riding rather than war-horses.

There is less information about larger cavalry formations, though it does seem that the term *eschiele* or squadron could mean something bigger than a *conrois*.[303] The *Old French Rule* stated that the knights fought in such *eschielles* under nominated leaders and that the *gonfanon* or small flag around which the squadron operated should have ten knights to defend the standard-bearer himself.[304] In the Occitan-speaking regions of southern France the term *escalus* was used for these squadrons, and it was in such an *escalus* that knights entered the mêlée.[305] Further south, in Castile, the *Siete Partidas* attributed to King Alfonso X advocated a cone-shaped formation for comparable squadrons when attacking a numerically superior enemy, with the front rank consisting of three horsemen, the next six, then twelve, twenty-four and so on. Smaller conical formations could start with a single man at the head,[306] but whether the *Siete Partidas* was reflecting the reality of late 13th century cavalry tactics in the Iberian peninsula is less unclear. The author may merely have borrowed the idea as a theory from a 10th century Byzantine military treatise attributed to the Emperor Nikephoros Phocas (see below).

The effectiveness of the Western European style cavalry charge in Crusader warfare varied a great deal, and could achieve victory if it found and hit a suitable target. Being something of a one-off tactical weapon, it tended to be reactive rather than proactive. In other words it could only be launched if the opposition presented the Crusader cavalry with an opportunity to charge. This was rare because Islamic armies, cavalry and even infantry, rapidly learned how to anticipate and to avoid the Latin knights' fearsome charge. This Islamic lighter cavalry did by simply getting out of the way or opening their formations to allow the charge to career through harmlessly. Thereupon the close-packed and less manoeuvrable Westerners were vulnerable to attacks against their own flanks or rear.

Even Islamic infantry forces were eventually able to avoid the charge, especially when operating in broken or otherwise difficult terrain. This was why cooperation between the Crusaders' heavily armoured cavalry *conrois* formations and their infantry crossbowmen became so important, the foot soldiers protecting their cavalry from enemy harrassment until a suitable moment came for the horsemen to charge.[307] Often that moment simply never came. Even as early as the siege of Damascus by the Second Crusade in 1148, an Arab chronicler recorded how the Latin cavalry formed up to '*make their famous charge*', but when they tried to do so those who came into range were struck down by the Muslims' arrows, javelins and stones.[308] In reality it was probably the Crusaders' horses that were felled, rather than the armoured men themselves. By the final decades of the Latin States in the Middle East, the Westerners' heavy, close-packed cavalry charge was most effective against other Westerners or those using Western tactics in the civil wars which wracked the declined Kingdom of Jerusalem.[309]

Although mounted infantry were often mentioned in Western European texts of the Crusader period, evidence for the use of mounted infantry in the Latin Middle East is less clearcut. Sometimes the accounts of Arab observers can be interpreted in this way, for example when Baha al-Din described the men defending Jaffa against Saladin towards the end of the Third Crusade. His statement that '*They sent only about three hundred knights against us, the great part of whom were riding mules*'[310] is usually understood to mean that the Crusaders were so short of horses that they fought on mules. Yet such an idea seems impossible, especially given the knights' training and expectation of combat, so it is more likely that Baha al-Din was referring to mounted infantry.

During the same campaign King Richard is specifically stated to have sent a high-speed column to intercept an Islamic supply convoy coming from Egypt, the knights carrying infantrymen on their horses' cruppers.[311] They would not, of course, have fought in such a position. A generation later in the aftermath of the Fourth Crusade the *Marshal* of Romania, who was one of the most senior military figures in the newly established Latin Empire of Constantinople, went on a raid which included *turcopoles* and mounted crossbowmen, both of whom were employed as scouts.[312]

Most Western European and Crusader infantrymen were, of course, simply foot soldiers: men who travelled and fought on foot. These troops were also significantly more effective than is generally realised. In mid-12th century Normandy and France the poetic chronicler Wace described infantry defending a river crossing,[313] or being joined in an open battle-array by knights who had dismounted while archers and crossbowmen were placed in the flanks.[314] Outside Rouen in 1174, an infantry formation arrayed by the Plantagenet king of England, Henry II, was said to number five to six thousand men, divided into three *batailles* each about twelve men deep. Yet its flanks still remained vulnerable to cavalry attack.[315]

Dismounted knights would, according to Wace, shorten their lances and remove the pennons to be better able to wield these weapons on foot. Yet they still formed up in their usual *conrois* formations, so closely packed that no man had room to turn and flee.[316] In his *chanson de geste* about the siege of Barbastro, the late 12th century poet Aimeri de Narbonne describes such men on foot thrusting the *aretueil* or butts of their spears into the ground to level them against the enemy as pikes.[317] The Arab nobleman, poet, warrior and scholar Usama Ibn Munqidh describes Crusader cavalry dismounting and doing precisely the same thing in defence of the entrance to their castle.[318]

During the siege of Acre by the Third Crusade, the besiegers were themselves surrounded and effectively besieged by Saladin's field army. According to Imad al-Din, the Latins *'stood like a wall behind their mantlets, shields and spears, with levelled crossbows'*.[319] Yet only a few months later King Richard, who was by now the sole remaining senior leader of the Third Crusade, is credited with using an entirely novel defensive tactic when his camp outside Jaffa came under sudden and unexpected attack. Here he formed his men into a line, on foot, and according to his chronicler: *'Our men prepared themselves as best they could to receive their furious attacks, each fixing his right knee in the ground, so that they might the better hold together, and maintain their position; the thighs of their left legs were bent, and their left hands held their shields or bucklers. Stretched out before them in their right hand they held their lances, of which the lower parts were fixed in the ground and their iron heads pointed threateningly towards the enemy. Between every two of the men who were thus covered with their shields, the king, versed in arms, placed a crossbowman, and another behind him to span the crossbow as quickly as possible, so that the man in front might discharge his shot while the other was loading'*.[320] It was not, of course, a new idea. It had been described in detail in Arabic military manuals for several centuries (see volume II) and if it was new for King Richard's Crusaders, they are likely to have learned of it from their northern Italian allies if not from their Islamic foes.

In battle the role of Western European foot soldiers was still essentially defensive and static, often within some sorts of field fortification. Such tactics were highly developed in Italy which, with its well-trained communal militias, also had the best European infantry until the 14th century. Here, in the 13th century, and excluding siege warfare, the classic method of using infantry was to group crossbowmen and *palvesari* into teams. The *palvesari* carried large shields, *pavises*, which they rested on the ground as mantlets to create a shield-wall behind which crossbowmen could span and shoot their weapons, both being protected from attack by spearmen. Crossbows and especially *pavises* were heavy and cumbersome, so it was normal for this equipment to be carried in carts or on baggage animals.[321]

On the other hand this tactic made an infantry formation even more static and unmanoeuvrable than before, so it is no surprise that there were cases where small forms of siege weapons were used against them and their shield-wall. In 1275, for example, the *Gibelline* (pro-Imperial) commander Guido Novello used particularly heavy crossbows to smash the resistance of a *Guelph* (pro-Papacy) infantry formation near Faenza.[322] Once again the remarkable Islamic military colony known as the Saracens of Lucera played a significant part in breaking this tactical mould. Armed with their traditional composite hand-bows and now also with light forms of crossbow, they were employed as light infantry just as so many of their infantry co-religionists were in North Africa and the Middle East. In Italy these Saracens were more than mere skirmishers and, in cooperation with light cavalry, introduced a style of manoeuvrable light infantry tactics which would eventually be adopted by other foot soldiers both in Italy and beyond the Alps.[323]

COMBAT SKILLS AND TRAINING

In the *Roman de Renart*, which dates from the late 12th or early 13th century, it was said to be normal for a warrior to shave his chin and cut his hair before battle, so that his helmet fitted better and there was nothing for an enemy to grasp in the bloody hand-to-hand combat of a *mêlée*. Furthermore, not doing these things was to show an unchivalrous contempt for the foe.[324]

Meanwhile changes in tactics led to changes in the way weapons were used. On the other hand, technological developments in weaponry itself had a relatively small impact upon tactics. In some parts of Western Europe and the Latin States such changes were obvious, most notably in the Iberian peninsula. With the introduction of essentially French-style heavily armoured cavalry in close *conrois* formations came the *couched* lance. Or perhaps it would be more accurate to say that the *couched* lance moved from being just one of several techniques of using a spear on horseback to become virtually the only method.[325]

This technique had different names in other parts of the world, where it remained just one of several skills. In Europe or the Latin States it meant that a long and heavy cavalry spear,[326] normally called a *lance*, was grasped at a place well to the rear of its point of balance and was then held between the rider's chest and upper-arm with the rear part of the shaft secured snugly beneath his armpit. The result was that the point of the weapon protruded further forward than would be the case if it were held at its point of balance, and it was also held very strongly, so much so that the horseman became one with his weapon. When riding in a deep saddle with high cantle and pommel and long stirrups, the rider, weapon and horse became a single immensely powerful projectile. The main disadvantage, of course, was that the *couched* lance could only be pointed forwards within a small arc. When a substantial number of cavalrymen holding their lances in this manner made their fearsome charge, the moral impact must have been huge and to have seemed unstoppable. However, if they themselves were attacked from the sides or rear they were virtually unable to use their weapons, like tanks whose guns only aim forwards.

The limitations of heavily armoured Crusader cavalry, even when well trained or skilled, were apparent to their Islamic rivals. As Abu Shama wrote of the Latin knights at the battle of Hattin: *'A Frankish faris (*élite cavalryman or knight*), as long as his horse was in good condition, could not be knocked down. Covered with a coat of mail from head to foot, which made him look like a block of iron, the most violent blows made no impression on him. But once his horse was killed, the knight was thrown and taken prisoner. Consequently, though we counted them (*Frankish prisoners*) by the thousands, there were no horses amongst the spoils, whereas the knights were intact. The mount had to be felled by spear or sword to bring down the faris from his saddle'.*[327]

Other aspects of the skills and equipment needed by the knight can be gleaned from a close reading of poetic *chansons de geste*, chronicles and surviving contracts for the hire of mercenaries. In *La Mule sans Frein*, which was written in the Champagne region of France in the late 12th or early 13th century, the hero takes seven shields when he goes on a warlike adventure because these wooden protections so often got damaged or broken.[328] The number might be a poetic exaggeration, but we may accept that spare shields were available. Having a warhorse that was too aggressive is likely to have been unhelpful as the control and discipline of a knight's mount would have been essential in the *conrois* and probably also in the *mêlée*. *Condotte* military contracts from 13th century Italy frequently required that, to be hired, the horseman must have horse-armour.[329] Although mail was not very effective against arrows shot at anything less than a reasonable distance, this insistence might indicate that heavily armoured Italian cavalry were already having difficulty closing with disciplined archers and cross-bowmen. Mail horse-armour was also notoriously heavy and cumbersome while all horse-armour tended to make the animal overheat and thus tire quickly.[330]

During the 11th and 12th centuries any attempt to make a clear distinction between heavy and light cavalry in Western Europe is likely to prove misleading. Differences in equipment still tended to reflect wealth and status rather than specific military roles. Light cavalry in the proper sense of the word would appear in some parts of Europe during the 13th century, but even then they seem to have been a limited local phenomenon. If a horseman appeared in the written sources wearing little or no armour, there was usually a reason for it. One of the most obvious is described in the memoirs of Usama Ibn Munqidh, who recalled that an early 12th century Crusader opponent had removed his *dir'* and *tijfaf*, mail hauberk and the soft armour worn beneath. This he did *'for lightness but was then killed by lance thrust in his chest'.*[331] Normally the wearing of a *gambeson* or other form of soft armour on its own was considered a sign of poverty, but since the Second Crusade there is clear evidence that French cavalry undertook scouting or harrassment duties – both of which could be seen as typical light cavalry actitivities – protected only by their padded gambesons.[332]

Amongst the earliest groups of Western European cavalry specifically described as 'light' were the *berrovieri* of 13th century northern Italy.[333] Their armour typically consisted of light *chapel de fer* brimmed or *barbuta* open-faced form of helmet, *panzere* mail hauberk, *corettum* cuirass, gauntlets and *iubba* or *jubba* quilted soft armour. The latter was another form of soft armour, the name coming from Turkish via Arabic. Each man carried a large *scutum* or *talamaccium* shield, a *coltello* light sword or large dagger, sometimes a spear and sometimes a crossbow.[334] The French term *talevas*, comparable to the Italian *talamaccium*, referred to a large shield used for skirmishing in late 13th and early 14th century northern England, as distinct from close-combat *'buttinge with sharpe speres'*. It was also distinct from the ordinary *sheld* carried by heavy cavalry knights.[335]

The only specialised light cavalry in the Latin or Crusader States were the *turcopoles* whom William of Tyre described as *equites levis armaturae*. They were distinguished not only by their tactics but also by their appearance which included archery equipment. By the 13th century these troops usually wore a *haubergeon* meaning a smaller or more limited form of mail *hauberk*. The Templars' *Old French Rule* states that, as well as scouting and harrassing the enemy's flanks or rear as horse-archers, these *turcopoles* could charge alongside or in support of the knights.[336] They proved themselves particularly effective in broken terrain.

Some of the clearest information regarding the skills required of infantrymen is found in sources concerned with urban militias in the Iberian peninsula. They were most effective when facing the small and similarly urban-based armies of the fragmented *ta'ifa* Islamic states and in wars between the Christian states of northern Iberia. Against the more powerful armies of the Murabitun and Muwahhidun, such militias were much less successful.[337] Militia infantry equipment was also far from uniform, as shown in the military regulations of Madrid, drawn up in the year 1264. They stated that a *ballesta* crossbow could be substituted for a spear, while men from the nearby mountainous Sierras could substitute a *cuchiello serranil* long knife for a sword.[338]

Other sources shed light on the armour worn by Western infantry. Anna Comnena having noted that the heavy mail *hauberks* of Latin knights were a disadvantage when they were fighting on foot.[339] Two centuries later, and again within Byzantine territory, the southern French troubadour Raimbaud de Vaqueiras took part in the Fourth Crusade's siege of Constantinople in 1204. There he recalled fighting on foot and declared that he was proud to be equipped like a Brabantine infantryman, *'a ley de Bramaso d'elm e de'ausberc e de gros guambaizo'*.[340] That is with a helmet, a hauberk and a large *gambeson* or padded soft armour.

Raimbaud was, in fact, the only troubadour known to have been knighted, and here he had been armed for close combat. The evidence, both written and pictorial, suggests that infantry archers were usually, though not always, more lightly protected. Archery was perhaps more significant in Western European warfare in the 11th and 12th centuries than is generally realised. We know that several senior men were killed by arrows in Britain and France,[341] as well as on Crusade in Italy and in Spain where archery featured more prominently.

Modern experimental archery shows that an arrow shot from a so-called longbow could penetrate mail from a range of two hundred metres.[342] There was, of course, no such weapon as a 'longbow' during the medieval period. All medieval bows of simple rather than composite construction were more or less 'long' and were simply referred to as 'bows'. Their power came from the weight of their arrows rather than the power or range of the bow. Certainly it did not come from the speed with which they could be shot, which was far slower than that achieved with a Middle Eastern or Asian composite bow (see volume II).

Yet archery was already potentially so dangerous to the knightly élite that, when Henry of Anjou captured Crowmarsh from King Stephen early in the 12th century, he had the sixty archers in the garrison beheaded. Meanwhile in France the Church tried to ban the use of bows in war in 1120.[343] More famously, the Church's great Lateran Council included in its wide-ranging reforms of 1139 a clause which sought to prohibit the use of crossbows, and probably ordinary bows as well, against fellow Christians.[344] This was not only to protect the knights, who were seen as the 'proper' people to settle disputes when war seemed the only answer, but also to protect their very expensive warhorses and avoid the danger of promoting blood feuds. Loss of one or more warhorses could ruin a knight financially,[345] and horse-armour was as yet virtually unknown outside Islamic- or Byzantine-influenced regions, so it was not only a matter of saving blood but of preserving the financial viability of an established military class.

Even the Lateran Council allowed that crossbows be used against non-Christians, and the attempted ban was largely ignored anyway. The popularity of crossbows as war-weapons spread rapidly while that of the ordinary hand-bow slumped almost everywhere during the 13th century.[346] Only towards the end of the reign of King Henry III of England did the military potential of what are now called 'longbowmen' begin to be recognised, and this was almost entirely restricted to England. Yet even here such archers remained far fewer than crossbowmen and also tended to come from specific parts of the country, especially from the most forested counties where widespread use of the simple bow had survived for hunting, or in many cases for poaching.[347]

The bow also remained common in Scandinavia as well as some more isolated or backward parts of Germany and its eastern neighbours. Elsewhere the crossbow's main competitor as a missile weapon was the hand-held composite bow which continued to be used in several areas under strong Byzantine or Islamic military-technological influence. Most of the composite bows in question also seem to have been in the earlier Byzantino-Arab tradition of quite large infantry weapons, though there may have been some adoption of shorter forms of Turkish composite bow developed for use on horseback. In late 13th century southern Italy, most of the Saracens of Lucera and other military colonies who served in Angevin armies against the Aragonese invaders of Sicily clearly used composite bows as well as being equipped with *rotelle* small round shields and spears. Some were mounted infantry or even light cavalry, and very few now used crossbows.[348] Apart from the *almogavars* and other light infantry of Moorish origin or inspiration in the armies of Christian Iberian kingdoms, the other most distinctive group of infantry archers in Christian service against Islamic armies during the 13th century were the Maronites of Lebanon. Jacques de Vitry described them as using bows and arrows and being both swift and skilful in battle.[349]

Elsewhere the overwhelming majority of Western European infantry 'missile' troops were now crossbowmen. There is strong evidence that the armies of late 10th and 11th century Anjou in France included crossbowmen,[350] but it otherwise seems to have been in the north of the Iberian peninsula and south-western France that the crossbow first became widely popular. Here this process began in the late 11th century.[351] All these were, of course, areas where fortification and thus siege warfare were relatively advanced at an early date. Quite why the crossbow came so late to urbanised and otherwise militarily advanced northern Italy remains a mystery, though the weapon was then adopted with great enthusiasm. Yet this did not stop captured crossbowmen from occasionally facing cruel treatment. For example the Genoese crossbowmen captured by Milan in 1246 had caused their foes such losses that they were mutilated in retaliation.[352]

Mounted crossbowmen are an especially interesting group. Most references to them in sources such as surviving 13th century Italian *condotte* mercenary contracts almost certainly indicate mounted infantry, and they were clearly more numerous than elsewhere in Europe.[353] References to crossbows actually being used on horseback are rarely clear, though this seems to have been done on a number of occasions against static infantry formations in Tuscany during the last quarter of the 13th century.[354] Yet even this may have been an ad hoc tactic rather than standard practice.

A much more ancient missile weapon, the javelin, continued to be used in many regions, though only in a few was it considered a local military characteristic. One such area covered the Pyrenees and substantial provinces to the north and south of these mountains. Large numbers of infantry *dardiers*, javelin or 'dart throwers', were mentioned during the Albigensian Crusade, notably during the siege of Toulouse. Furthermore, the Gascon *dard* was a feared weapon, fully capable of piercing even the best armour of that period.[355] Infantry javelins also appear frequently in art from the same areas, especially from Navarre on the southern side of the Pyrenees.

The most important cavalry weapon in Western Europe and the Latin States during this period was undoubtedly the *couched* lance. Traditionally it has been accepted that the *couched* method of handling and using the weapon was 'invented' in Europe, probably 'near Normandy' in the mid-11th century.[356] Yet it is now quite clear that a virtually identical, and perhaps actually identical, method of combat had been used by Byzantine heavy cavalry by the 10th century, if not earlier. More recent research into Arabic military training manuals shows that it was used even earlier by armoured cavalry in the 9th and probably also in the later 8th century (see volume II).

Whereas in eastern armies the *couched* lance was just one of several available methods of using a spear on horseback, it is sometimes thought to have been almost the only method amongst Western knights and other armoured close combat cavalry. Nevertheless, a closer look at reliable written sources as well as iconographically more dubious pictorial ones shows that, at least in the 11th and 12th centuries, Western horseman were fully capable of and willing to use their lances in other ways. Usamah Ibn Munqidh, for example, described Crusader horsemen reversing their lances to strike downwards at a man on the ground.[357] Nor was it necessary to transfix an opponent right through his body, as beloved of heroic *chansons de geste* and illustrations of Christian heroes slaughtering wicked infidels. As Jean de Meun wrote in 1284 in his *L'Art de Chevalerie*, a freely updated translation of the late Roman *De Re Militari*, a penetration by a spearhead of only two fingers depth was enough to defeat or even to slay a foe.[358] Detailed information on how spears were used on foot is much rarer, though a section of the *Roman de Renart*, dating from around 1190, refers to an infantry spear being supple, bound with leather thongs and used in conjunction with a round shield.[359]

Several Eurocentric myths also surround the use of the medieval sword. Most notable is the idea that fencing in the modern sense of the word, using the weapon both defensively and offensively and giving preference to the thrust rather than the cut, was 'invented' in later medieval Italy.[360] On the other hand, 12th century sources such as the epic poem *Aucassin et Nicolette*, when describing combat between sword-armed knights, emphasise cutting blows to the head and arms. There was also one remarkable reference to a man being dragged away by the nasal of his helmet, strongly suggesting that the poet had close knowledge of the brutal reality of warfare in the period.[361]

Other details are found in chronicles, especially when written by men who took part in the wars they describe. In the mid-13th century, the Crusader De Joinville drew a second sword from a scabbard attached to his saddle when unable to draw the sword that hung from his belt.[362] In contrast, Islamic training manuals insist that the saddle-sword should be used before that at a man's waist, as the latter was regarded as his final line of defence, to be reserved for the most desperate of circumstances (see volume II). De Joinville proves to be a particularly valuable source of detailed and sometimes gruesome information, noting, for example, the appalling cutting power of the single-edged *fauchon* or *falchion*.[363]

The mace has usually been considered a medieval weapon which first came into widespread use in the Turco-Islamic Middle East. This geographical association appears to be correct but not the dating because a remarkable mace, identical in most respects to some of the earliest medieval examples, was found in the ruined 3rd century Roman frontier fortress of Dura Europos in Syria. Nothing like it seems to have been found elsewhere in the Roman Empire, so perhaps it should be seen as an Iranian weapon, either used by Parthian refugees of ultimately Central Asian origin now in Roman service, or by the Sassanian Persians who were attacking the fortress.

The history of the mace in its various forms certainly went back a long way in Islamic history, so it is perhaps not suprising to find some of the earliest Western European references to this weapon in the Christian regions of the Iberian peninsula. One of the first is an epic poem, rewritten in the late 13th or early 14th century but otherwise still using 12th century military terminology, where it is called a *maza*.[364] An early 13th century Catalan epic described it as a weapon for heavily armoured élite cavalry,[365] and of course the mace was always intended as a stunning or smashing weapon for use against armoured or well-shielded opponents. The mace then appears in the Occitan literature of southern France in the late 12th and 13th centuries, this time in the context of heavily armoured men riding armoured horses: '*Chavaliers e chevaus armatz. Massas e brans, elms de color, escutz tranchar e desguarnir*'.[366]

Further north, in French-speaking regions and those dominated by French military culture, the *maçue* mace was initially linked with the simple club as the weapons of low-status warriors, peasants and mythical monsters, perhaps reflecting a prejudice against a weapon seen as Islamic and unsuitable for a knight.[367] On the other hand a practical and open-minded monarch like the French King Philip Augustus, who had himself been on Crusade and presumably seen the effectiveness of such weapons, soon included a specialised group of mace-armed cavalry sergeants in his army. They demonstrated their worth and that of their weapons in the French victory at the battle of Bouvines.[368]

The use of staff weapons is more of a problem and it is still not entirely clear what weapon was meant by a specific medieval term. The *jusarme* or *guisarme* is a case in point. One of the earliest references to such weapons which also gives some indication of what they were is found in *La Mule sans Frein* which was written in the Champagne region in the late 12th or early 13th century. On this occasion it was used by a peasant, was heavy, was carried on his shoulder, was wielded in a cutting action and could take off an enemy's head.[369]

Meanwhile the power and effectiveness of the crossbow was not necessarily as great as might be expected. It has actually been suggested that the range of the European crossbow during the Crusader period was around two hundred and fifty metres, with an effective killing range of seventy-five to one hundred metres and an ideal point-blank range of some fifty metres.[370] That would have been less than the Turkish hand-held composite bow, though the crossbow did shoot heavier arrows,[371] bolts or *quarrels*. It is also clear that the penetrating power of any missile against armour depended on its weight rather than speed, assuming a similarly sharp arrowhead.

Proper training was, of course, required for all these varied Western European weapons. Unfortunately far less information survives than it does for training in medieval Byzantine or Islamic armies. What are recorded are occasional episodes where a lack of skill or training, or perhaps simply tiredness, resulted in something worthy of note by a chronicler or poet. One such event happened in the summer of 1097 when Duke Godfrey de Bouillon was wounded in a fight with a bear, the worst damage being done not by the animal's teeth and claws but when Godfrey struck his own leg with his own sword leading to an 'unstaunchable stream of blood' which caused him to faint.[372]

Scattered evidence concerning the training of youngsters has them skirmishing with swords and spears in the late 11th or early 12th century *Song of Roland*.[373] A generation or so later it becomes clearer that the military education of a member of the knightly élite began around the age of twelve, before which their education had focussed on literacy and other more peaceful accomplishments. Now they had to learn to ride, use a spear and shield, give and evade blows, take part in hunting to improve their skill as horsemen as well as being able to 'read the terrain'. Other required skills included archery and throwing javelins against moving targets while some men from the upper aristocracy also learned how to play chess, perhaps to stimulate their tactical skills.[374] The Norman poet Wace makes it clear that knightly cavalry training could be dangerous, and fatal accidents were not uncommon.[375] In the Latin States of the Middle East, rather than merely training in the use of arms, young men of the aristocracy were commonly involved in warfare at under fifteen years of age.[376]

Otherwise, training was usually undertaken as part of a group of similarly aged *jeunes* or adolescents who were then expected to become a band of *amis* or friends within the *compagnie* or *maisnie*, all usually being dubbed as knights together when arms and money was distributed amongst the group.[377] *Chansons de geste* and comparable epic poetry in other European languages can add further details. The *quintain* or practice target for using a couched lance on horseback was mentioned in the late 12th early 13th century French *Elioxe*,[378] while the great German *Nibelungenlied* of around 1200 mentions young warriors exercising by throwing weights and javelins.[379]

Combat training manuals existed in the 13th century, which suggests a substantial degree of literacy at least amongst those responsible for military training. Only fragments remain of the earliest known examples, and the oldest to survive intact is a late 13th century Latin text from Germany on the use of sword and buckler and the associated skills of wrestling. Some of the skills, and certainly the very 'unchivalrous' practical attitude towards combat, seem to show an approach more like that of modern commando training than the refined sword-fencing of later centuries. It is also worth noting that the thrust was already being given precedence over the cut.[380] In the *mêlée* the main blows were aimed at an opponent's head, and later sources also focus on the need for a horseman to control his mount, especially when fighting in the *mêlée*, as well as the advisability of not tiring his animal too much.[381] Later training texts from the 14th and 15th centuries recognise the importance of psychological preparation before combat and there is no reason to suppose that such requirements were not appreciated earlier. Other information on knightly training and physical exercise from these later centuries shows that fitness and dexterity were more highly regarded than bodily size and brute strength, which is again likely to have been just as true of the 11th to 13th centuries. The *Master of Arms* emerged as a specialist in such training, but for various social and political reasons he was viewed with less favour in medieval England than on the continent, though still accepted as a necessity.

Military training was more than a necessity in the Military Orders; it formed a central part of their daily life and their reason for existence. Amongst the Hospitallers, and probably other Military Orders as well, military exercises seem largely to have been done in the afternoons. Late *statutes* or regulations indicate that these took place three times a week and included gymnastics, wrestling, drill, exercises with weapons and crossbow-shooting at targets, prizes for marksmanship being given every two months.[382] The Templars' *Old French Rule* stated that brethren were only allowed to use crossbows against targets, not simply for amusement or for hunting, and the same applied to jousting on horseback, which was only permitted in the presence of the Master.[383]

Most information about infantry training comes from those parts of Europe where communal militias were important and highly organised. In northern Italy there were clearly quite sophisticated training systems for urban militias from at least the mid-11th century. These involved the use of weapons, teaching men to work as a team, and for infantry and cavalry to cooperate effectively.[384] Such training continued throughout the 13th century, and as a result the best Italian communal infantry were capable of fighting in disciplined formations in defence of their city's *carroccio*, driving off enemy cavalry, using ditches, trenches or field fortifications, and delivering successful counter-attacks when the right moment came.[385] In addition to regular training, these militias were also expected to look after their own weaponry. In later 13th century Verona, for example, each man had to maintain his crossbow in good condition, yet the archives indicate that a few decades later there was only about one crossbow for each fifty to one hundred inhabitants even in the rich quarter of Verona, and only one to every three hundred people in the poor quarter.[386]

As so often happens, several aspects of military training evolved into participatory or spectator sports. Crossbow contests remained a popular pastime in Genoa well into the 14th century,[387] but in England non-lethal sword and buckler combats or displays as a form of public entertainment were condemned as a public nuisance in 1281.[388] *Masters of Arms* usually came from ordinary rather than aristocratic backgrounds, as did the majority of later medieval mercenaries, but still had higher status than the *pugils* who taught the art of boxing and remained shadowy figures on the fringes of the law in medieval England.[389]

MILITARY EQUIPMENT

There was a remarkable degree of similarity in the military equipment used within Western Europe during the period of the Crusades, though it was not as great as has sometimes been suggested. Some outlying regions preserved their own traditions of weaponry and even to some extent armour, as well as being generally old-fashioned or poorly equipped when compared to the core states of medieval Latin-Catholic civilisation. Some regions which differed in language and to some extent culture were nevertherless almost identical in military equipment. One such 'military technological zone' included Occitan-speaking southern France (Languedoc), French-speaking northern France, and England which was dominated by a French-speaking ruling class. Thus the list of equipment needed by a knight in the 1170s, according to the Occitan *troubadour* Guilhem de Marsan, would apply throughout France, the English-ruled regions of the British Isles, and to a greater part of western and central Europe as a whole. The troubadour's list consisted of a good horse, a lance, a shield, an *ausberc conugut* (meaning the mail hauberk and the man's identifying surcoat or simply the surcoat which might also be padded and thus protective), a saddle, a bridle, a '*really fine peytral so that nothing is unsuitable*' (this being a broad breast-strap rather than a horse-armour), a saddle-cloth, a pack horse to carry his mail *ausberc doblier* or 'doubled hauberk' (see below), and his weapons. He also mentions a 'double' helmet and iron chausses for the legs.[390] Guilhem was particularly specific where the knight's horse was concerned: '*One that is swift running and apt for arms ... And have the saddlecloth made with the same emblem as the saddle and the same colour as is painted on the shield; and the pennant on the lance in the same way.*' A slightly earlier source, which is also more relevant to Crusading warfare, might be the earliest so-called primitive *Rule of the Templars*. This is believed to have been translated into French between 1136 and 1149.[391] However, many of the pieces of military equipment this primitive rule mentions are not generally believed to have come into use until half a century or more later. These include the *chapeau de fer* brimmed 'war hat' style of helmet and the arming gauntlet. Otherwise the list includes mail *hauberks* which are presumed to incorporate some form of hand protections, as *hauberks* which specifically lack this protection are mentioned elsewhere, mail *chausses* for the legs plus presumably captured and reused 'Turkish maces' and 'Turkish swords'.[392] Information for the 13th century can be drawn from numerous sources, and most show that the military equipment used on Crusade or in the Latin States was virtually identical to that used in at least the warmer Mediterranean regions of Western Europe.[393]

Until recently it was generally accepted that the Western European warriors who took part in the First Crusade rode bigger horses than their Islamic foes and were more heavily armoured. Doubt has recently been thrown on this assertion, at least when drawing comparisons between the best-equipped military élites of both sides, and most especially where their horses are concerned. Nevertheless it does seem that Crusader Christian infantry were generally more heavily equipped than their Muslim counterparts, though in both cases a distinction must be made between real foot soldiers, low in status on both sides, and mounted troops who had, for one reason or another, dismounted to fight.

Although there was remarkable uniformity in the arms and armour of France and its immediate neighbours at least from the late 11th to mid-13th century, greater variety could be seen further from this cultural heartland of High Medieval Europe. In southern Italy and Sicily, for example, the influence of Byzantine and western Islamic military technologies was clearly seen.[394] How far these influences and their resulting alternative and sometimes very advanced military-technological traditions extended up the Italian peninsula is a matter of debate, but might well account for the substantially different styles that emerged in Italy in the very late 13th and 14th centuries.

Within the Christian regions of the medieval Iberian peninsula the process of military technological change took a somewhat different course, at least until well into the 14th century when Italian styles began to be imported. Here the main outside influences came from France to the north, and Islamic al-Andalus to the south, beyond which lay the technologically somewhat backward region of North Africa. Al-Andalus was, however, far from being backward (see volume II), though it was to some extent separate from the technological and economic powerhouse of the Islamic Middle East. It also preserved several now seemingly archaic military traditions dating from the earlier centuries of Islamic civilisation. Thus its influence upon the Christian 'Reconquista' states along its northern borders was in many respects different from that of the Islamic Middle East upon its closest Christian neighbours.

Until the 11th century, iron body armour had been rare in these Christian Iberian states and seems to have been almost entirely reserved for the military élite. In this respect northern Iberia was comparable to France a century or so earlier. Nevertheless, there is little evidence that these states were particularly poor and there was no reason why they should have been short of iron as there were several significant mining areas in northern Spain. Instead, the apparent preference for light cavalry and virtually unarmoured infantry probably reflected military and tactical traditions which had more in common with the westernmost regions of the Islamic world than they did with France and other Christian states beyond the Pyrenees.[395]

Although styles and traditions had changed by the later 13th century, it seems that Christian Iberian arms and armour remained generally lighter than those of France, England, Germany or Italy. Remarkably detailed information survives from this period in the form of laws stemming both from rulers and local urban authorities which stipulated what was expected of the fighting men who took part in various types of campaign. For example the *Fuero Real* of King Alfonso the Wise of Castile shows that a *caballero* cavalryman, when summoned to the army, must bring with him more abundant and considerably more costly equipment than had been required a century earlier. His horse was to be worth at least thirty *maravedís*. In addition he should have a shield, a lance, a 'metal' helmet which might suggest that other types perhaps of hardened leather were also available, a sword, a *loriga* mail hauberk, a *perpunt* quilted soft armour which could be worn either beneath or over the hauberk, and finally the *brofuneras* which protected his legs.[396] Other laws from other kingdoms or from the warlike cities of the frontier regions tended to differ only in detail or emphasis.[397]

Before looking at the particular items of equipment used by Western European warriors during this period, it is interesting to note that such equipment had to be both stored and distributed as well as manufactured in the first place. While high-status warriors may have owned and maintained their own arms and armour, even professional soldiers such as hired mercenaries sometimes had to rely on equipment from somebody else. For example, in late 11th century Castile a king or member of the higher aristocracy might give a man a horse and weapons in return for military service, though most professional members of the military élite had their own.

In many areas specific castles were used as securely defended weapons stores. During the 12th century the Latin Principality of Antioch seems to have used the fortress of Darbsak (Trapesac) as such an arsenal from which military equipment was distributed when an army was mobilised.[398] This practice was also mentioned in fictional sources such as the *Roman de Cléomadés*, a 13th century epic poem, where such an arsenal contained *épées*, *guisarmes*, *maçues*, *miséricordes* and *fauchons*[399] (see below). More prosaically the authorities in the late 13th century Italian urban commune of Perugia were responsible for the procurement and distribution of weapons for the city's militia. As a consequence Perugia demanded a certain number of crossbows from the surrounding *contado*, the rural area subject to the city, because these were needed to defend the castles of the city and *contado*.[400] Similar arrangements were seen in many parts of Italy and are likely to have been present in other relatively urbanised regions of Mediterranean Europe, perhaps including some of the Latin or Crusader States.

Throughout human history, the cost of military equipment has been a prime concern for governing authorities. Arms and armour have always tended to be expensive, with the richest states maintaining the best-equipped armies. Documentary and other evidence from the medieval period is, however, usually more useful in enabling historians to compare the relative costs of these items, including the horses which remained central to all such calculations. One of the earliest sources for the period under consideration is a Norman charter of between 1043 and 1048 which stated that a mail *hauberk* was worth seven *livres*, a considerable sum at the time, while other sources from the same period put the cost of a suitable horse at between twenty and thirty *livres*.[401] Just over two centuries later it cost the Order of the Hospitallers two thousand silver *deniers de Tours* to equip a knight, again a substantial sum, which remained much the same in 1303 when it also cost the Order one thousand five hundred *deniers de Tours* to equip a sergeant.[402] Converting medieval money into modern terms is difficult and often fruitless, but the fact remains that full military equipment for a fighting man, especially a mounted knight, was very costly at the start of the Crusading era and was even more so at its conclusion.

It seems that, as a rough generalisation, interest in the finery and decoration of weaponry also increased within the Western European military élite during these centuries. Nevertheless, in the late 12th or very early 13th century sections of the *Roman de Renart* the author and his audience had little interest in decorated weapons but were fascinated by their utilitarian capabilities.[403] Complaints about excessive finery diverting men's attentions from the religious motivation of Crusading warfare were already being voiced, and regulations were drawn up to control it, but it was not until the 13th and 14th centuries that military sumptuousness came to be seen as a serious threat to morale as well as a waste of resources.

Romantic modern interpretations of knighthood and indeed of Crusading warfare clearly give undue prominence to the sword as a weapon of war. In reality it was the simple lance that bore the brunt in Western European cavalry combat during this period. In literary sources such as the late 12th–early 13th century epic *Elioxe* its shaft was described as being made of spruce or fir,[404] while both pictorial and archaeological evidence shows that its iron point became smaller but thicker as the years went by. This clearly reflected the ongoing struggle between offence and defence, blade and shield or armour, with stronger but smaller lance-blades being designed to punch through the protection rather than to inflict broad wounds as in earlier years.

By the late 11th century the javelin, or thrown spear, had virtually ceased to be considered a suitable weapon for a member of the knightly élite, probably because it was largely redundant in the warfare of core regions like northern France. Instead the javelin became associated with the supposedly less civilised peoples of fringe areas, with lower-status warriors and with 'infidels' in general. It was in fact scorned by the Western European élite, though still being feared. It is interesting to note that in the *Song of Roland*, one of the earliest *chansons de geste*, there are many references to javelins, usually in the hands of Moors. On two such occasions this weapon is called a *múserat* which probably came from the Arabic *mizraq* meaning a javelin.[405] Not surprisingly, javelins appear in great detail in the late 12th century illustrated *Pamplona Bible* from Navarre which had particularly close military contacts with its Islamic neighbours at this time.[406] A few decades earlier, Spanish sources describe *ausconas* as javelins having a blade with a 'ridge'. Around 1270, Spanish or Catalan sources still describe the *azcona* as a Navarrese weapon. The similarity between these terms and the Berber-African *zagaya*, *zaghaya* or *asagai* raises further possible sources of military influence. Other forms of Christian Iberian javelin included simple *dardos* and perhaps the *venablo*, though this latter may have been a staff weapon that was not normally thrown.[407]

Western European swords varied in size and in the style or decorations of their hilts, though there was considerable uniformity in the basic forms of their blades which remained straight and double-edged. Although European sword-blades did evolve from the mid-11th to the mid-14th century, the 'current fashion' tended to be adopted by military élites throughout Latin European society. The *falchion* should, meanwhile, be regarded as a separate weapon (see below) and it was not until the late 13th century that the first evidence for single-edged or curved swords appeared in Western sources. Amongst the earliest was the somewhat obscure *badelaire*, mentioned in various French texts from around 1300, which has sometimes been interpreted as a sabre or early form of cutlass.[408] Even so, such weapons remained rare and the whole concept of the curved sword-blade continued to be associated with 'aliens', infidels and even demonic warriors for many centuries.

Evidence concerning scabbards and sword-belts suggests more variation.

Although such belts were usually of leather, they could be quite finely decorated and have gilded or at least highly polished mounts. In some southern regions, especially in the Iberian peninsula, sword-belts could also be made of very colourful galoon webbing; this being further evidence of strong Islamic stylistic influence.[409] Archaeological evidence from Spain tends to focus attention upon the splendid appearance of the scabbards and sword-belts of the military aristocracy. Meanwhile archaeological evidence from the Baltic region provides more prosaic information, such as scabbards being carved from the finest wood and then being lined with oil-soaked fur to stop sword-blades rusting.[410]

The dagger seems, like the curved blade, to have been regarded as a somewhat unknightly or ungentlemanly weapon at the start of the Crusading era. But this attitude soon changed in the brutal reality of Crusading warfare. As a result some of the earliest references to a *couteau d'armes*, fighting knife or dagger, are found in the records of the Military Orders. This weapon had, in fact, become part of a Templar brother-knight's standard equipment by the later 13th century.[411] Nor was it reserved for such fanatical warriors, the *coltello con punta* being a required weapon in Angevin armies fighting the Aragonese for control of Sicily and southern Italy around the same time,[412] while the Italian *coltellaccio* seems to have been a large dagger or short sword.

The mace was, for many years, also regarded as an 'infidel' and rather suspect weapon, at least in most of the core regions of High Medieval European civilisation where it was initially considered suitable for low-status infantry. For example, Graindor de Douai, in his account of the First Crusade in *Le Chanson d'Antioche* written in the late 12th century, placed the *maçue* in the hands of the almost wild Tafurs.[413] On the other hand the Occitan *troubadours* of southern France began to refer to *masses* or maces in the late 12th century, the small *masseta* being mentioned in the early 13th century and the larger *gran maza* appearing in the later 13th century.[414] Across the frontier in Catalonia, the 13th century mace could apparently be made of iron weighted with lead.[415]

In the very late 12th or very early 13th century German *Nibelungenlied*, the 'war-flail' so beloved of Hollywood film-makers was placed in the hands of a semi-monstrous character.[416] Although this peculiar form of weapon, with iron balls on straps or chains attached to a short staff, does appear in the hands of demons in some 12th and 13th century Western European art, it was until recently widely dismissed as a demonic fancy invented by medieval artists. More recently, however, smaller versions of just such flail-headed maces have been found in early medieval archaeological sites in southern Russia and the Ukraine. Clearly the weapon was used by some nomadic steppe peoples of these regions, and then caught the fancy of medieval artists and poets. However, there is still no evidence that it was used any further west, except perhaps in 10th or 11th century Magyar Hungary.

The axe clearly was used. At first it was regarded as an infantry weapon, but during the 13th century the war-axe was seen in the hands of Western European cavalry, partially as a response to the development of stronger armour, though also as a reflection of Islamic military influence. By the late 13th century such fighting axes came in a variety of sizes and shapes, some clearly descended from the large and famous 'bearded' or Danish Axes commonly associated with the Vikings. These remained infantry weapons and shared the battlefield with other long-hafted and generally longer-bladed weapons which are normally categorised as staff weapons (see below). The lighter axes wielded by some horsemen probably owed more to those used by Islamic and Byzantine cavalry in the Middle East. Other even more specialised military axes included those designed to cut enemy rigging during naval warfare.[417]

Medieval infantry weapons pose a number of problems, not only in Europe but also in the Islamic world, though to a lesser extent in China. This is a problem of terminology and identification. Many infantry weapons are mentioned in the literary sources, usually with little further elaboration because they were associated with low-status troops of little interest to the generally knightly audience for such literature. For example, Wace, writing in the mid-12th century, included amongst such non-noble infantry weapons the *besague*, *gisarme* and *truble*, some of which were for cutting, others for thrusting, and on some occasions apparently doing both.[418] Similarly, a great variety of weapons appear in the hands of foot soldiers in medieval art.

The main problem remains linking terminology with illustrations.[419] Nevertheless, by gathering together scattered if occasionally seemingly contradictory evidence from the written sources it is sometimes possible to suggest what a particular weapon may have looked like, and then to find the closest parallel in manuscript illustrations, carvings or other such pictorial sources. Some terms also remained in use into later centuries when terminology was more clearly defined. One may assume, though with reservations, that the words still meant roughly the same thing. For example, the *picois* and *pius* were clearly a form of infantry hafted weapon in the 12th century French poem *Beatrixe*, and can fairly be assumed to have been *pikes* or long-hafted spears.[420]

The *guisarme* is more difficult, but was also a much more important infantry weapon. The name might stem from the early German *getisarn* or 'mower', but seems to first appear in mid-12th century French.[421] Within a very few years *granz gisarmes* are in the hands of an urban burgess militia in the *Roman de Thèbes*[422] and a generation later Graindor de Douai arms some of the fearsome Tafurs of the First Crusade with *gisarmes* in his *Chanson d'Antioche*.[423] A little more information emerges around a decade later in *La Mule sans Frein* from the Champagne region, where a peasant warrior carries a clearly heavy *jusarme* on his shoulder and wields it as a cutting weapon against his enemy's head.[424]

Other evidence suggests that the late 13th century Italian *guisarma* had a long, single-edged blade which had some similarity with that of the *coltellaccio* large dagger or short sword, perhaps by being curved.[425] Although this staff-weapon was regarded as being quite distinct from the axe, it may have included considerable variations. For example, the English *Tower of London Wardrobe Receipt* of 1353–60 refers to *gisarmes vocant hasegaies* or 'like *hasegaies*'. The latter was related to the Berber *zaghayah*,[426] a hafted weapon with a blade for both cutting and thrusting which is widely regarded as the ancestor of the general African *asagai*. Unfortunately this further confuses the picture because the *zaghaya* is also often seen as the prototype of the Navarrese *ausconas* or *azcona* which is interpreted as a heavy javelin (see above).

The 12th century *truble* may have been *guisarme* with an additional thrusting point,[427] but does seem to have been rare, or at least the word was rarely used. The *fauchart* and other variations on this term also first appeared in the 12th century and became a much more significant though still occasionally obscure infantry weapon. Amongst the earliest references may have been the *faussó* in a mid-12th century Spanish text that was rewritten, without apparent alterations to its terminology, in the late 13th or early 14th century.[428] The context shows that it was not a sword-like weapon, and so was not a fully developed *falchion*. At the end of the 12th century a French text by Aymeri de Narbonne shows the *fauchart* to have been a large-bladed infantry weapon,[429] though the length of its haft remains unclear and a decade or so later it was sometimes called the *faussart*.[430] This has been tentatively linked with illustrations of a massive single-edged blade on a short haft, sometimes with a curve at the end like that on a traditional umbrella handle. Essentially the same shape of blade was being mounted on an ordinary sword-hilt during the second half of the 13th and the 14th centuries when such a weapon was called a *falchion*. The similarity in terminology clearly strengthens the idea of a gradual technological evolution which ended with a heavy blade, originally designed for an infantry staff weapon, becoming a massive form of single-edged sword or sabre-like weapon used both on foot and on horseback.

Archery remained an almost entirely infantry affair in the Latin Western European armies of the Crusading era. Three forms of weapon were involved: the simple or 'self' bow, the composite bow and the crossbow which could itself incorporate a simple, a composite or, in later centuries, a steel bowstave. The simple bow was made of one piece or stave of wood. Though widely referred to as a longbow in modern writing, it was, in the medieval period, known simple as 'the bow'. Some were longer, some were shorter, and there were variations in cross-sections of the stave as there were variations in the wood from which they were made, yew being preferable but not universal. There was no such thing as a 'short bow' as distinct from a 'longbow'.

The simple or self bow would earn itself a fearsome reputation in the hands of English archers in the later 13th to 15th centuries. In many respects it seemed, and indeed was, a primitive weapon with many disadvantages when compared to more sophisticated composite bows and crossbows. Yet it also had several advantages, above all in being cheap and quick to manufacture in large numbers. The large, simple bow had great power but also required great strength, skill and training to be used effectively. It was, in fact, later medieval England's archers rather than their unsophisticated bows which should take credit for the 'longbow's' remarkable success in the period immediately following the Crusades.

During those earlier years the weapon and the archers enjoyed little or no prestige. Their simple bows lost strength if kept strung for too long, which was not the case with composite bows.[431] When such a bow 'all of wood' was captured during the First Crusade and shown to the Seljuk Turkish commander Kerbugha, it was described by the probably southern Italian author of the *Gesta Francorum* as being 'useless'.[432] Another such bow was captured during the course of the Third Crusade, and was shown to Saladin as a primitive curiosity. Here it is, however, worth noting that in the context of the Mediterranean and Middle Eastern Crusades, simple bows made from single staves of wood may actually have been more common in Islamic rather than Christian armies, being the traditional weapons of militarily poor or backward groups such as the Arab bedouin and the Nubians (see volume II). It's possible that the effectiveness of these simple weapons was noted by some Crusaders, perhaps including Richard the Lionheart and his followers, this realisation being brought back to the British Isles where simple bows remained in wider use as hunting weapons than in most other parts of Europe. Simple bows were still not included in surviving English records of military stores before the mid-13th century, though they were often mentioned in legal documents as civilian hunting weapons. Even as late as as 1254–6 a forty days Papal indulgence was offered to English Crusading volunteers if they trained in the use of the crossbow in companies organised by local sheriffs.[433] Not until the reign of King Edward I (1272–1307), another ruler with personal experience of Crusading in the Middle East, did the simple bow start to play a major role in English warfare.

The composite weapon was far more complex and expensive, and has sometimes been seen as almost the 'miracle weapon' of the medieval world. Though characteristic of Central Asia, China, the Islamic and Byzantine worlds, it was certainly not unknown in parts of Europe. In the Iberian peninsula, for example, there had probably been no break in the manufacture and use of the composite bow since Late Roman times. The Muslim Arabs who conquered most of the peninsula in the early 8th century would merely have strengthened an existing military tradition and there were certainly more references to composite rather than simple bows in medieval Iberian written and pictorial sources.[434] The composite bow was similarly known in medieval Italy, though it was largely relegated to hunting rather than warfare as crossbows increased in popularity from the 12th century onwards.[435] Even in England such composite bows were known, though perhaps only as curiosities, as when King Henry III purchased two 'Turkish bows' from Walter Marshal's executors in 1246, along with fifty-two assorted crossbows, all of which also seem to have been of composite construction.[436]

Information about arrows comes from archaeological and documentary evidence because most pictorial sources lack sufficient detail to be very useful. Thus archaeological surveys of battle sites in the Iberian peninsula show a greater concern for armour-piercing capability in arrowheads than is seen in comparable surveys of medieval battle sites in the Middle East.[437] On the other hand this interpretation was made before the discovery of substantial quantities of medieval hardened and layered leather armour in Syria (see volume II). Such leather armour poses very different penetration problems to that posed by the largely iron mail armour of Western Europe.

Simple or so-called longbows also required very different arrows to those used in most composite bows, reflecting the weapons' different energy conservation and release characteristics as well as different tactical traditions in the use of the weapons themselves. Arrows for simple bows tended to be somewhat longer and substantially heavier. Their arrowheads were often huge in comparison to those shot from composite bows. There were, of course, variations for both weapons, and the arrow that killed a certain Simon de Skeffington in 1298 may have been a singularly massive hunting missile with a very broad blade. We know about the latter arrow in remarkable detail because the resulting inquest was recorded in the surviving *De Banco Roll*.[438]

The crossbow became by far the most important missile weapon in Western European warfare during the Crusading era, at least from the mid-12th century onwards.[439] It ranged from the structurally primitive weapon with a simple one-piece bowstave of the later 11th century, to the mechanically more sophisticated crossbow with a composite bowstave and sometimes elaborate spanning aids of the late 13th and early 14th centuries. On the way the Europeans learned of, and on occasions seemingly sought to experiment with, multi-shot weapons of almost certain Chinese and Middle Eastern inspiration. One such monstrosity, supposedly capable of shooting fifteen darts from a single loading, was apparently mentioned in 12th century Venice,[440] within a few years of the similarly experimental and perhaps equally fanciful sixteen-shot multiple crossbow 'engine' described and illustrated in al-Tarsusi's manuscript written for Saladin. Both of these weird machines were, of course, substantially before the invading Mongols brought the latest Chinese military technology to the Middle East and

Eastern Europe. Clearer Venetian evidence for an experimental crossbow with an eight-shot magazine had to wait until 1411.[441]

Where realistic, practical crossbows were concerned, manuscript illustrations show simple one-piece wooden bowstaves continuing to be used right up to the end of the 13th century, especially in the Iberian peninsula. A large version of such a crossbow stave carved from yew was found in the silted moat of Berkhamsted castle in England, having probably fallen there during the siege of 1216.[442] It is very thick and about a metre and a quarter long, thus qualifying as a siege crossbow rather than one to be carried and used by infantry in open battle.

Crossbows with composite bowstaves were able to achieve a much better power-to-weight ratio than those with simple bowstaves.[443] The fact that their bows were made of largely the same materials as composite hand-held bows was at one time taken as evidence of an oriental inspiration behind the technique. Then a series of fundamental structural differences between the two classes of weapon were noted, which undermined the theory of eastern origins. Now, however, several Islamic Middle Eastern crossbow staves have been discovered and studied, once again indicating considerable similarity between the eastern and western weapons. Those from the Middle East are generally older, but the age difference is not great enough to prove that the construction technique spread westwards. One such European composite crossbow stave was found in Germany in a fragmented condition which showed its internal structure to be very similar to those from Syria.[444] Most European examples do not have a layer of horn along the belly of the bowstave, though some do incorporate a central core consisting of one long horn. Their internal structures have very thick layers of whalebone along most, though not all, of their length, while up to half the entire volume of the bowstave consists of surrounding layers of sinew.[445]

One of the earliest European literary references to a crossbow supposedly 'of horn' is found in the *Roman de Cléomadés*;[446] however, the dry lists of weaponry stored in various French castles, drawn up for King Philip Augustus in the early 13th century, are a more reliable source of information. These include large numbers of crossbows of various sizes, but only three were specifically stated to include *balistas de cornu*, or 'crossbow of horn', these being in the particularly important fortifications of Gisors, Pont d'Arche and Laon.[447] Given the fame of Genoese crossbowmen in later decades, it seems surprising that the first mention of composite crossbows in Genoese hands was in 1224, and this is not very clear.[448] Even the late 13th century military supply archives of the Angevin Kingdom of Naples in southern Italy, while laying considerable emphasis on the three usual types or sizes of crossbow, only occasionally specify that any of these are *di corno*.[449]

It is generally accepted that crossbows with steel staves were a late development, though they may have been known as experimental novelties much earlier. The most remarkable evidence is the crossbow with a blue stave in the hands of the First Horseman of the Apocalypse in a Christian Iberian manuscript made in 1086. There is nothing in the standard Biblical text which would encourage an artist to interpret the verse in this manner, or even to give the Horseman a crossbow rather than the usual hand-held bow. Indeed it became traditional in much Christian art to portray the First Horseman of the Apocalypse as an Asiatic horse-archer, a Turk or a Mongol, or at least a frightening 'enemy alien'. So might the artist of this copy of *Beatus' Commentaries* have been reflecting the notably advanced metallurgical workshops of Islamic Cordoba to the south?[450] Such a possibility should not be entirely dismissed for, only two hundred years later, orders for the purchase of substantial quantities of military equipment at Toulouse for Philip the Fair seem to include some crossbows with steel arms, though again this could be interpreted differently.[451] Strong contrary evidence comes from Genoa where crossbows were made of wood and other organic material until 1460 when, it was stated, 'some foreign craftsmen imported iron crossbows'.[452]

Meanwhile there had been notable advances in the release mechanisms used in medieval crossbows, though primitive systems also continued to be used where suitable or where local technology seems to have been backward. For example the simple rising peg form of release seen in crude hunting crossbows found at Charavines in the Savoyard Alps of south-eastern France and dating from around 1000[453] was still being used centuries later in Switzerland, Scandinavia, parts of the Western Islamic world and Africa (see volume II).[454] Negative evidence is unreliable, yet it is interesting to note that highly detailed late 13th century Angevin military archives from southern Italy referred to carved horn nuts for crossbows of the one foot and two feet varieties, but not for the significantly larger *balista de torno* type, perhaps because the stresses involved in the latter were too great for a revolving nut release mechanism.[455]

The more complicated but also more efficient revolving nut form of crossbow release mechanism had been known in later Roman times, and archaeological evidence shows that it remained in use well into the early medieval period, into the misnamed Dark Ages. This was not the system used in Chinese crossbows, though it was used in the Islamic world. In fact it remains unclear how far the revival of the European crossbow as a war rather than merely as a hunting weapon reflected changing military priorities. Similarly the widespread use of a revolting nut, normally carved from horn, demanded a high degree of accurate craftsmanship, perhaps again reflecting technological influence from the neighbouring Islamic world (see volume II for the earlier adoption of crossbows as war weapons in some parts of the Islamic world).

Discounting for a moment massive 'giant crossbows' supposedly mounted on wooden frames or pedestals which should be regarded as siege weapons, ordinary crossbows came in three basic sizes. The smallest soon had a stirrup attached, into which the crossbowman placed one foot while spanning his weapon. This had been known in Europe since at least the late 11th century, which is considerably later than the stirrup crossbow's appearance in the Islamic world. The two-feet crossbow was spanned by the crossbowman placing his feet on the bowstave on either side of the central stock, rather than incorporating a stirrup large enough for two feet. It was clearly a larger and more unwieldy weapon, normally used in siege or naval warfare rather than open battle, and was particularly characteristic of the 13th century. These two versions, the *baliste ad estrif* and the *baliste ad duas pedes*, appear in the French military register drawn up for King Philip Augustus in 1204. So does the third version, the *baliste ad tornum* which was only used in sieges.[456]

Also known as the *arbalete à tour*, the latter was spanned with the help of some sort of 'turning' mechanism and was in use in Portugal as early as 1184. During that year the Muwahhid ruler Abu Yaqub was reportedly killed during his siege of Santarem by what an Arabic chronicle called a *qaws al-lawlab*, or 'windlass bow'.[457] From the Western European viewpoint, 12th century Portugal was an isolated and backward part of Christendom, so the presence of such an advanced crossbow almost certainly reflected military influence from the Islamic south.

Several mechanical spanning aids were known during the later medieval period, but in the 13th and early 14th centuries the most common remained a relatively simple windlass.[458] This could be seen as a development of the belt and *croc* or hook, adopted in Europe during the late 12th century, which enabled a crossbowman to use the strength of his legs to pull back the bowstring or span his crossbow. References to the *croc* increased considerably from the early 13th century onwards.[459] By the later decades of that century in southern Italy the spanning belt was sometimes called a *bandoliere* which suggests a shoulder belt rather than a waist belt.[460]

The most common word for a crossbow arrow or bolt was a *quarel*, *quadrel* or other variations on that term, and its earliest appearance seems to be in the very late 11th century.[461] It indicated a missile with a four-sided, rectangular or diamond-section head. Many of these boltheads have been found by archaeologists, and all seem to be substantial blades designed to punch through shields, armour or helmets. *Quarels* for two-feet crossbows cost slightly more than those for stirrup crossbows, being larger and including more iron.[462] Most though not all Western European crossbow boltheads were of the socket rather than tanged variety, as was also the case with European arrowheads, and by the 13th century they tended to become even shorter, thicker and sturdier.[463] From the late 12th century onwards the larger type was sometimes known as a *materas* in French-speaking areas.[464] This term may have had a Celtic Gaulish origin, via colloquial

Latin, or may have been a punning corruption of the Arabic word *mitrad* which meant a form of small spear or javelin.

While crossbow bolts with paper flights would be charactistic of the Islamic Middle East (see volume II), leather flights were added to crossbow bolts during a siege of Bamborough in the 1220s.[465] This may, however, have been unusual, yet wooden flights have been found on a few of the largest surviving later medieval crossbow bolts. They may also have been the reality behind the crossbow bolts supposedly fletched with *latone* or *latten*, which was similar to brass.[466] While *laton* meant the mixed metal alloy *laiton* in medieval French, there might be a misunderstanding in its application to medieval crossbow bolts. *Lat* and *late* can mean a lathe or thin sliver of wood in colloquial Italian while *later* can mean 'add *lathes* to' something else. In medieval French *lat*, *late* or *lete* came from the low Latin word *latta* meaning a long piece of wood,[467] which would seem more likely where crossbow bolts were concerned.

During this period a warrior's first line of defence was his shield, and at the start of the Crusader period the most typical Western European form was the elongated 'kite shaped' cavalry shield. It was not the only form in current use, nor was it only used on horseback, but it was characteristic enough to be used as a way of identifying 'good' warriors in much medieval art, whereas the round shield came to be used as a means of identifying 'evil' enemy or Islamic troops in such iconography. At one time it was thought that the kite-shaped so-called 'Norman shield' had been invented in northern France in the 11th century. Now, however, it is clear that it had been used in Byzantine armies much earlier and may actually have first appeared in the Islamic world as an infantry defence. In fact one of the first Western European illustrations of such a kite-shaped shield is said to be on an early 11th century Portuguese carving, perhaps reflecting Islamic Andalusian influence.[468] By the second half of the 12th century the kite-shaped shield had not only been adopted by the knightly élite throughout virtually all of Latin Europe, but had become even larger and heavier in presumed response to an increasing threat from crossbows. So it is hardly surprising that it was sometimes supported by a doubled rather than a single *guige* or shoulder-strap.[469]

There seems to have been great variety in infantry shields, as there was in infantry weapons. During the 12th century the largest was the *talevas* which may originally have been designed as a protection against arrows during 'skirmishing' warfare and might also be used by light cavalry in such skirmishing.[470] Pictorial sources suggest that it could be roughly rectangular in shape, and it may indeed always have been so. The term *targe* was used more widely, but generally seems to have meant a round shield. In Europe these would normally have been of wood, but *targes* of *cuir bouilli* hardened leather were used in an attack on Toulouse during the early 13th century Albigensian Crusade according Geoffrey de Tudela. Such technology almost certainly reflected contact with al-Andalus or North

Africa where the *lamt* of hardened leather was the most prestigious of all shields (see volume II).

The *pavise* may have been a further and heavier development of the *talevas* and first appears in a document of 1229, the *Storia di Bologna*, as the *pavensibus*, possibly named after the city of Pavia where it may have originated.[471] The *pavise* was certainly an infantry protection, heavy and normally rested on the ground as a form of mantlet. At the other end of the scale the 13th century saw the adoption of quite small wooden shields or bucklers held in the fist and used by sword-armed foot soldiers in what became a highly developed system of sword-and-buckler fencing that persisted throughout the rest of the medieval period. One such probably 13th century buckler of this form was excavated in Amsterdam and was found to be made of local willow and poplar wood.[472]

The most dramatic changes in Western European armour had to await the 14th century, yet there were still significant developments from the 11th to 13th centuries. Many were almost unseen, taking place beneath the outer layers of armour or clothing illustrated in medieval art. Others involved more detailed or subtle improvements in existing technology or styles which can be seen in pictorial sources if the observer looks closely. In many cases, however, we have to rely on documentary sources, literary, historical or tediously bureaucratic. Sometimes significant information emerges from what might otherwise be little more than a poetic aside in some greater literary work. For example, in the famous German *Nibelungenlied* epic of the very late 12th or early 13th century, men are recognised as secretly wearing armour beneath their ordinary clothes since they appear unnaturally broad-chested.[473] This is turn points to their wearing some form of soft armour with their mail hauberks because mail alone added little bulk and other forms of plated armour were not as yet in use in Germany.

There is, in fact, no real evidence for the use of any form of larger plates in Western European armour, with the notable exception of helmets, before the very late 12th century. Small mounts were adopted as protection for the limbs in the 13th century but even this did not become really common until the 14th.[474] Meanwhile the use, forging and sophisticated shaping of substantial iron plates in the manufacture of helmets shows that this lack of other plate protections was not a result of technological inability, as has so often been claimed. Rather it was a reflection of military fashions, tactics, current requirement, and perhaps of the availability of sufficient quantities of good quality iron. When small elements of plate were introduced, they protected limb joints; at first *poleyns* to cover the knees after 1250 and then *couters* to shield the elbows no earlier than 1260.[475] This again reflected perceived current needs, with the vital organs of the chest and abdomen adequately protected by other means.

The era of the Crusades was still the age of mail where a history of armour is concerned. Throughout this period, at least in Western Europe, the mail *hauberk* remained the primary protection, plus helmets and shield, for men fighting on horseback and on foot. During the 11th and 12th centuries this mail *hauberk* weighed around 11.5 kilograms. Documentary sources of this period, especially those of a poetic and literary character, frequently refer to such *hauberks* being 'doubled'. One of the earliest supposed references to such a doubled *hauberk* may, however, result from a mistranslation. Here, in the late 11th century *Song of Roland*, the statement that '*De son osberc les dous pans li desaffret*' actually means 'of his *hauberk* the two parts he undecorates (separates)', this being done with a mighty blow, but the two parts in question could well be the left and right sides or hems.[476] Elsewhere the *Song of Roland* refers to Saracens in triple mail *hauberks*. This is surely a poetic exaggeration,[477] but might reflect a belief, current at the time the poem was written, not only that the Muslims had access to more abundant armour but that multiple layers of mail were characteristic of the Islamic military élite. There is, in reality, strong evidence to support such a belief (see volume II).

Later sources are more specific, but it is interesting to note that one of the next references to multiple layers of mail again comes from the Iberian peninsula. It is found in a mid-12th century Spanish poem, rewritten in the late 13th century but unaltered in terms of its military equipment, which refers to the *alberc doblier*.[478] The military élite in the slightly later French *chanson de geste* of *Aucassin et Nicolette* similarly wear doubled *hauberks*.[479] A distinctly unpoetic Latin list of equipment drawn up for Philip Augustus in the early 13th century stated that *loricas duplices* were stored in the castle of Evreux,[480] but other *loricas* in this extensive inventory were not, however, doubled. A Catalan source of around 1270 again frequently mentions *lorigas dobladas*,[481] but thereafter this style seems to disappear, presumably because other more effective, lighter or more convenient methods of increasing protection had been developed.

It is possible that the second layer in such defences consisted of a more limited mail armour, for example like that mentioned in the will of a north Italian Crusader who died at Damietta in Egypt in 1219 during the Fifth Crusade. This stated that: '*To the Hospital of the Germans (*Teutonic Knights*), where he wished to be buried, he left all his arms and armour, and his panceriam with one long sleeve and coif*'.[482] On the other hand this might also mean the style of mail *hauberk* with only one mitten, for the right or sword-arm, as shown in Italian art of this period.

Another very interesting variation was the *jazrain hauberk*, which certainly had Middle Eastern Islamic origins. It was, in fact, a copy or development of the mail-lined, fabric-covered and padded or quilted *kazaghand* from which its European name also stemmed. The *jazerenc hauberk* first appeared in Western Europe in the *Song of Roland*, though here it was only mentioned once.[483] There then seems to be a gap of almost half a century until the *jaserant*, *jazerant* or *jaseran hauberk* is again mentioned. In all these early cases the armour in question was being worn by Moors or Saracens,[484] and its external fabric was sometimes stated to be of a specific colour. Not until the late 12th century was the *jaseran* worn by Christians in such poetic sources.[485]

The question of the use of scale and lamellar armour in Western and Central Europe during this period remains a matter of debate, and indeed controversy. There are certainly many medieval illustrations of apparent scale armour but almost all can be interpreted either as highly stylised representations of mail or as symbols that the wearer is 'evil'. In the latter case the artist was drawing upon a tradition of dressing the 'wicked' in what were, at the time, believed to be Saracen or Turkish forms of armour. Only in a very few, very dubious cases might any current reality of Western European armour lie behind these apparent scale-covered body armours.

The only real exceptions come from the 13th century Iberian peninsula which was itself under notable military influence from the western regions of the Islamic world. Here a form of armour called *fojas* or 'leaves' was initially given to 'enemy giants' in a Catalan epic. It could be fragmented by blows, was worn with a mail *loriga* and a *gorget* for the throat and consisted of *launas* which seem to have been metal scales.[486] Unfortunately, it is unclear how the *fojas* differed from the *corazas* or plate-lined cuirass. By the end of the 13th century, other Spanish sources like *Las Siete Partidas* show that the *fojas* was a real rather than merely poetic protection.[487] Armours which fit this description appear in Christian Iberian art, being worn by Christians as well as Muslims and fanciful or demonic warriors. The most detailed representation of an armour of this type is, however, found on an almost unique effigy in northern Italy. This shows the Marchese Guido Pallavicino, a Templar brother knight who died in 1301 and was buried in the Abbey at Fontevivo of which he was a 'protector'.[488] As a Templar and perhaps Crusader, it is tempting to look for a Middle Eastern inspiration for Guido Pallavicino's highly unusual armour, but it is probably more correct to look to the western, Iberian or North African regions of Islam for its origins.[489]

Lamellar armour was known in Scandinavia, being found in both art and archaeology, and was probably also taken to Ireland by some Vikings. Yet in all cases these armours were almost certainly rarities of eastern Baltic, Russian, Byzantine or Middle Eastern Islamic origin. Another archaeological puzzle is posed by some iron scales excavated at Charavines in French Savoy, and dating from around 1000 or slightly later. They are so unlike anything else yet found in Western Europe during this period, and have sufficient similarity with Byzantine 'loose riveted lamellar', that they may have been imported rarities, probably from neighbouring Italy.[490] Clearer evidence for probable lamellar armour suddenly appears much later in the Crusader enclave of Acre in 1291. Here, according to the *Anonymous Account of the Fall of Acre*, armour of scales or plates was used by the defenders during the final siege. If this was lamellar, then it had almost certainly been captured or purchased from the Latins' Muslim neighbours.[491]

The use of leather armour in medieval Europe poses problems of its own. It clearly existed, but the terminology remains difficult. The very name of the *cuirie* shows it to have been of leather, probably hardened or of rawhide. It began to appear in the written sources in the late 12th century, being worn over a mail *hauberk* but beneath a *surcoat*, which is presumably why this early form of *cuirie* cannot be easily identified in pictorial sources.[492] The late 12th and early 13th century Provençal troubadours knew it as the *coirassas*,[493] a term which would eventually become the cuirass. During the first half of the 13th century *corazas* were worn by infantry rather than knights in Spain and Catalonia, often with a mail *capellina*, and could have a *xamete* decorative fabric covering of a distinctive colour.[494] As such they would appear in art, though usually being almost indistinguishable from other forms of fabric costume. Meanwhile there were increasing references to leather armour and even leather helmets in the training regulations of various northern Italian urban militias.[495] Leather armour is mentioned more rarely in northern Europe, though in 1298 the arsenal of Berwick on the frontier between England and Scotland contained an 'old armour of *cuir-bouilli*', namely hardened leather.[496]

The *coat-of-plates* which incorporated iron elements is likely to have evolved from the leather *cuirie* or *cuirasses*. One of the earliest illustrations of a body armour which can be identified as a *coat-of-plates* or *pair-of-plates*, as it was otherwise known, is in a version of *Beatus' Commentaries on the Apocalypse* painted in all probability in northern Spain.[497] Once again it is worth noting that this early evidence comes from a region in close military and technological contact with the Islamic world; in this case al-Andalus. It was also a few years before 1225 when the French chronicler, Guillaume le Breton, mentioned *pales* being worn under a mail *hauberk* and an *aketon* soft armour. This is normally interpreted as an early reference to iron splints or plates, perhaps forming an addition to an ordinary leather *cuirie*.[498] Around 1230 a French romance mentioned a *cuirie bonne ... largement ferrée*, a 'good cuirie ... largely ironed (having iron added)', but offered no further details.[499] Twenty or so years later the French Crusader and chronicler, De Joinville, stated that a 'special jousting *hauberk*' proved more effective against arrows.[500] Perhaps this was another early form of *coat-of-plates*. Illustrations now start to become clearer. It is interesting to note that while externally worn *coats-of-plates* in late 13th century Germany and its neighbours to the east and north normally incorporated substantial vertical plates,[501] the *coat-of-plates* which found favour in France and its cultural colony of England tended to have a hoop-like construction, probably inspired by or even directly copied from the hardened leather hoop armours currently in widespread use in the Islamic Middle East and Mongol empires.[502]

Separate or additional defences for the limbs were at first of mail, and included the *braoneras* mentioned in a Catalan source of 1151. They, like the *brassonieras* worn by Roland in a mid-12th century but subsequently reworked Spanish epic, appear to have been separate from the main *hauberk.*[503] The long mail sleeves shown beneath some of the short-sleeved mail *hauberks* on the Bayeux Tapestry have been interpreted as comparable separate pieces, though they might also simply be part of a second, long-sleeved *hauberk.*

Extensions to the sleeves of such larger mail *hauberks* soon developed into full hand-protecting mittens or *mufflers*, though the versions seen in late 12th century art sometimes still do not cover the wearer's fingers.[504] One of the first written references to a hand protection called it a *manicle de fer* and, given its late 12th century date, this is more likely to mean a mitten attached to the *hauberk* sleeve than a separate *gauntlet.*[505] The next development was rigid, disc-like *couters*, strapped to the outside of the elbows to protect vulnerable joints, but these did not appear until the very end of the 13th century, or more likely the early years of the 14th century. Whalebone *gauntlets* were mentioned in 1285, metal plated *gauntlets* eleven years later, and in both cases they probably consisted of small plates or scales between layers of fabric.[506]

Separate shoulder defences can be regarded as extensions or protections for the head and neck (see below). The earliest written references include an account of the siege of Barbastro on the northern frontier of al-Andalus, written by Aimeri de Narbonne over a century later. Here some of the troops had either a *broine* or *hauber* mail hauberk, sometimes *dobliere* or doubled, and a *clavain* or *claviere* for their throat which probably also protected other parts of their neck and shoulders.[507] The *espalliere*, with other variations in its spelling, was more obviously a protection for the shoulder (*espalle*) and was first mentioned in the *Roman de Perceval* of around 1170. It was still being used in 1248 when its function as a shoulder defence was clearly specified.[508] The *Rule of the Templars* also referred to the *espalier*, noting that it should be stored separately from the *hauberk.*[509]

Separate leg defences had been known at the time of Charlemagne, but were reserved for the highest members of the military élite and, in all probability, had been exotic imports from the Byzantine, Khazar or perhaps Islamic worlds.[510] Separate mail protections for the legs very occasionally appear in manuscript illustrations from the period between the Carolingians and the 11th century, but they then rapidly become more common. This may have reflected changes in warfare and the rising threat to cavalrymen from foot soldiers, but is more likely to reflect a growing European economy which made these mail additions more affordable. These *chausses* almost became standard equipment for the knightly class in the second half of the 12th century, remaining so throughout the Crusader period and well into the 14th century. In Christian Iberia they were generally known as *caussas de ferre* and were worn by both Christian and Muslim armoured cavalry.[511] The French *Old Rule of the Templars* made the interesting observation that mail *chausses* for brother sergeants lacked the feet which were included in those for brother knights, so that it was easier for them to walk and fight as infantry.[512]

First appearing as the *cuissot* in a late 12th century French document, *cuisses* as they became more commonly known in French and English, were separate protections for the thighs and knees. Usually worn with and over the upper parts of the knee and lower leg-protecting *chausses*, they were of quilted or padded construction rather than mail, at least until later years. In the Christian realms of the Iberian peninsula such leg defences were known as *cuxa*, *cuixa* and *cuja* in the 13th century.[513]

Knee-covering *poleyns* did not come into use, or at least into widespread use, until the second half of the 13th century and initially took the form of relatively small rigid additions to the *cuisses*. A possible but otherwise obscure early version of the knee-protecting poleyn may have been the *genellieres* which were described as being like *fenestres pendoient*, 'pendant window-shutters', in a late 12th or early 13th century section of the French *chanson de geste, Elioxe*.[514] By the close of the 13th century much more substantial *poleyns* had appeared in Italy, but at first these were of hardened leather rather than metal. It has been suggested that the Italian *cistarelle* made of willow withies was another form of semi-rigid leg armour, though it seems more likely to have been a light helmet (see below).

Before looking at helmets, there is another form of armour made of organic material – so-called soft armour. This provided padding and protection, enabling other forms of armour to 'give' and thus absorb the shock of blows, while itself absorbing such blows and stopping metallic armour from chafing its wearer. Something of the sort must surely have been worn under mail armour in all periods of history, but the centuries prior to the Crusades are virtually silent on this matter, at least in Europe. On the other hand the term *afelter*, which could literally be translated as covering with felt, was used to mean preparing oneself for combat.[515] This could indicate that felt was used as the necessary padding beneath a mail hauberk before more sophisticated techniques of quilting were reintroduced from the Byzantine and Islamic worlds in the 11th and 12th centuries.

Documentary sources from the latter half of the 12th century suddenly start to include a variety of terms for such soft armour. Some of their origins are clear while others remain obscure. Similarly the differences between a *pourpoint*, an *aketon* and a *gambeson* are still unclear, though 12th and 13th century Spanish and French sources indicate that both the *perpon*, *pourpoint* and *gambeson* were usally worn over other armour.[516] In this context the early appearance of such armours in Spain may again be significant.

The importance of soft armours certainly should not be underestimated, particularly for infantry. This was certainly the case in the 13th century when both written and pictorial sources make it clear that crossbowmen as well as other foot soldiers were frequently protected by soft armour of various sizes and shapes. It is rare enough for medieval iron armour to survive, so the preservation of a probably 13th century sleeve and mitten from a quilted soft armour in the reliquary of a French church is even more remarkable.[517]

Perhaps the descriptive French word *pourpoint* was used as a general term for anything quilted. The *gambais*, *gambaisel*, *gambeson*, or in German the *wambeis*, seems to have been a more decorative or decorated form of quilted soft armour, sometimes of richer material and occasionally worn outside the iron armour.[518] The name may be a corruption of the Byzantine *kabadion* which was itself a padded soft armour, sometimes richly decorated, and it first appeared in the French epic *Roce* written by Wace in 1169.[519] In the Christian regions of the Iberian peninsula it was variously known as a *cambays* or a *gambax*.[520] This style of soft armour remained in use in most of Europe throughout the 13th century, and a substantial purchase of military equipment that King Philip the Fair of France ordered in Toulouse in 1295 included *gamboisées* tunics in which most of the padding had to be in the chest.

Aketon stemmed from the Arabic *al-qutn* meaning cotton, but the earliest known French use of the term *alqueton* was in a *chanson de geste* from around 1125 entitled *Gormant et Isembart* and referred to a flag, not to a form of protection. Probably the first French use of the term in the latter sense was in *Le Chanson d'Antioche* by Graindor de Douai, written around 1190, in which there was a reference to *un paile d'auqueton*, 'a mantle of *auqueton*', but even this may merely have been a cotton cloak.[521] The normally plain quilted cotton garment subsequently known as an *aketon* was usually, though not invariably, worn beneath a mail *hauberk*.

Another form of quilted garment was the *jupau*, which came from the Turkish–Persian word *jubba*, which was itself a form of cloth-covered and padded armour which sometimes, though not apparently always, included some element of mail. In the *Rule of the Templars*, however, the *jupeau d'armer* was clearly a soft armour,[522] as was the widespread southern Italian *iubba* of the late 13th century. During the 14th century the quilted *jupau* became a tight-fitting and fashionable item of aristocratic male clothing, and formed part of a fascinating process whereby various aspects of military attire were adopted in civilian life, seemingly as a means of expressing virile masculinity.[523]

The most typical helmet or *galea* of the early years of the Crusades, and well into the second half of the 12th century, was the conical so-called Norman helmet, often though not necessarily forged from a single piece of iron and with a substantial nasal bar at the front, again often but not necessarily forged from the same piece as the skull of the helmet. In the Iberian peninsula, southern France and Italy, another form of helmet had survived from late Roman and early Byzantine times, subsequently reinforced by military influences from the Islamic world. This was a rounded rather than conical helmet, normally forged from either one or two pieces of iron and initially lacking a nasal, though nasal bars were increasingly seen on helmets of this shape in European art. During the later 12th century a notably taller and sometimes rather bulbous but still rounded style appeared. Perhaps they were being worn over some smaller form of protection, as hinted at in some documents. In France at the time of Philip Augustus, for example, there were references to *galeas dublices* as well as *galeas singulares*. However, this remains unclear and could indicate an early form of the close-fitting *cerveliere* worn inside a *great helm*, either over or inside a mail *coif*.[524]

Before the introduction of the *great helm*, helmets which lacked nasal bars only gave protection to the head rather than to the face or neck, though some seen in Iberian and Italian pictorial sources seemed to extend some distance down the back of the neck. Other snippets of information from written sources suggest that these late 11th and 12th century helmets were 'laced behind' at least as often as they were secured with a chin-strap,[525] such lacing behind the wearer's head being very clear in some manuscript illustrations, carvings, seals and metalwork.

The introduction of the face-covering and eventually fully head-enclosing *great helm* is much easier to trace in art than in documents,[526] since the terminology remained largely unchanged, with the word *helm* referring to virtually all helmets until more specialised forms made their appearance during the course of the 13th century. The first step in the evolution of the *great helm* was the addition of a fixed face-mask, sometimes being little more than a considerably enlarged nasal bar. Around the same time flat-topped helmets also appeared, initially with no more facial protection than the old conical or rounded forms. The *great helm* could, perhaps, be said to make its real appearance when complete face-masks were added to these flat-topped helms, and sometimes to rounded or conical ones. After this the sides of such face-masks soon extended backwards, eventually providing all-round head and neck protection. In so doing they also posed problems of ventilation as well as greatly reducing visibility, so it is hardly surprising that, though popular with medieval artists, the fully developed *great helm* never became universal, even amongst knightly cavalry. It was even more unsuitable in the hot and dusty conditions which so often characterised Crusading warfare.

While the great helm was being developed to provide almost complete head protection at the expense of other considerations, other types of helmet developed in an effort to improve protection while not sacrificing ventilation and visibility. The most obvious was the brimmed helmet, generally known as the 'iron hat', *chapel de fer* in French.[527] Its history remains a matter of debate, having been known in classical times and probably being used by some Byzantine troops before reappearing in Western Europe late in the 12th century. Its popularity may subsequently have been increased as a result of Mongol influence in the later 13th century, the Mongols perhaps having adopted the brimmed helmet from their Chinese enemies.

The *bascinet* is normally regarded as a typical 14th century form of one-piece helmet which covered both the back and sides of the neck as well as the skull. However, it was being widely used in Italy as an infantry protection from the mid-13th century onwards, appearing in an Italian document of 1281 as the *bazineto*.[528] *Bacinets de cuero* of hardened leather were also mentioned in some 13th century Iberian texts.[529] The obscure *cistarelle* is mentioned above in the context of leg defences. These were made of wood, perhaps of plaited or interlaced willow,[530] were included in a list of armour stored in the castle of Robbia near Vercelli in northern Italy in 1203, and seem most likely to have been a form of light but brimmed war-hat.[531] The question of the use of hardened leather and wooden helmets in the neighbouring Islamic world will be discussed in volume II.

The mail *coif* or close-fitting armoured hood was a much more common, indeed almost universal form of head protection. The concept was clearly of Asiatic, probably Iranian or other Middle Eastern, origin but had been adopted by Roman armies by the final century of the Roman Empire in Western Europe. Whether the mail *coif* really dropped wholly out of use in all of Western Europe during the early medieval period remains unknown, though it continued to be a primary item of military equipment in Byzantine and Islamic armies. Whether either of the latter two civilisations was responsible for returning the mail *coif* to Europe is again unknown, though it is likely. Certainly it was widespread amongst the military and knightly cavalry élites of the 11th century and became almost universal during the 12th. There are even a few references to decorated, cloth-covered or more probably padding-lined *coifs* in some texts. For example *Beatrixe*, written in France during the second half of the 12th century, twice mentions a *coife fort et turcoise*, or simply *turcoise*.[532] Cloth-covered coifs also appear, albeit rarely, in later 12th century art. Such head protections, when worn in conjunction with otherwise uncovered mail *hauberks*, must surely have been separate *coifs*. Doubled *coifs* are also mentioned in *Elioxe*, which dates from only a few decades later.[533]

While the *espalier* can be characterised as primarily a shoulder protection, the *clavain* or *claviere*, first mentioned in the late 12th century French *Chevalier du Cygne*, was primarily intended to protect the front of the neck or throat.[534] As such it sounds like an early form of gorget, yet it is almost impossible to identify this *clavain* in 12th or even early 13th century pictorial sources. Separate protective *colerias* were included amongst the armours stored at Chinon at the time of Philip Augustus,[535] but are again virtually impossible to identify in art. Perhaps they were metallic, hardened leather or stiffly padded elements which formed the basis of the upstanding, seemingly almost rigid collars seen in some of the more detailed manuscript illustrations of quilted soft armours. Amongst the clearest are those in the mid-13th century French *Maciejowski Bible*.[536]

The last decade of the 13th century also saw the emergence of the *gorget*, *gorgiere* or *bevor*. Unlike the *clavain* or *coleria*, it seems only to have protected the front of the throat and uppermost part of the chest and was first mentioned in French in the *Roman de Ham* dating from 1278.[537] Seventeen years later King Philip the Fair's substantial purchase of military equipment in Toulouse included *gorgerettes* made in the same way as quilted *gamboisées*, and which were intended to be worn underneath unspecified mail collars.[538]

It has been suggested that the use of horse-armour, presumably of a late Roman form, continued in Brittany well into the early medieval era;[539] however, this may be a misunderstanding of the only literary Latin text to mention such a defence. The only parts of Europe where horse-armour clearly was used during the early Middle Ages were the Byzantine Empire which of course included substantial parts of Italy as well as the Balkans; Islamic al-Andalus in what are now Spain and Portugal; and amongst some of the semi-nomadic peoples of the steppe regions of southern Russia and Ukraine. On the other hand the latter extended their military presence deep into Central Europe on several occasions, under the Avars, Bulgars, Khazars and finally the Magyars or early Hungarians. Given these facts, knowledge of the existence of horse-armour if not horse-armour itself, may have been more widespread than is generally realised.

Even when horse-armour does begin to make a clear reappearance in Western Europe, well before its reappearance in the art of these regions, the terminology remains difficult. For example, the word *poitrine* has been translated as the front or breast section of horse-armour in an 11th century French source, yet it might better be translated as the broad breast-strap which stopped a war-saddle from being pushed backwards by the impact of a *couched* lance against the shield of its rider.[540] There is greater justification for translating the similar terms *poitrail* and *poitral* as the front section of a horse-armour in Gaimar's *L'Estoire des Engles*, written in 1138,[541] as is also the case with the *peytral* in a mid-12th century Spanish poetic source, redrafted in the late 13th or early 14th century.[542] Matters are more straightforward in *De Re Militari et Triplici via Peregrinationis Ierosolimitare* by Radulfus Niger, an Anglo-Norman text written just prior to the battle of Hattin. This uses elements of military equipment for allegorical purposes and clearly includes horse-armour amongst such items:

> *De armatura equi – Habet equuus etiam armaturam suam testeriam, que caput munit, et coleriam que collum, et pectus protegit et cruperiam, que posteria munit et operit.*[543]

The *Roman de Thèbes* was written a decade or so earlier under the influence of the Second Crusade. In it the white horse of Hermagoras de Salemine was all covered as far as its feet with a *cendal* (fine cloth) of vermilion red, but there is nothing to indicate that this included any protective element.[544] Similarly *Beatrixe*, dating from the second half of the 12th century, mentions a *couverture* which might be a horse-armour, a non-defensive *caparison* or merely a large saddle-cloth.[545]

The most straightforward description of a piece of Western European horse-armour is actually found in Baha al-Din's Arabic account of the Third Crusade, in which he describes a Crusader horseman who was killed in a skirmish with Saladin's troops. This man was riding a horse covered in *zarad* or *zard*, mail, which hung as far as its hooves, the rider being armoured in the same fashion.[546] Given the increasing German influence upon Hungarian military styles during the 12th century, and the Magyar Hungarians' own now somewhat distant steppe warfare traditions, it is interesting to note an account of the battle of Semlin by the Byzantine chronicler Nicetas Choniates. In it he claimed that the Hungarian army, defeated by the Byzantines, consisted entirely of fully armoured cavalry riding armoured horses,[547] though these protections apparently only covered the animals' head and breast. If this is a correct interpretation, then it sounds as if a steppe tradition of horse-armour which went right back to the Avars of the 6th and 7th centuries had survived in Hungary.

The German connection emerges again in Robert de Clari's account of the Fourth Crusade's first assault on the Byzantine capital of Constantinople, during which horse-armour was used by the cavalry of Henri de Hainault and the Germans.[548] The Military Orders were especially vulnerable to a loss of horses because of their very exposed role in defence of the Latin States in the Middle East. Although these Orders were soon regarded as being rich, horse-armour was so expensive that it remained very rare in the Crusader States. Furthermore almost all iron items of military equipment had to be imported from Western Europe. Yet it was once again a German knight who attracted a chronicler's attention because of his possession of horse-armour.[549] At the other end of the Mediterranean, some laws from mid- to late 13th century Castile refer to a *loriga de cavallo*, or mail horse-armour, being so valuable that it resulted in several military privileges for any *caballer* cavalryman who owned such an item.[550] Even so, the Spanish army which was defeated by an invading Marinid force from Morocco at Ecija in 1275 included sufficient numbers of armoured horses for these to be noted by the North African chronicler Ibn Abi Zar'.[551]

MANUFACTURE, TRADE AND STRATEGIC MATERIALS

The manufacture, procurement and distribution of military equipment was of paramount importance for the effectiveness of armies during the Crusades. The Crusades actually began during a period of remarkable economic expansion in Western Europe and may in many respects have been stimulated by that expansion. On the other hand this period of growth had been going on for longer in some regions, and had also reached greater heights, than in others. For example southern Italy had enjoyed considerable economic and population expansion since the 7th century, sharing in the economic expansion of the Islamic world with which it was in close trading contact. Mining, metalworking and shipbuilding, each of which had major military implications, were particularly well developed.[552]

In addition to being a time of intellectual ferment and creativity in Europe, the later 11th to 14th centuries also witnessed notable experimentation in technology, not least in military technology. To look at the design and manufacture of armour alone, this saw experiments – some successful, others less so – with the use of whalebone, horn, *cuir-bouilli* hardened leather, as well as iron, steel and a brass-like alloy called latten.

Iron and steel remained, of course, the most significant materials. Before the Crusading period, many if not most European swords were made by twisting iron strips together, these then being hammer-welded and shaped into a coherent blade because real welding was not yet possible. In some other technologically more advanced parts of the world, blades were already being forged from a single bar of iron, a technique which was now spreading into Europe. In some privileged regions of Asia and the Islamic world, blades were forged from early forms of steel (see volume II), but this would not reach Western Europe for some centuries. Experimental archaeology suggests that it took forty-three man-hours, and one hundred and twenty-eight heatings, to make a pattern-welded blade of average quality. It was also found easier to make good quality slag-free iron in small rather than large strips and that these were the best raw material for a sword-smith. A really fine sword with modest decoration took at least two hundred man-hours to make when the hilt, scabbard, belt and other fittings were included, and required 100 to 150 kilograms of charcoal for the forging.[553]

Leatherworking was perhaps the second most important technology where military equipment was concerned. This involved not only the making of horse-harness, belts and straps, but also the linings of helmets, coverings and fittings of shields, and some pieces of armour.

During the early medieval period the European leather industry had been dominated by Islamic influences, and European craftsmen had generally tried to imitate the products of the Islamic world. The 12th and 13th centuries then witnessed major changes and by the late 13th century new methods of tanning had been developed in Italy, especially in Pisa, shifting from the cold water to new hot water tanning techniques. This resulted in the mass production of cheap but still good quality leather goods, even including some items which had previously been regarded as luxuries. A further consequence was a fundamental change in patterns of trade, with Europe now exporting to the Islamic world while the latter became little more than a supplier of unworked hides.[554] It was surely no coincidence that this period also saw a sudden increase in the use of hardened leather armour, especially in Italy. On the other hand there does seem to have been a continuing fundamental difference between the hardened leather armours of Europe and those of the Middle East and perhaps also of North Africa. Whereas medieval European techniques produced hardened leather armour made of a single shaped layer, sometimes consisting of remarkably large sheets,[555] the leather armour of the 12th to 15th century Islamic world consisted either of lamellar defences made in an already ancient tradition, or of relatively small elements consisting of several layers stitched and perhaps also glued together (see volume II).

Although weapon-smiths had worked as small-scale itinerant craftsmen in early medieval Europe, a number of regions soon emerged as significant iron-working centres. Some had been important in Roman times and had probably never ceased production, even during the most economically stagnant centuries. By the 11th century it is clear that arms production was becoming increasingly concentrated in regions with access to iron ore, water and wood for charcoal. These included parts of western Germany and northern Italy which would virtually take over the European arms industry by the end of the Middle Ages. During the 12th century Pisa and Genoa became famous for iron goods, including military equipment. The Genoese *ferrarii* or iron workers were the second biggest group of artisans after those involved in the wool and cloth trade,[556] making swords and armour while other guilds made shields and above all crossbows.

Catalonia in the Iberian pensinula rose to significance in the 14th century but it is unclear how important this region had been as an arms production centre before that date.

Most countries also had their own regional or localised iron-working centres, Genoa emerging as a major centre of crossbow manufacture. Genoese archives still contain considerable documentary evidence of this industry, including deeds of apprenticeship as well as records concerning the sizes and dimensions of crossbows plus their prices.[557] Further south the the Sicilian kingdom became renowned for the manufacture of crossbows, some of which were used by the famous Saracen archers of Lucera, though these men generally preferred to use composite hand-bows which they again manufactured themselves. The Islamic or at least Middle Eastern connection is also seen in the name of a *Magister*

Balistarius or master of crossbowmen, Symone de Syria, who worked for the Imperial Curia of the Emperor Frederick II in southern Italy around 1240.

Five named crossbowmakers appear in English *Pipe Rolls* for the year 1204. Two had names which linked them with the Islamic world, Peter Saraczenus (the Saracen) and Benedict the Moor, both of whom may originally have been captives taken on Richard the Lionheart's Crusade.[558] A remarkable amount is actually known about Peter Saraczenus. First appearing in 1204, he continued to work for King John until 1215 and was always the highest-paid amongst the crossbowmakers, receiving twice the pay of an ordinary crossbowmaker. He also received the most perks, including a clothing allowance for himself and his wife. The last mention of Peter Saraczenus was when he was given the annual income of a royal mill.[559]

Peter and the other named crossbowmakers in King John's service produced weapons with composite rather than simple bowstaves, which again reinforces the Middle Eastern connection. Elsewhere in England the Forest of Dean produced staggering numbers of crossbow bolts in the 13th century, some 50,000 being ordered at one time, their heads forged from locally mined iron and their shafts shaped from local timber.[560] This sort of specialisation was common in the crossbow-making business, and in early 13th century Paris separate groups of craftsmen seem to have made the *quarrels* and others the crossbows.[561] Amongst the armourers of early 13th century Paris there was again a craftsman named Richard the Saracen.[562]

Rather then being mere artisans, skilled armourers enjoyed significant status. In early 13th century Paris, a crossbowmaker was paid 2 *sous* a day, his assistant 1 *sous* and a junior assistant 6 *deniers* a day, an assistant armourer being paid 18 *deniers* a day, a fully qualified armourer 3 or 4 *sous* a day, with a helmet maker earning the top rate.[563] The degree of skill and the length of time it took to make a fine piece of military equipment is occasionally acknowledged in 12th century *chansons de geste* which were, of course, written for a knightly or aristocratic rather than a craftsmen audience. In *Beatrixe*, for example, the hero laces on *chausses* which, the poet maintained, had taken a Saracen craftsman 'thirteen years' to make.[564] Muslim craftsmen played a major role in making military equipment, especially huge quantities of crossbow bolts, for Aragonese armies during the second half of the 13th century.[565] Later that century the Muslim craftsmen of Lucera in southern Italy played a vital but controversial role in making weaponry for the Emperor's wars against fellow Christians.[566]

Men who could straddle the religious and cultural frontier physically as well as technologically were clearly very useful. According to the Crusading chronicler, De Joinville, John the Armenian was 'artilleryman to the king' and was able to travel to Damascus to buy horn and glue to make crossbows.[567] Such activity may not have been that unusual as, after a treaty between a previous Crusade and

Damascus had been signed in 1239, 'Franks' were permitted to visit Damascus to buy weaponry.[568]

Although considerable documentary information survives about the medieval arms trade, especially in Italy and parts of France, certain aspects of this business were sufficiently discrete for records to be camouflaged. The Genoese records are again amongst the most useful. They make it clear that Genoa was exporting mail *hauberks* and *gamberas* to Sicily and southern Italy in the late 12th century and may have been doing so for many years.[569] The Genoese and other Italians were an important source of crossbows for England during the reign of King John, which may also have been the case during the previous rule of the Crusading King Richard.[570] Genoa remained a major centre and transit point for the arms industry through the rest of the medieval period,[571] and it has been suggested that amongst the unusual items disguised under the generic term 'spices' from the orient were steel sword-blades, technologically far in advance of anything yet manufactured within Western Europe.[572] Occasionally such documentary souces shed light on otherwise seemingly insignificant aspects of the trade in, or transportation of, military goods. In England new crossbow bolts were, for example, usually packed into bran barrels, with 500 bolts to each barrel.[573]

Trade in military or strategically important items between Christendom and the Islamic World was, at least theoretically, strictly limited. For example the laws of late 13th century Aragon and Castile restricted the taking of weapons or horses into Islamic territory,[574] whether they were for sale or not. Even within Europe such trade was controlled. Again in the late 13th century, the commune of Perugia stationed two *superstites* or supervisory guards at each gate of the city to supervise movement during a period of conflict with a rival neighbouring city as a form of economic warfare.[575]

A significant defeat could also have economic as well as more immediate military consequences, as when the failure of the Fifth Crusade at Damietta in Egypt greatly weakened the Kingdom of Jerusalem in terms of money and military material.[576] So it is not surprising to find captured equipment being used where possible. The *Rule of the Templars* referred to the use of 'Turkish' weapons,[577] while a Hospitaller legal document drawn up in Cyprus in 1303 makes a clear distinction between 'Turkish saddles' and *selles de croce* or *selles de cronce*. The latter were the normal peaked saddles with high pommels and wrap-around cantles used by European knightly cavalry. It also noted that 'warriors of Syria' should not use *selles d'armes* or war saddles because they were *turcopoles* and other such light cavalry, not knights.[578]

FORTIFICATION

For over a century historians have been trying to determine who had the most advanced fortifications during the period of the Crusades, and who was influencing whom. This may, however, be a largely meaningless exercise as there was so much variation within each of the participating civilisations. These variations not only reflected differing 'states of the art' within, for example, Latin Catholic Western and Central Europe, but also widely differing economic conditions. These latter had a direct bearing upon what sort of fortifications a governing or local power could erect, and upon the nature of warfare in the region in question. Differing military circumstances resulted in differing emphases within fortification, be they urban or rural, riverine or coastal, associated with strategic routes or set upon seemingly isolated hilltops.

It might also be misleading to assume that an area where archaeologists have found more sophisticated fortifications than elsewhere was necessarily therefore a leader in this field of military technology. So many structures have been lost, completely rebuilt at a later date or not yet investigated that such assumptions are very risky. Furthermore, it was not necessarily the case that fortifications which resisted the ravages of time, most obviously those of well-cut ashlar masonry, were therefore the most 'advanced' in terms of military function. Timber and earth, rubble and concrete, could in strictly functional terms be just as 'advanced' or effective as the finest soaring limestone towers.

On the other hand it is unclear whether the mid-12th century Norman-French writer Wace was still reflecting current practice, or merely reporting the behaviour of a century earlier, when he described how troops *'from a ditch and a barrier of stakes made a small fort'*, and that *'wood and wattle are well interlaced, crenellations remade, doors constructed'*.[579] His reference to prefabricated castles or forts being transported in barrels during William the Conqueror's invasion of England may also concern materials used in temporary field fortifications rather than castles in the normal sense of the word.[580]

Anjou in western France was already erecting advanced and particularly sturdy stone tower or *donjon* castles in the 11th century. Further south, in the French Midi, there had been a remarkable increase in the numbers of fortifications during the first half of the 11th century, reflecting changes in the local political, military, social and economic landscape. Here a class of local *milites* or what might be regarded as proto-knights had emerged, living in local castles and wielding local power.[581] It was factors like these, ranging from the architectural sophistication of Anjou to the castle-mentality of the Midi, which, with many others, had a direct bearing upon the behaviour of the First Crusaders when they came to erect their first fortifications in newly conquered territory.

Even before the First Crusade, the Norman invaders of Islamic Sicily built small castles to consolidate their hold. These varied a great deal, some being simple structures on naturally defensible outcrops of rock while there might also have been an earth *motte* at Petralia Soprana, built around 1060–1 and recalling the *motte and bailey* castles of Normandy itself.[582] Very soon, however, the Norman conquerors of southern Italy and Sicily were drawing upon more advanced existing Italian, Byzantine and Islamic ideas of military architecture. Thereafter the *castra* fortified villages helds by knights or sergeants remained an important feudal and military feature in the Norman Kingdom of southern Italy and Sicily.[583]

The progress of the First Crusade was initially different. What these First Crusaders saw and sometimes overcame on their journey east, and what they found in existence when they arrived there, included fortifications that were far stronger than anything yet existing in Western Europe. Most striking, perhaps, were the famous triple land walls of Constantinople (Istanbul) and the less well-known triple walls of Tyre in Lebanon. Yet the newly established Frankish founders of the Latin States in the Middle East did not adopt this idea of multiple, even double, let alone triple, lines of defence for many decades. It was military pressure from their revived Islamic neighbours which, from the end of the 1160s onwards, forced the Western settlers to adopt a different approach to the building or restoration of fortifications. This in turn resulted in the erection of multiple walls and subsequently of concentric castles, forms of fortification which they already clearly knew about but only now found it necessary to copy.[584]

By the later 12th century it was clear that the siege machines and mining techniques used by Islamic armies were effective against smaller Latin towers and simple enclosure castles, especially those in level or low-lying terrain or low hills. This obliged the Latins to start building more carefully planned and ambitious fortifications, the most famous of which was the concentric castle of Belvoir.[585] This might also be taken as evidence that the larger or wealthier Islamic states were already using early forms of counterweight stone-throwing *trebuchet* capable of breaking the relatively flimsy walls of the earliest Crusader fortifications.

The importance of outlying castles, which provided some degree of defence in depth for the main urban centres of the Latin States, was not lost on their builders, nor on their attackers. In the wake of Saladin's great victory at the battle of Hattin in 1187, his chronicler Imad al-Din wrote of Antioch: '*To take away her fortresses is to take away her life*'. Several were indeed taken by Saladin, but not all, and Antioch would remain in Latin hands for many more years. Many documentary sources, including those from the Islamic side of the struggle, emphasised the inaccessibility of some of these northern Crusader castles. This feature is, nevertheless, likely to have been exaggerated. It was not that enemy infantry or miners were unable to reach such sites. It was usually that enemy siege machines could not approach close enough to batter the walls or provide cover for the miners.[586]

Military, political and indeed economic circumstances were different in the other Latin or Crusader States of the eastern Mediterranean. In Cyprus fortification remained a royal prerogative, with only a few large castles being built, plus those erected by the Military Orders. The latter included the so-called Castle of Forty Columns outside Paphos. It is a geometric concentric defence, perhaps inspired by the slightly earlier Hospitaller castle of Belvoir in Palestine which is regarded as the earliest 'scientifically planned' concentric castle. In addition to the more important coastal forts and defended harbours, there were only a few small isolated tower or *donjon* castles in the lowlands. Some of those in the mountains were, on other other hand, quite dramatic and had similarities with the upland castles of Cilician Armenia.[587] This may have been partly as a result of a shared Byzantine architecture heritage in the two areas and partly because they developed a close military-political relationship.

A lot of scholarly attention has been focussed on the admittedly picturesque and romantic Latin Crusader castles of the Peloponnese in southern Greece, while those of central Greece have been relatively ignored.[588] This is particularly so where their real functions were concerned. In Latin Greece, most castle building was not done by the Crusader conquerors themselves, but by their second or third generation successors.[589] These men and their military architects followed local Byzantine tradition in using rugged natural locations, mostly in the mountains, to provide the main elements of defence. The fortifications themselves are usually divided into upper and lower castles, with the inner using a hill or mountaintop to dominate the lower. The *donjons* or keeps were often polygonal or irregular while the outer walls were generally plain with few towers and very simple gates.

In several respects their design and forms of construction were like inferior versions of what the Latins built in Syria, and there was also overwhelming evidence of the continued use of Byzantine methods of construction, and almost certainly of local Byzantine builders.[590] Armies in this region were mostly small and lacked very effective siege trains. In fact the threat of Byzantine reconquest was not as yet very serious, and the prospect of Turkish invasion lay far in the future. Furthermore, the newly established Latin states in Greece remained poor throughout their remarkably long existence. The Latin Empire of Constantinople, centred upon the ex- and future Byzantine capital itself, was soon in an even weaker economic and financial position, surviving for a much shorter period. For all these reasons, the fortifications of Latin Greece were generally old-fashioned and of low quality even when compared to those of Western Europe. Indeed it is often difficult to identify what is Latin construction, what Byzantine, or what early Ottoman Turkish, as there were no major changes in design or structural techniques from the Byzantine, through the Crusader into the late medieval Ottoman period.[591]

The only supposedly Crusader castle to stand as an exception is that of Clermont in the north-western Peloponnese.[592] It is a superb, well-made and very differently designed fortification. Unfortunately it might also not be Latin at all, but may largely date from the final Byzantine period of rule in the 15th century. Elsewhere, the Crusader castles of Greece were numerous but rarely splendid or indeed strong. Yet they remained as dramatic statements of Latin authority. So, perhaps, did the tall but simple single towers which dotted some parts of Crusader Greece and Venetian-ruled islands, especially Evoia. These usually dominated one or more villages rather than overlooking strategically significant locations. In military terms they could only have provided limited, entirely passive defence and may have been held by the non-noble but locally powerful *sergeant* level of Latin feudal society.[593]

Latins held other enclaves in the Balkans during the later Middle Ages, usually on the coast or offshore islands, most notably the Epirus region of north-western Greece and in Albania. The very little that is known of their fortifications suggests that they made use of existing structures and construction techniques, plus some ideas reflecting styles of Italy from which they themselves mostly came. The main indigenous traditions of Balkan fortifications north of Greece and outside the main centres of Byzantine power continued to largely rely on earth and timber until the 15th century. This was also the case at the northernmost extremity of the Balkans, in what is now Romanian Transylvania and Wallachia.[594] The Crusading Military Orders which played a brief role in these regions in the 13th century seem to have used traditional earth and timber defences, with the addition of some Central or Western European stone elements introduced by the Orders themselves. However, this subject has as yet received little study.

Much more attention has been given to the castles of Spain and Portugal which date from the period of the Reconquista. Here an interesting mixture of local, Islamic Andalusian, imported French and Italian influences resulted in a tradition of castle-building which changed considerably between the 11th and 14th centuries. At first it was Western Islamic military-architectural styles which dominated, including those from both Andalusia and North Africa and perhaps even from distant Egypt. By the close of the period, however, it was influences from beyond the Pyrenees which dominated, with more regular or geometric plans and less use of terrain.

Even so the high citadels and keeps, particularly elaborate curtain walls and a continued delight in decorative brickwork betrayed a lingering Andalusian, or now perhaps more correctly Mozarab, influence.[595] In fact, the Christians continued to make use of the already advanced fortifications they conquered while modifying them where it was considered necessary. A particularly interesting and well-studied example of this process during the early 13th century can be seen at Alcala de Chivert in southern Aragon.[596] Another Arab-Andalusia feature seen on both sides of the religious and cultural frontier was the major importance of small, seemingly isolated frontier watchtowers called *almenara* and *atalaya* in the Christian realms, terms which again came from Arabic.[597]

The earliest Latin fortifications in the Middle East consisted of simple towers but soon included a large *enceinte* or walled enclosure, though as yet without *donjon* keeps.[598] Bayt Jibrin or Gybelin in southern Palestine is an interesting example of these early developments. Built in 1136, it was the first castle to be granted to the Hospitallers. The first phase of Latin construction used the existing ruined Romano-Byzantine city walls and towers while adding a new wall. The *inner ward* was similarly based upon the remains of an Umayyad, early Islamic structure. A second stage of Latin building saw the construction of outer walls and a moat, thus creating what was in effect a large concentric defence which may have served as the model for later Crusader fortresses in this region.[599]

Most of the fortifications held by the Military Orders within the Kingdom of Jerusalem were enclosure castles rather than isolated towers, despite the current emphasis on towers within those parts of Europe from which most members of the Military Orders came. The only real exceptions were a few small refuges along dangerous roads such as that used by pilgrims between Jerusalem and the Jordan valley.[600] Elsewhere many initially simple tower refuges later developed into full-scale castles.[601]

'*A castle destroyed is already a castle half-built*' was a favoured proverb in the Latin Crusader States,[602] and it was certainly true that the demolition of fortifications rarely involved the physical removal of the materials, including finely cut masonry, from which they had been built. Only recently, however, have detailed studies been made of the actual methods of construction as distinct from overall design and defensive function.[603] One particular Crusader castle, which was destroyed in 1179 before being completed, and where work never restarted, sheds an astonishing amount of light not only on the process of construction but on the people and animals involved as well as those who had to defend the incomplete building site.[604] This is the site of Vadum Iacob or Jacob's Ford overlooking a strategic crossing point on the river Jordan. Erecting a castle here, on what was in effect a disputed frontier, was a military operation just as much as it was a building project. The job had to be done as quickly as possible, hopefully before the Muslims could assemble an army to disrupt or destroy it. In the event the Crusaders failed in this attempt, Saladin using available forces in and around Damascus to lauch a rapid preventative campaign. The gruesome result was that everything, bar the timber structures which were burned and some of the walls which were mined or pulled down, remained as it was when Saladin's victorious troops withdrew, including workmen's tools, workmen's bones and the astonishing number of arrows which had rained upon them.[605]

As yet the archaeological record has proved less dramatic elsewhere. Close scrutiny of masonry techniques, chiselling patterns on smoothed stones and the mason's marks left by craftsmen can, on the other hand, point to strong Armenian influence or involvement in the castles of the Principality of Antioch. These were often very well made. In contrast the line of small fortresses that the Crusaders seized or built in Oultrejourdain, in what is now southern Jordan, were far more rudimentary. These stretched from Salt to the Gulf of Aqaba, and briefly included the ruins of Roman Jerash slightly further north. In most places the conquering Latins used ancient or Islamic masonry where this was available. At Jerash they attempted to convert a massive Roman temple into a fortress, though this was not, of course, a new idea. The occupiers also made sometimes remarkable use of natural features, including weird vertical gulleys and massive boulders in the semi-desert landscape around the largely abandoned ancient city of Petra. Elsewhere their masonry was exceptionally rough, incorporated minimal decoration and resulted in generally small castles, now largely hidden inside much larger fortresses dating from after the Islamic reconquest.

To some extent the masonry of Crusader, and indeed Islamic, fortifications changed in response to the increasing power of the siege machine pitted against such walls. Bossed masonry had, for example, been used in the Middle East by the Romans but then dropped out of use until it was reintroduced by the Crusaders. This bossed masonry was not, however, the same as what is now known as rusticated masonry. Whereas the former may have been merely stylistic and involved greater labour than a flat surface, the latter left the centres of each external block of masonry projecting a substantial distance and with a very rough surface. At first this looks like corner-cutting by the builders, but in fact the projecting surface protected the more vulnerable masonry joints and had the effect of dissipating the force of a missile thrown by a siege machine. Furthermore the rough surface meant that very few such missiles actually struck the surface squarely, again reducing the power of their impact.

The purpose of other elements within the design of a castle or urban fortification is usually more obvious. Their presence or otherwise, and the way in which they are incorporated into the overall structure, can indicate the age and sophistication of the defences in question. At Sahyun the archery embrasures are high up the exterior wall and the merlons along the summit are not pierced. Nor is there any direct communication between the curtain wall and some of the main towers. All these are regarded as early features showing strong and continuing Byzantine influence. Recent archaeological surveys have, in fact, shown that the pre-Crusader Byzantine castle at Sahyun was considerably larger than had been thought. There is no structural use of timber,[606] as would have been normal practice for most of the newly arrived Crusader conquerors, despite the fact that this was, and is now once again becoming, one of the most wooded parts of Syria. Taken altogether Sahyun sometimes seems more like a Byzantine than a Crusader castle, yet its strongest outermost elements certainly date from the 12th century. The most dramatic feature at Sahyun is, of course, the vast man-made ditch. Clearly within a Byzantine tradition of fortification within Syria, it is nevertheless generally accepted to be Latin work and its excavation involved the removal of an estimated 165,000 tonnes of rock. Several other large Crusader castles in the Principality of Antioch also incorporated substantial previous Byzantine work, but most such previous work, like that at Baghras, are either demolished or hidden within Latin or Armenian fortifications.

The lack of timber elements such as the wallhead hoardings and other elements characteristic of Western European fortifications during the Crusader period has usually been ascribed to the lack of available wood in the Latin States. However, this is probably misleading as areas like that around Antioch, coastal Syria, Lebanon and even parts of Palestine were not short of trees. Some of the available trees were very substantial indeed, most notably in Lebanon. It is much more likely to have been a combination of the very advanced pyrotechnic capabilities of the Middle East, and the sophisticated stone and brick military architecture which to some extent itself mirrored the threat from fire weapons, that accounted for the abandonment of timber by those who commissioned Crusader castles.[607]

Thereafter castle design within the Latin States saw a steady increase in the number of defensive features, including stronger and more numerous walls, larger and closer towers, which boosted the natural defensive nature of the site on which a castle had been erected. Walls also became thicker, often higher, and a sloping *talus* of Arab-Islamic origin was often added to their base. This was an additional protection against mining which, during the medieval period, normally attacked the base of a wall rather than seeking to drive deep beneath it. Ancient columns could be laid horizontally within the structure of a wall, increasing its lateral strength and stability, especially in low-lying areas where the fortifications were not firmly bedded in bed-rock. Walls and towers had an increasing number of embrasures or arrow-slits, sometimes for observation rather than shooting purposes. Curtain walls often had defensive galleries within them, sometimes more than one above the other, and on the outside there were many projecting box *machicolations* or *machicolated galleries* which enabled defenders to drop or shoot down on enemies at the base of a wall, door or gate. An earlier version of this concept was the slot *machicolation* which consisted of a sloping groove down the exterior of a wall, again enabling defenders to strike those beneath them.

The growing size, strength, closer spacing and greater projection of towers around the walls was another feature, especially in the 13th century. Outside these main walls and towers were increasing series of outworks ditches or moats. Small postern gates, usually hidden from direct bombardment by enemy siege machines but in no other sense really 'secret', enabled defenders to launch flanking sorties against enemies who attacked their walls too closely. Meanwhile the main gates similarly became stronger and more complex in design, with drawbridges, portcullises and enfilading embrasures within the gate complex. In castles these became so strong that they themselves were rarely attacked.[608]

The smaller and in some cases temporary fortifications of the Latin States included some interesting examples of 'counter-castles'. These were built during a major siege to face and hopefully isolate an enemy fortification. Two or perhaps three were erected during the siege of Antioch by the First Crusade, and another was recorded during the siege of Damietta in Egypt in 1218–19. This also seems to have consisted of a man-made *motte*, probably reflecting the traditions and concepts brought on Crusade by men from Flanders and low-lying regions of Germany where such otherwise old-fashioned ideas of castle-building were still used.[609]

Caves were also used as refuges and, in a few cases, virtually as castles. This practice had a long tradition in the Middle East. The most famous Crusader cave-fortress was that of the Cave de Sueth, Habis Jaldak or as it is now known, 'Ayn Habis. Its astonishingly dramatic location overlooking the deep valley of the river Yarmuk had previously been a Byzantine Orthodox Christian *lavra*, monastic retreat.[610] In addition to as yet unidentified Crusader cave-fortresses in this same area, the Latins used others in the coastal mountains of Syria,[611] while their local Maronite allies had a cave-fortress in the Jabal Bishri south-east of Tripoli during at least one invasion by the Mamluk Sultan Baybars.[612]

The urban defences of the Latin States in Syria, Lebanon and Palestine have only recently started to receive the same sort of scholarly attention given to the more dramatic Crusader castles. Nevertheless, they were in many respects more interesting and certainly posed great challenges to those who designed, built and defended them. During most of the Crusader period the areas enclosed by urban fortification were not filled with buildings. This was clearly the case in the 12th century, and, even when cities like Acre and Jaffa expanded into suburbs beyond their walls in the 13th century, this still left some open spaces inside. Only fourteen of the towns or cities occupied by the Latins had circuit walls, and all but two of these had been built before the Crusaders arrived. The two exceptions were the newly fortified suburb of Montmusard on the northern side of Acre, and the *faubourg* or new town facing the coastal castle of 'Atlit.

What the Latins did, once they recognised the need to do anything, was repair and in some places greatly strengthen the existing Arab-Islamic urban defences.

Their biggest efforts came after the Third Crusade and during the 13th century, such projects often being financed by the leaders of Crusades from Western Europe. Amongst the most noticeable resulting changes were larger and more projecting towers within a city's curtain-wall.[613] Most were rectangular but some were round or keel-shaped, essentially five-sided but presenting an angle to the exterior. Not all coastal fortifications were actually on the coast. Margat (Marqab), for example, was set on a high and steep hill overlooking the shore but, in terms of fortifications, effectively separated from it. Here the castle was so large that it actually enclosed a small town on the northern side of the main citadel.

Fortified gates of cities remained the main targets for a besieger, perhaps because such gates, though getting stronger, still had to provide practical access in and out of bustling commercial centres in times of peace. At Acre the old single circuit wall was eventually doubled, but even in the later 12th and early 13th centuries most Latin-held coastal towns still lacked modern, uprated or in several cases any outer defences. Instead the first phase of urban strengthening focussed on the construction of powerful citadels. These formed castles within or more normally on one edge of a city or town where they served as refuges for people and moveable property if the town itself was attacked. A change of priorities came in the mid-13th century, during and after the Crusade of King Louis IX of France. It also reflected a change in the strategic intentions of the newly established Mamluk Sultanate which now virtually surrounded the land frontiers of the Latin States. Instead of mere raiding and prolonged economic warfare, the Mamluk Sultan Baybars instigated a programme of steadily taking Latin fortifications one by one.[614] The corresponding Latin programme of urban fortification and strengthening continued until the fall of Acre itself, the last recorded work being carried out in 1287.[615]

The suburb of Montmusard was also walled, but this had the effect of isolating and rendering virtually worthless the existing citadel of Acre which now stood alone in the centre of a walled urban area, unable to play any defensive role other than that of a final refuge after the city had fallen. Meanwhile there were several other fortifications within Acre, as there were in some other Latin cities of the Middle East. The *convents* or headquarters of the three main Military Orders of Hospitallers, Templars and Teutonic Knights were powerful structures, especially that of the Templars which stood like a castle overlooking the sea. Other defensible buildings were owned by various Italian merchant communes, though their purpose was usually to defend the interests of one Italian city against another rather than facing any external foe. Thus these towers too often appear in the chronicles fighting against each other.[616] Little is known about such communal fortifications but they seem to have been similar to those in the rival merchant cities of Italy itself, ranging from the tall and perhaps slender *torre* tower, to the broader, lower *casa-torre* and the sturdily constructed warehouses.[617]

SIEGE WARFARE AND WEAPONRY

Until recently it has been widely assumed that the siege technology and techniques of Western Europe were inferior to those of the Byzantine Empire and major Islamic states of the Middle East at the time of the First Crusade. However, this once again fails to take into account profound differences between various parts of Western Europe during the 11th century. Some places, like southern Italy and the Iberian peninsula, were in such close military and other forms of contact with the Byzantine and Islamic worlds that they appear to have shared the same array of military machines. Here the most significant hindrance to the Westerners was that they were generally not as wealthy as their rivals, and so could not afford such elaborate or abundant devices. On the other hand it has been suggested that the siege artillery skills widely demonstrated in southern Italy were more likely to be local developments than resulting from Byzantine or Islamic technological influence.[618]

Meanwhile there is even stronger evidence that northern Italy, or at least some of its most thriving and outward-looking merchant cities, had access to military technology at least as advanced as that seen anywhere else around the Mediterranean during the late 11th and 12th centuries. Under such circumstances it is hardly surprising to find that men from Genoa, Pisa, other northern Italian cities and from neighbouring regions of southern France proved to be the most effective siege engineers and siege combatants during the First Crusade. This would continue to be the case throughout much of the rest of the 12th century.[619] European military commanders, especially those involved in major Crusading expeditions, had profound respect for qualified siege engineers and were prepared to pay them handsomely for their services. Yet even as late as the 12th century there were still members of the European knightly and aristocratic élite who looked askance at the increasingly technological nature of warfare. Amongst them was Guiot de Provins who complained: *'Did Alexander have sappers or King Arthur use siege engines?'*.[620]

Perhaps the biggest such engine available to the Crusaders was the *belfry* or wooden tower which was sometimes moveable, though on rollers rather than wheels.[621] This had been used in Western Europe since at least the 10th century and there is no reason to suppose that knowledge of the device had ever been lost since the fall of the Western Roman Empire, at least not in areas which retained elements of Roman civilisation or contacts with the surviving Eastern Roman, namely Byzantine Empire. *Belfries*, which also went by several other descriptive names, were used by Normans against Byzantines in southern Italy, by Christian Iberians against Muslim Andalusians during all stages of the Reconquista, and of course during the First Crusade.

Wooden siege towers continued to play a very prominent role in 12th century

Western European siege warfare. In the Latin States of the Middle East they were prominent during the early decades of the 12th century, though not necessarily very successful. The Crusaders brought such a *belfry* against the walls of Beirut in 1109/10 but the defenders broke it with stones thrown by a *manjaniq* or *mangonel*.[622] Another was used to attack Sidon the same year, being covered with brushwood, matting and the hides of freshly slaughtered oxen as a protection against mangonel stones and incendiary weapons. This *burj* or tower as it was called by Arabic chroniclers, was supposedly mounted on wheels and contained both offensive weapons and quantities of vinegar to douse fires.[623] Two years later, when besieging Tyre, the Crusaders mounted rams inside their towers,[624] but a Fatimid naval officer in the garrison of Tyre used iron hooks to deflect these rams (see volume II). One ram was later found to be over sixty cubits long, about thirty metres, and had an iron or iron-reinforced head weighing over ten kilograms, the whole device being hung on ropes inside a moveable tower.[625]

Comparable siege machines were used by the Spaniards, one siege tower during a 12th century invasion of Majorca being defended by dangling ropes and osiers to absorb the shock of the *mangonel* stones that were shot against it. An earlier attack on Ibiza in 1114–15 had involved a battering ram similarly protected, but again it was driven back.[626] Elsewhere there were other more sophisticated developments of the *belfry*. One large example built for the Emperor Frederick I during his siege of Crema in 1160 had a very long counterpoised bridge on top which was to be lowered onto the opposing city wall.[627] Also in the mid-12th century a floating siege tower was used to attack a castle on the banks of the river Rhône.[628] The Pisans brought a similar siege tower mounted on boats against the Tower of Flies in the harbour of Acre in 1190, but here the idea failed, perhaps because even the Mediterranean Sea was rarely as calm as a river. Nevertheless, the idea was used successfully by a Crusader army in 1218 against Damietta's Chain Tower, but here again the ambitious structure was floating on a river, the Nile.[629]

Less dramatic but generally more successful were the 'armoured sheds' or sturdy wooden roofs that were used to protect miners from rocks and other missiles dropped or shot at them from the wall which they in turn were attempting to undermine. Such defences could enable men to tip material into the defenders' moat, hopefully this filling it and enabling attackers or their siege towers to approach the wall more closely. The *Roman de Thèbes*, written in mid-12th century France and influenced by the enthusiasm of the Second Crusade, called such devices *charcloies*. Beneath them miners attacked the masonry foundations of the wall with picks and chisels, though the timber defence above them was also vulnerable to *feu grejois* Greek Fire.[630] One of the most effective weapons used by the Third Crusade in their siege of Acre was another massive iron-tipped ram, supposedly from the mast of a ship and this time beneath an armoured roof rather than being inside a moveable tower. But once again it was burned by the Islamic defenders.[631] A threat from incendiaries would, in fact, be largely responsible for almost removing such vulnerable wooded structures from the Crusaders' siege armoury.

Stone-throwing weapons were made almost entirely of timber but could be used at a greater distance from fortified walls and were thus less vulnerable to fire either thrown from the walls or brought against the machine during a sortie by the defenders. By the time of the First Crusade the old torsion-powered stone-throwers of Graeco-Roman siege warfare had been almost entirely replaced by beamsling weapons of ultimately Chinese origin. The latter had been brought west by the Avars and pre-Islamic Turks in the 6th and 7th centuries, being adopted with enthusiasm by the Byzantines and even more so by the Muslims.

Mangonel or beamsling artillery pieces were easier to make, assemble, dismantle, transport and reassemble.[632] They were also easier to repair if damaged during a siege, and even the man-powered versions used before the invention of the more massive counterweight version, known in Europe as the *trebuchet*, could hurl a larger missile than the dauntingly elaborate machines used by Greeks and Romans. In Italy and during the Crusades these *mangonels* were very often closely linked with maritime powers, sailors or other men associated with the sea, just as they were in the Islamic world. Even in 13th century England, the ropes needed for siege machines were mostly made in Bristol,[633] the kingdom's main western port where even larger quantities of ropes were presumably required for shipbuilding. Another skill which naval personnel brought to this aspect of siege warfare was that of handling large and heavy pieces of timber, namely masts, spars and booms, again by using ropes and pulleys.

The written sources range from Egidio Colonna's technological treatise entitled *De Regimine Principum* written around 1280, to sometimes remarkably sober accounts in chronicles and occasional interesting details in poetic epics. *De Regimine Principum* divided these machines into groups, including those pulled by men on ropes; those with a counterweight fixed to the beamsling which was considered the most accurate; and those with a counterweight which hung from an axle at the end of the beam which achieved the greatest range. The latter was supposedly called a *biffa*. A siege machine called a *biffa* or *buffa* had been known in Italy a generation earlier, becoming the *biffe* as used in France.[634] The name is believed to mean buffalo, which might reflect the weapon's power or the sound it made when shot. Egidio Colonna's fourth version has sometimes been dismissed as a fanciful invention called a *tripantum* and which supposedly included both types of counterweight.[635]

In the Iberian peninsula during this period, beamsling siege machines were known by a variety of names including *manguanel*, *trabuquetz* and *algarrada*, the last stemming from the Arabic term *al-'arrada*.[636] The latter was one of the man-powered versions, as it also was in its original Arabic form (see volume II), and may have been similar to what was known in some other parts of Western Europe and on Crusade as the *Turkish perriere*.[637] Unfortunately the European literary sources tend to be imprecise in their use of terminology, but an early 13th century French military inventory did specify that the four hundred *cordes ad petrarias* ropes were for *petraria turquesa* rather than other forms of stone-throwing engine.[638] This type could also come in a variety of sizes, as indicated by mention of a *Turcorum more* or large Turkish mangonel in an early 13th century account of the life of King Philip Augustus.[639]

Quite when and where the counterweight *mangonel* was invented remains a matter of scholarly argument, and even the term *trebuchet* did not always necessarily mean that the *mangonel* in question was of the counterweight type. It normally did so, and was probably initially adopted as a descriptive term relating to the sudden drop of the counterweight. In the late 11th century *Song of Roland*, before the appearance of counterweight mangonels in Europe, though not necessarily before these were seen in some parts of the Middle East, the word *trebuchier* was used to describe the dead 'falling headlong'.[640] The word *trebuchel* was first used in French for a form of siege machine in the late 12th century *Chevalier Ogier*,[641] and the defenders of Cremona in northern Italy in 1199 were said to have used a *trebuchet*, but this account was written some time after the event.[642] The first clear reference to a counterweight stone-throwing machine being used by Westerners was during the Third Crusade's siege of Acre in 1189 where these weapons were so effective that they were said to have reduced a fortified wall to the height of a man.[643] Man-powered *mangonels* are most unlikely to have been capable of that.

Medieval *mangonel* and *trebuchet* operators were also concerned, where possible, to cut their missiles from stones which would not shatter and so reduce their impact against their fortified target.[644] The range of *mangonels* is believed to have been between eighty-five and something less than one hundred and fifty metres, the longest ranges probably being achieved by the largest counterweight versions whereas those powered by teams of men or women pulling ropes would have been less.[645] Missiles weighing some hundred kilograms were reportedly possible with man-powered *mangonels*, and up to two hundred and fifty or more kilograms with the largest counterweight weapon.[646] Recent experiments with a reconstructed counterweight *trebuchet* achieved a maximum range of one hundred and eighty metres shooting a fifteen-kilogram ball. The heaviest missile that this machine threw weighed forty-seven kilograms and flew one hundred metres. The accuracy proved quite astonishing and was comparable to that of modern infantry mortars.[647]

Evidence from medieval sources indicates that large *trebuchets* were nothing out of the ordinary. That used by Simon de Montfort during his siege of Toulouse in the Albigensian Crusade had a beamsling arm some twelve metres long and a counterweight calculated at 26,000 kilograms. Most counterweights are assumed to have consisted of iron-reinforced wooden boxes filled with stones, but the *trebuchets* stored in Carcassonne in 1293 had counterweights of both stones and lead. Other equipment, presumed to be for these same weapons, included substantial winches to pull down the shooting end of the beamsling.[648] Iron was stored at Berwick on the border of England and Scotland in 1298 for the counterweight of a particularly large *trebuchet*, along with some brass. Both these materials may, however, have formed part of the weapon's structure: the iron to reinforce the counterweight box, the brass forming some other more delicate part of the machine or its axle.[649]

Some idea of the shooting rate of even counterweight *trebuchets* can be gained from King Edward I's attack on Holyrood in Edinburgh in 1296 where his three weapons threw one hundred and fifty-eight missiles over three days. Even assuming that the garrison's surrender came at the close of the third day, this meant that each *trebuchet* shot seventeen or eighteen times a day or about once every twenty minutes during daylight hours.[650] Smaller manpowered *mangonels* could shoot much more quickly, especially if they were of the smallest type mounted on a single pole which could be traversed in any direction. These were, however, anti-personnel rather than castle-breaking weapons.

Such weapons may have been more characteristic of the Islamic states than of Western Europe, but they were probably used by the final defenders of Latin Acre in 1291. Here a weapon which the sources call a *bible* or *biblieta* might be a refence to what was otherwise known as a *brigola* or *bricola*. This had first been mentioned in early 13th century Genoa and was, in turn, a larger version of the weapon mounted on a single pole but having two weights which swung down on either side of that now larger pole.[651] On the other hand, the name *bible* might come from the medieval Latin *bubalus* meaning a female buffalo, in which case the weapon is more likely to have been a version of the *biffa* mentioned above.[652]

The ancient Roman system of using torsion power to propel a missile in siege warfare had not been entirely abandoned. It has been suggested that the *chadable* or *chaable* siege engine mentioned in the *Song of Roland* might be such a weapon, yet this could supposedly 'cast down towers' and break walls which no torsion weapon could do.[653] Where proved to exist, they were fearsome anti-personnel machines. The *caable*, *chadabula* or *chaablum*, all of which probably stemmed from the medieval Latin word *cabulus*, were still being used in early 13th century France and some historians have again interpreted them as torsion-powered weapons.[654]

Whatever the *chadable* was, another form of torsion-powered anti-personnel siege weapon clearly came into use in the mid-13th century. It was new for Western Europe, and perhaps even for the Latin States of the Middle East, but had been known for at least a century in the Islamic world and even longer amongst Byzantine military technicians. This was the *espringal*, a crossbow-like machine in which the two separate bow-arms were placed under huge twisting tension by separate skeins of horsehair or animal tendons.[655] These cords, always in pairs for the two arms, were amongst the stores in Carcassonne in 1293, the weapon itself being called a *springallis*.[656] Known as *springalds* in late 13th century England, they remained very small in numbers compared with the largest forms of siege crossbow.[657] 'Great' *balistas* or crossbows had been used in defence of Latin fortifications in the Middle East since the early 13th century and reportedly caused heavy casualties amongst various attackers.[658] Large *balistas* were actually credited with defeating Saladin's assault on Tartus in 1188.[659] Quite what if anything distinguished the largest *arbalete à tour, treuil* or *ballista de torna* from a virtually fixed, frame-mounted '*great crossbow*' is unclear, the latter also being spanned by mechanical means such as a windlass.[660]

Many of these machines, including both stone-throwing *mangonels, trebuchets, espringals* and *great crossbows*, were at least as important in the defence of fortifications as they were in attacking such places. Nor was defensive siege warfare merely a matter of passive endurance. Castles in the 12th century Latin States, and probably in many other regions as well, were essentially designed, provisioned and garrisoned to resist a single campaigning season; that is a siege of several months' duration.[661] However, Marqab was at one time reportedly provisioned to withstand a siege of no less than five years.[662] It therefore seems surprising that the main water cistern or *birka* at Marqab was outside the walls. In time of close siege the defenders and other inhabitants would have had to rely on a smaller cistern and well inside the circuit walls.[663] Castles often also served as supply centres for their surrounding regions, and some clearly contained reserves to be used by a Crusader army operating in their area. William of Tyre stated that Artah and the surrounding Latin-held towns fulfilled this function as early as 1119.[664]

In times of peace the gates of a fortress, and very often of towns, were closed at night. This was similarly the case in medieval Europe, but the Rules of the Hospitallers are very specific. These state that the gates of a frontier castle must be shut after *Compline* or evening prayers and were not to be reopened until morning.[665] The size of a fortress, or more particularly the length of its walls, could on occasions be a disadvantage, especially if the garrison was depleted and the attackers numerous. This happened at several places after Saladin's destruction of the Latin field army at the battle of Hattin. At Bourzay Saladin launched small attacks against several parts of the walls to divide and exhaust the already demoralised defenders. Shouts by the many Muslim prisoners already held within the castle then made the garrison of Bourzay think that the enemy had broken in somewhere else, leading them to surrender.[666]

The size of Latin garrisons clearly varied a great deal, reflecting not only the size and importance of the place in question, but the level of political or military tension, the ability of castle-holders to pay these garrisons and the availability of suitable troops. At one end of the scale the wartime garrison of the newly rebuilt Templar castle of Safad in Palestine in the mid-13th century was said to number as many as 12,000 people. This was reduced to 1,700 in peacetime, including fifty brother knights, thirty brother sergeants, fifty *turcopoles*, three hundred archers most of whom would have been crossbowmen, eight hundred and twenty support staff and labourers, and four hundred slaves.[667] In contrast, Hospitaller-held Marqab had, in 1212, a night patrol of only four brother knights and twenty-eight other soldiers out of a total population of a thousand people.[668] Elsewhere there are records of minor fortifications having no permanent garrison in time of peace, apart from a caretaker and perhaps his assistants.

The Latin States' shortage of troops was a permanent feature of their military history. Nevertheless, even at the very end, the city of Acre was defended by a substantial and professional or at least trained force; so much so that the Christians were initially confident of holding the city in 1291.[669] Unfortunately these numbers were achieved only by reducing other garrisons to a bare minimum, and when Acre fell the remaining Latin-occupied enclaves were virtually indefensible. Most made either a nominal resistance or surrendered, or their garrisons slipped away before being besieged.

Defending a medieval fortification was not merely a matter of enduring and holding on until help arrived in the form of a relieving army, though this remained the basic strategy. There are plenty of documentary sources, historical and literary or poetic, which describe the defence of walls and towers. In the mid-12th century, for example, Wace stated that non-noble defenders, burgesses or citizen militias, were armed with the *funde* sling and *plumee* perhaps lead-weighted javelin which were also used in street fighting.[670] The French *Aucassin et Nicolette* epic poem described how, during the defence of the castle of Beaucaire, knights and sergeants – namely the professional soldiers – manned the gates and towers while the local burgesses manned the walls where they used bows, crossbows and javelins.[671]

A generation or so later, in the German *Nibelungenlied*, all ranks including knights used javelins in siege warfare, especially when fighting inside a castle.[672] Bows, slings and dropped stones were used against the Crusader King Richard's men when he attacked the defences of Messina in Sicily,[673] while early 13th century French *troubadours* wrote of defending archers standing near the *barbacana*, ready to shoot while around them the wall lost its *dezanvana* parapet to the enemy's bombardment by stone-throwing machines.[674] The effectiveness of the defenders' weapons is recalled in the mid-12th century *Roman de Thèbes*, in which a *serjanz* shot a *carrel*, quarrel or bolt from a crossbow, piercing both the shield and mail hauberk of an attacking knight.[675] The defensive importance of crossbowmen was also shown in the dry bureaucratic records of 13th century Genoa where such men played perhaps the most important role in protecting not only Genoese ships but Genoa's fortified overseas possessions.[676] So it was not surprising that the archaeologists who excavated the Castle of Forty Columns at Paphos in Cyprus found a store of crossbow boltheads as well as about 1,500 stone mangonels balls which seem originally to have been stored on the roof.[677]

Archery and crossbows were fundamental to the design of the fortifications themselves, with the towers of early Crusader castles being about thirty to forty metres apart; in other words a normal effective bow-shot. These towers were primarily intended as archery emplacements, though early forms of man-powered *mangonels* could also be mounted upon them. The arrow embrasures or loopholes are more difficult to understand. They were another feature of virtually all fortifications during this period but it remains unclear just how they were used. Modern experiments in a 13th century English castle found that it was impossible to use a longbow within the embrasure. The weapon was too big and the arrow yawed considerably during the first eight or so metres of its flight. This may also have been true of an arrow from a composite bow, though the weapon itself was smaller and thus more practical within the embrasure. Arrows or bolts shot from a crossbow do not yaw, but the weapon had to be held horizontally and therefore had a much more limited traverse than a hand bow.[678] Archers could shoot out of the embrasure if they stood back from the arrowslit while the problem of yawing could be overcome with practice, but by standing back they also had even more limited vision, so it was found that a man could stand in close to 'spot' his target, then step back to shoot. Crossbowmen also had a slightly greater arc of fire if they stood back in this way.[679] Perhaps they worked in teams, with an observer and a shooter. On the other hand it was found that about a third of the arrows shot against the arrowslit by men outside, when operating from a reasonable range, actually came through the slit to endanger those inside.[680]

Stone-throwing mangonels and other such 'missile' siege machines were at least as important in defence of fortifications as they were in attacking them. Their role was either counter-bombardment to break the besiegers' stone-throwers, or to destroy the besiegers' siege works, offensive towers or mining operations. One of the most detailed early descriptions of such a use of mangonels comes from early 12th century France where siege technology was precisely the same as that available to the early Crusaders. Here the siege of a tower at Amiens known as Le Castillon was described by the Abbot Guibert of Nogent in his memoirs. Siege towers had been brought against Le Castillon, and knights were assigned to them. A man in the town, named Aleran, who was skilled in such matters, erected two 'catapults' opposite these siege towers and set almost four-score women 'cranking' the stones that he had also piled up. As a result the wooden siege towers were smashed, and after the enemy retreated the defenders took their timber inside their town.[681]

It has been suggested that the first counterweight *mangonels* were simply the old man-powered types with a weight replacing the men or women on ropes, and that a hole had to be excavated beneath their frame to stop this weight hitting the ground as it swung down. This was clearly the case with the machine described by al-Tarsusi in his manuscript for Saladin, which is the earliest clear account of such a weapon (see volume II). Other sources indicate that these machines were especially useful if mounted on fortified towers, so it is interesting to read of a hole or trench in the summit of the biggest or 'great tower' of the late 12th-early 13th century castle of Bressuire in western France.[682] Perhaps it was to take the downwards swing of the earliest type of counterweight *trebuchet*, perhaps inspired by what French knights had seen on the Third Crusade.

Another very important tactic for the defenders was, of course, the sortie. This could be a small number of defenders suddenly emerging from a gate or postern to destroy a particularly troublesome enemy siege-machine. Or it could be a full-scale attack by virtually the whole garrison. Both were risky, and the latter could endanger the entire defence if defeated. This is what happened when Richard of Salerno emerged from Edessa to attack the besieging Seljuk Turks in 1105–6, against the advice of local military leaders. The attack resulted in the loss of four hundred and fifty foot soldiers, mostly Armenians. The remainder regained the safety of the fortress but Richard now lost local support and had to leave the city shortly afterwards.[683]

Offensive siege warfare has tended to receive greater attention, especially when it succeeeded and led to a castle or more substantial territory changing hands. Amongst the most significant successful sieges was the taking of Toledo in central Spain by the Christians in 1085, which has been widely seen as the start of the great period of the Reconquista. Another major siege and seizure of a great Islamic city some century and a half later could be seen as marking the end of that dramatic period. This was the fall of Seville in 1248 after a two-year siege and blockade which provided a well-documented example of how such wide-ranging and long-term operations were conducted.[684] The siege of Bedford in England in 1224 was on a much smaller scale. Here, however, the survival of a wide array of documents sheds a remarkable light on the costs, the siege weapons involved, as well as the numbers of men involved, both soldiers, craftsmen, labourers and other support personnel.[685]

Archers and crossbowmen were as vital in offensive siege warfare as they were in defence of such places. This seems to have been even more true in Spain and Portugal than in most other parts of Western Europe.[686] English archers were credited with driving the Islamic defenders from a tower during the siege of Lisbon in 1147. Here it seems the archers came close to the tower in order to shoot, in one of several examples of such bowmen shooting showers of arrows as they advanced.[687]

Archers were also vital in the Latin or Crusader States of the Middle East but they could not alone breach or overcome walls, so another tactic was to try and lure the defenders into an ill-advised sortie. In the small-scale warfare of early 12th century Syria, a Crusader raiding force attacked 'Gistrum', an unidentified location with a bridge over the Orontes which may have been Shayzar, and tried to lure the Islamic garrison out by drawing up in battle lines then burning the suburbs. However, the garrison refused to respond, and so the Crusaders were obliged to withdraw.[688] On another occasion, Tancred of Antioch's men formed a *testudo* to fight their way through a breach in the wall of Azaz in 1111.[689] This tactic in which men on foot covered their formation with large interlocked shields was more associated with Romans than with medieval troops and it required considerable discipline as well as training.

Wooden siege towers may have been vulnerable to counter-bombardment by the defenders, both with rocks and incendiary weapons, but they still played a significant role in the 11th and 12th centuries. In fact they were considered important enough for the Italian fleet which attacked the island of Pantelleria in 1087 (then ruled by the Zirid *Amir* of Tunisia) to bring with them prefabricated timber, nails, ropes and 'armoury' for such towers. Pantelleria itself, like Malta, probably lacked sufficient timber for siege towers to be constructed from local resources.[690] Only ten years later the First Crusade constructed similar wooden siege towers during its siege of Nicaea (Iznik). Crossbowmen and archers played a major role in this first significant siege operation of the First Crusade.[691] On reaching Syria, the First Crusade was involved in even more desperate sieges. At al-Bara a man with a horn was stationed on top of the Crusaders' moveable tower, apparently to communicate instructions over the din of battle.[692] At Jerusalem one of their first siege towers got stuck too far from the wall for its men to get across the gap, so a bridge was either constructed or extended using timber which had been seized or had fallen from the Islamic defences. Clearly shortage of wood could be a significant problem during Palestinian sieges, though it does not appear to have been so in the more wooded lands of Lebanon and coastal Syria.[693]

Again during the siege of Jeruslaem by the First Crusade, the Fatimid defenders had to move their counter-bombardment artillery from the tops of the walls and towers inside the defences. This was because of the intensity and effectiveness of the Crusaders' *mangonels*, and resulted in the defenders having to rely on less accurate shooting with the aid of spotters on the wall. On the other hand, the defenders at least had such spotters. The besieging Crusaders could now only estimate the position of the Muslims' *mangonels* which they could no longer see.[694]

During their siege of Haifa in 1100, the Crusaders protected a wooden siege tower with a battery of seven stone-throwing machines for what would, in modern terms, be called suppression fire.[695] Here it is also worth noting that a *mangonel* damaged by enemy shooting could sometimes be repaired and returned to action, as was recorded in northern Italy in 1155.[696] A besieger's stone-throwers might themselves be protected by earthworks or embankments, as happened during the siege of Acre by the Third Crusade.[697]

Earthworks and mining would, of course, have been supervised by skilled men. Various crafts and skills were required in siege warfare, offensive and defensive, and men with the most highly rated such abilities could command substantial salaries. They ranged from carpenters and miners to engineers and architects.[698] The engineers who operated Simon de Montfort's largest *trebuchet*, *Bad Neighbour*, during his siege of Minerve during the Albigensian Crusade were paid 21 *livres* a day which was a very handsome sum.[699]

During the first years of the First Crusade the skills available to the Crusaders seemed somewhat varied. At the siege of Nicaea, for example, their first armoured roof collapsed under the defenders' bombardment. The next was better designed while that built by the Italians was better than that of the Germans.[700] Once again it was the handling of large and heavy pieces of timber which distinguished the best from those less skilled, and again it tended to be men from the great maritime cities who excelled in these skills. The Genoese had been famed for their ability to use timber from ships to make siege machines in the late 11th and early 12th centuries. Not surprisingly they were soon selling their expertise.[701] Italian technological support was present not only in the Crusading warfare in the Middle East but also during the Iberian Reconquista.[702] Here they were not alone, and the skills which the sailors of the northern European fleets of the Second Crusade brought to the siege of Lisbon proved decisive. Yet even so it was an engineer man from Pisa in Italy whom the chroniclers picked out for particular praise.[703]

Once the Latin States had been established, and the Military Orders had risen to prominence in their defence, these Orders developed their own siege trains. Unfortunately very little is known of the men who designed and operated them.[704] Most would probably not have been brethren of the Orders. We do know that one of the main skills required of an artilleryman or *mangonel* master was accuracy and his ability to hit the enemy's machine with the stones thrown by his own. In the early 12th century Latin States one such highly regarded man was an Armenian named Haverdic.[705] In 1238 a Spanish engineer named Calamandrinus had been expected to command the Emperor Frederick II's siege train against Brescia, but he was captured and then welcomed by the Brescians who also presented him with a bride. Calamandrinus now agreed to work for Brescia, and his stone-thrower was so accurate that he destroyed those used by his previous employer, forcing the Emperor to abandon his siege.[706]

Ability rather than nationality or even religion was what mattered, and the Norman rulers of southern Italy and Sicily soon learned to appreciate the military engineering skills of their conquered Muslim-Arab subjects. These men built mobile towers for King Roger during his attack on Montepeloso in 1133, and King William used a similar tower against Alexandria in 1174.[707] Just over a century later, Charles, the French Angevin ruler of southern Italy, had his famous 'Saracens of Lucera' operate four *mangonels* during a campaign in Sicily.[708] As in several other aspects of Crusading warfare, there is considerable evidence for Islamic, Byzantine or Armenian influence in European siege techniques. In the Iberian peninsula, for example, it has been suggested that Islamic elements in the design of Christian castles resulted from the employment of captured Muslim military architects.[709] However, there is also strong Fatimid Middle Eastern influence, especially in the design of 12th and 13th century gates, which might suggest a more peaceful exchange of ideas.

Occasionally an individual military engineer rose to sufficient importance for his origins and career to be recorded, rather then merely his name. These unusual men included Master Jordan who built *trebuchets* for the English king in the early 13th century,[710] and Master Bertram who served the king of England in the mid-13th century.[711] Other evidence highlights the degree of technical specialisation amongst such men, Master Thomas de la Réole, a *fossator* miner or sapping expert, and Master Bernard the *carpentarius bridarum* who constructed the large stone-throwing engine both being in English service in Gascony in 1297.[712]

Much less is known about the humbler labourers who worked under these highly paid experts, but it is clear that in most parts of Western Europe it was the urban population who provided the bulk of the semi-skilled craftsmen required. Their numbers could be considerable, not only in construction, excavation and the moving of supplies but also in the operation of some *mangonels*. At the Crusader siege of Lisbon in 1147, teams of fifty men operated two such weapons and were able to throw five thousand stones in ten hours. That is approximately eight every minute, assuming that the figures are in any sense realistic and that the hours included only daytime. What is not clear is how many of the men were working at any one time. Did the fifty form smaller teams who served in rotation, or were there two teams of twenty-five drawn from a larger but unspecified number?[713] As already stated, women operated the early 12th century *mangonel* in defence of Amiens in northern France (see above) and women also operated *mangonels* in defence of Toulouse during the Albigensian Crusade in 1218, one of their missiles killing the Crusader commander, Simon de Montfort the Elder.

PYROTECHNICS AND CHEMICAL WARFARE

The use of fire and noxious substances in warfare was an area where, until the adoption of gunpowder firearms in the 14th century, Western Europe was clearly inferior to both the Byzantine and Islamic worlds. This did not, however, mean that fire was rarely used. On the contrary, efforts to burn enemy fortifications, siege machines, ships and indeed anything made of wood were common. Cases of offensive siege towers being destroyed by fire in 12th century southern Italy might indicate that pyrotechnics were relatively more advanced here as a consequence of Byzantine and Islamic military influence.[714] Fire weapons were also a common and terrifying aspect of naval warfare in the European Mediterranean from at least the 11th century onwards, having been prominent in Byzantine and Islamic naval warfare since the early Middle Ages.[715] Such weapons did not, of course, always succeed; for example the fireships sent by the Genoese against the Pisans at Karalin in 1207 failed to achieve their objective.[716]

Back on land, during one of the many 12th century Spanish raids against Majorca, the defenders built a wooden counter-tower to face that of the attackers. However, the troops manning the latter took a spar from one of their ships, attached incendiary material on one end and with this managed to burn down the defenders' counter-tower.[717] Fortune almost veered the other way during Simon de Montfort's siege of Minerve during the Albigensian Crusade. Here the defenders made a determined sortie and tried to set fire to de Montfort's biggest *trebuchet* using animal fat, bales of straw and flax carried in baskets, but the alarm was raised in time and the fire was extinguished.[718] A variation on this theme was attempted when ships tried to destroy a bridge of boats across the river Seine in the early 13th century, using boiling pitch which they then ignited.[719]

Such incendiary materials were far inferior to the famous *Greek Fire* of the Byzantine Empire which, known as *naft*, was used even more enthusiastically by the Muslims both on land and at sea (see volume II). This technology spread to France, perhaps as a direct result of experience during the Crusades, and was mentioned in the mid-12th century *Roman de Thèbes* as *feu grejois*.[720] Knowledge of making and using the simpler forms of *Greek Fire* probably reached northern Europe in the late 12th century, King Richard I of England paying two shillings and six pence for pitch to make *Greek Fire* in 1193.[721] A generation later in Italy the Sienese defenders of Montefollonica used *Greek Fire* against attackers from Orvieto.[722]

As yet it seemed that such knowledge was limited and was handed down through generations of military specialists with very little scientific or theoretical interest in the subject. Around the year 1280, however, a certain Marcus Graecus, 'Mark the Greek', wrote a *Book of Fires for the Burning of Enemies*. He was probably a Byzantine and his incendiary recipes were almost as sophisticated as those of the Middle East. Marcus Graecus' main ingredients were sulphur, tartar, sarcocolla, pitch, boiled salt, petroleum, ordinary vegetable oil, all of these being boiled together then soaked into tow before being lit. He also included distillates of this mixture for fire-arrows.[723] As protection from such fire weapons the Crusaders learned to use vinegar, this being recorded during the First Crusade's siege of Jerusalem where local craftsmen, presumably Christians, showed the invaders how to protect their wooden siege machines. There were far fewer references to what might today be called chemical warfare in medieval Europe. On the other hand the defenders of Beaucaire placed slow-burning sulphur and other substances in a sack, creating gases which drove back enemy miners.[724]

COMMUNICATION, TRANSPORT AND SUPPORT SERVICES

Medieval armies had a supporting 'tail', just as do modern armies, and the fighting men were similarly dependent upon many other personnel. As in all periods of military history, this essential support tended to slow down an army's rate of march. Some of the early Crusades covered staggering distances overland, though not necessarily very quickly, while the later Crusades and the Latin States were almost entirely dependent upon naval transport over equally long distances.

During the First Crusade the contingent commanded by Godfrey de Bouillon averaged a daily march of just under twenty-five kilometres, whereas the less well organised and disciplined horde led by Peter the Hermit did rather better, at nearly twenty-nine kilometres per day. Later forces again averaged around twenty-five kilometres per day, with the Emperor Frederick Barbarossa's army reaching almost twenty-nine kilometres on good roads. Other evidence shows that small groups of mounted men could maintain thirty-two to forty kilometres a day, but only for limited periods because a horse's stamina was less than that of a man on foot.[725] Good roads were a rarity in Europe during this period, especially in less developed regions such as the Balkans. Nevertheless the necessity of sending pioneers ahead of the main body, to clear a way with axes, was probably not so much for the benefit of men and horses as for waggons or from fear of ambush.[726]

In addition to pioneers and labourers, the Crusader élite, like others knights of this period, required squires, horse-handlers, horse-breeders, armourers and other highly skilled support,[727] while their commanders similarly depended upon clerks and a variety of literate non-combatants.[728] Once established in the Middle East, the Latin conquerors and settlers quickly took advantage of the bureaucratic and other skills of the indigenous inhabitants, mostly though not invariably relying on local Christians. Here it is interesting to note the influence of more complex Middle Eastern tent design on Western European tents which seem to have previously been based on Roman models.

Even before setting out, let alone reaching the Middle East, Crusader commanders naturally had to deal with substantial financial, logistical and administrative problems. Sometimes these were very down to earth, as when King Richard I of England ordered fifty thousand horseshoes from the ironworking centre of the Forest of Dean as part of his preparations for the Third Crusade.[729] Even King Richard, though a notably enthusiastic Crusader, was a part-timer. It was the Military Orders which became the professionals and experts. By the second half of the 13th century they were bearing massive financial and administrative burdens while themselves still suffering from the same shortage of horses, though not necessarily of manpower, suffered by the Latin States.[730]

The problems faced by the Latin States in Greece were even greater in this respect because they attracted much less support, financial, active and even emotional, than did the Crusader States of the Holy Land. Even after the Principality of Achaia came under the control of the generally quite prosperous Angevin rulers of southern Italy in the later 13th century, its garrisons were sometimes not properly paid nor its castles properly maintained. The Neapolitan Angevins were aware of these difficulties and tried to solve them by sending food and supplies to Greece until almost all military equipment came from Italy, but it was never quite enough.[731]

If communications between Italy and Greece were sometimes difficult, those between Western Europe and the Latin States of the Middle East were even more problematical. As the overland route was gradually strangled by the Turkish states of Anatolia, so the maritime link became absolutely essential.[732] This was not simply a matter of transporting men, animals, food supplies, munitions and other goods, but also of maintaining the flow of information, diplomacy and, for the Military Orders, instructions to their subordinate houses in Europe. The unreliability and slowness of such communications were seen as a major problem and there was great fear of the power of rumour or false information, compounded by a tendency to mistrust local interpreters, at least in the early days.[733] As the Military Orders earned a reputation for the reliability of their own international communications system, so rulers and other senior people began to use them as couriers and transmitters of information.[734] Even when the Military Orders were not used, there was a deep-seated preference for personal messengers of officially acknowledged status. Similarly, great efforts went into ensuring the safe arrival of such men.[735]

The Latins came to recognise the usefulness, and indeed the reliability, of pigeons. The carrier pigeon had been used in the Middle East for hundreds of years and pigeon-posts were a well-established means of communication, at least within states which could afford to maintain the infrastructure. The Crusaders learned fast, not least by intercepting a pigeon which was on its way to besieged Tyre with a message in 1124. The original message urged the garrison to hold on as help was on its way. This the Latins changed, advising the defenders to surrender as help was not forthcoming, and as a result Tyre duly gave up the struggle. Even so the Latin States never used carrier pigeons to the same extent as their Islamic neighbours.[736]

Short-range and battlefield communications were a different matter, and at least one Master of the Templars employed a *turcopole* as a sort of dispatch rider.[737] The mid-12th century *Roman de Thèbes* may have been more than usually influenced by the practices of Crusading warfare when it mentioned musical instruments such as the *buisines*, *tabours* and *troynnes* being used on campaign, along with the *frestiax*, which was a form of multiple flute, and the *chalumiaux* which may have been bagpipes.[738]

The importance of the road systems of the medieval Middle East had not, until recently, been properly appreciated. Even so there is still a tendency to assume that any significant roads that existed during this period must have been the crumbling remains of those dating from the time of the Roman Empire. Many Roman roads did exist, of course, but the early period from the 7th to 11th century had witnessed a huge upsurge of economic activity and trade, both local and long-distance. As a result an even more complex road network had developed by the time of the First Crusade and would then have a direct bearing on subsequent Crusader warfare.[739] Most of these roads were not, however, paved like the better-known Roman main roads. They were instead designed for pack animals and horses rather than wheeled traffic.

Much the same was the case in Western Europe, even in regions which either retained the old Roman network or saw the development of new roads in the medieval period. Supply waggons were used by most Western European armies during this period, the army of the French Crusading King Philip Augustus allocating two cars for every eight to ten *sergeants*.[740] The presence of wheeled vehicles also required suitable bridges over some rivers, and here again specialist engineers or builders were in demand. In 1098 Roger of Sicily was able to call upon the skills of his newly recruited Sicilian Muslim troops to erect a wooden bridge over the Volturno during the Normans' siege of Capua.[741]

Although waggons were used, pack animals were now more important for large armies on the move. For example, the Emperor Frederick I Barbarossa conducted several large-scale campaigns in northern Italy. These involved much the same logistical problems as he faced when leading a Crusading army overland to the Middle East. The distances were smaller, but Frederick's German army had to cross the Alps, which was no small feat at that time. Each knight had his own servants, warhorses, mail *hauberks*, weapons, pack horses with saddle-bags of cash, provisions, extra horseshoes plus their nails, and goatskin coats against the cold of the mountains. The *ministerials*, who, though already a military élite, were still of legally unfree status, were not expected to bear the full cost from their own fiefs. So they received grants of clothing and other necessities from their lords.[742]

The *Nibelungenlied* described the appearance of such a German army on the march around 1200. The knights loaded their armour and other clothing on pack horses, but still carried their shields and swords, especially when riding through unfriendly territory. However, they only put their shields on their shoulders when an enemy came near, which suggests that these shields might previously have hung from their saddles or on their backs.[743] More specific details are found in the Templar *Old French Rule*. This decreed that, at the start of a campaign, the brethren mustered and brought with them horses, pack animals and livestock for food. The *Marshal* and his assistants organised them into one or more *caravans* or groups which were then usually placed under command of the *Gonfanonier*. At the end of a day's march the brethren set up tents for themselves and their retainers around a chapel-tent which stood at the centre of the encampment. All their gear must be placed inside the tents, whereupon the squires were then sent foraging '*with horse and saddle*' for firewood and water. The work of squires was again under the command of the *Gonfanonier*.[744]

As already stated, naval transport soon became vital in Crusading warfare. In fact there is evidence that travelling from Acre and Ramla was considered easier by coastal ship from Acre to Jaffa then a ride along the coast during the 11th and 12th centuries.[745] This may, however, have reflected local security conditions rather than the state of the roads. By the second half of the 13th century the Latin States in the Middle East had to be supplied with virtually everything by sea, including large quantities of food. This was partially paid for by selling Muslim slaves to Europe.[746] Italian shipping dominated, but by the late 1230s the Military Order of the Hospitallers owned its own vessels. These were based in various Western European Mediterranean ports, particularly Marseilles where a new official called the *Commander of Ships* may have been responsible for their construction and fitting out.[747] As yet the Military Orders had no warships of their own.

The chance survival of certain records gives us an idea of how the transport of people and goods operated in support of the Latin States and some Crusading expeditions. In 1251, for example, a large ship called the *Damixela* sailed from Genoa to Constantinople which was still then under Latin Crusader rule. It was escorted by a fighting galley, though the larger vessel carried soldiers, weaponry and horses. Amongst the passengers were a Genoese named Ansaldus Gatiluxius and his four sons who had either been, or were on their way to serve as, mercenaries in the Byzantine Empire of Nicaea.[748]

Some of these passenger ships were large. In 1172 a three-masted Venetian vessel sent to evacuate people from Constantinople astonished the Byzantines by being able to carry between 1,400 and 1,500 people.[749] This was, of course, an emergency, but such ships did not remain unusual for long, five of them bringing seven thousand Crusaders against Constantinople during the Fourth Crusade.[750]

Other surviving documentation concerns a ship that set sail from southern France to the Middle East. Its passengers included many *peregrini* 'pilgrims' who were on their way to Damietta. In fact they were Crusaders who intended to join King Louis IX's army campaign in Egypt. Damietta was, however, retaken by the Muslims by the time this ship reached Messina in Sicily, so the passengers demanded be taken to Acre, there to join the defeated Crusading king. The passenger list shows that there were 453 such Crusaders on board, including fourteen knights and group leaders. At least ten of the knights were themselves the leaders of *socii* or people travelling as a group, two being Templar brethren. These leaders had ninety unnamed retainers, while the largest contingent of *socii* consisted of thirty-six people led by a Czech *zupan* or nobleman named Markwald. The other groups ranged from three to twenty people. There were also seven clerics on board, who did not have retinues.

Just over three-quarters of the remaining passengers were commoners travelling alone; some of their names indicated that they were of middle-class urban *burgess* origin. Of the forty-two women on board, twenty were with their husbands, the others travelling without male chaperones. Whether this was unusual is unknown and it is possible that some of these independent women were prostitutes. Only one commoner was described as a *serviens* or servant, which might also mean *sergeant*, and the others included various craftsmen. One of the better-known passengers was Oliver de Termes who had taken the cross and become a Crusader as a penance for his fighting against the Albigensian Crusade. It would be the start of a brilliant military career in the Middle East, and it is possible that there may have been other 'ex-heretics' amongst his fellow passengers.[751]

The merchants of 13th century Acre dealt in iron, copper, bows, arrows and horses from neighbouring Islamic territories, some of this merchandise probably being exported to Europe. In return some of them were seemingly involved in the contentious export of Italian timber to the Islamic Middle East.[752] The transport of munitions may have been small in terms of bulk, but it was large in terms of importance and value. Just one Venetian vessel captured by Maltese and Genoese ships near Greece in 1205 was found to have a cargo which included 1,200 shields, many other weapons, two hundred bales of cloth and nine hundred men.[753] Elsewhere it is clear that larger siege weapons such as *trebuchets* were transported, presumably dismantled, by sea or river in preference to being carted overland. This was certainly the case in 13th century England.[754]

It was, however, the ability to transport horses in substantial numbers and over long sea distances which had the biggest impact on warfare. The Normans might have learned how to do this while in Byzantine service, during the failed invasion of Islamic Sicily in 1038.[755] Twenty-three years later the Normans launched their own attack on Messina and are estimated to have carried around twenty-one horses in each ship.[756] This was, of course, only a short hop from the toe of mainland Italy, but in 1091 the Norman rulers of Sicily were able to get thirteen horses to Malta, alive and fit enough for combat, during their invasion of the island. This was a much longer voyage.[757] The Arabs had, meanwhile, been able to transport forty horses per ship since at least the late 10th century, and over notably longer distances.[758]

By 1100 the southern Italians were building larger cargo ships than the Byzantines but had still not solved the problem of providing adequate fresh drinking water to be able to transport horses over longer distances, despite the fact that Islamic shipping had been doing this for centuries.[759] It seems that the animals remained standing, but were cradled in canvas slings during these long voyages. Quite what else the Venetians learned, which enabled them to do this for the first time in 1123, is unknown, but they quite suddenly seemed able to transport horses directly from Italy to the Middle East. This was, paradoxically, a major step in establishing Italian naval domination in the Mediterranean.[760]

Another significant military-naval technology was the ability to land troops and horses directly onto a beach. This tactic became increasingly common from the late 12th century onwards,[761] and the French *chelandre* seems to have been a specialised horse-transporting galley whose name came from the Byzantine *chelandion*. In 1224 the *chelandres* built for the Emperor Frederick's Crusade were still powered by oars, and were similar to *taride* landing craft.[762] The last such vessel recorded in Western Europe is the *salandria* which King Louis ordered from Genoa in 1269, though by that date it was a sailing ship rather than a galley.

Once again, surviving documentation has enabled maritime historians to attempt theoretical reconstructions of the ships built for King Louis during his Crusade in the mid-13th century, though such reconstructions have varied somewhat.[763] It was not, of course, only the Crusades themselves which spurred technological developments at sea. In the 1260s the threat of a revived Byzantine Empire and Genoa joining forces against Venetian interests in the Aegean was a major factor in Venice redesigning and reorganising its merchant fleet. The result was increasing tonnage, stronger defences and a policy of sailing in convoys in dangerous waters. This continued well into the 14th century and was given further encouragment by the fall of Latin-held Acre to the Mamluks in 1291.[764]

The Venetians were not alone in developing more advanced vessels. For example the *tarida* long-distance landing-craft built in Genoa in 1246 for King Louis of France's Crusade had three sternposts with two ports or openings between them. There may also have been a simpler or smaller version with a single stern port, perhaps between two sternposts.[765] Such a vessel would have been remarkably similar to a bronze lamp in the form of a model galley which, made in Egypt around the time of the Islamic conquest, was one of the finest representations of early medieval Mediterranean shipping until it was lost during the Second World War.[766] It may also have represented the form of beach landing-craft or horse-transport which gave the Muslim Arabs naval domination until shortly before the Crusades. Even more detailed information survives concerning the galleys built for Charles I of Anjou, the ruler of southern Italy in the second half of the 13th century.[767]

Almost as important as ships were harbours and arsenals.[768] Many smaller craft could beach directly while larger vessels usually relied on small boats and barges to transfer people, goods and perhaps horses to and from the shore.[769] Sometimes other facilities were required and at Otranto in 1071 Robert Guiscard had a ramp excavated into a low, rocky cliff enabling warhorses to be embarked directly into ships in the deeper water below the cliff.[770] Presumably this was considered easier or more efficient than ferrying them out from a shallow water beach. Within what became the Latin Kingdom of Jerusalem there were already man-made harbours at Acre, Arsuf, Atlit, Caesarea, Beirut, Tyre and Sidon. At Jaffa a somewhat exposed natural harbour was partially protected by an offshore reef, but at Ascalon men and goods were probably landed onto the open beach.[771] Little seems to have been done to improve what the Phoenicians, Greeks, Romans and Muslim Arabs had built and there were clearly difficulties of maintaining these harbours. This, of course, remained a problem throughout the medieval Mediterranean.[772]

Over and above the problems of communications and transport there was the question of money, without which no medieval state or its army could function. The Military Orders were amongst the most efficient in raising and distributing these financial 'sinews of war'. In addition to their increasingly wealthy and well-administered estates back in Europe, the Military Orders also tended to use their properties within the Latin States of Greece as sources of money.[773] Once such money had been raised, it had to be spent and while Crusading warfare was the very purpose for the Military Orders' existence, direct military expenditure was only one demand upon the resources of those European states which participated in the Crusades. Particularly detailed records of medieval state expenditure on arms, armour and such matters relate to the Angevin Kingdom of Naples' wars against the Aragonese in late 13th century southern Italy and Sicily.[774] Significant defeats could lead to major losses of military materiel, perhaps resulting in short-term embarrassment while the victors might suddenly find themselves with more weaponry than they were accustomed to. This seems to have been the one result of an Angevin defeat by the Byzantines in Albania in 1281.[775]

The massive amounts of wine consumed by medieval European armies were not, of course, a matter of drunkenness nor even of maintaining morale. Wine was needed because water was dangerous to drink, especially in the vicinity of a military encampment with its lack of sanitation and general filthiness.[776] Horses were another major source of expense, especially warhorses. The 'knightly charger' was normally neither as large nor as heavy as has sometimes been thought, but it was certainly highly trained, often intensively bred and in some cases remarkably expensive.[777]

The skeletal remains of horses found during archaeological excavations in London included a great variety of sizes of animal. They are unlikely to have included knightly destriers or warhorses but ranged from ten and a quarter hands to sixteen hands. Sixteen hands is currently considered the minimum height for a modern London police horse, an animal daunting to rioters, who might, in this case, stand in for disorganised medieval infantry. Evidence from London and elsewhere, including the Latin States, suggests an average of around thirteen and a half hands for medieval horses, including riding, pack and draught animals. Nor does this evidence support the widespread thesis that European horses generally increased in size from the Roman to the medieval period.[778] On the other hand there is some evidence that medieval European horses were less robustly built than Roman horses, at least until the later medieval period when new blood had been introduced from the Islamic world.

The popular idea that the Crusaders were able to bowl over or barge aside their Islamic opponents because the Europeans rode much larger horses is now seen to be a myth. Most of the horses used during the First Crusade were probably quite small, the largest being something like a small modern hunter. Whereas it is true that the nomadic Turks still rode small steppe ponies, these formed only part of the cavalry forces of Middle Eastern Islamic armies. The professional élites of such forces were much better mounted on horses which were probably larger than those of the majority of the invading Crusaders, especially when the latter reached Syria.[779]

It is also clear that the First Crusade suffered a massive loss of horses during its long march across Anatolia. Of the estimated seven hundred to one thousand still alive in the autumn of 1097, only one one or two hundred remained by June the following year. Big efforts were then made to capture remounts in Syria which was, at that time, a major horse-raising region which continued to export high quality animals to the Byzantine Empire throughout the medieval period. Some knights were obliged to ride mules or donkeys, though they did not fight on them. These men had, in fact, been reduced to the status of mounted infantry.[780]

In the light of the existing very limited ability of ships to transport horses long distance, it is not surprising to find that the first settlers and occupiers of the Latin States made great efforts to capture and breed warhorses. Two hundred were, for example, taken from a defeated Damascene force in 1106, others being seized from the Egyptian Fatimids the following year.[781] Even after it became possible to ship horses directly from Europe to the Latin States, the problem remained acute because so many animals were lost to enemy archery. The rulers of the Kingdom of Jerusalem also agreed to replace any animal killed or mutilated in battle, their value having been assessed before the campaign. This system was known as *restor* and was organised through the *Marshal.*[782] Within the Order of the Templars, according to the *Old French Rule*, the *Commander* was responsible for the breeding and raising of horse herds which was done at some of the Templars' *casals* or farms.[783]

Large numbers of horses were needed. All countries tried to maintain the required herds and in Europe the cost of a warhorse was normally equivalent to that of twelve head of cattle during the Crusader era.[784] Generally speaking, horses seem to have been rather cheaper in southern Europe than in the Middle East, though the prices roughly equalised in the 12th century. In other respects the cost of such animals fluctuated according to the distance from threatened frontier regions or the frequency of invasions. It was, as always, a matter of supply and demand.[785]

In a French army of 1231 both knights and most mounted sergeants had three animals, a destrier or warhorse, a palfrey or ordinary riding horse, and a pack horse,[786] though this force might have been particularly well supplied. To the south, Spain became one of the most famous horse-breeding and -exporting countries of the Middle Ages. It was probably this large-scale operation, resulting in sufficient horses being available, that accounted for the fact that prices remained remarkably stable whether the Iberian peninsula was in a state of peace or war.[787] In 1268 the official price of a standard warhorse in the frontier town of Jerez was fixed at 400 *sueldos*, compared to 30 *sueldos* for a bull and 40 to 50 *sueldos* for an ordinary riding horse.[788] To the east, horse-raiding had been the main agricultural activity in Hungary but, for reasons which are not entirely clear, this declined from the late 12th century onwards.[789] The Emperor Frederick II of Germany and Italy imported horses from North Africa.[790] Elsewhere in Italy, a generation or so later, the commune of Perugia imposed an annual levy of horses upon its inhabitants, these animals being needed by the cavalry militia.[791] Other cities probably made similar demands.

Then there was the matter of medical support. This was in some respects more advanced than might be expected, even for such a supposedly backward area as Western Europe.[792] Those who survived into adulthood in the medieval world seem to have been remarkably tough and there are well-documented cases of both Crusaders and their Muslim opponents recovering from huge combat wounds without dying of infection. This was, of course, before the introduction of gunpowder firearms changed the nature of battlefield wounds.[793]

An ongoing study of wounds on skeletons found at Vadum Iacob and dating from Saladin's capture of this incomplete castle has produced a far higher incidence of blade injuries that amputated limbs or cut right through bones than has been found in comparable battlefield excavations within Europe. The reasons are as yet unexplained but might reflect the fact that so many of the men caught at Vadum Iacob by Saladin's sudden attack were craftsmen and labourers, presumably lacking any form of armour.[794]

Another skeleton that has been studied in detail is that of a young adult male found in a Latin context at Le Petit Gerin in Palestine. He suffered a severe shoulder wound which then partially healed, suggesting that the unfortunate young man lived for at least two weeks after his injury. A lack of other bone injuries might also indicate that the actual cause of death was a soft tissue injury elsewhere on his body.[795] Less well-dated evidence of a skull injury found in a medieval Islamic cemetery on the same site shows a very severe cutting blow which had nevertheless completely healed, allowing the victim to live for many more years.[796]

Having initially been closely involved in medicine during the early medieval period, the Christian or at least Latin Catholic Church changed its attitude and, by the 12th century, seems to have disapproved of surgery because it involved the spilling of blood. Churchmen then reentered this field during the 13th century, making efforts to control the activities in expanding medical schools. Meanwhile surgery enjoyed a higher status in southern Europe than it did in the north, probably because of the south's closer cultural links with the Islamic world.[797] This was particularly the case in southern Italy. Not only did King Roger of Sicily's Muslim troops provide valuable military medicine during the siege of Nocera,[798] but the city of Salerno was becoming the greatest centre of medicine and surgical knowledge within Europe. Even here, however, it is noticeable that the section dealing with head wounds in the late 12th century *Chirurgia*, attributed to Roger of Salerno but actually written by one of his students, remains less detailed than that in the late 10th to early 11th century Arabic work by al-Zahrawi, known in Europe as Albucasis.[799]

A mid-13th century English copy of an Anglo-Norman translation of the *Chirurgia* included three interesting if gruesome examples of how to deal with military wounds. When an arrow is to be removed from a headwound, the patient's head must be shaved so that the surgeon can see the entry and exit wounds. He should then ask the patient his position at the moment he was struck, after which the surgeon moved the arrow gently to loosen it, possibly also enlarging the hole in the skull by trepanning. The arrowhead was then removed through this hole whereas the rest of the arrow was extracted through the entry wound. Before removing a barbed arrow, the barbs should be closed with forceps to make them flush with the shaft and thus facilitate withdrawal, or the surgeon could place a brass or goosequill cannula on each barb to stop them snagging in the wound.[800]

The *Chirurgia* interestingly noted that the soldiers most vulnerable to head wounds were *sergeants*, especially those not wearing a suitable helmet: '*There are so many ways that a sergeant can be struck when he is in the mêlée without an iron hat (*chapel de fer*) and poorly armed, I should be quite fatigued if I tried to tell you in verse and writing of all the wounds both great and small*'.[801] Furthermore, the surgeon was warned to be very cautious in trying to treat a man with a skull wound, especially if the brain was damaged, because a surgeon could risk his reputation by trying and then failing.[802] Other more straightforward wounds were stitched with a ligature much as they would be today, and the surgeon could look forward to more of his patients surviving, along with his reputation.

Within the Iberian peninsula, the militias of Castile and León often had their own *cirujanos* or surgeons. This appears to have been the case in virtually all frontier towns, where there were also specially designated *guardadors* to guard prisoners and *pastores* to look after the militias' animal herds.[803] The Latin States established by the Crusaders in the Middle East similarly had their own medical practitioners and medical laws.[804] Nor were these necessarily as primitive as we are sometimes led to believe. Even during the early Crusader period there is strong evidence that the available medical support, if only in the form of fellow soldiers and clerics, had a practical and effective approach to the treatment of wounds, draining infection, using bandages, incisions, surgery, bleeding and cauterisation where deemed appropriate. This practical if rudimentary knowledge may have been one reason why they and their successors so easily and so quickly learned from the more advanced medical practices which already existed in the Middle East.[805]

The Crusaders provided a channel whereby such knowledge spread back to Western Europe while Jerusalem became a significant centre of medical teaching during the decade before it was retaken by Saladin.[806] There were soon a number of hospitals in these Latin States while others were established on a temporary basis while on campaign, especially during prolonged sieges.[807] That maintained and run by the Hospitallers was the most famous and in the aftermath of the battle of Montgisard in 1170 it was recorded as having cared for seven hundred and fifty wounded men.[808]

NAVAL AND RIVERINE WARFARE

Because maritime communications and transport were so important in Crusading and related conflicts, naval warfare was necessarily also significant. Various peoples were involved but, amongst Western European participants, none played such a vital role as the Italians. Above all this meant the main maritime and commercial states.

The first to emerge as a significant naval power and rival to existing Islamic and Byzantine Mediterranean dominance was Amalfi, in southern Italy. The republic of Amalfi had been established in 840, independent of the surrounding Lombard principalities but theoretically still under Byzantine suzerainty. Amalfi's rise to prominence was sometimes in competition with the Muslims, sometimes as the ally of one or more Islamic ruler. Early in the 11th century, however, the republic's independence was threatened by the rising power of the Normans. Seized and sacked by the rival Italian maritime republic of Pisa in 1135, Amalfi was completely ruined as a naval power a few years later.[809] But even before that Amalfi did not play a significant role in the Crusades.

This left Pisa, Genoa and Venice to become by far the most important Italian naval powers; indeed the most important Christian naval powers in the Mediterranean. In each there was plenty of financial capital available in the early 12th century, and this was used to finance both trading expeditions, naval raiding and full-scale warfare. Even earlier, temporary 'companies' of shipowners had been formed to draw upon such resources to attack the Islamic coasts of Sardinia, Sicily, North Africa, the Balearic Islands and Iberian peninsula. Here the rival Muslim shipowners were sometimes almost reduced to piracy to survive.[810]

While Amalfi was slipping out of the picture, Genoa played a much more important role in assisting the initial Crusader conquest of the Syrian, Lebanese and Palestinian coasts while Pisa and Venice had yet to make a significant appearance.[811] Elsewhere geographical conditions meant that coastal communications were similarly important. One example was southern Italy where the extremely mountainous nature of the western coast meant that it was almost always easier to travel by sea than overland. The importance of maritime communications was even more obvious in Greece, with its mountainous, deeply indented coastline and abundance of islands. The latter had been relatively prosperous at the time of the Fourth Crusade in 1204, although increasing piracy had forced many communities to move inland. In fact some Greek islands had already summoned Genoese or Norman protection.[812]

In other parts of Europe the period of the Crusades saw changes in traditional attitudes towards the sea and naval warfare amongst the ruling and military élites. In France, for example, there was rising interest in the possibilities presented by naval power during the reign of the Crusading King Philip Augustus. This was clearly reflected in the French epic literature of the period.[813] Subsequently there was a comparable change in attitudes in England.

Technological advances in the design of ships and especially of their rigging were largely stimulated by the demands of trade rather than warfare. Nevertheless they did bring about slow changes the nature of naval conflict. Where larger transport ships were concerned, new technology actually made these vessels less manoeuvrable but did enable them to sail closer to the wind.[814] Larger and more numerous ships also demanded larger and more numerous sails, resulting in Italy developing its own cotton industry in the 12th century.[815] Such large transports also had to be able to defend themselves, at least against pirates, and many if not most had a remarkably high stern structure called a *bellatorum* which often overhung the water and served as a centre of defence. It remains unclear, however, whether these tall wooden structures were permanent fixtures until the late 13th century.[816]

One of the most common forms of Italian ship at the start of that century was the *sagenae* which is believed to have been a lateen rigged sailing vessel with some secondary use of oars rather than being a galley in the proper sense of the word. The *sagenae* was also similar to, but smaller and faster than, the *tarida*,[817] both forms of ship also being used by the Muslims. Southern Italy and Sicily seem to have preferred small, fast vessels whose design continued to show strong Islamic influence. However, it was the northern Italians and above all the Venetians who adopted the Arab-Islamic tradition of really big ships (see volume II). Even in 1096 the Byzantine Princess Anna Comnena described a three-masted Venetian galley with two hundred oarsmen.[818]

The hull of the medieval fighting galley would remain largely unchanged until the 18th century. What did change was the arrangement of its oars which, until the 14th century, were usually arranged in groups at one level on an outrigger, each oar being pulled by a single man. Around 1320 Sanudo wrote in his *Liber Secretum*: '*It must be known that in AD 1290 in nearly all galleys two men rowed on the same bank (bench)*',[819] a system known as *alla sensile* or 'simple fashion'. Sometimes the oars were grouped into threes and historical confusion may have resulted from the fact that the galleys in question were often called *biremes* and *triremes*. In neither case, however, were the oars on two or three levels as had been the fashion in the ancient and classical Mediterranean. During the 14th century oars arranged *alla sensile* were gradually replaced by a smaller number of larger, evenly spaced oars, each pulled by five to seven men.

While the centre of defence for a sailing transport or so-called 'round ship' was the tall *bellatorum* at its stern, the most important fighting position on a war galley was at the prow, beyond which was the *calcar* or beak. This had replaced the ancient ram during the early Middle Ages and served as a boarding rather than a ship-breaking device. It could also wreak havoc amongst the oarsmen in the midships of an enemy galley.[820] The galleys ordered from Genoa by King Louis of France in the late 1260s also had *mangonels* in or near their prows, presumably in the hope of bombarding enemy shore positions rather than enemy ships. The ships were meanwhile protected by large *pavois* shields or mantlets and had a 'castle' or fighting top on their main or middle masts.[821]

Although the Mediterranean, Aegean and to a lesser extent the Black Sea lay at the heart of naval warfare during the Crusades, there was also a brief period of conflict in the Red Sea. This came about when Reynald de Châtillon launched a small fleet to challenge the long-established and virtually total Arab-Islamic domination of the waters between Egypt, Arabia, the Sudan (then generally included in 'Nubia') and Ethiopia. His ships were reportedly made at Kerak in what is now southern Jordan, before being carried in disassembled pieces to Aqaba. Recently it has been suggested that the vessels are more likely to have been made at Ascalon on the Mediterranean coast.[822] Nevertheless it needs to be noted that the hills of central and southern Jordan were probably more forested in the 12th century than at any time since.

The struggle between Islam and medieval Christendom extended into the Atlantic. Here there is recently published evidence of the survival of what might be called a third tradition of shipbuilding. To the north was the well-known Scandinavian or Viking tradition which had spread to much of the British Isles and northern France by the 11th century. To the south, in that stretch of water between the Iberian peninsula and north-west Africa which is sometimes called the 'Mediterranean Atlantic' there is powerful evidence of an essentially Mediterranean tradition of shipbuilding. This had either survived from Roman times or been reintroduced by the conquering Muslim Arabs in the 8th century, or most likely was a combination of both factors. A shipwreck found in the Saintonge region of west-central France now shows that elements of a typical medieval ship in neither the Viking nor the Mediterranean traditions was already present in the 7th century.[823] Instead it includes elements of a much earlier Celtic and Gallo-Roman tradition which could be seen in a wreck from the Roman period in the Channel Islands.[824] Furthermore it is important to realise that a highly developed shipbuilding and maritime heritage flourished in what became southern Portugal, the Algarve or in Arabic the *al-Gharb* ('the west'). This had been built up during the Islamic period,[825] and was not broken by the Christian-Portuguese Reconquista in the 13th century. It was also in just this region that the Arabic *karib* became the medieval *caravo* and thus the *caravel* of the great age of European discovery little over two centuries later.[826]

Despite their own naval heritage, the Norman conquerors of southern Italy and Sicily largely relied on Greeks, Lombards, other southern Italians and Greek-speaking Calabrians.[827] In fact the crews of ships involved in Crusader and other Mediterranean naval campaigns varied considerably. Here, as in northern waters such as the English Channel, the word *piratae* did not mean pirates in the modern sense, but referred to sailors who were trained to fight.[828] Men who had earned a reputation as effective corsairs could also rise high in medieval Mediterranean society. For example, Count Henry of Malta had originally been the Genoese corsair Enrico Pescatore. As Count Henry he became admiral of the Emperor Frederick's fleets in Sicily and south Italy.[829]

During this and earlier periods Mediterranean ships tended to have large crews, partly because ships defended themselves by hand-to-hand fighting.[830] Surviving documents dealing with a Venetian naval expedition in 1224 reflect this need to repel boarders, the ships in question consisting of war galleys and *galleons* which were at this early date probably smaller ships relying on both sails and oars. Each had a crew of one hundred and one sailors plus eleven marines, only three crossbowmen plus the captain. The full-scale war galley had one hundred and thirty-nine sailors and oarsmen, thirteen marines, just four crossbowmen, the captain and, if the commander of the expedition was on board that ship, also a servant. One other ship was mentioned, a small *sagita* carrying four crossbowmen.[831] In 1255 the Venetian *Doge* (elected Duke) Zeno introduced a law which insisted that all seamen had a full set of proper military equipment suitable to their role on a ship, again illustrating a reliance on numbers and close combat.[832]

This began to change in the second half of the 13th century and eventually led to a slump in the status and numbers of sailors required. A reduction in the number of sailors may also have been associated with a gradual move from lateen to square-rigging during this same period.[833] Ordinary sailors now had less of a voice in the running of ships while that of masters, owners and merchants was increasing.[834] This was in many respects a social revolution and eventually caused serious social problems in some Mediterranean coastal cities. The biggest factor for change was an increasing reliance upon crossbows operated by a smaller number of more highly trained and better-paid marines. These men became a naval élite as ships defended themselves from a distance rather than repelling boarders. Later 13th century Venetian naval regulations were also more concerned to ensure that key personnel had sufficient body armour, again reflecting the growing threat from crossbows.[835]

The contract between King Louis of France and Genoa, ordering ships for the king's proposed Crusade against Tunisia, referred to galleys to be rowed by one hundred to one hundred and twenty oarsmen. The marines to defend these vessels included crossbowmen commanded by a master crossbowman though most of these naval troops were still equipped for close combat, *muniti ad ferrum* or 'armed in iron'.[836] Nevertheless most late 13th century Mediterranean European naval crossbowmen also served on the benches as oarsmen. Apparently it was only in the Catalan fleet that such crossbowmen were dedicated professionals. Perhaps as a result, Catalan ships were particularly effective in naval battle.[837]

The provision of food and water for ships' crews was less difficult than it was for horses aboard transport ships. The range and distances squadrons of galleys could cover was sometimes astonishing, just as long as they had ready access to water at regular intervals. If they were denied access to such sources on the coasts along which they sailed, their operations became virtually impossible. It is now believed that ships from northern or Atlantic Europe played a significant role during the First Crusade's operations around Antioch. These vessels and crew would have got their supplies from Byzantine or perhaps Cilician Armenian territory, and may indeed have been under some degree of Byzantine command. Yet they had needed to get to the eastern Mediterranean in the first place, and this meant sailing through the Straits of Gibraltar. Many northern vessels had done this before, and would continue to do so, but they must also have had the acquiescence of the Islamic rulers of neighbouring coasts. Italian ships operating in the eastern Mediterranean at the time of the First Crusade and its immediate aftermath would have brought supplies directly from Italy, but thereafter they too would have resupplied in Byzantine-held ports.[838] Then, of course, there were almost certainly Byzantine imperial ships operating in this area (see below).

While Islamic garrisons continued to hold the ports and sources of fresh water on the coast of Syria, Lebanon and Palestine, there was no mention of Christian galleys carrying large numbers of people operating further south than Tripoli. Not surprisingly, therefore, the Crusaders focussed a great deal of their early effort on capturing the coasts after having seized Jerusalem.[839] Once they achieved this, maritime communications with Western Europe were opened and remained open until the fall of Acre in 1291. The distances remained great, and adequate drinking water was always a serious concern. Otherwise it was a case of carrying enough *biscoti* or ship's biscuit, dried foods and money to purchase other necessities during a voyage, whether it was a peaceful trading expedition or a naval campaign. An interesting and quite well-documented example of the latter was Count Henry of Malta's campaign in 1206, with Genoese support, to stop Venice taking control of Crete in the aftermath of the Fourth Crusade. This again entailed assembling ships, men, *biscoti* and money to purchase horses, presumably locally.[840] It resulted in a difficult and little-known sideshow of the Crusades which ended in Venetian victory in 1212.

Naval battles between substantial numbers of ships were very rare during the Middle Ages, though there were a number in the Mediterranean. None took place on the high seas out of sight of land, where ships rarely ventured anyway, and several were actually fought in or immediately outside harbours. On other occasions the weaker fleet could beach its galleys stern-first and close together, thus forming a powerful defensive position because the main strength of such galleys was in their prows.[841] A reference to Venetians tying their ships together to form a fixed battle formation in 1084 has been disputed as unlikely, not least because in the open sea such a formation could be attacked from the flanks or rear.[842] In more constricted waters it might have been more practical, and does seem to have been carried out by the fleet defending Malta harbour in 1283.[843] In the subsequent fighting, the Catalan galleys had sufficient crossbowmen and javelin-throwers to decimate the French galleys' crews while the French found themselves unable to board the Catalan ships and take advantage of their heavier close-combat armour. This might also suggest that the Catalan galleys rode higher in the water on this occasion.[844]

Eleven years later, during a naval battle between the Genoese and Venetians at Ayas in Cilicia, the Genoese prepared for combat by 'taking down masts', 'lashing together prows' and then awaiting the Venetian attack. In other words they adopted a defensive array. This time the Venetians proved overconfident and were defeated when the wind took them broadside to the enemy, exposing their vulnerable flanks to enemy fire.[845] If communications between troops on land was a problem during this period, communication between warships was similarly difficult. Quite how flags and other visual signals were used is practically unknown. Instead it seems that vessels tried to remain close enough for auditory messages, as when trumpets sounded the challenge which started a major battle in Malta harbour in 1283.[846]

The most important offensive weapons aboard ship at the start of the Crusading era were bows and javelins, though crossbows were already being used at sea by Islamic mariners. By the 13th century the crossbow had become by far the most important naval weapon on board Christian shipping, both in the Mediterranean and increasingly aboard Atlantic and northern vessels as well. These weapons included the usual types and sizes, though the large *balista a tour* or windlass-spanned version may have been particularly effective.[847] Even the largest *great crossbows* proved to be less vulnerable to damp than was the torsion-powered *espringal* and so were occasionally also used at sea, for example by the Emperor Frederick II in 1239.[848]

Different naval powers employed different systems to equip their naval troops. Before one Venetian naval expedition of 1224 the overall commander had to provide arms for himself and many of the men, the rest apparently being furnished by the state.[849] Other naval weaponry, in addition to personal weapons used on land, included *rochets* which seem to have been specialised long-hafted axes to cut the enemy's rigging, *triboli* calthrops to pierce the enemy's feet, soft soap to make his decks slippery, perhaps quicklime or chalk dust to blind him and fire arrows to burn his sails. There were also cases of spars being slung on ropes to serve as battering rams.[850]

There had long been a tradition in the Mediterranean for specific fighting galleys to be armed with particular weapons, and thus to serve in a particular way in battle, but this habit was not adopted in northern waters until the late 13th century.[851] Similarly the frequent references to English and French ships having large stone-throwing siege engines aboard almost certainly meant that these weapons were being transported, and were not normally for use at sea. In the Mediterranean, however, such engines were used aboard ship, though against shore-targets rather than other vessels. The Genoese and particularly the Pisans seem to have been skilled in such ship-to-shore bombardment. Various Crusades then adopted the idea against Constantinople in 1204, against Damietta in 1223 and 1249. During the latter campaign such *mangonels* were used against enemy ships in the Nile but this was a limited target area and sometimes several stones were seemingly thrown at once because the targets were moving and fragile enough to be easily damaged.[852]

Fire-weapons were not an area in which the Western Europeans excelled, yet they were sometimes used in naval conflict. The Venetians may have used them in 1081, though this is unclear.[853] A ship's superstructure could be covered in felt soaked in vinegar or sour wine as a defence against such *Greek Fire*, though this surely suggests that the vulnerable masts and rigging must already have been removed. A late 13th century Italian source, the *Documenti di amore*, describes one such protection: '*Wrap the ship around with good hides to turn away fuoco* (Greek Fire) *in battle*'.[854]

During the period of the Crusades, naval strategy seems to have been considerably more advanced than naval tactics. All naval actions, including major Crusades, were dominated by the prevailing patterns of wind and weather, as were more peaceful trading voyages. The islands which dotted the Mediterranean clearly played a major role in strategy, though not in quite the same way they did in later centuries. Malta, for example, provided a naval springboard for Sicilian Norman campaigns in North Africa but could not serve as a significant naval base because it lacked timber. On the other hand it was fertile in cotton, which had probably been introduced by the previous Arab-Islamic rulers to provide replacement sails for passing ships. Thereafter Malta remained an important trading and military staging post for the rulers of Sicily throughout the 12th and 13th centuries.

Cyprus was much bigger, more fertile, more wooded and was strategically located close to the Islamic heartlands of Syria and Egypt. It therefore served as a naval assembly point and source of provisions for various Crusades, especially after being seized from the Byzantines by King Richard of England during the Third Crusade. At the opposite end of the scale in terms of size was the tiny offshore island near the Islamic city and naval centre of Mahdia on which Roger of Sicily established his base when invading Tunisia. In the event the Normans suffered a major defeat on the mainland and had to withdraw in a great hurry, but, having based themselves on this little island, they were able to take all their military equipment and valuable horses with them.[855]

One of the least known but strategically most ambitious aspects of the military struggle between Latin Christendom and the Islamic world during the period of the Crusades was a series of Spanish naval attacks down the Atlantic coast of Morocco in the 13th century. These may have been to seize the valuable grain supplies of a fertile region which had enjoyed considerable economic expansion under the Murabitun (Almoravids). It may even have been an early effort to disrupt trans-Saharan trade and to get closer to the sources of African gold and slaves which were believed to be the main source of North African wealth.[856] The Murabitun who had incorporated the Islamic regions of the Iberian peninsula into a vast, largely African empire had themselves originated beyond the Sahara in what are now Senegal and southern Mauretania. Apart from earlier attacks on Sabta (Ceuta) on the southern side of the Straits of Gibraltar, the first recorded attacks on the Atlantic coast were by Castile against Sala in 1260 which was an attempted conquest; against al-Ara'ish by 'Rum' who may have been Castilians or Portuguese which was for plunder; then again by Castile against Tangier in 1292 which was to disable an enemy fleet.[857]

When rival fleets or smaller squadrons did commit themselves to battle, the most common tactics were to keep the ships close together, sometimes, perhaps surprisingly, including both galleys and sailing 'round ships' which otherwise manoeuvred in entirely different ways. Islands were used as cover from which to ambush isolated enemy ships, smaller convoys or squadrons.[858] As the vessels closed, the archers and crossbowmen tried to shoot down on the enemy's decks, which was why fighting castles at the stern and sometimes prow, as well as fighting tops on the main mast, were so important.[859] Some Venetian ships had fighting tops as early as 1084, from which men could also throw weights to smash through the enemy's hull.[860] In northern waters there were references to ships, especially the type called a *cog*, being lightened so that they rode high in the water and thus gained a height advantage in combat.[861] In addition to the crossbows the largely unarmoured and famously nimble *almugavars* employed as marines in Catalan fleets also used javelins as a final barrage before boarding enemy vessels.[862]

The size of naval expeditions, and thus of fleets, naturally varied. Some were very large, such as the Genoese campaign against Pisa in 1120. According to the *Annals of Genoa* this involved eighty galleys, sixty-three other ships, four special transports for equipment and siege machinery, and 22,000 soldiers of whom 5,000 were heavily armoured.[863] Another major Genoese naval expedition was sent against Islamic Almeria in Iberia in 1147 and reportedly consisted of sixty-three galleys plus one hundred and sixty-three other ships carrying men and equipment. It was accompanied by six of the ten consuls of Genoa and cost a huge sum, at least 17,000 Genoese *lire* to build and outfit the fleet, which has been calculated as equivalent to the total overseas investment by Genoa's leading commercial families in a good trading year during the 1150s. Furthermore the fleet included ships from other Ligurian communes like Ventimiglia.[864] Even so it ended in disaster.[865]

Few medieval rulers had more than a tiny handful of their own 'royal' ships during this period. There was, for example, no French 'navy' during the 13th century, despite France playing the leading role in most Crusades. Transports and fighting galleys had to be summoned as a form of feudal obligations, or hired, purchased or commandeered as and when required. Such systems varied from country to country. Under Norman rule the coastal towns of Sicily had heavier naval obligations than did the coasts of the southern Italian mainland.[866] This presumably enabled King Roger to lend fifty ships to Barcelona in 1128 for use in a Crusade against the Muslims of al-Andalus.[867] In 1191 a Sicilian fleet sent against those of the invading German Emperor is said to have comprised seventy-two galleys, plus four smaller *sagittiae* and *scurzatae*.[868] On the other side the Emperor Henry had to rely to a considerable extent upon Pisan and Genoese fleets when attacking the Norman coastal cities of southern Italy.[869] Long after the fall of this Norman kingdom in the south, southern Italy remained a significant naval power using a variety of types of ship. In 1274, for example, the Neapolitan fleet sent to Valona in Albania still included what was called a *tarite*, presumably meaning a *tarida* which is likely to have served as a horse-transport.

The Latin Kingdom of Jerusalem had no real fleet of its own, though some vessels could be summoned from Tyre, Tripoli and the Military Orders when needed.[870] In contrast the County of Tripoli is believed to have created a small fleet after a squadron of Saladin's warships from Egypt entered the 'harbour' or more probably the roadsteads of Tartus in 1180, ten galleys of Tripoli being mentioned in 1188.[871] Though the rulers of Jerusalem sometimes called upon the Military Orders, the latter normally hired ships and were very rarely involved in naval warfare during the 12th and 13th centuries. They eventually had a few transport vessels, but only in the very late 13th and 14th centuries did such Military Orders, especially the Hospitallers, start to play a major role in naval warfare.[872]

While major clashes or naval battles were rare, other forms of naval warfare were so frequent as to be a normal aspect of maritime life, especially in many parts of the Mediterranean. The most traditional of these was coastal raiding. The skills that are required of commanders, sailors and marines were clearly widely available. Usually such raids were launched at weak, vulnerable or undermanned targets. Sometimes, however, a fleet was sent against a more formidable foe, for example in 1188 when the Crusader admiral Margaritus brought his galleys so close inshore that his crossbowmen and archery could hit the coastal road, hindering Saladin's march. Here the water was deep because the coast was so steep, leaving Saladin's troops little alternative but to erect palisades manned by their own archers who thus tried to keep the Christian ships at a distance.[873] An unusual variation on this coastal-bombardment tactic was seen during the final Mamluk siege of Acre in 1291, when the Christian defenders stationed archers and crossbowmen in ships protected by wooden hoardings or vaulting covered in fire-proof ox-hides. These men shot at the flank of the enemy siege-lines where they touched the coast, and at an encampment behind the lines. Another ship even had a stone-throwing *mangonel* but this was broken in a storm and was not repaired.[874]

Christian piracy against Islamic coasts was a more common strategy, and in response the Islamic states of North Africa and Sicily started building small coastal defensive towers during the 11th century. Comparably small, isolated fortifications based upon those earlier Islamic models then appeared on the Italian mainland during the 12th century where they became known as *saraceno* towers.[875] Christian coastal piracy became more intense against Mamluk-ruled Syria and Egypt from the mid-13th century onwards, but, even before this, Crusader raiders had been able to reach al-Warrada and Qatya in the eastern part of the Nile Delta in 1243. On this occasion the Latins were defeated, despite what was by then a supposedly overwhelming Christian naval superiority.[876]

Very occasionally there were more determined and larger-scale Western European attacks upon Islamic or Byzantine fortified ports. It was on such occasions that the use of ship's spars as battering rams, wooden siege towers erected on board ship and the building of flying bridges from a vessel's superstructure to the opposing wall made their appearance.[877] They were rarely successful. In many respects the defenders on land always enjoyed certain tactical advantages over attackers from the sea, though the strategic initiative correspondingly lay with the latter. For example, the large Sicilian fleet which attacked Alexandria in Egypt in 1174 had to bring its own *mangonel* stones from Italy.[878] Might these also have served as part of a ship's ballast during the outward voyage? On this occation the Sicilian fleet included thirty-six *taride* with 1,500 horses and cavalrymen; that is forty per ship. Other vessels carried the siege machines and general supplies.

The Sicilian cavalry outside Alexandria were not all landed at once and it might have been that only a few of the *taride* had a suitable beach-landing capability. It is also important to note that these medieval landing-craft had to use their oars to get their sterns on the beach, since that was where their disembarkment doors were located.[879] One of the best descriptions of a medieval naval landing comes from the pen of the Norman writer Wace in the mid-12th century. He wrote that: '*The archers disembarked, the first to set foot on land, each with his bow bent, his quiver (coivre) and bowcase (tarchais*, from the Persian word *tarkash* and more likely meaning a different kind of quiver*) hanging at his side*'. Once these infantry archers had secured a bridgehead, the armoured knights disembarked with their horses and formed up on shore.[880] When King Richard landed at Jaffa in July 1192 it seems that the beach had already been cleared of opposition by crossbowmen on board his ships.[881] Two generations earlier, during the Sicilian Norman attack on Mahdia, there was a clear reference to five hundred cavalrymen landing directly onto the beach in the face of stiff resistance.[882] The Fourth Crusade was able to do much the same outside Constantinople and in both cases such cavalry proved unstoppable.[883]

Riverine warfare played only a small part in the Crusades and, indeed, in medieval Western European warfare as a whole. Nevertheless, the fleet that the Emperor Frederick II assembled for his intended invasion of Egypt in 1220 was specifically designed to be able to penetrate some distance up the Nile. As a result it included large numbers of shallow draught galleys which were inefficient as military transports,[884] including many *chellandes*.[885] These might actually have been serving as horse-transports. In the end the Emperor's armada sailed to Palestine instead.

2

Byzantium and the Orthodox Christian States

THE MILITARY TECHNOLOGICAL BACKGROUND

The study of medieval Byzantine military affairs poses very different problems to those posed by Western Europe. While there is an abundance of relevant and highly detailed written material, most notably in the form of military manuals or texts, there is correspondingly little reliable pictorial evidence and a poverty of archaeological artefacts. The frustrating conservatism and indeed archaism which permeates Byzantine art, and that of most neighbouring cultures under strong Byzantine influence, makes such pictorial evidence very difficult to use. Yet it should not be dismissed as wholly misleading. Several of the same difficulties also apply to Byzantine literary sources which can be as frustratingly prone to the use of archaic terms and images as the pictorial sources. Yet they again do provide considerable information, once the stylistic literary chaff is removed. A good example is Nicetas Choniates whose writings focus on much of this period and show that the author had vivid powers of description as well as an interest in military matters. Yet even Choniates was prone to use misleading terminology, and as a result some attempted statistical studies based upon his work have proved misleading.[1]

Although it is clear that Byzantine military effectiveness had declined since the great territorial expansions of the 10th century, the armies of the following decades were built upon essentially the same principles and traditions. The Empire's military forces had rarely been evenly spread and it would, paradoxically, be the traditionally stronger eastern frontier which collapsed in the final quarter of the 11th century. In the late 10th century the evidence strongly suggests that the eastern frontier *themes* or provincial armies were more effective, and certainly larger, than those elsewhere, at least outside the capital of Constantinople. A few of the eastern *themes* could raise around one thousand cavalry, others only seven hundred or so, while some of the European *themes*, including those of the vulnerable Balkan frontiers, could raise or maintain far fewer troops.[2]

There were also differences between the armies of the Asian and European provinces, largely reflecting local traditions and sources of recruitment as well as ecological factors and the influence of neighbouring cultures. Western European influence was still slight and was in any case itself rooted in some of the same military traditions. The influence of the largely nomadic Turkish peoples of the steppes had been the most persistent and significant external factor since the 6th century, if not earlier. By the 10th century the neighbouring Arab-Iranian-Islamic world was also exerting a profound military influence, though this might have been more apparent in Anatolia and the eastern frontier *theme* armies than in those of the capital or of the European provinces.[3]

Here it is worth noting that the political and military land-frontier between the Orthodox Christian Byzantine Empire and the Islamic world of the Middle East was not as much of a barrier between rival cultures as has sometimes been maintained. Though the frontier itself may generally have been clearly defined, on the ground as well as on maps, there were substantial regions on both sides which were more like a cultural and even a religious no-man's-land. In these mountainous fastnesses of what is now eastern Turkey, several religious minorities found refuge. They were not always or invariably persecuted but they were outside the mainstreams. The most significant were the Armenians who maintained not only their separate language, culture and church but also a distinct military identity and, for much of the time, separate state structures which enjoyed greater or lesser autonomy (see below). Very different were the Paulicians who, adhering to dualist religious beliefs rooted in Manichaeanism, were regarded as the worst of heretics by Christian Byzantines. The Islamic authorities were generally more tolerant, which inevitably meant that the Paulicians of Anatolia were regarded with justifiable suspicion by the Byzantine civil and military authorities. Large numbers were forcibly removed from the strategically sensitive eastern frontier to the Balkans. Here, however, they continued to resist Byzantine oppression by occasionally allying themselves with invading Pecheneg Turks from the western steppes in the late 11th century. It was in this respect that they featured during the history of the First Crusade.[4]

Local disaffection was only one of the many problems which weakened Byzantine defences during the second half of the 11th century. These resulted in the eastern frontiers of the Byzantine Empire being notably poorly manned at precisely the time when the previously weak and fragmented Islamic side of the frontier was being reunited by the Seljuk Turks. One might even suggest that the Byzantine imperial government's failure to appreciate what was happening in the Islamic Middle East fatally undermined the Empire's defensive capabilities. Yet it was a failure based upon Byzantium's previous remarkable military revival, a sequence of astonishing victories and the overconfidence which this recent history engendered.

Not only was the Byzantine Empire's eastern frontier poorly manned, but it proved easy to penetrate and as a result many raiders were able to get deep inside Anatolia during the 1060s. A major assault upon the Byzantine Empire was not Seljuk policy, which instead focussed on extending Seljuk domination of the Islamic heartlands of the Middle East. Nevertheless the Byzantine Emperor Romanus IV chose to extend his large-scale campaign against frontier raiders into a challenge to the Seljuk Great Sultan himself. The result was a catastrophic defeat at the battle of Manzikert in 1071, followed by a palace coup against the Emperor Romanus and a subsequent civil war which left the Byzantine eastern frontier weaker than ever. The remaining local authorities and forces were largely left to fend for themselves, either resisting or coming to terms with increasingly 'official' Seljuk and other Turkish invaders.

By the time the newly established Byzantine Emperor Alexius I requested military help from Western Europe, and thus set in train a series of events which culminated in the First Crusade, the greater part of Anatolia and even some offshore Aegean islands were under the control of various Turkish lords. Most of them owed real or nominal allegiance to the Seljuk Great Sultan whose own power was based in Iran and Iraq. Nevertheless, a Byzantine recovery was already under way by the time the First Crusade appeared on the scene. Most of the northern or Black Sea coast had never been lost and various Christian Armenian lords still preserved their independence in the Taurus and other inaccessible mountain ranges of south-central and south-eastern Anatolia. Some acknowledged some degree of Byzantine overlordship, though usually recognising the more immediate suzerainty of the Seljuk Turks.

It was into this complex and confusing military-political situation that the First Crusade marched at the close of the 11th century. Meanwhile, and in its wake, the armies of the Byzantine Emperor Alexius I continued to regain a substantial part of western, northern and southern Anatolia. This reconquest had begun with an expedition to the occupied eastern Aegean islands in 1092.[5] By and large, the recovered provinces were the most fertile or the most mountainous, but above all they were those which could be reached, invaded, defended or resupplied by sea. This Byzantine military dependence upon the sea, though not a new phenomenon, became paramount during the 12th century.

Despite a reoccupation of western Anatolia, Byzantine relations with the newly established Crusader or Latin States in the Middle East cooled rapidly, partly over the status of the Latin Principality of Antioch. This in turn contributed to a steadily worsening relationship between the Orthodox Christian Byzantine Empire and the Latin or Catholic Christian states of Western and Central Europe. There were, of course, other factors undermining trust between the two 'Christian worlds', and the eventual collapse of such trust which resulted in the diversion of the Fourth Crusade. This was followed by the conquest and Latin occupation of the Byzantine imperial capital of Constantinople itself.

As a clear result of this shift in military capability, the Byzantines never regained the high plateau of central Anatolia, still less the mountainous regions further east which had previously formed the Empire's main line of defence against eastern invaders. On the other hand a remarkably similar line of defence was established in the lower but still rugged mountains of western Anatolia, resulting in the revival of several very traditional Byzantine military systems.[6]

At the same time, and in almost complete contrast, Western European military ideas, tactics and their associated styles of arms and armour had a greater impact upon Byzantine armies under the Comnenid imperial dynasty founded by Alexius I than had ever been seen before. These included a greater emphasis on close-packed cavalry formations using the *couched* lance and long or so-called 'kite-shaped' shields which, though probably developed and certainly used in both Byzantium and the Islamic Middle East in earlier centuries, had now become firmly associated with Western European heavily armoured cavalry tactics.[7] The failure of these in the unsuitable military circumstances of 12th century warfare against the Seljuk Turks in Anatolia almost exactly mirrored the ultimate failure of comparable Crusader heavy cavalry charging with *couched* lances in the Latin States of Syria and Palestine. The most dramatic Byzantine failure in this regard was at the battle of Myriokephalon in 1176 which virtually destroyed the Comnenid military system and was followed by a dramatic, though far from steady, Byzantine military decline.[8]

This decline further encouraged the regional variation which had been a feature of Byzantine military affairs for many centuries.[9] Yet at the same time the Comnenid emperors continued with a policy of attempted centralisation. This achieved mixed results and itself resulted from specific aspects of the Byzantine Empire, its culture, society, political and military traditions. For example, the Byzantine 'Reconquista' of western Anatolia was very different from the Spanish–Portuguese 'Reconquista' of most of the Iberian peninsula which was taking place around the same time. The Comnenid campaigns were imperial governmental enterprises and barely involved any spontaneous military activity on the part of the local Christian populations, as was so often a feature of the Iberian Reconquista. Following catastrophe at Manzikert in 1071, Byzantine military resources had been very limited. Furthermore, the Byzantine aristocracy were far less enthusiastic about taking part in these imperial campaigns, largely because money rather than land remained the basis of political power within the Byzantine state. Military campaigning was expensive, and the territorial rewards were far less attractive to the Byzantine élite than they were to the relatively poor and land-hungry élites of the Iberian Christian states. Even the Comnenid family itself had shown this relative lack of interest in land. They were of Anatolian origin and had held huge estates in Anatolia, but had not remained to fight in defence of their landed assets in the wake of the battle of Manzikert.[10] Instead Alexius Comnenus chose to use the family's financial and other more 'liquid' assets to strive for, and eventually to win, the imperial crown in the capital of Constantinople.

The Angelus dynasty, which ruled from the fall of the Comnenids until the Fourth Crusade took Constantinople, largely continued their predecessors' attempts at military centralisation, though with even less success. After losing Constantinople to the Crusaders in 1204, the fragmented Byzantine successor states were all 'provincial' in the sense that they no longer controlled the imperial capital. The most powerful was that of the Lascarids which re-established a Byzantine 'Empire' in western Anatolia with its capital at Nicaea (Iznik). Here the Lascarid Emperors initially tried to achieve a sort of balance of power with their own tumultuous military aristocracy, but eventually attempted a return to the traditional Byzantine policy of centralisation. Their successors of the Palaeolog dynasty continued this policy, especially after regaining Constantinople from the Latin (Crusader) Emperors in 1261, but with uneven results. Another period of military collapse began in western Anatolia only a generation after the Byzantine Emperor Michael VIII Palaeologus returned to Constantinople. The fertile Meander (Menderes) valley was lost to the Turks by the 1280s, and as a result the new Turkish *beylik* or mini-state of Aydın was able to develop into a significant naval power in the Aegean – a sign of greater dangers to come.[11]

A closer look at the different regions or frontiers of the Byzantine Empire highlights a number of points already touched upon. The eastern frontier had, of course, been the most important since at least the 7th century. Here rivalry and often overt conflict between Greek- and Armenian-speaking troops had become a significant source of military weakness by the 11th century.[12] The Byzantine annexation of the previously independent Kingdom of Armenia in the mid-11th century had been intended to strengthen the Byzantine imperial position and more immediately to regularise a confused military situation.

As part of this annexation, the Byzantine authorities replaced the local Armenian feudal levies by a system of heavy taxation but this, in addition to replacing a military burden with a financial one, also left the Armenians largely leaderless and to a considerable extent disarmed. Furthermore, much of the Armenian élite now found itself without a clear or local military role.[13] Many moved westward, deeper into Byzantine territory where they served in Byzantine rather than Armenian armies. Many others moved south and to a lesser degree east, into the Islamic world where Armenian mercenaries suddenly changed from being rare to being remarkably numerous (see volume II). The still independent Christian kingdom of Georgia was another potential employer. Armenian troops were even recorded fighting for Russian Kiev against the Poles in 1064, though there is no evidence of a substantial Armenian military colony within Russia until the second half of the 13th century, after the Mongol conquest of Armenia itself.[14]

The situation was, and had been for a long time, different along the north coast or Black Sea littoral of Anatolia. During the 11th century there seem to have been no real *theme* armies in this region for the simple reason that the Black Sea was regarded as a Byzantine lake. Since there was no perceived threat to the Byzantine provinces of the northern Anatolian coast, there was little need for local armies.[15] The western coasts of the Black Sea were largely under Byzantine rule and here any threats came from the land, from Turkish nomads or local Christian rebels, or at most from fellow-Christian though Catholic Hungary.

Part of the commercially strategic Crimean peninsula had been Byzantine for centuries, and further north the steppes were dominated by potentially dangerous and frequently unpredictable Turkish nomadic *khanates*, but these rarely if ever ventured to sea. Beyond the nomads was the fellow-Orthodox Christian power of Kievan Russia. This was, however, fragmenting into numerous competing principalities, one of which was Chernigov which itself had inherited the Kievan Russian outpost of Tmutorokan on the Taman peninsula east of the Crimea. Between 1097 and 1118 this Russian '*khanate*' of Tmutorokan came under Byzantine rule from neighbouring Crimea.[16] Thereafter it remained a significant local power, though not a naval one, until at least the mid-12th century.[17]

Meanwhile the eastern coast of the Black Sea was largely controlled by the fellow-Christian and largely friendly Kingdom of Georgia. This happy state of affairs was barely interupted by the loss and partial reconquest of those provinces of Anatolia south of the coastal mountains, at least until the Fourth Crusade shattered the political unity of what remained of the Byzantine Empire. One of the most significant successor states was the Empire of Trebizond (Trabzon) which continued to be ruled by members of the Comnenid imperial family. Once the situation had settled down in the aftermath of the Fourth Crusade, this 'Empire' was only rarely and marginally involved in the affairs of the Byzantine heartlands to the west. Trebizond seemingly concentrated on its own survival and its own considerable wealth as a major hub of Black Sea, and thus of European and Asian, trade. Its only 'imperial territory' was the Byzantine province of the Crimea, and that not always. Nevertheless, commercially preoccupied Trebizond still faced military threats, most notably from the Turkish states of the Anatolian interior and from the Mongols who threatened practically everyone from the mid-13th century onwards. Another neighbour was a greatly expanded Georgia,[18] but, in general, the Byzantine Empire of Trebizond maintained friendly relations with Georgia.

Until the 13th century, the Balkan provinces of the Byzantine Empire seem to have been of secondary military importance, despite the fact that they were at least as often invaded as the Anatolian provinces. Perhaps the threats faced by the Byzantine authorities in the west were seen as less 'mortal' than those coming from the east. Perhaps they tended to be more susceptible to diplomatic solutions, or at least the invaders could be more easily turned against one another. Even when the Byzantine Empire lost local control to local states such as Serbia and latterly Bulgaria, these were at least usually fellow Orthodox Christians.

The nature of Byzantine frontiers in Europe was also different and perhaps more varied than those in Asia. Some were notably blurred and easy to cross. Paradoxically the Paristrium region along the lower Danube was like this, despite the presence of the broad river Danube seemingly providing a clearly defined and defensible line on the map. As a result regions such as Paristrium became linguistic and cultural melting pots, many of whose inhabitants were regarded by the 'real' Byzantine citizens of Constantinople as *mixobarbaroi* semi-barbarians who included Byzantine families that had 'gone native', to use the terminology of 19th century imperialism.[19]

A potentially more serious threat to Byzantine power in the western Balkans was posed by the newly established Norman Kingdom in southern Italy and Sicily. This was not only rich and ambitious, but was ruled by Latin Catholic Christian monarchs whose invasion of the Balkans in 1107 caused a significant diversion of Byzantine military efforts away from Anatolia.[20] Although this Norman threat was eventually defeated, other Italian powers would inherit the Italo-Normans' ambitions, while in places like Epirus, in what are now northern Greece and Albania, a tradition of local leaders making common cause with westerners persisted. This was exacerbated by the fragmentation of the Byzantine Empire after the fall of Constantinople in 1204.

One of the successor states was the Despotate of Epirus which, unlike Nicaea or Trebizond, did not claim to be a Byzantine 'Empire' in its own right. Its Despots did, however, often find common cause with the Latin or Crusader States established in Greece after the Fourth Crusade, none wishing to be incorporated into the reunited Empire of the Palaeolog Emperors. Indeed the Despots of Epirus developed particularly strong military and naval links with the Italian rulers of the Ionian Islands,[21] but were themselves soon threatened by the Angevins of southern Italy who saw Albania and perhaps even the entire Byzantine Empire as their zone of expansion. Consequently there was a fundamental shift in Byzantine priorities by the later 13th century, with more troops being stationed in the Balkans than in Anatolia.[22]

Despite the Byzantine army inflicting a significant defeat on Charles of Anjou, ruler of southern Italy and Sicily, in 1280, western European and more specifically Italian influence upon western Balkan military organisation and equipment remained strong. The effectively autonomous Byzantine-Greek province of Thessaly, for example, had, according to one European report, an army of thirty thousand in 1303, including six thousand cavalry in eighteen *battalions* each commanded by a *baron* and under the overall authority of a *Marshal*.[23] The latter was said to be a Greek or with the status of a *Vucomity* which was clearly a corruption of the common western European title of *Viscount*. The western Balkans would remain a complex arena of rivalries until virtually all existing local powers were swept away by the rising power of the Ottoman Turkish Sultans in the late 14th and 15th centuries.

Although the Byzantine Empire was the biggest and most powerful Orthodox or non-Catholic power in south-eastern Europe and the Middle East, it was not the only one. The Armenians have already been mentioned and, prior to its annexation by the Byzantine Empire in the mid-11th century, Armenia had itself been a significant military player.

Quite when those Armenians who had been living under Byzantine rule began once again to look to their own defences is unclear. It might have been as early as the Seljuk Turkish ruler Tughril Beg's campaign of 1054, especially as the depleted Byzantine garrisons were increasingly restricted to a series of strongly fortified bases.[24] If that was so, then there would have been no real break in indigenous Armenian military traditions. After Manzikert, however, it became increasingly clear that, as the Turks took over the central Anatolian plateau in 1074, they were not only able to force the Byzantines further west but were also able to turn and attack the Armenian mountain fastnesses from the west – in effect from the rear.[25] It was from this time onward that substantial elements of the Armenian aristocracy and their supporting military élites migrated south-west into the even more rugged Taurus Mountains overlooking the fertile coastal lowlands of Cilicia. As a result Cilicia, or at least its mountainous hinterland, became a warlike but largely isolated Christian enclave, virtually surrounded by Islamic states.[26] It remained so until it finally fell to the Mamluks two and a half centuries later.

The Seljuk Great Sultan Alp Arslan, the victor of Manzikert, had sound strategic and political reasons for allowing autonomous Armenian principalities to remain in existence not only in the Taurus Mountains and northern Syria but also further north, in the ancient Armenian heartland around Mount Ararat. They could be used as pawns in the greater powerplay of the Middle East and also maintained local stability without much need for Turkish or other Islamic garrisons in some notably rugged and inaccessible regions. In this respect Seljuk rulers were merely continuing a policy of military and political devolution that dated back at least to the 'Abbasid Caliphate of the 9th century and perhaps even earlier to the Umayyad Caliphate.

Other Armenian military families moved to the still substantially Syrian Christian urban centres of what was then regarded as northern Syria or the northern Jazira. These areas had formed an integral part of the Islamic world since the 7th century. Here, in the foothills of a broad and fertile region now divided between Turkey and Syria, they established themselves as autonomous town-based authorities usually recognising some degree of tenuous Seljuk Turkish, and thus Islamic, suzerainty.[27]

One of the most enigmatic personalities in this confused period and region was an Armenian leader named Vahram Varajnuni, better known in Byzantine and Latin sources as Philaretus. He established an ephemeral but none the less militarily significant state based upon the fortified city of Edessa (Urfa) but also including the great trading city of Antioch. It has sometimes been called an *akritic* state because Vahram Varajnuni and his army emerged from the long-established frontier community of *akritoi* or indigenous warriors which had played, and would continue to play, such a vital role in Byzantine military history.[28]

The supposed chaos of this region in the decades immediately before the arrival of the First Crusade may well have been exaggerated. Vahram Varajnuni took control of Antioch in 1079 and managed to reach some accommodation with the Byzantine Empire which still claimed the city as its own. It is worth noting that Venetian merchants still reached Antioch to trade that same year, as did their rivals from Amalfi. Meanwhile Vahram Varajnuni also paid tribute to the Uqaylid Arab rulers of Aleppo and Mosul, becoming one of their staunchest allies against the advancing Seljuk Turks. These Uqaylids were nevertheless overthrown by the Seljuk Great Sultan in 1085, after which Vahram Varajnuni disappears, perhaps killed alongside his Uqaylid friend and ally.[29]

When the First Crusaders arrived only thirteen years later, they found effectively independent and militarily potent Armenian proto-states already existing in the mountains as well as virtually autonomous Armenian élites in several towns including Edessa. It might almost be true to say that, to a substantial extent, the work of the First Crusade had already been done for them in what became the Latin Principality of Antioch and the County of Edessa.

The Armenian state firmly established in Cilicia in the wake of the First Crusade would, in the event, long outlive all the Latin Crusader States on the Middle Eastern mainland. This Kingdom of Lesser Armenia, as it was often known, nevertheless remained virtually surrounded by usually hostile Islamic states while its relations with the Byzantine Empire were generally bad and those with the Crusader Principality of Antioch not always good. By the 13th century the Kingdom of Lesser Armenia had virtually become a 'Crusader state' in terms of its military organisation as well as its diplomatic and trading links.[30] The Western European Crusading Military Orders had been given responsibility for the defence of some its most vulnerable frontier castles, yet Cilician Armenia remained vulnerable to Islamic attack. This was despite its numerous and, until the late 13th century, highly regarded troops.[31] In fact comments by Marco Polo, the famous Venetian traveller in the closing years of the 13th century, that the military qualities of the Cilician Armenian had greatly declined should not, perhaps, be taken at face value.[32]

The Mongol conquest of Turkish Anatolia in the 13th century fatally undermined the Seljuk Turkish Sultanate of Rum, but, paradoxically, this caused a big increase in Turkish, or more strictly tribal Turcoman, raiding against Cilician Armenia.[33] In fact the Armenian alliance with the Mongols against the remaining Islamic powers of the area, though logical enough at the time, proved fatal once the Mongol Il-Khanate of Iran, Iraq and eastern Syria itself became Muslim. The Mongol Il-Khans' great rivals were, of course, the Mamluk Sultans of Egypt and Syria who regarded Cilician Armenia not only as the Mongols' consistent military ally but as a potential Christian beachhead for future Crusades. Thus they tried to isolate it from the West and eventually conquered it outright.

The Mamluk Sultanate also launched campaigns against the sprawling Christian kingdom of Georgia, but these were motivated by purely strategic rather than religious considerations.[34] Fewer studies seem to have been made of Georgian military systems, traditions and equipment during this period than of the Armenians. Yet sources such as a Georgian epic poem *The Man in the Panther's Skin*, written down in the late 12th or early 13th century, show very strong Iranian and Turkish Islamic influences, not only in the story itself which has parallels with the better-known *Shahnama* epic, but also in arms, armour and styles of warfare.[35]

The peoples of the southern and eastern Balkans were in most respects so similar to the Byzantines in military matters as to be virtually indistinguishable. Most of them had, of course, formed part of the Byzantine Empire for centuries and even when they achieved independence they emerged as local variations on an essentially Orthodox Christian Byzantine cultural, political and military civilisation. Only the Wallachians and Moldavians of what is now Rumania built states beyond what had been the traditionally accepted frontiers of the Byzantine Empire. The independent Serbia which emerged in the 13th century was militarily an offshoot of Byzantium, as was the independent Albania that had emerged in the late 12th century. At first fragmented under its own local *archontes*, Albania was briefly and superficially united under a *magnus archonte* but soon lost its independence again in 1216, this time to the Byzantine successor state of Epirus.[36]

The first Bulgarian state was, of course, an exception having been established by Turkish conquerors from beyond the Byzantine realm. Yet by the 11th century this First Bulgaria was a distant memory which had left very little behind and almost nothing military that could be traced back to the original semi-nomadic Turkish or Turco-Mongol Bulgars of the 7th to early 11th centuries. On the other hand the Second Bulgarian Kingdom was open to further military influences from steppe peoples further north.

It has been suggested that, under John Asan II in the early 13th century, the new Bulgaria included territory north of the Danube in Wallachia, in what is now Rumania. This remains a matter of debate, yet there is no doubting the prominent role of Vlachs or Wallachians in the rebellion against Byzantine rule which resulted in the creation of the new Bulgaria. Such military and political links across the Danube also resulted in increased Byzantine military and cultural influence, via a now independent Bulgaria, within Wallachia. This would seem to have been welcomed as a counterbalance to Hungarian and thus Catholic rather than Orthodox pressure.

These trans-Danubian links weakened after the death of John Asan II while Hungarian military influence correspondingly strengthened after a Hungarian victory over the Bulgarians at Vidin in 1230.[37] Seventeen years later the Hungarian king gave the Crusading Military Order of the Hospitallers considerable rights over the provinces of Severin and Cumania. The former was one of the most strategic locations in Europe, dominating the narrow gap where the Danube river broke through the Carpathian Mountains from the great Hungarian plain of central Europe into a broadening plain which stretched eastward to the Black Sea.

Cumania was, of course, named after the Kumans or, as they are more correctly known, the Kipchaq Turks who currently dominated the lowlands of Wallachia. This area was, in effect, the easternmost extension of the vast Eurasian steppes. West of the river Olt the Hospitallers largely left the existing local Wallachian administrative units of *knezats* and *voivodates* in place. Thereafter Severin became known as Oltenia while Cumania became Muntania, each with its own local troops and military aristocracy.[38] However, it was not until the 14th century that these regions, plus territory further east, achieved autonomy and then independence as the Principality of Wallachia. Similarly the region north-east of the Carpathian Mountains, which became Moldavia, also achieved its independence during the 14th century.

RECRUITMENT

The Byzantine Empire was in several respects unlike virtually any other European state and had more in common with its Middle Eastern Islamic neighbours. Like several of them, it had inherited a great deal from its Roman past. The result was a highly bureaucratic state with a professional core to its armies. Patterns of recruitment varied according to circumstances, but the degree to which the Byzantine full-time military units consisted of mercenaries, often of non-Byzantine origin, was regarded by most Western observers as both strange and as a sign of weakness. The relatively low status accorded to military men and military activities by Byzantine society also seemed peculiar to visitors from places like France, Germany or even much of Italy.[39]

Contrary to the impression given by several Byzantine chroniclers, and still accepted at face value by many modern historians, the 'Frankish' or Western European mercenaries who served in large numbers on the eastern frontiers of Byzantium from 1047 onwards proved quite reliable. This was true even of Norman mercenaries from southern Italy whose reputation was tarnished by the wild ambitions of a few within their ranks.[40] Furthermore, it was only in the crisis of the late 11th century that foreign mercenaries began to outnumber locally recruited troops.[41] Some parts of the 11th century Byzantine Empire had, in fact, been virtually demilitarised. In the one-time Byzantine provinces of southern Italy, for example, many local communities offered no resistance to the Norman conquest, regarding it merely as a change of masters.[42] However, in the aftermath of the great defeat by the Seljuk Turks at Manzikert,[43] Byzantine society in general and the landed aristocracy in particular did become gradually more militarised. Nevertheless, this militarisation would not reach the level common in Western Europe where, paradoxically, there was a trend in the opposite direction.

The Byzantine army was not as ineffective as Western historians, medieval and modern, have so often maintained. Nor was the Byzantine Empire entirely defensive in posture, even in relation to its Western European neighbours. For example a close political and military as well as economic alliance developed between Byzantium and the effectively autonomous Italian trading city of Ancona in the 12th century. As a result the defence of Ancona in the face of German Imperial ambitions was often bolstered by a Byzantine garrison. Yet this military activity on the western side of the Adriatic Sea declined after the death of the ambitious Emperor Manuel I in 1180.[44] In fact a general military decline now set in, though major efforts continued to be made to defend what remained of Byzantine territory in western Anatolia. The fragmented Byzantine successor states of the 13th and 14th centuries remained militarily as well as economically important, even to states as far away as England. So much so that an English embassy travelled all the way to Trebizond in 1292–3.[45] Meanwhile English recruitment to the Byzantine Emperor's famous Varangian Guard continued much later than is generally realised (see below).

Before looking at the details of Byzantine recruitment it is worth noting the major role played by disease in defence of the Byzantine Empire. This shattered the military potential of several invading peoples and rendered their survivors ripe for recruitment. Largely Turkish nomadic invaders from the steppes north of the Black Sea seemed particularly vulnerable to epidemics after they penetrated the settled and urbanised Balkan provinces of the Empire. This happened to the Pechenegs in 1046–7,[46] after which they were easily defeated by Byzantine forces. Their survivors were settled as military colonies tasked with defending Byzantium against further invasion – a policy which had been pursued since Roman times and which would continue almost until the very end of Byzantine history.

Unfortunately, modern nationalist historians have tended to obscure rather than illuminate the reality of this Byzantine policy of absorbing ex-nomads from the steppes, especially where its impact on existing populations is concerned. This has also been the case in parts of the Balkans that lay beyond the generally accepted Byzantine frontier. For example, when other Turkish tribes pushed the Pechenegs south from their old power centre in what are now the lowlands of eastern Moldavia in the early 11th century, they moved into the plains of the lower Danube, into territory dominated by the Byzantines. It has then been suggested that the local populations which had garrisoned this area for the Byzantine Empire retreated into the mountains, not only southwards into the Balkan Range of Bulgaria but northwards into the Carpathian Mountains where they supposedly fortified themselves as predecessors of the Vlach or Rumanian-speaking Wallachians.[47]

External or non-Greek-speaking recruitment was also a feature of the eastern frontiers of the Byzantine Empire. Here the regions of south-eastern Anatolia which the Byzantines had reconquered in the late 10th and early 11th centuries were largely populated by Muslim Kurds, Christian Arabs, Armenians and heretical Paulicians. According to the Christian Syrian chronicler Bar Hebraeus, many Paulicians were recruited by the Byzantine Empire and proved to be good soldiers, especially when raiding Muslim states to the south, but they were also undisciplined.[48] Arabic sources similarly noted the presence of new units in Byzantine armies from the mid-10th century onwards, often referring to them or their units as *zirwar*. This term clearly came from the Armenian *zorovar* or 'general' which may itself have been equivalent to a Byzantine rank of *strategios* in the *theme* armies of newly occupied Armenian territory. The role of Armenians has already been noted and the Byzantines clearly used such troops to garrison newly conquered or constructed fortresses in the mountains of what is now north-western Syria.[49]

Throughout the 10th and 11th centuries Armenians were the most important non-Greek minority within Byzantine armies, most of the leading Armenian families being largely Byzantinised in culture if not in the version of Christianity they followed. This process was clearly under way before the Byzantine Empire actually occupied the independent Armenian regions in the mid-11th century. The fact that Armenian troops were at least as prominent in defending the European provinces as they were the Anatolian ones could be interpreted as a sign of their reliability and effectiveness or as a sign of their potential unreliability in what had been their home territories.[50] Their importance declined in the 12th century, after Byzantium lost control of eastern and central Anatolia. Nevertheless the Armenian population of Tal Hamdun in Cilicia was transported to the Byzantine island of Cyprus in 1136/7, probably to establish a military colony.[51] Just under five hundred years later, additional Armenian troops might have been taken to Cyprus by the rebel governor Isaac whose wife was a daughter of King Thoros of Cilician Armenia.[52] It seems clear that Armenians were amongst those who unsuccessfully resisted the Crusader King Richard of England's conquest of Cyprus in 1191. Another important Armenian colony with at least some military role existed on the Asiatic side of the Dardanelles at the start of the 13th century. This made the fatal decision to ally with the invading Fourth Crusade, but Armenian troops were still present in these or neighbouring regions for several more decades, many deserting their unreliable current employers to take service with the Byzantine Empire of Nicaea.

The role of Arabs in Byzantine service went back to the initial Islamic conquests of the 7th and 8th centuries, when several Christian Arab tribes from Syria and the Jazira (Mesopotamia) migrated into Byzantine Anatolia rather than accept Muslim Arab domination. The following centuries of frontier life and frontier war saw the military élites of both sides occasionally changing allegiance and, although this trend was usually from Christian Byzantium into the Islamic world, there was a pronounced Arab-Islamic impact upon Byzantine frontier forces in this region. It can be seen in, for example, the famous medieval Greek epic poem of *Digenes Akritas* whose earliest surviving text was probably written in the mid-11th century in the Syria-Commagene region, now those provinces of Turkey immediately north of Syria. In it the hero's military followers are called *goulabios*, which stemmed from the Arabic term *ghulam* or élite soldier of freed slave origin.[53] This early medieval Arab-Islamic influence is also seen in the military equipment, clothing and horse-harness of the *Digenes Akritas* epic.

Nor did the Byzantine army only recruit Christian Arabs, for in the early 11th century a local Muslim leader named Mansur was allocated a fief near the frontier with the rich and still unconquered Syrian city of Aleppo. Here he was allowed to maintain his own small army.[54] The Maronite Christians of what are now Lebanon and Syria were also largely Arabic-speaking. For centuries their military role had been strictly local though they became generally reliable allies of the Latin Crusader States in the 12th and 13th centuries. Many also migrated from the mainland to Byzantine-ruled Cyprus during the first half of the 12th century. Their military role on the island is, however, not very clear.[55]

One of the most striking features of the Byzantine army was its mixed character and in this the Byzantine imperial authorities were continuing a tradition of military recruitment that went right back to late Roman times. For example foreign troops in the army of Emperor Alexius I in the late 11th and early 12th centuries included 'Russians', who themselves included Scandinavians, plus Germans, pagan Pecheneg Turks from the steppes and Balkans, Muslim Turks from Anatolia, Alans who were a semi-nomadic people from the Caucasus and the adjacent steppe who followed the Orthodox Greek Christian rite, Bulgars, 'Franks' who included Frenchmen, Normans and perhaps Italians, and Anglo-Saxons from England. Of those only the English were a new source of recruitment.[56]

Thereafter the proportion of such foreigners within Byzantine forces as a whole fluctuated, as did the proportion of men from specific sources. Yet a century and a half later, the army which initiated the partial Byzantine reconquest of southern Greece from its Latin-Crusader occupiers in 1262 included Muslim Turks, largely pagan Kipchaq Turks, Germans, Hungarians and Greeks from western Anatolia and Thrace. No local forces from southern Greece seem to have been involved at this stage, though local infantry from the mountains of the Peloponnese would soon be playing a very significant role in Byzantine campaigns against the Latin Principality of Achaia and Duchy of Athens.[57]

Despite the preponderance of foreigners in the armies of Emperor Alexius I, founder of the Comnenid imperial dynasty, he recruited native Byzantine citizens as far as was possible. His successors tried to increase local recruitment, as did Isaac II, the first ruler of the subsequent Angelus dynasty. However, it is often more difficult to identify the origins of internally or domestically recruited Byzantine troops than it is those from beyond the Empire. It can also be difficult to separate those of internal Orthodox Christian background from similarly Orthodox Christians from regions of the Balkans currently outside Byzantine control. For example, locally recruited troops from Epirus and Albania included both Greek and Albanian speakers, plus Slavs who may today be identified as Serbs or Macedonians but at that time probably thought of themselves simply as Christians of the Orthodox pursuasion. Such troops played a significant role in Greece and the western Balkans from the 11th to the 13th century,[58] as they did later. Some generations fought beneath central or local Byzantine banners, others for local lords against Byzantine authority, yet others for or against various Crusader or Latin or Italian rulers. There is even evidence of forced recruitment by the Byzantine authorities of one child in five in Albanian and Slav regions.[59] Although this was not necessarily for military service, it is remarkably reminiscent of the later Ottoman *devsirme* forcible recruitment of children from largely Slav and Albanian Christian families for élite *Janissary* infantry regiments. There is no doubt that during the late 13th century the Byzantine Empire enlisted large numbers of Slavs as soldiers in what is now Greece,[60] while the following century was characterised by a major migration of Albanians into northern and western Greece where they continued to play a leading military role well into the 19th century.

Then, of course, there were the nomadic or semi-nomadic Vlachs who spoke a language descended from Latin which was the ancestor of modern Rumanian. They dominated many upland regions from Greece in the south, through Albania[61] to Bosnia in the north, and were at times militarily very important; so much so that Thessaly in what is now central Greece was at times known as *Megalo Vlachia* – Great Wallachia.[62] Further north, in the mountains of Bulgaria, local Vlach tribes had a considerable military role during the mid-12th century.[63]

Still further north they were already a locally dominant linguistic and cultural group in parts of the Carpathian Mountains where, of course, the Vlach or Rumanian principalities of Wallachia and Moldavia would eventually emerge.

Elsewhere, in what could be regarded as the traditional heartlands of the Byzantine world, local troops were often not available in sufficient numbers nor were sufficiently trained. After the fall of Constantinople to the Fourth Crusade the re-established 'Empire of Nicaea', which was the strongest Byzantine successor state, faced warfare on three fronts, against the Latin-Crusader occupiers of Constantinople, against the Seljuk Turkish Sultanate in Anatolia and soon against Bulgaria. After regaining Thrace and much of Macedonia in the Balkans, the Empire of Nicaea had to maintain two armies, one in Asia and one in Europe. The lands they defended and indeed expanded across were insufficient as sources of soldiers, so that in the winter of 1254–5 Emperor Theodore II reportedly sent 'untrained huntsmen' against the Bulgarians and suffered a significant defeat.[64] This may have been part of a hurried attempt to raise indigenous troops.

Clearly the most effective fighting men available to the Empire of Nicaea were drawn from the state's eastern borders facing the Turks. Here a frontier élite in north-western Anatolia maintained the old traditions of the *akritoi* who had earlier defended Byzantium's provinces in eastern Anatolia. The Paphlagonians from the mountainous regions north of the modern Turkish capital of Ankara were, for example, renowned as highly disciplined archers. They played a significant role in the Nicaean Empire's European provinces, often fighting the similarly Orthodox Christian and largely Greek-speaking Epirot warriors who formed the backbone of the rival Byzantine Despotate of Epirus. They also fought against the Latin-Crusader Empire of Constantinople and the Latin-Crusader States in Greece as well as defending the Anatolian frontiers. In contrast, Balkan troops from Macedonia were not so well regarded nor as reliable.[65] It is interesting to note that infantry archers from essentially the same provinces of Anatolia would be vital to the success of early Ottoman armies in the 14th century, the men in question almost certainly being the now Muslim descendants of those who fought for the Byzantine Empire of Nicaea.

Another distinctive group which earned itself a relatively new military reputation during the latter part of this period were the Cretans. Crete itself had been occupied by the Venetians, though not without fierce resistance, in the aftermath of the Fourth Crusade. Resistance continued, either passive or active, throughout the 13th century and resulted in many of the island's militarily active population fleeing as refugees into Byzantine territory, mostly to the Empire of Nicaea in Anatolia. Cretan refugees were still available as an identifiable group in 1293 when the ruler of a now substantially reunited though shrunken Byzantine Empire recruited them during his effort to re-establish an *akritoi* frontier defence system in Anatolia. They proved initially successful and even managed to get some of their Turkish foes to come over to the Byzantine side. Only two years later, however, their general Philanthropenos rebelled against the Emperor and was abandoned by his Cretan troops, after which Byzantine control of western Anatolia rapidly collapsed and the Cretans largely disappeared as a distinct military group.[66]

The Turks themselves were an important source of recruits for the Byzantine Empire, as they had been in earlier centuries, and would remain so until the fall of Constantinople in 1453. Until the mid-13th century, the majority of these Turks were not Muslims, nor did most of them come from the newly established Seljuk and later Turkish-Islamic states established in Anatolia. During the period under consideration, the first significant group were the Pechenegs who had been pushed westward along the steppes north of the Black Sea by other more powerful Turkish tribal peoples. Eventually these Pechenegs 'fell off the map' of the steppes, being driven away from the broad grasslands, which maintained their semi-nomadic way of life, into the forested, cultivated, mountainous and urban regions of the Balkans.

Although there were steppe-like grasslands in the Balkans, especially in Thrace and eastern Bulgaria, these were relatively small, almost like islands of steppe which may have been able to support the Thracian horse-cultures of ancient times but were now insufficient to enable a horse-based nomadic culture to achieve anything more than the briefest local domination. For these and other reasons, the Pecheneg invaders or refugees were soon defeated by Byzantine forces, despite being supported by local and similarly semi-nomadic Vlach tribes. Their survivors were settled in the wooded mountains between Sofia and Nis, but soon rebelled, largely because the terrain was unsuited to their way of life. Defeated again, they were moved eastward to a more suitable area bordering the Black Sea. This had been the heartland of the first Bulgarian state several centuries earlier, and was one of the largest 'islands of steppe' within the Byzantine Balkans.[67] In 1094 the Byzantine Emperor Alexius defeated the Kipchaq Turks who had been pushing the Pechenegs ahead of them, thus regaining a traditional Byzantine frontier along the lower reaches of the river Danube. Some of the best descriptions of these Pechenegs, both as invaders, as Byzantine auxiliaries and as military supporters of rivals to the Byzantine imperial throne, are found in princess Anna Comnena's *Alexiad*, an epic biography of her father the Emperor Alexius I.[68]

Relations between the Byzantine Empire and the new nomad 'steppe empire' of the Kipchaq Turks remained generally stable for over a century, until the Kipchaqs themselves fell victim to yet another wave of steppe-conquerors from the east – the Mongols. Their fate, or rather that of their defeated political and military élites, was much the same as that of all previous nomadic peoples who had been pushed westward along the steppe corridor north of the Black Sea.

They fled from the steppes and sought refuge amongst neighbouring settled states. Many were eventually absorbed by Russia, others crossed the Carpathians into Hungary while yet others turned south into the Balkans, into the recently recreated Kingdom of Bulgaria and into the Byzantine Empire beyond.

Confusingly known by different names in each state or culture that gave them refuge, these Kipchaqs almost always proved to be an effective and largely reliable source of troops. They also managed to retain many aspects of their own military traditions, including the horse-archery skills which made them so valuable in the eyes of their new employers. The Byzantine Emperor John Vatatzes of Nicaea reportedly settled ten thousand Kipchaqs in Thrace and in the Meander (Menderes) valley of western Anatolia in 1241. Many Kipchaqs had become Christian even before their steppe-empire was overthrown by the Mongols, though mostly adopting the Latin Catholic rite. Once settled in Byzantine territory virtually all became Orthodox Christians. Thereafter they formed a standing army and light cavalry reserve which played a vital role against Nicaea's enemies in the Balkans and in the retaking of the imperial capital of Constantinople from the Latins. The Kipchaqs had not always proved loyal, however. Some deserted to the Bulgarians in 1256 and defeated their previous Byzantine masters near Didymoteichon. Those who remained in Byzantine service settled down as semi-nomads or even as farmers, being summoned from their settlements for specific campaigns, then returning home afterwards. They were last recorded by name in 1292, while a smaller élite unit of full-time soldiers may have remained closer to the Emperor though never quite rating as a guard regiment.[69]

As far as the Byzantine army was concerned, the name 'Turk' largely seems to have been reserved for Muslim Turks from Anatolia. During the Byzantine reconquest of western Anatolia before and in the aftermath of the First Crusade, many Turkish leaders and tribesmen deserted to the Byzantines. Many had, of course, been only nominally subject to the Seljuk Great Sultan, some had never accepted Seljuk overlordship and a great many were at most only superficially Islamic. These people rapidly converted to Christianity and were absorbed within the re-established Byzantine military structure.[70] Those Turks who subsequently deserted the independent Seljuk Sultanate of Rum in Anatolia during the course of the 12th century usually did so for internal political reasons, and from the mid-12th century onwards would have been more genuinely Muslim. They were presumably absorbed within a Byzantine-Turkish military group known as the *myrtaïtai* who were recorded as garrison troops in the later 12th century.[71] It is equally likely that this group itself evolved into the *Mourtatos* of 13th century Byzantine armies, the name stemming from the Arabic *Murtidd* via the Turkish *Murtat* meaning 'renegades'. Despite this unflattering name, the *Mourtatos* formed a high-status Byzantine guard unit under the Palaeolog Imperial dynasty.

Anatolian Turks clearly became more important in the armies of the Palaeolog Byzantine Emperors after they regained Constantinople in 1261, having already been present at the battle of Pelagonia where the Byzantine Emperor defeated a Latin Crusader army. Here such Turks were commanded by a Christian Turk named Nikephoros Rimpsas.[72] By this time the Seljuk Turkish Sultanate of Rum was already in decline, having been defeated by Mongol invaders at Köse Dağ in 1243. As the authority of the Sultanate fragmented, that of various Turcoman or Turkish tribal leaders increased. Some groups eventually succeeded in establishing their own small states, often referred to as *beyliks*, while less successful groups or others who feared Mongol retribution fled into Byzantine territory. Large numbers actually moved overseas, into the distant Byzantine province in the Crimea. Yet others, perhaps arriving via the Crimea, were settled by the Byzantine Emperor in the Dobruja region on the southern side of the Danube delta where they served as a frontier defence force for many years.[73] By the later 13th century Byzantine sources might also have been using the term *Tourkopouli* 'sons of Turks' to distinguish the Christian descendants of such troops from *Turks* who would appear to have been Muslims and others who had not yet converted.[74]

A closer study of Western European soldiers in Byzantine service shows that a great many were not really mercenaries. Many were political refugees while others settled down and attempted, not always successfully, to be accepted as Byzantine citizens. The sources are, meanwhile, not necessarily as clear as one might wish, merely referring to these assorted westerners as 'Franks'. Some so-called 'Franks' who had served in the Byzantine army commanded by George Maniakes in Sicily and Italy in the late 1030s and 1040s subsequently settled in Illyria on the other side of the Adriatic, in what is now Albania. Here they were known as *Maniakates* after their old commander. Some, or perhaps their sons, still formed a military unit in the 1090s under the command of a certain Constantin Humbertopoulos 'son of Humbert' who was himself of Western European family origin.[75]

Other troops of 'Frank' or Frankish family background fought in the Byzantine army which defended Nicaea in 1113 and in that which defended the island of Corfu in 1149.[76] Even after the Fourth Crusade, which seized Constantinople and established a Latin Empire in the heart of the now fragmented Byzantine world, troops of Western European origin continued to be recruited by the Byzantine successor states. Now often referred to as Latins as well as Franks, they formed almost half the army of the Empire of Nicaea which defeated the Seljuks at Antioch-on-the-Meander (not to be confused with Antioch on the Orontes on the Syrian frontier) in 1211, though they were almost wiped out in the process. Over the next three years the Nicaean Emperor rebuilt his victorious but shattered army with Turks, Armenians, Germans and Latins from his supposed great enemy, the Latin Empire of Constantinople.[77] The latter was, of course, already in such dire financial straits that it often could not pay its own soldiers.

Significant as such Western troops were in Byzantine armies, their importance has often been exaggerated by Western historians, especially where men from their own countries were concerned. This is particularly true of the admittedly very interesting and colourful but rarely very numerous 'English'. The main wave of Anglo-Saxon military migration to Byzantium was not immediately after the Norman Conquest of 1066 but came after 1069. On that occasion many in the Anglo-Saxon aristocracy and military élite of *thegns* had sympathised with a Danish invasion of England. Following the defeat of this little-known assault, the new Norman King William the Conqueror dismissed many of those Anglo-Saxons *thegns* who had been accepted into the new ruling class of England, seizing their lands and denying them and their descendants any significant military role.

Further Danish attacks in 1070 and 1075 deepened the Normans' suspicion of the Anglo-Saxons. Rather than accept such social and indeed financial demotion, many, though not of course all, of the sons of the defeated 'generation of 1066' left England and sought military service in Denmark. Like the other Scandinavian countries, Denmark had strong trading and military links in the east, not only with Russia where the Kievan state had largely been created by Scandinavian adventurers, but also with the Byzantine Empire. Here the *Varangians* who included both Scandinavians and what might be called Scando-Russians, had already earned a high military reputation as mercenaries during the 11th century. Large numbers of dispossessed Anglo-Saxons simply followed in their footsteps.[78]

Within a few years the Emperor was recruiting more such men, directly from 'isles of the sea' which must surely have meant the British Isles.[79] It is also worth noting that these later Anglo-Saxon recruits seem to have been largely young and militarily inexperienced, almost certainly youngsters from families whose fortunes had slumped in the new Norman-ruled Kingdom of England. This was why they now sought their fortunes in Constantinople,[80] the 'Great City' which had for so long featured prominently in Scandinavian and Anglo-Saxon tales of adventure and heroism. A particularly large contingent left England by sea around 1075. Another such supposed 'Anglo-Saxon fleet' was operating in the eastern Mediterranean when the First Crusade arrived at the close of the 11th century. In neither case can such an exodus have taken place against the wishes of England's Norman rulers. On the contrary, the Normans were probably glad to see such potential troublemakers leave.

There is some evidence that the Emperor Alexius I sent numbers of Anglo-Saxon volunteers to garrison an outlying Byzantine province in the Crimea,[81] and in 1088 there is the first clear reference to Anglo-Saxons in the Emperor's still largely Scandinavian *Varangian Guard*. Like their Scandinavian colleagues, the 'English' guardsmen were armed with large battleaxes.[82] A tradition of English recruitment was thus formed, English *Varangians* forming part of the Byzantine army that suffered defeat at Myriokephalon in 1176.[83] Although the survivors reportedly returned home, there is some evidence of a continuing English presence in the later *Varangian Guard*, though the latter became little more than a small ceremonial unit with clearly limited duties. It is possible that these later *Varangians* were actually Byzantinised descendants of English troops who still maintained a pride in their Anglo-Saxon heritage.

Norman mercenaries and military settlers were certainly more important from the late 11th century onwards. While the *Varangians*, Scandinavian or Anglo-Saxons, served as infantry or at most as mounted infantry, the Normans were cavalry. They were first recorded quite early in the 11th century, generally arriving in groups of more than one hundred men, often under leaders who had already proved successful in southern Italy where, of course, another more gradual and harder-fought 'Norman conquest' had begun.[84] Several of these Norman military leaders, or at least those who remained loyal to their Byzantine paymasters, subsequently founded Byzantine families who had a prominent military role for several generations.[85]

Other groups of Western mercenaries included Flemings and Germans. Count Robert of Flanders sent a contingent to help the Byzantines around 1090, before the First Crusade got under way. They formed a clearly defined regiment which fought against the Pechenegs in the Balkans rather than against the Muslim Turks in Anatolia, and appear to have served as heavily armoured cavalry. Most settled in the Byzantine Empire rather than returning home, and their descendants may have been absorbed into the *Varangian Guard*.[86] According to Princess Anna Comnena, Germans 'had long served in the Imperial army',[87] but little else is known about them during this early period. Even less is known about Hungarians in Byzantine service, though they do appear to have included men captured during various frontier wars between the Byzantine Empire and Hungarian Kingdom in the 11th and 12th centuries.[88]

Italians were more important and probably more numerous. They played a vital and increasing role in the Byzantine fleet, though Italian soldiers were also present on land alongside Germans in the army commanded by the Caesar, Nikephoros Bryennius, in the early 12th century.[89] Pisans fought in defence of Constantinople against the Fourth Crusade, though this was probably at least as much to protect their commercial interests as from loyalty to the Byzantine Empire.[90] An Italian named Aldobrandini was in command of the port city of Antalya when it finally fell to the Seljuk Turks in the early 13th century,[91] and significant numbers of Italian mercenary cavalry were operating in northern Greece in the early 1260s. They had probably been fighting for Charles of Anjou during his invasion of Byzantine territory, then served John the Bastard, the rebel son of the Despot Michael II of Epirus who ruled Thessaly, before ending up in the army of the Emperor Michael VIII Palaeologos.[92] Such multiple and indeed frequent changes of paymaster would become a feature of the confused warfare and politics of the declining Byzantine successor states and empires. The Italian admiral Licario from the Venetian-ruled island of Evoia was firmer in his loyalty to the Emperor Michael VIII, commanding a fleet and army which retook many of the northern Aegean islands in the 1270s, thus temporarily restoring Byzantine naval domination in the Aegean. His forces included not only Byzantine Greek troops and sailors but also Catalan and other Spanish mercenaries as well as Sicilians who had been in the invading Italian army defeated by Michael VIII at Pelagonia.[93]

Given the increasing hostility between the Crusader States in the Byzantine Empire as well as the desperate shortage of military manpower in these same states, the prominent role of mercenaries from various Crusader States in Byzantine armies might seem strange. Relations were still generally cordial when the Byzantines recruited knights from the Latin Crusader States of the Middle East for a naval assault upon Egypt in the mid-12th century,[94] but the political atmosphere was very different in the early 13th century. Nevertheless, the Byzantine successor Empire of Nicaea saw Latins not only serving as heavy cavalry but forming an influential part of the Byzantine imperial retinue. The majority apparently arrived from the rival Empire of Constantinople, though others came via Venetian colonial territory around the Aegean and even from the Crusader States in Syria.[95]

The 13th century Byzantine successor Empire of Trebizond similarly recruited mercenaries from a wide area. The bulk of the population probably consisted of indigenous Laz and Tzan tribes whose language and culture were essentially the same as those of neighbouring Georgia. The state was, however, dominated by Pontic Greeks who similarly traced their ancestry back to Classical if not Ancient times.[96] Alexios Comnenos had taken control of this outlying region of the Byzantine Empire in 1204, largely relying on Georgians to provide his military power base, while his brother David Comnenos briefly controlled Paphlagonia to the west with Georgian and local troops. Subsequently Alexios recruited 'Frank' mercenaries or auxiliary troops in his rivalry with the other main Byzantine successor empire, that of Nicaea, but most were reportedly killed in an unsuccessful campaign.[97]

Georgia itself was an independent and sometimes very powerful state. In the later 11th and early 12th century King David III of Georgia attempted to make the monarchy less dependent upon the old system of feudal levies by breaking away from existing military traditions. As a result the Georgian army no longer consisted solely of local feudal levies but included mercenaries, paid by and therefore more directly loyal to the king. Most of these troops were, however, not drawn from fellow Christian states but from the largely pagan Kipchaq Turkish tribes of the steppes north of the Caucasus Mountains.[98] On the other hand it might be rather misleading to see these Turks simply as mercenaries. As was the case in so many other parts of the medieval world, including Western Europe, paid foreign troops were actually drawn from states or peoples that were already close allies. This seems to have been the case in Georgia, at least in 1120–1 where there appears to have been a perhaps informal alliance between the Georgian King and the Kipchaq *Khan* or *khans*.[99]

The Despotate of Epirus was the third Byzantine successor state and it was based in a region of the old Byzantine Empire which had long been renowned for its Albanian and Vlach warriors. These communities, rather than the Greeks of the lowlands and the cities, subsequently formed the backbone of the Despotate's armies. The greatest and most ambitious of the Despots of Epirus was probably Michael II Doukas who ruled from around 1237 to 1271. He is known to have recruited 'Latin' or Western mercenaries, but very few other details are known about his army, or that of the other Despots.

ORGANISATION

The Byzantine military system which developed during the early medieval period, prior to the battle of Manzikert in 1071, was essentially based upon two separate but mutually supportive structures. At the centre were the metropolitan Imperial armies, largely based in or around the capital of Constantinople and under the immediate control of the Emperor. The other provinces of the Empire, and most particularly the frontiers both land and maritime, had their own regional forces, traditionally known as *themes* or *theme* armies. They would supposedly deal with all but the most serious invasions while themselves raiding enemy territory. In an emergency they could expect support from the central or imperial regiments. The latter were also available and designed for offensive operations beyond the imperial frontiers. That, at least, was the theory.

By the 11th century several aspects of classical Byzantine military structure had declined in effectiveness or were in disarray. One such was the *strateia* system in which families of middle but not aristocratic status owed military service in what was, in some respects, an almost feudal relationship with the government. This had emerged in the 10th century and had proved highly effective, not only in defending vulnerable frontier regions but in expanding Byzantine territory. By the 11th century, however, many such *stradioti* or provincial troops had commuted their military duties in favour of paying taxes with which the government hired more professional, though not always more reliable, mercenaries.[100]

As a result, in the well-recorded year of 1057, the eastern and south-eastern frontiers facing the Islamic world were defended by five separate corps of full-time soldiers, two of which consisted of Western mercenaries. The latter were dispersed in fortified strongpoints including the city of Edessa which would feature so prominently in the First Crusade. Their main base was, however, Malatya, a strongly walled city which had been one of the keys to domination of mountainous eastern Anatolia under earlier Islamic and now Byzantine rule.[101] The Byzantine authorities did not necessarily control the rural and still less the mountainous lands between their fortified garrison centres.[102]

Before Manzikert these were often dominated by disaffected Armenians and other local forces. After Manzikert many fell under the control of Turkish tribal raiders, infiltrators and outright conquerors, leaving the remaining Byzantine garrisons effectively isolated. Initially the latter held out in hope of relief from Byzantine field forces which were, however, now largely tied up in civil wars as various Byzantine leaders fought for the Imperial throne. On the other hand the Byzantines may have sent up to eight thousand 'Franks' or Western mercenaries to Vahram Varajnuni (Philaretus), the increasingly autonomous and eventually independent *Dux* of Antioch who took control of that city in 1079.[103] These troops formed the nucleus of Vahram's army and it is possible, indeed probable, that some of them or their sons were still in the area when the First Crusade arrived. A similar though less desperate situation developed in the Balkan provinces of the Empire.

During and after the Byzantine reconquest of western Anatolia, the new Comnenid dynasty of Emperors made a number of significant changes to Byzantine military organisation. New regiments included one called the *Archontopouloi*, meaning 'sons of *archons*', which was initially recruited from the children of men who had been killed during the loss of eastern and central Anatolia. Significantly perhaps, many of these new recruits came from military families which had lost their lands in the east and were therefore no longer able to maintain themselves or equip themselves as soldiers. The *Archontopouloi* gradually became an élite and almost a minor aristocracy based at the Byzantine imperial court, most of whom entered military careers after their training at court. These men maintained themselves with *pronoias* which were fiefs allocated by the government but only for the lifetime of the holder and which could be withdrawn at any time.[104]

The massive employment of external mercenaries during this period resulted in the appearance of new officials and new titles. One such was the *Sebastius* who was first recorded in the late 11th century and was the commander of foreign troops and, perhaps a few decades later, of those troops of non-Byzantine origin who had been assimilated into Byzantine society. Thereafter the *Sebastius* and other variations on this term remained an important office. In the 14th century he commanded Slav troops and, perhaps, Vlachs or Albanians.[105]

Following the successful experiment with the *Archontopouloi*, the 12th century Comnenid Emperors John and Manuel continued with efforts to rebuild a national or indigenous Byzantine army, including the settlement of prisoners of war in military colonies. Some of these men were supported by a new or at least enlarged and modified *pronoia* system of military fiefs, though this only became widespread after the further catastrophe of the Fourth Crusade in 1204.[106] The system of *themes* or military regions with their own small armies had declined by the late 12th century but was now rebuilt in the reconquered provinces of western Anatolia, including a new one called Neokastra. The latter still had its own army in the early 13th century as part of the Empire of Nicaea, though it is unclear if the same was true of all the other reconstructed *themes*. These later *theme* forces are likely to have garrisoned local forts and towns, probably under the command of the regional *Dux* or governor who also administered the local *pronoia* fiefs, and by the local *Stratopedarch*.[107]

Other attempts at military reform in the late 12th century improved the capabilities of local Balkan forces but seemingly had little impact on those in Anatolia.[108] It was a time of administrative weakness, even fragmentation, and as a result the local *archontes* of places like Greece became a sort of semi-official network of leading men who were not yet a distinct or recognised social group. They had nevertheless usurped many local military and administrative rights by the time Greece fell to invading Latin forces following the Fourth Crusade.[109]

The army of the Byzantine successor Empire of Nicaea under its initial Lascarid emperors was based upon existing 12th century Comnenid structures but built around a nucleus of Western mercenaries,[110] especially of men who had abandoned the already failing Latin Empire of Constantinople. It was notably expensive to maintain, especially after regaining substantial Byzantine territory in the Balkans. There was further development and extension of the *pronoia* system of fiefs which were introduced to the Izmir region for the first time. During this early Nicaean period some *pronoia* were known as *zeugelateion*, meaning that they were granted in perpetuity and were thus much more like Western European feudal fiefs.[111] Though they varied considerably in size, most *pronoias* were small and were given to local *stradioti* troops.[112] Some may only have been capable of supporting a single soldier without any followers. Other larger *pronoias* were allocated to members of the aristocracy who were expected to maintain a military retinue.[113] It proved to be a highly effective system and remained so under the subsequent Palaeolog Emperors, at least until the early or even mid-14th century.

The central corps of units which remained close to the ruler was still called the *Tagmata*, which was a term that had been used for many centuries. It included guards and soldiers of the imperial court and household, plus the field army. Elsewhere it seems likely that remnants of the old *theme* or provincial armies still existed. Some of these had already been subdivided into small units, the better to deal with Turkish raiding. They were now either revived or remained as effective local defences, each under their local *dux* or military governor throughout much of the 13th century.[114] The Byzantine higher aristocracy provided the senior command of Nicaean armies, usually being led by the Emperor or his *Grand Domestic*. Next in theoretical seniority came the *Protostrator* as the *Grand Domestic*'s deputy.[115]

In the 1250s Emperor Theodore II of Nicaea intoduced wide-ranging military reforms. He reduced the recruitment, pay and privileges of Western mercenaries while continuing his predecessors' policy of enlisting a larger proportion of local soldiers. He also created the new posts of *Grand Stratopedarch* as head of the commissariat, and *Grand Archon* responsible for the reorganisation of the imperial retinue as the élite core of the field army. New or modified military ranks were similarly introduced. They included that of *allagator* in charge of an *allagion* formation of indeterminate size, and *Grand Tzaousios* or senior *tzaousios*,[116] the latter rank being of Turkish origin, from the term *çau*. It was given to officers in command of garrison troops in a fortified town.[117]

Another command position was that of a *Stratopedarch* commander of a formation known as *Monokaballoi* who are likely to have been cavalry; of the *Tzaggatores* or crossbowmen; of the *Mourtatoi* who are generally believed to have been ex-Muslims; and of the *Tzakones* who originated as a regional force from southern Greece but were later an élite light infantry formation.[118] Two military units which had been prominent in the 11th and 12th centuries, the *Vardariots* and the *Varangians*, were now firmly attached to the Nicaean Imperial retinue. The former were under the authority of the *Primmikerios* and were responsible for maintaining order in camp, while the *Varangians* now guarded the imperial treasury at Magnesia (Manisa) and supplied bodyguards for the Emperor on his travels.

The entire imperial retinue was under the immediate command of the *Grand Primmikerios* and would theoretically remain so until the mid-14th century, though by then the *Grand Primmikerios* had few men to command. This senior officer was sometimes placed in command of the major garrisons in reconquered Macedonia.[119] One of the lowliest ranks in the imperial court was that of *paidopoula* or page. These youngsters were mostly selected around the age of seventeen, not always from aristocratic families, and were trained for both administrative and military careers.[120] Some rose to seniority and it is interesting to note that the system was copied or more likely absorbed intact by the Ottoman Turkish Sultans, in whose court such high-status trainees and pages were called *payks*. In contrast the *tzouloukonai* were servants or even mere camp-followers who were poorly armed and fought only in exceptional circumstances.[121]

The Nicaean Byzantine army was, or attempted to be, a highly structured and well-administered force, unlike the still largely feudal forces of the Latin Crusader Empire and States in Greece which were one of its major foes. Estimates of the

Right: 1. The eastern wall of Sahyun (Saone) castle, overlooking the massive man-made fosse. Sahyun is of particular importance because, with the exception of a Byzantine inner fort, virtually all its fortifications date from the 12th century Crusader occupation.

Below: 2. Yilanlikale is the most dramatic and well preserved of Armenian castles in what was the Kingdom of Cilicia or Lesser Armenia. It largely dates from the 13th century and typically makes full use of its location on a naturally defensible hilltop.

3. The substantially reconstructed southern walls of the fortified medieval city of Tarnovo, capital of t
Second Bulgarian Kingdom. Their design is typical of the strongly Byzantine influenced military architectu
of the later medieval Balkans.

4. The fortified port of Aigues Mortes, next to the Rhône delta in southern France, was built in the late
century by King Philip the Fair, primarily as a launching point for French Crusades across the Mediterran
Today the coast has receded some kilometres but during the medieval period the sea may have covered
reedbeds in the foreground of this photograph.

A series of 12th century carved relief on the façade of the church San Zeno in Verona illustrate the legend ˈ Roland and Faragut. Here the hero and the villain joust on horseback, both holding their lances in the •proved 'couched' manner as knights. The combat concludes in a subsequent panel, where they fight on foot with swords.

ι 13th century wall painting in the Crypt of Massenzio, beneath the Basilica at Aquileia in north-eastern ˏ, immitates a wall-hanging. It is particularly interesting because the subject illustrates a Christian knight suing a horse-archer. The latter, shown here, might be intended as a Saracen or Turk, but his military equipment and horse-harness actually look more Hungarian.

Above left: 7. A Byzantine wall-painting, showing Jesus being brought before Pilate, in the Church St. Neophytos in Cyprus was made around 1200 AD. Byzantine art is difficult to interpret as a source evidence for Byzantine arms and armour. However, this officer clearly wears a mail shirt, mail coif and carri a straight sword similar to those used in Western Europe. *Above right:* 8. An early 12th century capital the church at Mozac in central France. It illustrates the sleeping guards outside the Holy Sepulchre an though the carving is simple, it shows the chin-covering ventail of this man's mail coif hanging unlaced.

Above left: 9. Again the figures of sleeping guards outside the Holy Sepulchre provide information about arms and armour of the time and place when they were made, in this case later 13th century Germany. H the lower of the two carved figures inside the Mauritius Rundkapelle of Constance Cathedral has an e form of coat-of-plates which buckles at the back. *Above right:* 10. The Old Testament prophet Joshua, senior military leader, has been given the lamellar cuirass and domed one-piece helmet of the best equip Byzantine troops in this wallpainting in the monastery church of Osios Loukos in Greece. Dating from 10th century is also interesting for the 'pseudo-Kufic' or imitation Arabic writing on Joshua's helmet, w seems to have been fashionable in Byzantine armies around this time.

1. Othon de Grandson was one of the senior Crusader commanders during the final siege of Acre, which ·ll to the Mamluks in 1291. His exceptionally finely carved effigy in the Cathedral of Lausanne portrays the old warrior in old-fashioned mail armour, though he lived until 1328.

Although the wall painting of a huntsman with a crossbow from the Sanctuary of San Baudelio de ·langa dates from the 12th century and is therefore not amongst the oldest representations of this weapon, loes illustrate a very old-fashioned form, painted in an old-fashioned style, in in an area where Western :opean Christian and Western Islamic military technologies merged. The painting is now in the Prado Museum in Madrid.

13. Crac des Chevalier in Syria is often regarded as the finest of all Crusader castle. It is certainly spectacular and remarkably well preserved but, like virtually all Crusader castles in the Middle East, it was repaired and altered after being retaken by the Muslims in the 13th century. At Crac the southern outer wall, seen here on the right, was

4. This carved ivory box, dating from the 11th or 12th century, is a superb piece of Byzantine art. It is so typical in its use of ancient or classical motifs such as the nude figure, perhaps of Bacchus, on the left. evertheless the figure on the right, perhaps representing Mars, is shown in qute ordinary Byzantine military equipment of this period. The box is now in the Hermitage Museum in St. Petersburg.

Two other figures on the same Byzantine carved ivory box, dating from the 11th or 12th century, represent tly equipped infantry armed with sword and spear or javelin. Such soldiers formed the bulk of Byzantine armies. Now in the Hermitage Museum, St. Petersburg.

16. The circuit wall and towers of Avila in central Spain are perhaps the best preserved 12th century urb fortifications in Europe. Their design, with closely spaced towers protruding quite a distance from the m wall, probably reflects the adoption of mangonels as defensive stone-throwing machines, but the small s of these towers indicates that the machines in question were still of the relatively light man-powered rat than heavy counterweight form.

size of its individual units vary from three to five hundred men, though these may have become larger after the recapture of Constantinople in 1261. Groups of up to three hundred Kipchaq horse-archers were often attached to other units. Known as *Skythion*, the traditional Greek term for virtually all nomads north of the Black Sea, they were drawn from Kipchaq refugee communities that had been settled in the Balkans and Anatolia by Emperor John Vatatzes in 1241. Some of their chiefs entered Byzantine Imperial service but it seems that the warriors themselves were not under any particular commander. They did retain their tribal organisation and, more importantly, their valuable military traditions.[122]

More information is available about the army of the Palaeolog Emperors than on that of their Lascarid predecessors, especially after they regained the Byzantine Imperial capital of Constantinople. The first Palaeolog Emperor, Michael VIII, continued to build professional or otherwise élite units of *Latinikon* Western mercenaries and *Skythikon* settled, largely Kipchaq, Turkish refugees around the imperial retinue. Next came the *allagia* regiments drawn from or based within the Anatolian and Balkan provinces, those garrisoning some of the more important European cities being known as *megaloallagitai*. Whether this indicated higher status, larger numbers or greater strategic importance is unclear. It does, however, appear that such provincial regiments increased in number, perhaps reflecting a regionalisation of the army or at least a blurring of the distinction between field and provincial forces.[123]

The mercenaries remained vital, normally being employed in the field army and as expeditionary rather than garrison forces. Those of Latin origin were still regarded as potentially disloyal or troublesome, so the Palaeolog rulers tried to balance Latins based around the capital with indigenous Greek-speaking military units,[124] most particularly with the *Tzakones* who originally came from southern Greece. There they had been amongst the occupying Crusaders' fiercest opponents. In addition to considerably reorganising the *Tzakones*, who now became best known as marines, the Emperor Michael VIII created three new military formations or divisions after regaining Constantinople. These were the *Thelematarioi* consisting of Greeks living around the capital who had previously been under Latin rule, the *Gasmouli* who were supposedly descendants of mixed Greek and Latin marriages, and the *Prosalentai* who, like the *Thelematarioi*, were soldiers who supported themselves with relatively small allocations of land.[125] Service in all these formations was to some degree a hereditary obligation.

An interesting but not entirely reliable source maintains that the Nicaean army consisted of twenty-seven *allagia* or 'companies' at the battle of Pelagonia in 1259.[126] The Byzantine expeditionary force which began the partial reconquest of southern Greece from the Latin States in 1262 reportedly consisted of 20,000 men of whom six thousand were cavalry in eighteen *allagia*.[127] Thereafter Palaeolog Byzantine cavalry in the Peloponnese clearly consisted of *allagia* backed up by mercenaries under their own leaders plus local Albanian warriors, again under their own almost tribal leadership.[128]

After the retaking of Constantinople, the administration and to some extent the defence of the Empire's Balkan provinces was often delegated to senior members of the Imperial family. Those actually in command of local forces, defence, law and order were called *kephales*. However, there seems to have been overlap, and indeed competition, in responsibility between these imperial *kephales* and their supposed juniors, the local *kastrophylakes* fortress commanders and *prokathemenoi* senior civil officials, eventually contributing to an undermining of central government control.[129] Meanwhile the Byzantine provinces in Anatolia were increasingly dominated by a higher aristocracy to whom military responsibilities were delegated in a system comparable to that known in Western Europe as 'bastard feudalism'.[130] *Tourkopouli* remained an important element within Byzantine armies for the rest of the 13th and well into the 14th century. The militarily most significant of these Christianised Turks and their descendants were those who had settled along the Vardar river north of Thessaloniki and into Macedonia. Further south, the Slav peoples of the Peloponnese had retained their separate identity, tribal structure and military spirit throughout the Crusader occupation and continued to do so following the Byzantine reconquest.[131]

By the end of the 13th century it is possible, even perhaps likely, that the majority of soldiers in the central military formations under the Emperor's immediate command were *pronoia* holders. An interesting manuscript from the mid-13th century shows that a *stratior*, or soldier of the *stradioti*, was allocated his *pronoia* by the local *Dux* and then given proprietorial rights over a village, its people and its animals. This may, indeed, have been typical of the average *pronoia*.[132] The *Chronicle of the Morea*, which is an account of the Crusader conquest and occupation of southern and central Greece, only survives in a mid- to late 14th century Greek version and is therefore not entirely reliable. However, it might be more accurate where 13th and early 14th century Byzantines are concerned, suggesting that the local Byzantine *pronoia*-holding military élite consisted of cavalry followed by military dependants who may or may not have been mounted.[133] From the later 13th century onwards much of the *strateia* system appears to have been gradually demilitarised, with many *stradioti* commuting their military service in favour of paying taxes. As had happened several times in the past, the Byzantine government used such money to hire mercenaries. Although others continued to serve as soldiers, those of low status formed a local levy of auxiliary infantry and archers in support of the field armies.[134] One effect of these changes was to deny frontier communities their special military status, with an ultimately devastating impact on the morale of those defending Byzantine Anatolia against increasing Turkish pressure.

The little that is known about the military organisation of the Comnenid Empire of Trebizond suggests that in the 13th century it consisted of, or at least included, small cavalry units described by Western visitors as *lances*, a Western European term which might indicate some degree of similarity with Western armies.[135] Things would seem to have changed by the 14th century, and most available sources suggest that the army of Trebizond was by then small, ill-equipped and in many respects similar to that of the neighbouring Muslim Turks, though also warlike and bolder than the neighbouring fellow-Christian Georgians.[136]

The other main Byzantine rival to the revived Palaeolog Empire was the Despotate of Epirus which dominated Albania, much of north-western Greece and a substantial stretch of the Adriatic coast. Here Italian military as well as economic and cultural influence was growing stronger until, under the largely Italian Despots of the 14th century, the country and its military structures was largely feudalised. Its armies, like the state itself, were linguistically very mixed but still attempted to maintain sometimes anachronistic Byzantine terms. For example, the commander of the army of Epirus was sometimes known by the Byzantine title of *Protostrator* while some forces or regions were called *themes*, though they no longer had much in common with the highly structured Byzantine *themes* of earlier centuries.[137] The autonomous horse-rich region of Thessaly in central Greece similarly developed a strongly feudalised and even Westernised character during the second half of the 13th century. Its towns, though small, tended to be well fortified and were perhaps more important as *kastron* military centres than anything else.[138] Meanwhile the fully independent Balkan states of Bulgaria and Serbia based their military organisation and administration so closely and, it seems, so consciously upon those of the Byzantines that they were practically identical.

This was not the case with the independent Christian kingdoms east of the Byzantine frontier. Georgia, despite its close links with the separate Byzantine Empire of Trebizond in the 13th and 14th centuries, retained a distinctive military heritage which was rooted as much in that of Iran as that of Byzantium. Nor was this merely an ancient tradition that predated the Islamic conquest of Iran. Iranian, or perhaps more correctly Perso-Turkish, military influence was particularly strong in Georgia during the 12th century when Iran, like most of the rest of the Islamic Middle East, was ruled by the Seljuk Great Sultans and their increasingly independent regional governors. This was reflected in the adoption of Persian and Turkish military terms for much military equipment and in the continued use of some Persian ranks. The most obvious was the *Spaspeti* or commander-in-chief whose title came from the Persian term *ispahbadh*; a term which no longer retained its ancient military meaning in most Persian- or Turkish-speaking lands.[139]

Other, perhaps more complicated influences were at work in Cilician Armenia. Following the collapse of Byzantine rule in the late 11th century the frontier city of Edessa, and probably other Christian-dominated cities in this region, remained autonomous under Armenian governors who employed mercenaries when they could afford to pay them. Otherwise they had to depend upon their own urban militias. These mostly fortified cities along what is now the Turkish frontier with Syria were highly militarised, as were the neighbouring Arab-Islamic cities of northern Syria itself. Like them they usually had citadels and garrisons, and this was still the situation when the First Crusaders arrived at the end of the 11th century.[140]

To the west in Cilicia the newly emerging kingdom of Lesser Armenia was initially built upon essentially the same lines as the earlier kingdoms of the Armenian heartland of eastern Anatolia. Here powerful *nacharak'* barons were almost as powerful as the king in military and political terms. Their military obligations to the ruler were far from clear and were certainly not feudal in the sense of being in return for ownership of their lands. Beneath these *nacharak'* barons were the *azatk'* who did hold land in return for military service, and were the main source of Armenian troops. Beneath them in status were the serfs who lived in a state of hereditary servitude but did not have military obligations.[141]

King Leon II, who ruled from 1198 to 1219, is widely credited with major reforms of Cilician Armenia, both administrative, political and military. Under his rule a new and more Westernised feudal system was imposed, largely based upon that seen in the Crusader States of Syria and Cyprus. How far these changes really took root is a matter of debate, and the reality may not have reflected the theory. Nevertheless, King Leon II does seem to have reduced the autonomy of the *nacharak'* baronial class and to have bound it closer to the monarch; namely himself.[142]

Virtually nothing is known of the payment and organisation of the garrisons which defended Cilician Armenia for so long. Despite a superficial adoption of Western European feudal forms which saw the kingdom divided into counties and baronies, the *nacharak'* military system remained. The term *azatk'* was used more rarely, and instead seemingly a knightly class of *jiavors* appeared, probably with precisely the same origins as the old *azatk'*. Meanwhile the lowly class of bound peasants or serfs remained almost unchanged. The similarity between the Armenian term *jiavor*, the Turkish *çaus* and the Byzantine *tzaousios* was surely not coincidental. The army commander was still sometimes called the *Spasalar* but was also given the French title of *Connetable* while other officers included the *Bayl* (from the French *bailli*), the *Chantsler* (from the French *chancellor*), the *Marachakhd* (from the French *marshal*) and the *Avak Baron* or chief baron. Other titles such as *Sebastos* and *Proximos* came from Byzantine Greek.[143]

MOTIVATION

The Byzantine Empire had traditionally been a money-based commercial economy, more like the rival Islamic world and indeed modern societies. It was unlike early medieval Europe where land formed the basis of wealth and power for the great majority of those who had wealth or power in the first place. Yet things were changing, even by the 10th and 11th centuries, as great families maintained themselves through the possession of land as well as cash. Econonic, political and military changes further undermined the old Byzantine social order and its traditional attitudes, and as a result livestock became a major aspect of aristocratic wealth in many parts of what remained of the Byzantine Empire during the 12th and 13th centuries. This was apparent in Greece as well as the Balkans where it led to changes in attitudes towards the nomadic or transhumant and largely tribal peoples who dominated the uplands. Whereas these groups had previously been despised and feared, they now came to be seen as potentially wealthy as well as being sources of hardy warriors.[144]

Nevertheless, money remained central to the hiring of mercenary troops and for the maintenance of their morale as well as their loyalty. The most important mercenaries were also the most expensive; namely the armoured cavalry, a large proportion of whom came from Western Europe or the Latin Crusader States. Most were paid handsome wages, though some were provided with *pronoia* fiefs, in which case they seem to have been known as *kavallarioi*, from the French *chevalier* or knight.[145] *Pronoia* holders, whether indigenous or foreign, also received money wages and food supplies from the army stores while on campaign.[146] By the 1260s, however, it is clear that inflation and economic decline resulted in some *strateoiti* no longer being wealthy enough to equip themselves properly for a campaign and as a result they fell into debt. Indeed in many respects it seems that they now received less in real terms than their ancestors had done in the old *akritoi* frontier system, as it existed before the disastrous Byzantine defeat at Manzikert.[147]

Flags, banners and military music were used by Byzantine armies not only for command and control but also to raise morale. Anna Comnena's *Alexiad* describes military flags on poles decorated with silver nails,[148] while in the successor Empire of Nicaea each *allagion* military unit had its own banner.[149] A love of display is also apparent in the probably mid-11th century *Digekes Akritas* epic poem where an élite warrior's horse was described as being decorated with henna,[150] the red-brown dye similarly used to decorate horses' manes and legs in the neighbouring Islamic world. Perhaps this was another example of Arab-Islamic influence upon Byzantine frontier forces, the earliest surviving text of *Digenes Akritas* having been written on the frontier with Syria.

The *Digenes Akritas* epic also mentioned military music consisting of trumpets, horns, drums, cymbals and, rather more surprisingly, *organa* organs.[151] Anna Comnena certainly noted how Byzantine troops were roused from camp by drums and marched to the sound of flutes,[152] while military bands played a vital role during difficult manoeuvres.[153] Their enemies similarly noted the importance of military music in Byzantine armies, as seen in the *Danishmandname* medieval Turkish epic poem by 'Arif 'Ali of Toqat. Here the Christian Greeks were summoned to battle with essentially the same *naqar* drum, *nefir* trumpet and *zurna* large form of clarinet wind-instrument as used by the Turks themselves.[154]

Religion was a more important underpinning of military morale. Even so, the Byzantine Empire and its armies were much more diverse than those of Western Europe and while this diversity was largely linguistic or ethnic, there were significant religious divisions within the empire. The most significant had been that between the Orthodox Christian, largely Greek-speaking population and the Armenians who were so important as a source of troops. But as the military status and numbers of Armenian troops declined during the 11th and 12th centuries, so the tensions caused by their different version of Christianity largely dissipated.[155] Traditionally regarded as good soldiers but politically unreliable, such Armenians remained potentially dissident supporters of the Byzantine Empire until it was torn apart by the Fourth Crusade in 1204.[156]

Much of the Armenian military colony established by the Byzantine government on both sides of the Dardanelles Straits then allied itself with the European invaders, turning ruthlessly upon the local Greeks and, having then been abandoned by their new Crusader allies, attempting to form an alliance with the Bulgarians.[157] A similarly catastrophic sequence of events would soon be seen further east, in the Armenian heartlands of eastern Anatolia and in the new Cilician kingdom of Lesser Armenia. Here the arrival of the Mongols seems to have aroused hopes that Armenian power and glory could be revived as allies of these fearsome newcomers. Some popular stories of the time even portrayed the invaders as saviours of the Armenian Church and people.

Another dissident and more obviously persecuted religious group were the *Bogomils* who, in terms of their beliefs if not necessarily in terms of their ancestry, were descendants of the Manichaean or *Paulician* 'heretics' of earlier medieval eastern Anatolia. They are first recorded within Europe in 10th century Bulgaria. Their ideas then spread further westward to emerge as, amongst other so-called heresies, the *Cathar* movement in 13th century southern France. *Bogomilism* has been described as, at least in part, a social reaction against existing dominant élites, including rulers and church hierarchies. The movement tended to be more urban than rural, having a strong egalitarian and pacifist streak which limited its appeal to the military classes, while its ascetic and anti-marriage or anti-sex doctrines limited its appeal to ordinary people. For reasons which are unclear,

Bogomilism also tended be more anti-Catholic than anti-Orthodox, a factor which would be important in the later history of places like Bosnia under Ottoman rule. In fact the Balkan *Bogomils* survived persecution and marginalisation to become, briefly, a dominant military force in Bosnia shortly before its conquest by the Ottoman Turks. Thereafter many rapidly and voluntarily converted to Islam whose egalitarian doctrines were similar to their own.[158]

Secular motivation was a much more difficult factor to identify in all medieval military forces. Aristocratic pride and self-interest played its part in the Byzantine world, at it did everywhere else, but the provincial military minor aristocracy of the Byzantine Empire tended to be both more numerous, less influential and often more turbulent or unreliable than, for example, in many parts of Western Europe. This became increasingly the case during the mid- to late 13th century, especially in western Anatolia where such men and their families felt increasingly neglected by the Byzantine government. Here the *akritoi* local military class of the Sangarios (Sakarya) and Meander (Menderes) river valleys had always been more loyal to the old Lascarid dynasty of Nicaea than to the new Palaeolog Emperors. No longer even receiving reliable pay from their rulers, those that were not drafted to the Balkans to face Western threats to the Empire, now defected to the Turks in increasing numbers.[159]

With the probable exception of the Armenians and perhaps some tribal peoples of the Balkans such as the Albanians and Vlachs, pride in ethnic identity seems to have played little role in military morale amongst the 'native' peoples of the Byzantine Empire. One interesting exception was, however, the *Gasmoulis*. Their name is thought to be a combination of the medieval French *gars* or 'boy' and the medieval Greek *moulos* meaning 'mixed'. By origin these *Gasmoulis* were, in fact, regarded as the offspring of Latin Crusader fathers and local Greek Byzantine mothers. Despised by the Latins who carved out their new states in conquered parts of what are now Greece and north-western Turkey, they were welcomed as good soldiers by the 13th century Byzantine successor states,[160] because they supposedly combined the courage of Westerners with the intelligence of Byzantines.

Some soldiers of Byzantine origin had meanwhile tried to seek fame and fortune in Latin service in the wake of the Fourth Crusade. One such was Michael Ducas who came from a long-established Byzantine aristocratic and military family. However, Latin prejudice and arrogance towards Byzantines was such that he gave up the attempt and instead gathered sufficient indigenous local support around Arta in western Greece to establish the Despotate of Epirus as a separate state.[161]

Apart from death or injury in battle, captivity and the hope of ransom were important factors in the morale of Byzantine troops. At least as far back as the 10th century, the Byzantine and neighbouring Islamic government had developed systems for prisoner exchange. This not only included military personnel, but also the substantial numbers of captives taken either as slaves or for their ransom value.[162] As a result Byzantine troops could face the prospect of capture with perhaps greater confidence than could their Western European counterparts where, with the exception of the Iberian peninsula, there was as yet no comparable mutually acceptable system of prisoner exchange.

The sudden appearance of the Turks in the east, followed by the Crusades and the establishment of Latin Crusader States in the Middle East, upset this almost comfortable modus vivendi, especially where prisoner exchanges were concerned. It would soon be re-established with the Islamic Seljuk Turkish states but it took longer for the Crusaders and other westerners to learn to appreciate such more civilised attitudes towards at least some of the hazards of warfare.[163] Even then, savagery remained and it is worth noting that the wars between Bulgaria and the Latin Empire of Constantinople during the early 13th century were often little more than slave-raids. They certainly contributed a great deal to a decline in the Greek population of Thrace, leaving it open for Turkish colonisation following the Ottoman invasion which began in 1352.

STRATEGY

By and large the armies of the Byzantine and Orthodox Christian countries shared the same traditions of strategy, tactics and combat styles, but with stronger Turco-Persian and Arab-Islamic influences amongst the Georgians and Armenians. In broad strategic terms the Byzantine Empire's eastern provinces or border zones had traditionally been, and continued to be, regarded as an ideological frontier unlike that seen on the Empire's western frontiers. To the east the Islamic world had taken over from the Persian empires as the main cultural rival of Graeco-Roman and now Christian Byzantine civilisation. Beyond the Empire's western frontiers lay fellow Christian states, some of which shared the Byzantines' Orthodox faith while even those Latin Catholics who followed a slightly different version of Christianity were at least fellow-believers. While the Byzantines may have regarded the latter as virtual barbarians, they were not seen as real rivals, as were the Muslims. It was largely for this reason that the east was marked by a broad and barely populated no-man's-land which became a true military frontier.[164]

From the first eruption of the Muslim Arabs from Arabia in the 7th century until the 9th century the Byzantine Empire was the weaker party and had evolved a highly successful defensive guerrilla strategy known as 'shadowing warfare'. It was also used on the Islamic side of the frontier but was clearly more typical of Byzantine forces. During the 10th century, however, the political fragmentation of the 'Abbasid Caliphate and perhaps also some element of economic decline within the Arab-Islamic states led to a significant shift in the military balance.

This was accompanied by a series of increasingly ambitious offensives by Byzantine Emperors which involved significant changes in both broad strategy and battlefield tactics. The most dramatic of these was the revival of heavily armoured shock cavalry. Their tactics closely reflected those of previous generations of heavy cavalry on the Islamic side and were remarkably similar to the tactics of the supposedly newly invented 'knightly cavalry' of 11th and 12th century Western Europe. This even extended to their use of the *couched* lance and long, kite-shaped shield popularly known in Western Europe as the 'Norman shield'.

A period of dramatic Byzantine expansion and consolidation lasted into the 11th century but then petered out with a widespread feeling within the Byzantine Empire that the state was now secure. Certainly the Islamic Middle East, on the other side of a now more distant frontier, had become extraordinarily fragmented and militarily weak. Many of the Byzantine ruling élite seem, in fact, to have regarded a substantial army as an expensive luxury that was no longer really required. Consequently the Byzantine army declined in size, prestige and in funding. On the other hand, various forms of sometimes specialised troops developed during the age of conquest remained in place.

Paradoxically, the outpouring of tactical, strategic and other forms of military literature which had been seen in the 10th century continued throughout much of the 11th. Some of it was new and original while some was virtually a reworking or updating of respected ancient military texts such as that of the Greek *Elian the Tactician.*[165] Elian was similarly studied and incorporated into theoretical and practical military texts on the Arab side of the frontier. More original was the *Taktika* written by Nikephouros Ouranos, probably during his time as governor of the newly conquered Syrian city Antioch in the first years of the 11th century.[166] Parts of his text show the author's pragmatic approach to a number of military problems and clearly reflect firsthand experience of warfare against the Muslims of Syria, especially where siege warfare is concerned.[167] This interest in military writing continued after the catastrophic battle of Manzikert, the *Strategikon* by Kekaumenos probably dating from around 1075.[168]

Byzantium's military situation after Manzikert was, of course, very different to the rather self-satisfied assurance of the earlier 11th century. The Empire was now fighting for its survival, just as it had in the 7th century in the face of the first wave of Arab-Islamic expansion. Now the most threatening enemy were Muslim Turks, but, as had been the case in the 7th century, these enemies from the east were not the only ones beating at the Empire's gates. There were formidable enemies in the west as well. The question has sometimes been asked: why did Byzantine armies not return to the 'shadowing warfare' which had served so well during the

Empire's previous fight for survival? In reality the situation was very different. In the 7th century the Byzantines had lost the fortified cities of Syria and what was then known as Mesopotamia, rendering the surrounding open plains indefensible. They therefore fell back into the mountains which thenceforth formed a no-man's-land between two essentially urban civilisations.

Despite the severity of the crisis, the 7th century Byzantine state, government and armies had not collapsed into prolonged civil war as happened in the last quarter of the 11th century. Furthermore these new, largely Turkish invaders were nomads, far less vulnerable to mountain ambushes than the 7th and 8th century Arab armies had been. To some extent the Turks ignored the mountains once they had penetrated the central high plains of Anatolia where, in the 12th century, they established their own new and increasingly urbanised states. Here it is worth noting that theories of wide-ranging cooperation between Byzantine 'rebels' and some Turkish invaders in the years after Manzikert seem to have been overstated. One supposed case of concerted action was between Rapsomates who governed Byzantine Cyprus, Caryces who similarly governed Byzantine Crete, and Çaka the newly established Turkish *amir* of Smyrna (Izmir). Although this Turk's ambitions seem to have been huge, he, like the two Byzantine 'rebels', was merely reacting to the current chaotic situation rather than seeking to form alliances which would enable the participants to divide the Empire between them.[169]

Once the Byzantine Empire had regained a unified central government under Emperor Alexius I, its armies returned to the offensive in the broken but lower, less harsh and more fertile hill country of western Anatolia. This they regained with relative ease against greatly outnumbered and frequently divided Turkish opponents, employing normal offensive tactics, siege warfare and remarkably effective diplomacy. The situation was in almost all respects entirely different to that seen during the initial waves of Arab-Islamic conquest.[170] The subsequent centuries were far from being the most glorious in Byzantine military history, but they did produce one of the most interesting military manuals of the later Middle Ages. This was written in 1326 by Theodore Palaeologus, a prince of Byzantine origin who spent much of his life in northern Italy and thus could be seen as the product of two not entirely dissimilar military traditions. His work clearly contains Italian elements but by this time Byzantine warfare was already under strong Italian as well as Turkish influence. So it seems likely that Theodore's work reflects the Byzantine military ideas of his day or perhaps of a generation earlier.[171]

As already stated, Byzantine offensive warfare had largely focussed on the eastern frontier for many years. Having retaken a large part of the mountainous frontier zones in eastern Anatolia, Byzantine armies could turn south into the virtually open plains of northern Syria. This was an urbanised area where the cities, though powerfully fortified and with warlike reputations of their own, remained vulnerable because of their dependence on the intensively cultivated areas around them. Though not necessarily oases in the strict sense of the word, they were often oasis-like in economic terms. However, instead of striking directly towards the great cities of the Syrian interior such as Aleppo and Damascus, the Byzantines focussed on guarding their flank by trying to take control of the coastal mountains bordering the Mediterranean where Byzantine fleets now dominated at least the waters between Anatolia, Cyprus and northern Syria.

The resulting little-known but, from the point of view of Crusader history, significant struggle in 11th century northern and coastal Syria was a war of fortresses. There were already many strong castles in this area, and against them the large and notably well-equipped Byzantine armies brought the very latest in siege weaponry. Powerful siege trains formed part of most major Byzantine armies while comparable equipment was used to defend castles, cities and ports once these had been captured. Greek Fire was even used against men in fixed positions and, as was more normal, against wooden structures including ships.[172] Meanwhile the same technology was also available to their enemies, perhaps in even more advanced forms (see volume II), but the Muslims were politically, militarily and indeed religiously divided.

The Emperor Alexius I Comnenus was clearly focussing upon regaining the ports and coasts when his plans were interrupted and to some extent superseded by the arrival of the First Crusade.[173] Nevertheless, the Comnenid campaigns to regain the coasts and immediate hinterlands of Anatolia in the late 11th and early 12th centuries were so similar to the war of the Syrian coastal mountains that one is tempted to suggest that the records of the previous struggle must have been fresh in the minds of the Emperor and his generals.[174]

Following the Fourth Crusade and the temporary loss of the imperial capital of Constantinople to the Latins, Byzantine forces rarely undertook significant offensives against their Turkish Islamic eastern neighbours. Instead their offensive efforts were directed against the Latin Crusader States planted in the Byzantine heartlands. Nevertheless the people of the mountainous Anatolian frontiers of the Nicaean Empire did raid Seljuk Turkish areas for booty, or in reprisal for Turkish raids. These were not normally carried out by the Nicaean imperial army but by local militias whose activities thus enabled the core regiments to be focussed elsewhere.[175] Even in the Balkans and Greece, 13th and 14th century Byzantine forces tended to avoid direct clashes with their Latin or Western European enemies, relying on almost guerrilla campaigns of ambush, raid and ruse. The great battle of Pelagonia in 1259 was therefore something of an exception, and even this could be seen as an ambush on a grand scale.[176] Byzantine forces resisting Angevin-Italian invasion and occupation in Albania continued this same tactical tradition, putting particular effort into severing the enemy's communications between the coast and their few inland strongpoints.

One significant battle fought in 1281 resulted from an Angevin leader trying to cross a river with a force of heavy cavalry, perhaps to break a Byzantine blockade. Byzantine light infantry, lying in ambush, shot down the enemy's horses and then defeated the cumbersome armoured knights with ease, capturing their leader as the survivors fled.[177] This battle was, in many respects, similar to that of Pelagonia a generation earlier.

Byzantine defensive tactics in eastern Anatolia reflected the fact that there were only four practical invasion routes through the Taurus and Anti-Taurus mountain ranges to the plains and cities of the central plateau. The first ran from the north coastal plain of Cilicia through the Taurus via a pass known as the Cilician Gates to Tyana (now Niğde). The second ran north from Maraş through the eastern Taurus to Caesarea (now Kayseri). A third ran from al-Massisa in eastern Cilicia via the Seyham river valley, again converging on Caesarea. The fourth, from Malatya through the Anti-Taurus, similarly headed for the strategically key city of Caesarea or northward to Sebastea (Sivas).

Access from Iran and Azarbayjan through the mountains of Armenia and north-eastern Anatolia was more limited and the most important route followed the upper Euphrates valley to Koloneia (Kamacha) and Trebizond (Trabzon). Once through one or all of these, an invader had an extensive network of roads, mostly dating from Roman times but still in use, before him.[178]

The first Byzantine military reaction to their monumental defeat at Manzikert was to repair fortifications, at least where they still controlled them. This policy was continued throughout the reign of Alexius I who naturally concentrated on the coastal strongpoints. His son, the Emperor John, extended the policy inland, repairing, strengthening and building new fortifications to block potential invasion routes down the main river valleys to the fertile coast which was now firmly back under Byzantine rule. The largest of these fortresses also served as secure military bases for his own offensives and reprisal campaigns into the interior. John's son, the Emperor Manuel, did the same, constructing a sequence of frontier forts to block the upper reaches of the vulnerable valleys.

During the early 13th century John III Ducas Vatatzes, the second ruler of the Byzantine successor Empire of Nicaea, further strengthened these Anatolian frontier defences with a series of new 'military villages' while the castles themselves served as regional arms depots as well as garrison centres. Such garrisons often consisted of free men of non-noble, sometimes peasant status. Most were not from the immediate area but had been given land near the fortifications and undertook military service in return for tax exemption. In some regions archaeological research shows that during the 13th century the local populations were gradually becoming more concentrated in and around these fortifications. At Ephesus, for example, the ancient classical Graeco-Roman and early Byzantine city became little more than a fortress while the bulk of the inhabitants moved to nearby but more defensible Ayasoluk with its great castle of Selçuk.[179] It was clearly an effective defensive policy which survived until the renewed Turkish or Turcoman tribal infiltrations of the later 13th century.[180] Its failure was then a result of political neglect and a withdrawal of garrisons to face problems in the Balkans.

Defensible mountain passes, especially where dotted with fortifications, were essential to the protection of the isolated Empire of Trebizond during the 13th to 15th centuries. Here Turkish and any other raiders faced the problem of occasionally appalling, indeed almost subtropical, rain as well as dense forests in which the Turks and the flocks upon which they depended could easily be ambushed.[181] The Cilician Kingdom of Lesser Armenia lacked the subtropical climate and the dense forests. Instead its defence rested upon the high mountains and deep valleys of the Taurus Mountains. These shut off the fertile, but also often unhealthy, coastal plain not only from now Turkish-ruled central Anatolia but also from the centres of Islamic power in Syria. Because invaders had to use such a limited number of routes they could rarely hope to achieve surprise. Furthermore their own communications and their route home remained vulnerable to attack by defending troops.[182]

The mountainous heartland of the Cilician Armenian state was regarded as so vital that even the allied Crusader Military Orders were not allowed to garrison fortifications here. Instead they were permitted to hold and defend a few lowland and eastern castles, especially those in close contact with the sea. Nor was Cilicia's long coastline as vulnerable as it might at first appear, since it was shallow, very exposed to storms and had few good harbours. Furthermore, from the 12th to 15th centuries Christian fleets, mostly from Italy, dominated this part of the Mediterranean.

It was those self-same passes which the Byzantines had defended against Islamic invaders from the south and east, including from Cilicia itself, which Cilician Armenian forces now defended against Islamic raiders from the north and, as before, from the east. One major Turcoman raid broke through into Cilicia in 1187, reaching the fortified Armenian capital Sis, but was nevertheless defeated by the army of King Leon.[183] Like the Byzantines before them, the Armenians also occasionally launched counter-raids, but more often it seems that they were more concerned to resupply threatened castles. One such reprisal expedition was in 1264 against Turcoman tribes from Karaman. On this occasion an Armenian baggage train, carrying grain for the hungry garrison, was guarded by cavalry and infantry. The former included horse-archers who were able to ambush and defeat the opposing Turks.[184]

TACTICS

The abundant surviving tactical and other military treatises from the Byzantine Empire tell us a great deal about what Byzantine tactics were supposed to be like. They do not necessarily tell us what really happened on the battlefield. On the other hand, additional historical sources, including descriptions of warfare against Byzantine forces written by those 'on the other side of the fence', do indicate that the theory and the reality were not entirely separate. This in turn suggests that some, if not all, Byzantine manuals probably served a practical training purpose some way down the chain of command, and did not merely provide debating points for rulers and senior generals.[185]

A particularly detailed mid-10th century technical text stated that, as a battlefield ideal, 6,000 cavalry should operate from within a defensive infantry square of 16,000 heavy and light foot soldiers who were themselves in units of 1,000. A consistent overall ratio of four infantrymen to every cavalryman seems to have been preferred, though this did not apparently apply to what was regarded as the largest practical forces of 40,000 cavalry and 100,000 infantry.[186]

Further fascinating tactical details are found in Byzantine historical and biographical sources. For example Anna Comnena, in her *Alexiad*, mentioned that charging with a lowering sun in their eyes proved a problem for Byzantine cavalry around the turn of the 12th century.[187] This difficulty was also highlighted in greater detail in medieval Islamic tactical manuals. Nicetas Choniates, describing a final battle against the Hungarians in 1167 during the reign of the Emperor Manuel Comnenus, stated that the enemy did not form up with separated right and left wings as the Byzantines would have done. Instead they assembled in a single line with an ox-drawn 'banner cart' of *caroccio* in the centre. The Hungarians launched a massed charge but were defeated by the Byzantines' more flexible and controlled counter-attacks.[188]

A little under forty years later, Byzantine forces defending their capital of Constantinople faced a Western European enemy in the form of the Fourth Crusade. One of their mostly French opponents described the Byzantine army as having formed up in six battalions outside the city walls with *sergeants* and 'squires' on foot behind their cavalry, but with archers and crossbowmen in front of these cavalry. This was a normal frontal array for that period, but was quickly brushed aside by the invading Crusaders.[189]

Byzantine forces from the Empire of Nicaea had returned to more thoughtful, careful and considered tactics by the time of the battle of Pelagonia in 1259. Initially Emperor Michael Palaeologus of Nicaea had avoided direct clashes with the armies of his foes, King Manfred of Sicily and the Despot of Epirus. Meanwhile Michael's brother John held the higher ground with the Nicaean armoured cavalry while the lighter Greek, Kipchaq and Anatolian Turkish cavalry harried the enemy in the neighbouring plain. The Nicaean forces also misled the enemy by making their numbers appear larger than they were. This they did in the night by lighting more camp-fires than they needed and in the day by moving herds of cattle around to raise additional dust.[190] Eventually the opposing vanguards met while Michael's troops continued to harry the enemy. Then, before dawn, the Despot of Epirus fled, perhaps fearing that his Western allies would betray him. During the morning the Westerners also tried to flee but at this point the Nicaeans attacked and won a complete victory. Very few of their enemy escaped because the Byzantine light cavalry could move much faster.[191] The lighter equipment and greater nimbleness of Byzantine infantry archers and their Turkish light cavalry allies or mercenaries also enabled them to inflict a signal defeat on Sully, the military governor of Albania, on behalf of the Angevin ruler of southern Italy, near Berat in 1281.[192]

Military manuals indicate that Byzantine forces tried to pay particularly careful attention to their organisation while on the march, at least during their periods of military success. One treatise *On Siege Warfare*, probably written in the late 10th or early 11th century, deals with some aspects of such a march. In particular, it refers to an officer called the *monoprosopon* who was in charge of munitions while crossing enemy territory. He was similarly responsible for looking after the wounded.[193]

Another text, entitled *Campaign Organisation and Tactics*, seems to reflect the Byzantine military situation in the Balkan situation in the late 10th century, though the surviving text was written fifty or so years later. It maintained that when an army was on the march the cavalry should go in front, followed by the infantry with flank guards.[194] The major threat to such a column seems to have been from fast-moving enemy light cavalry, and, to guard against these, substantial numbers of infantry archers should be posted along the outsides of the line of march.[195] Other men, presumably used as pioneers, used axes to clear roads or passes of vegetation which would not only obstruct the road but could hide ambushes.[196] An army was particularly vulnerable when moving through a defile or pass, in which case javelin-throwers and light troops such as archers and slingers should control the slopes on either side as the rest of the army marched through.[197]

It seems to have been the Emperor Manuel's failure to follow such advice that led to his defeat at Myriokephalon in Anatolia in 1176. Here the Byzantines' foes were Seljuk Turks whose tactical traditions were as sophisticated and at least as effective as their own. This time the Byzantine army pressed their advance through a pass and were ambushed. Manuel's Latin heavy cavalry mercenaries had been placed on the right flank, perhaps because this would have become the traditionally offensive right wing once the Byzantine army opened out into its full battle array. This never happened, however, and the Western European knights, many of them from the Crusader Principality of Antioch, were routed by the Turks, igniting a panic which infected much of the rest of the army.[198]

The text entitled *Campaign Organisation and Tactics* also paid close attention to fortified encampments, for which the Byzantine army had been renowned since Late Roman times.[199] Foot soldiers were responsible for placing *calthrops*, pieces of iron with four spikes, one of which always pointed vertically, outside the camp. They were mostly a threat to horses' feet but could also also injure unwary infantry. These Byzantine *calthrops* were, however, apparently tied together with string so that they could be recovered even when hidden in grass, perhaps even from inside the camp.[200] There was also concern to avoid incendiary weapons falling onto the men in camp,[201] while the layout of the encampment itself varied according to the terrain.[202]

The *Taktika* military manual by Nikephoros Ouranos similarly mentioned *calthrops* as well as other devices to be placed in the ditches which surrounded a properly fortified military camp.[203] Nor was all this knowledge merely theoretical, even if it did not necessarily bring victory. In 1030, for example, the Byzantine Emperor launched a large and ambitious invasion of northern Syria. This took them beyond the mountains into the broad fertile plain north of the powerful Islamic city of Aleppo. The Emperor established a base-camp near Azaz (now a frontier town on the Turkish–Syrian border). This they fortified with palisade and ditch, but the Arab Mirdasid rulers of northern Syria had the support not only of their own bedouin and related tribes but also of the local settled peoples. As a result the Byzantine army found itself penned within its camp, running short of water and supplies while the Arabs controlled the surrounding countryside. Eventually the Emperor decided to withdraw but was then pounced upon by the lighter but well-equipped enemy cavalry.[204] The Byzantine retreat became a virtual rout, especially when the infantry 'shield bearers' who were defending the ditch feared being left behind and abandoned their posts. The local population then overran the Byzantine army's fortified camp and, joined by many Armenian soldiers who now deserted the Emperor, seized huge quantities of booty.[205]

Where specific cavalry battlefield tactics were concerned, the *Taktika* credited to the Emperor Leo VI and dating from the early 10th century described the background to the period under consideration. Here 'current tactics' had Byzantine horse-archers shooting while their horses stood in ordered ranks, loosing volleys at command. The front rank supposedly shot first, then bent forward over their horses' necks to allow a clear field of fire for the rank behind, this being repeated until the rear rank had loosed their arrows. It was, in fact, a version of the 'shower shooting' which had been characteristic of Sassanian Persian and other settled rather than nomadic horse-archers since pre-Islamic times, and would be brought to a peak of development within the Islamic Middle East (see volume II).

Similarly disciplined cavalry tactics remain the ideal, though not necessarily the norm, in Byzantine armies of the Comnenid period. According to Anna Comnena, the best Byzantine horse-archers still operated in disciplined units and could fight as infantry archers, spare arrows being brought up to their formations by mules.[206] Anna similarly described how the invading Norman cavalry under Bohemond of Taranto were defeated by archers who killed or wounded their unarmoured horses, though their heavily armoured riders were difficult to hurt.[207] The similarities between this confrontation and that between Crusaders and Islamic forces in Syria is striking. All the sources make it clear that Comnenid cavalry were divided into light and heavy. The former were employed as, amongst other things, fast-moving raiders whereas the latter were armoured and seem to have been used in much the same way as Western European knights. They rode Arab or Hungarian horses and were armed with maces as well as other normal cavalry weapons plus long kite-shaped shields.[208]

What was clearly different about Byzantine cavalry was that many of the heavily armoured men seem to have been equipped as horse-archers and, as such, had much more in common with the élite heavy cavalry of the Islamic world than with the knights of Western Europe. At the battle of Zimony against the Hungarians in 1167, according to Nicetas Choniates, the main Hungarian formation was attacked by Byzantine horse-archers in its rear and flanks, apparently after the Hungarians themselves had launched an all-out cavalry charge. It is also significant that this Hungarian charge did not break the Byzantine formation, though part of the latter lured the enemy forward with a feigned flight. Furthermore the Byzantine heavy cavalry were sufficiently well armoured to meet the Hungarians in a hand-to-hand mêlée where their own maces proved particularly effective against the armoured Hungarians.[209] The mace was, of course, primarily designed to stun or injure an opponent, even if it failed to penetrate or break his armour. On the other hand, little under fifty years later the Byzantine troops defending Greece were described as lightly armoured when compared to Westerners in the wake of the Fourth Crusade, and proved unable to resist the invaders in close combat.[210]

The *Taktika* credited to the Emperor Leo VI described an early 10th century Byzantine infantry defensive formation in which the front rank knelt behind their shields, those behind standing with their shields protecting their chest, and those behind holding shields over their heads. To what exent this level of discipline survived amongst Byzantine foot soldiers of the later 11th and 12th centuries remains doubtful. None the less, command and control as well as battlefield communications continued to be taken very seriously. The treatise entitled *Campaign Organisation and Tactics* made clear the paramount need for agreed and properly understood passwords and recognition signals, especially when fighting in dusty conditions, fog or at night.[211]

TRAINING

Military training is an area in which a highly structured, professional and reportedly disciplined army such as that of the Byzantine Empire might have been expected to excel. Certainly it was the subject of considerable thought, with different groups of soldiers, including those from different ethnic origins, seemingly being trained to use their own traditional weaponry. This did not, however, preclude élite units developing multiple skills. For example the *Varangians*, including those referred to as *Rhos* from Russia, clearly fought as mounted infantry with spear and shield as well as on foot from the late 10th century onwards.[212] They may even have served as cavalry, though perhaps not until the 11th century.[213] Stemming initially from Scandinavia, these 'eastern Vikings' might have been expected to serve on foot or aboard ship, yet it must be borne in mind that the Viking invaders of north-western Europe seized horses whenever they could, becoming high-speed raiders on land just as they already were at sea. Indeed it is possible that the Vikings played an important role in the spread of stirrups from the western steppes, Russia and Middle East to Western Europe.

Of course these *Vanagians* remained best known for their battle-axes which were used in defence of Constantinople in 1204 and were still mentioned in the mid-14th century at virtually the close of *Varangian* history. A much earlier source refers to a mid-11th century Varangian soldier in disguise, with his helmets and weapons hidden beneath his clothes. Of course he lacked the shield which would have exposed his identity, and was therefore obliged to wrap a cloak around his left arm as a rudimentary form of defence.[214] Exactly this behaviour was illustrated in a Byzantine or Lombardic manuscript from southern Italy, from the immediately pre-Norman period.

Ordinary, presumably non-élite Byzantine infantry archers were still sufficiently well trained to successfully defend the Emperor's fortified camp against the Turks before the battle of Manzikert in 1071,[215] though the subsequent battle itself resulted in defeat. Thereafter the Emperor Alexius I, as part of his efforts to revive the Byzantine army, was said to have trained infantry archers to shoot at an angle to their line of battle, in an effort to strike the right or unshielded sides of their enemies.[216] This again recalls more detailed archery instructions in medieval Arab-Islamic training manuals.

By the later 12th century, Byzantine infantry or urban militias were also using crossbows in open battle, as well as traditional handbows and slings, though little is known of their methods or standards of training. Though defeated with relative ease by King Richard of England in his conquest of Cyprus during the Third Crusade,[217] Byzantine crossbowmen may have become more formidable by the 14th century when the *Danishmandname* Turkish epic poem by 'Arif 'Ali of

Toqat made much of the danger they posed to the Turks' horses.[218] Further east, the Georgians were considered by the Italian merchant and traveller Marco Polo to be very good archers and fair soldiers, though he does not mention crossbows in this context.[219]

Cavalry, as usual, received more attention in specialist military manuals, chronicles and warlike epic literature. Consequently more is known or can be deduced about their specific styles of combat and thus of training. An emphasis upon the spear or lance, sword and shield was much the same in the epic *Digenes Akritas* poem from the mid-11th century frontier regions near Syria,[220] and in Anna Comnena's biography of her father, the late 11th and early 12th century Emperor Alexius I.[221] In her description of one particular combat Anna stated that a cavalryman attacked by another horseman with a sword did not draw his own blade but instead took the mace which was hung from his saddle and used it to stun and then capture his opponent.[222] A century and a half later a description of a Cilician Armenian army which inflicted a defeat upon the neighbouring Seljuk Turkish Sultanate of Rum only mentions spear-armed Armenian cavalry.[223]

According to the Syrian Christian chronicler, Matthew of Edessa, the lightly equipped Armenians of the Vaspurakan region in the old Armenian heartland of eastern Anatolia attempted to attack a Turkish force in 1021. The latter were still newcomers in this area, noted for their long hair and skill as horse-archers. When the Armenians attacked with drawn swords they lost heavily to the Turks' arrows, whereupon their commander announced: *'Let us withdraw and put on our armour to resist the arms we see in the enemy's hands and to protect us from their arrows'*.[224] Written a few decades later, the *Digenes Akritas* epic refers to light cavalry armed with *belesin* javelins.[225] According to the Byzantine chronicler Psellus, javelins from the hands of Georgian warriors could knock a man out of his saddle.[226]

Nevertheless it is clear that the bow and arrow remained the most important missile weapon amongst Byzantine light cavalry right up until the fall of the Empire in the 15th century. Indeed its importance may have revived in the 13th century and later, after witnessing something of a decline under the 12th century Comnenid Emperors. Horse archery had been a major aspect of the training of indigenous Byzantine élite troops since at least the 10th century [227] and would remain a vital part of the military education of the Byzantine aristocracy.[228] By the 13th century the aristocracy of the largely isolated eastern Empire of Trebizond also played polo which they had adopted from their Islamic neighbours.[229] Polo may have reached the Byzantine empire of Constantinople in the 14th century and was certainly being played there in the 15th.

MILITARY EQUIPMENT

Byzantine military equipment is a subject which has, until recently, been largely neglected by historians. It poses a number of difficult problems, largely stemming from the paucity of surviving artefacts, a lack of archaeological focus, the tendency of Byzantine written records to use archaic and sometimes inappropriate terminology, and above all the extraordinarily stylised and conservative character of most Byzantine art. On the other hand it is clear that Byzantine armies were often very well, even abundantly, equipped and that the Byzantine Empire was often, though by no means always, wealthy enough to import or manufacture arms and armour in substantial quantities. Some estimates have suggested that the Fourth Crusade alone seized 10,000 armours as booty from the Byzantine imperial capital of Constantinople in 1204.[230]

If true, then the military hardware captured by the Crusaders probably included material comparable to the remarkable but small and little-known array uncovered by archaeologists during their excavation of the Byzantine imperial Great Palace shortly before the Second World War. This consisted of nine iron masks, some elements of lamellar armour, tanged rather than socketed arrowheads, the cheek-pieces of a horse's bit and other harness fragments, plus a spearhead. A coin from the reign of the Comnenid Emperor Manuel I was found stuck to the armour, which suggests that the finds dated from the 12th or very early 13th century, and the arrows were much closer to those used by medieval steppe and Middle Eastern archers than those of Western Europe. The iron face-mask visors had holes for the eyes but not the mouth, plus small paired holes at the top and sides of the edges, presumably to fasten the mask to a helmet.[231] Once again the closest parallels have been found in the steppes and steppe-influenced parts of European Russia and the Ukraine, though the iron visor-masks from these regions tended to have mouth- as well as eye-holes and were usually attached to a helmet by a hinge at the brow.

The arms from the Great Palace have sufficient features that link them with warriors of the western steppes that one might suggest that the troops who used them were mercenaries or refugees of steppe origin. On the other hand the admittedly limited evidence of earlier medieval arms and armour from around the Black Sea could suggest a broadly shared military technology and that some aspects of western steppe arms actually reflected Byzantine influence rather than the other way around.[232] Indeed it seems highly likely that a mutual sharing of military technologies was as characteristic of the Byzantines' relations with the largely Turkish peoples of the western steppes as it was of their relations with the Arab, Iranian and subsequently Turkish peoples of the Islamic Middle East.[233]

The weapons of élite cavalry, as reflected in the 11th century *Digenes Akritas*, were the sword, *kontarion* lance and mace.[234] This epic poem was, however, written in the frontier region facing Arab-Islamic Syria where it is clear that the Byzantine and Arab military élites shared common combat traditions. In other parts of the Empire, especially in frontier regions facing Turks and perhaps Iranians, other weapons may have shared prominence. Nevertheless, the spear or lance was the most important close-combat cavalry weapon. Again the *Digenes Akritas* epic provides additional details, noting that the hero wielded a 'green' Arabian spear.[235] Others were described as being made of what could be translated as Arabian spring-wood, green wood or cypress.[236] This same source also refers to an *akontion* spear painted 'all iron by the painter's art'.[237] The *akontion* is normally translated as a spear, but here it may possibly have referred to a heavy javelin.

Exceptionally few Byzantine swords are known to survive, though it seems probable that some from neighbouring regions including parts of the Caucasus, western steppes, Russia, the Balkans and even the early Islamic Middle East may actually have been of Byzantine manufacture. Byzantine illustrations may actually be more realistic and thus useful in their representation of swords than most other pieces of military equipment. These show that, throughout this period, most swords were at least superficially similar to the straight-bladed, double-edged weapons used in Central and Western Europe. At the same time, and to an increasing extent, other forms of sword were also used by Byzantine troops. The most obvious variation was the single-edged blade, initially straight or almost straight, but gradually becoming what would normally be regarded as a curved sabre. According to the chronicler Psellus, élite troops used the single-edged *rhomphaion* by the early 11th century.[238] These were issued to *Varangian Guards* of Scandinavian and Russian origin in the mid-11th century: *'All armed with shields and the rhomphaia, a one-sided sword of heavy iron which they carry suspended from the right shoulder'*, thus indicating that its scabbard was attached to a baldric rather than a sword-belt.[239] Perhaps the unusual single-edged swords found in Viking age Scandinavia itself were of Byzantine origin, or were at least inspired by such weapons brought home by returning mercenaries.[240]

Similar weapons have been found in Russia, but here, as almost certainly in the Byzantine Empire itself, the true sabre was copied from the nomadic Turco-Mongol peoples of the steppes, amongst whom the medieval sabre almost certainly originated. A similar process of adoption took place at virtually the same time in parts of the neighbouring Islamic world and amongst the Christian peoples of the Caucasus region. Perhaps the most interesting sabre in this context was found far away in the northern end of the Ural Mountains. Its blade was decorated with an Armenian inscription whose style and content has been taken to indicate an 11th century date.

The blade itself is, however, more similar to those used by steppe peoples in the 12th and even 13th century. On the other hand the blade is not of the technologically advanced one-piece so-called Damascene forging normally associated with these and later weapons. Instead it consisted of an inner layer sandwiched between outer layers then beaten together. Currently this fascinating weapon is thought likely to have been made in the Caucasus region or Islamic Iran, then decorated by Armenians before somehow finding its way to a resting place close to the Arctic Circle.[241] Nevertheless, this assumption reflects the fact that we know more about sword-making in the medieval Caucasus and Iran than in Armenia or, indeed, the Byzantine Empire and there seems to be no specific reason why the blade should not have been made in either of these Christian regions. Yet another suggestion has recently been made by the Russian arms scholar, Michael Gorelik, who believes that this blade was actually made in the Volga Bulgar region north of the steppes and east of medieval Russia, before receiving its Armenian inscription.

The prominence of various forms of mace sets Byzantine armies apart from most of their Western or even Central European contemporaries while placing them closer to their Middle Eastern Islamic rivals. Once again the 11th century *Digenes Akritas* epic is useful, with several references to an *upokonta rabdia* or *opathorrabdin* which seems to be a mace or club or heavy staff-weapon. It may have been similar to the slightly earlier *opathobakion*.[242] This was distinct from the *rabdin* 'club' which served as the weapon of poor, humble or peasant warriors in *Digenes Akritas*.

Of course the bow and its associated equipment was more important in overall military terms. Byzantine bows were, as far as one can tell, invariably of composite construction and shared essentially the same technology and forms as were used by the nomadic steppe people to the north as well as the Muslims to the east and south. As in the latter region, if not necessarily in the former, there seem to have been certain differences between bows primarily for use by infantry and those intended for use on horseback, though the overlap between these two general categories is likely to have been larger than any differentiation between them. As in virtually all other cultures which took archery seriously, bows were primarily designed for the size and strength of the man who was to use them. Beyond that, however, we know remarkably little about Byzantine military bows.

Surprisingly, perhaps, we know more about Byzantine crossbows but here it must be made immediately clear that the *solenarion* was not a crossbow. Seemingly first mentioned in the Byzantine Empire as a device for use by infantry in the *Strategikon* attributed to the Emperor Maurice at the close of the 6th century it was an arrow-guide, a slit tube or groove held against the belly of the bow.[243] This enabled an archer to shoot arrows or darts whose overall length was shorter than the distance between the bowstring and the bow when the weapon was fully drawn. Such a device was used to an even greater extent by Islamic archers and also in medieval Korea – the archers of all these regions having to face Turkish or

Mongol horse-archers as perhaps their most dangerous archery rivals.

In technological terms the crossbow had been known since at least late Roman times when small hand-held versions had been used in hunting while much larger forms may have served as siege weapons. The fate of the crossbow in the early medieval Byzantine Empire, if not of the technological knowledge upon which it was based, is unclear. However, it almost certainly reappeared in various forms by the 10th century, in much the same period that the crossbow appeared as a military weapon in the eastern and central Islamic lands. Until the 11th century all, or at least almost all, of these Byzantine *toxobolistrai* crossbows were substantial weapons to be used in siege or naval warfare.[244] During the 11th century some hand-held *cheirotoxobolistra* seem to have appeared, though even this is not entirely clear since references to the 'hand' in their terminology might concern their spanning mechanisms rather than their supposed size. Whereas most Byzantine *toxobolistrai* were mechanically spanned, perhaps usually with some sort of winch, the 10th century Byzantine *cheirotoxobolistra* is considered to have been a smaller hand-spanned but not hand-held crossbow that was still normally mounted on a frame.[245] Sometimes these substantial weapons were also mounted on carts.[246]

The well-known statement by Anna Comnena that Byzantine soldiers did not use the *tzangra* form of hand-held crossbow already used by Byzantium's Italian, Norman and other Western European foes in the late 11th and early 12th century poses almost as many questions as it provides information.[247] For a start there had already been clear references to such a *tzangra* crossbow in early 11th century Byzantine sources, then again in the *Strategikon* of Kekaumenos written around 1075, all of which predate Anna Comnena's *Alexiad*. Kekaumenos seems to use the word *tzagrai* as a general term in assocation with, or sometimes perhaps as a replacement for, *toxoballistra*.[248]

Nevertheless, it is clear that the light or hand-held crossbow, especially when used by infantry in open battle, was still regarded as a weapon of Western European 'barbarians' even in the early 13th century. Things then began to change rapidly in the armies of the fragmented Byzantine Empire. Crossbows steadily increased in popularity, both at sea and on land. In the latter case this was probably because the Byzantines were now largely on the defensive and, throughout its history, the crossbow proved most effective in static, siege warfare. Indeed by the late 13th and 14th century almost all the Greek Byzantine written sources and those of their foes make it clear that crossbows formed an essential part of the defence of Byzantine fortifications.

Such weapons also began to appear in 14th century and later Byzantine art, sometimes in the hands of warrior saints whom Byzantine artists had previously armed with normal composite bows. Amongst the gifts which the Comnenid Emperor of Trebizond sent to a Crusading ruler in the mid-13th century were supposed crossbows of horn or cornel wood, though it is also possible that these were composite bows of horn and wood construction rather than crossbows.[249] Archaeological evidence from the 13th–14th century Carevac Palace in the medieval Bulgarian capital of Tarnovo suddenly starts to include new forms of arrowheads which may be armour-piercing crossbowbolt heads.[250] They were uncovered in essentially the same archaeological context as the remains of what seem to be large rectangular shields, similar to the infantry mantlets used by crossbowmen in Italy and other parts of Western Europe during this period. It was also the period when the armies and military equipment of the independent kingdom of Bulgaria were virtually identical to those of a rapidly declining Byzantium.

During most of this period the round shield was most common amongst Byzantine troops, especially infantry, though other more varied forms were widely adopted from the 12th century onwards. It also seems highly likely that the elongated 'kite-shaped' cavalry shield was adopted by Byzantine heavy cavalry before it was taken up in Western Europe. It may, indeed, have first appeared as a form of cavalry protection in the Islamic world (see volume II) and might have developed from various large or elongated infantry mantlets.

Such interpreations are entirely based on the literary and pictorial record, as no organic materials from Byzantine shields, or those of Byzantium's Orthodox Christian neighbours, are known to have survived from earlier than the late 13th or more probably 14th century. One particularly fine shield-boss was, however, excavated at 'Ayn Dara on what had been the Byzantine frontier north of Aleppo. It dates from before the Byzantine collapse in the 11th century and is made of gilded bronze, with an engraved decoration of running animals around its broad rim.[251]

Another fascinating fragment of information is found in an Icelandic saga written around 1030 which describes a *Varangian* mercenary returning home with rich arms and armour which included a shield with a 'knight' painted on it. In reality this picture is more likely to have been a typical Orthodox Christian military saint in full armour.[252] It has recently been suggested that a substantial rectangular shield that once hung over a tomb in Belgium was that of Baldwin of Flanders, the first Crusader ruler of the Latin Empire of Constantinople, and dated from the early 13th century.[253] It only survives in a 16th or early 17th century antiquarian's drawing but would seem to have had similarities with the archaeological evidence of large, rectangular 13th or 14th century shields from the Carevac Palace in Tarnovo, Bulgaria.[254]

Little has as yet been published on Byzantine armour when compared to that of medieval Western Europe.[255] There has, however, been considerable debate about whether Byzantine armourers and weapon-smiths ever used real steel.[256] What is clear is that they manufactured a greater variety of forms of protection than was normally seen in Western Europe and in many respects used technologies, and indeed forms, which had much in common with those of the steppes and the Islamic Middle East. The troops who purchased this equipment, or to whom it was issued, similarly had a tradition of wearing multiple types and layers of protection, again similar to what was seen amongst at least élite troops elsewhere in the Middle East.

A few notable points can be found in the albeit difficult literary sources. For example, the chronicler Psellus indicated that fully armoured Byzantine cavalry wore mail armour on their bodies and probably their arms. They also used leg armour which, by the 11th century, is likely to have been of mail comparable to the mail chausses already worn by the best-equipped Western European horsemen. What set Byzantine cavalry apart from their Western neighbours was their additional wearing of lamellar cuirasses.[257] Furthermore, padded or quilted soft armour was more common, abundant and was used at an earlier date in Byzantium than in Western Europe with the possible exception of the Iberian peninsula. The 11th century *Digenes Akritas* epic sheds some light on the multi-layered character of Byzantine cavalry attire, describing a hero dismounting from his horse. Because of the heat he took off his *upolorikon* which may have been like a surcoat or like a padded *epilorikon*, though here being worn over armour because of the heat. He then tucked up the skirts of clothing to make walking easier, and put a *kamilaukitzin* hat or hood on his head.[258]

During the same period the Emperor Isaac was assaulted by four *Varangians* who simultaneously thrust at him with their spears but were unable to penetrate his full armour, nor did they topple him from his saddle because all four were pushing from different directions.[259] Haraldr Sigurdson, who would later be killed during his failed invasion of England in 1066, returned home from his time as a *Varangian* guardsman in the Byzantine Empire, bringing with him a calf-length armour, probably a mail hauberk which he liked so much that he nicknamed it 'Emma'.[260]

The abundance and fully-covering character of Byzantine armour was still a noted feature in the 14th century, when the Turkish *Danishmandname* epic poem described fully iron-covered infidel warriors wearing two armours at once, sometimes specifically identified as *cebe* hauberks and and *cevşen* cuirasses.[261] Whether these were still in the earlier Byzantine tradition of mail and lamellar, or indicated a Byzantine adoption of Western European mail and plate is less clear.

The most important item of mail armour was the *lourikin* or hauberk which, according to colourful literary sources such as *Digenes Akritas*, could be decorated with gold. If true, then the gilded links would probably have been made of brass or bronze. There is certainly archaeological evidence for this practice further east, both at earlier and later dates. The cuirass had sometimes been called a *thorak* from the 6th to 11th century and could apparently be of iron or organic lamellae, perhaps horn, though hardened leather would seem more likely. This lamellar cuirass, or perhaps a modified smaller version of it, would be known as a *klibanion* from the 9th century, a term which became very common from the 10th century onwards.[262] The adoption of this more limited form of lamellar cuirass is thought to have resulted from Byzantium's need for fast-moving light cavalry during its period of defensive 'shadowing warfare'. As such it was also practically identical to the sleeveless, little more than hip-length lamellar *jawshan* cuirass which was widespread in the Islamic world.

The question of the use, or more particularly the nature of limb protections within Byzantine traditions of armour is much less clear. A warrior gravesite excavated by Soviet archaeologists at Gelendjik (Tuapse) close to the north-eastern shore of the Black Sea dates from the 8th to 9th centuries when this region was dominated by the Turkish Khazar Khanate. The Khazars were, more often than not, allies of the Byzantine Empire and enemies of the Islamic Caliphate. The armour found here, and in a few other Khazar sites, shows that either the Khazars were themselves astonishingly advanced in their armour technology,[263] using methods of construction rarely if ever seen elsewhere amongst steppe peoples, or they imported advanced military equipment from their Byzantine allies.

The objects in question include plated shoulder, arm and leg defences of a sophistication not seen in Europe until the 14th century, in addition to more usual styles of armour and weapons including curved sabres.[264] Elaborate forms of limb protection also appear in the art of the Khazars, some of their subject peoples and have interesting parallels in splinted limb defences from early medieval Scandinavia, perhaps indicating a technological link between these regions even before the Vikings began their epic adventures across Russia and down the road to *Mikkelgard*, the Great City of Constantinople.

Several centuries later, there is further specific evidence concerning limb defences as part of Byzantine armour. This now appears in the 14th century Turkish *Danishmandname* epic in which Christian warriors are described wearing *qolluq* arm defences and *budluq* thigh defences against Turkish arrows.[265] These may have been comparable to the *qolluq* and *budluq* used by Turkish heavy cavalry, though by this date it seems more likely that the Turkish poet was using Turkish terms for pieces of armour the Byzantines had copied or purchased from Western Europeans.

Soft armour was an aspect of protection in which the Byzantines clearly had a profound influence upon Western Europe. However, they themselves were probably under even greater influence from their Turkish and Islamic neighbours to the north and east. Within the Byzantine Empire the normal term for such quilted soft armour of cloth was *kabadion*. Most appears to have had short sleeves, though the term could also be used for horse-armour, suggesting that *kabadion* indicated a method of construction rather than a specific garment.[266] It is similarly possible that the Byzantine Greek word *kabadion* lay behind the rather later Western European term *gambeson* and its variants which came to mean a high-quality item of soft armour for a man. Another Byzantine word for padded soft armour for a man, horse or ordinary infantry soldiers was *kentouklion*.[267] On occasions a *kentoulion* could also be, or be used as a descriptive term for, a hood or hat attached to, used with or made in the same way as a *kabadion*.

Another form may have been the *epilorikon*, though this might have been more like a surcoat. In *Digenes Akritas* the *epilorikon* of a senior commander was 'sprinkled with gold', rather suggesting that it could be used decoratively, either on its own or worn outside normal armour.[268] Another garment was called the *linothorax* which, seemingly made of linen, appeared in the late 12th or early 13th century.[269] It was sometimes mentioned in a ceremonial or court context and may again have been a form of surcoat, perhaps mirroring that adopted by Western European knightly élites who were influencing the contemporary Byzantine military aristocracy in so many ways.

The description of a *Varangian* guardsman who returned home to Iceland in 1030, though written down many years later, stated that his rich arms and armour included a gilded helmet.[270] A perhaps more reliable description by Cinnamus of the Emperor Manuel's war against the Hungarians in 1150 states that the Emperor's armour was gilded and, though it does not specify that his helmet was similarly decorated, it does say that it included protection for his eyes which was proof against a sword cut. Nevertheless, the blow, which seems to have struck a mail aventail rather than an iron visor, left an impression on Manuel's face.[271] Once again this sounds closer to the sort of head and face protection currently being used by Byzantium's eastern rather than western rivals.

The question of horse-armour in the Byzantine Empire is particularly interesting during this period. Various forms of such horse-armour had been used by the most heavily armoured Byzantine cavalry in earlier times and probably during the first wave of Arab-Islamic conquests. It had included a so-called Avar style which protected only the front part of the animal, as is most clearly illustrated on the magnificent over-lifesized rock-cut high relief statue of a late Sassanian Iranian ruler at Taq-i Bustan. This also dated from very shortly before the Arab-Islamic conquest of Iran.

References to Byzantine horse-armour then seem to disappear until the 9th or more clearly 10th centuries. Then, however, the style, shape and method of construction seems to have changed, perhaps as a result of Islamic influence. By the mid-10th century, Byzantine heavy cavalry in combat with the army of the Arab Hamdanid rulers of northern Syria sometimes used metallic horse-armour, perhaps of mail but more likely of lamellar construction. Sometimes this reached far down the animals' flanks. One such occasion was described by the Arab poet

Mutanabbi who wrote; '*They* (the horses of the Byzantines and their Russian or *Varangian* mercenaries) *rode against you, armed* (their horses) *in iron, so that you would think they rode on horses with no legs*'.[272] On the other hand, quilted horse-armour would have been much more common than either lamellar or mail and was made of the same *kentouklion* padded material used in soft armour for men.[273] In this respect the Byzantines would again have had much more in common with their Islamic rivals, where padded horse-armour was even more widespread, than with Western Europe where horse-armour seems to have been virtually unknown during the early medieval centuries.

Much later the Turkish *Danishmandname* epic poem included a description of a completely iron-covered infidel and his similarly iron-armoured horse.[274] A close reading of the text shows that only the chest or front of the animal was protected, which was remarkably similar to the front-only horse armours also used in the Iberian peninsula. Perhaps this indicated that this distinctive style was either introduced to Byzantium by Catalan and other Spanish mercenaries who featured so prominently during this period, or was taken back to Spain by returning mercenaries.

A seemingly strange remark by Friar Ricoldus de Monte Crucis, in a report he sent to his superiors in Western Europe shortly after the fall of Acre in 1291, deserves more attention than it has received. Having been sent east just before the fall of Acre, and having travelled through Byzantine territory to Iraq where he wrote his report, Ricoldus described how 'Greek farmers' in Anatolia *caparisoned* or armoured their horses when they left the safety of their town walls for fear of the Turks.[275] By 'Greek farmers' he probably meant the low-status *akritoi* local and rural militias, many of whom still cultivated their own land, while the availability of even the simplest forms of *caparison* or protective covering for their horses suggests that such equipment was widely used against the persistent threat from Turkish archery.

Most of the available information about Byzantine military horse-harness focusses on a high degree of decoration and magnificence. This is a constant theme in the *Digenes Akritas* epic, where the decoration in question sounds remarkably similar to that used in the Islamic Middle East and was subsequently echoed in the Armenian *David of Sassoun* epic as well as later Turkish poems from the same part of the world. The retired *Varangian* guardsman whose return home to Iceland in 1030 was described in a slightly later source, brought with him not only rich arms and armour but a decorated saddle. Sadly, however, almost nothing is known of the styles of harness and saddle decoration used by Byzantine cavalry during these centuries.[276]

At the other extreme there is documentary evidence for the use of non-metallic stirrups, presumably by low-status horsemen. During one of his battles against the Byzantine garrison defending Cyprus during the period of the Third

Crusade, King Richard of England seized a riderless enemy horse '*with cords for stirrups*' which he then rode.[277] A little later a Turkish epic poem, the *Book of Dede Korkut* which is believed to have first been written down in the mid-13th to early 14th century in eastern Anatolia, contains a reference to Christian 'infidels' of the Caucasus region who similarly rode with rope stirrups.[278]

MANUFACTURE, TRADE AND STRATEGIC MATERIALS

The little information which survives concerning the manufacture and distribution of arms and armour in the Byzantine Empire confirms a broader impression that the Byzantine state was in economic decline relative to many and perhaps even most of its neighbours. Having still been hugely rich at the end of the Roman period, the surviving Christian Roman provinces of the Near and Middle East that became what is now generally known as the Byzantine Empire gradually changed from being a major centre of military production to relying almost entirely on imported military equipment, though this took many centuries.

It did not, however, mean that local production for local use came to an end. With the collapse of the Late Roman system of state-owned and -run *fabricae* making arms, armour and horse-harness, their role seems to have been taken over by seemingly more independent local craftsmen. They became a feature of Byzantine cities and some large towns, though there were still state-run factories and arsenals in major urban centres such as Constantinople. Salaried craftsmen continued to manufacture military equipment in the main Byzantine towns at least until the first half of the 13th century when they were still recorded during the reign of Emperor John Vatatzes of Nicaea.[279] Much such production may have been centred around the palace. This certainly seems to have been the case in the independent but essentially post-Byzantine Kingdom of Bulgaria during the 13th and 14th centuries. Here archaeological evidence points to substantial arms production in or around the Carevac Palace at Tarnovo.[280]

On the other hand it was apparently becoming more common for specialised military groups, ranging from settled ex-nomadic Turkish refugees to the élite *Varangian Guard*, to produce some of their own weapons. In the latter case this might have been a case of recruits entering Byzantine service with weaponry brought from their Scandinavian, Russian or English homelands, then being responsible for maintaining this in proper condition.[281]

Despite clear technological and stylistic similarities between Byzantine and Arab, Iranian or Turkish military equipment, there is no real evidence of trade in military goods across the Byzantine Empire's eastern frontiers. A completely different state of affairs would develop across the Empire's western borders where imports of arms, armour and raw materials, mostly from Italy, would eventually become the Byzantine armies' major sources of supply. This was even the case when, following the Fourth Crusade, the Byzantine successor states were largely hostile to their Latin, Crusader and other Western European neighbours. In 1238, for example, the Pope sent a rebuke to the Crusading Military Order of Hospitallers, accusing them of providing horses and military equipment to the ruler of the Empire of Nicaea in return for land and *casales* or farm-estates.[282] Whether this accusation was based on fact remains unknown.

The Italian maritime and mercantile republic of Genoa also forged a firm alliance with Nicaea, becoming a major source of military equipment for Byzantine forces in a relationship which continued long after the Byzantines regained their capital city of Constantinople.[283] During the late 13th century, and perhaps earlier, the autonomous Dalmatian maritime city of Ragusa (Dubrovnik) was a major channel through which military equipment reached Albania and the Byzantine Despotate of Epirus, much of the material in question almost certainly having been manufactured in Italy.[284]

Like all armies, those of the Byzantine Empire reused captured military hardware when it was suitable to their needs. Sometimes the volumes of such material seemed huge. It could also serve as diplomatic gifts. This was the case when Saladin and the Byzantine Emperor exchanged 'embassies' to cement what was in effect an unofficial anti-Latin alliance after Saladin retook Jerusalem but before the resulting Third Crusade reached the eastern Mediterranean. On this occasion Saladin is said to have sent the Emperor fifty Turkish saddles and one hundred Turkish bows plus quivers and arrows. The Byzantine ruler responded by sending Saladin four hundred *loricas* or mail hauberks, 4,000 lances and 5,000 swords captured during the course of King William II of Sicily's unsuccessful invasion of the Byzantine Empire.[285] The numbers quoted come from a hostile Western European source and are therefore suspect, at least where the Byzantine gifts were concerned. However, it is worth noting that Saladin sent Islamic equipment to the Byzantines, presumably in the knowledge that it would be useful, whereas the Emperor sent captured Western material to the Muslims, suggesting that it was either unsuitable or surplus to requirements.

FORTIFICATION

Siege warfare, both offensive and defensive, featured prominently in Byzantine military operations before, during and after the period under consideration. Byzantine armies are also widely assumed to have been particularly skilled in these operations. Yet, with the exception of such notable fortifications as those of the great cities of Constantinople (Istanbul), Thessaloniki, Antioch and a few others, early Byzantine military architecture rarely looks very impressive at first sight. Most Byzantine isolated fortresses or castles within the Empire were rectangular with corner towers that were usually though not invariably square, often with wooden rather than stone stairs linking their various floors. Those on or close to the mountainous frontiers were mostly small, relying for their strength more on the natural features of their location rather than walls or towers. These frontier defences consequently tended to be irregular in plan with small towers and often also incorporating covered internal galleries.[286] Few seemed designed to overawe an attacker, and they were certainly more functional than impressive. Nevertheless, they proved effective over many centuries.

Different terrain resulted in different types of structure, as the Byzantines do not seem to have inherited the Romans' passion for uniformity. Changing military circumstances also had a clear impact upon the design, size and strategic importance of such fortifications. For example, a detailed study of Byzantine military architecture in Anatolia shows that the defences of the Comenid period were significantly different from those of earlier centuries. Now, after the huge territorial losses that followed defeat at the battle of Manzikert and as part of the process of partial reconquest, massive effort was put into defending what remained of the Byzantine Empire's Asian provinces. The defences became larger, more sophistated and in general terms more numerous. They also had many stylistic features in common and were clearly part of a broad defensive strategy directed from the centre.[287]

Later Comnenid and Lascarid fortifications in Anatolia, dating from the second half of the 12th and first half of the 13th centuries, clearly began to incorporate new ideas. They reflected the adoption of new siege weapons such as the counterweight *mangonel*, both by the defending garrisons and by their attackers. This resulted, amongst other features, in larger and bulkier towers.[288] Many Lascarid fortifications in western and north-western Anatolia also had large arched embrasures which are believed to have been firing points for heavier machines.[289] The similarity and near-identical dating of these new developments parallel what was happening in the Islamic Middle East to a remarkable degree.

Syria had been lost to the Byzantine Empire by the late 7th century, but parts of the north-western coastal mountains and the foothills north of what is present-day Syria were subsequently regained during the Byzantine offensives of the late 10th and 11th centuries. This resulted in a number of extremely impressive, though subsequently largely rebuilt, castles. One of the most dramatic was at Sahyun (the Saone of the Crusaders).[290] Here a great deal more of the late 10th century Byzantine fortress remains, forming an essential part of the later and much better-known 12th century Crusader castle. Certainly the archaeological evidence shows that Byzantine efforts to strengthen Sahyun in the later 11th century were more extensive than had once been thought.[291] Might the huge rock-cut ditch which is seen as the glory of Crusader Saone have been at least started by the Westerners' Byzantine predecessors? Unfortunately there is no surviving documentary evidence indicating quite who cut away these millions of tonnes of rock.

Other rock-cut ditches in much the same area are sometimes credited to the brief Byzantine reoccupation of parts of north-western Syria, including that at Shayzar overlooking the river Orontes south-east of Sahyun.[292] The Byzantine occupiers also restored and refortified Marqab on the coast in 1020, as well as other locations in the hills behind.[293] So did their Muslim rivals in what was, in effect, a 'war of castles' to dominate this region during the 10th and first half of the 11th century.

Byzantine fortifications in Europe mostly seem feeble in comparison to those epic eastern castles. Even in the 13th century, when the Balkans became the primary focus of most Byzantine military efforts, few large or indeed very modern fortifications seem to have been built. In the Despotate of Epirus, for example, a walled city or *kastron*, administered as the military centre of each district under the command of a *kastrophylax*, might be dramatically located and picturesque but its design rarely incorporated new or even up-to-date ideas.[294] At Butrint (Buthrot) in Albania, for example, the Despot Michael II fortified the site in 1236, though he probably did little more than improve the existing Byzantine defences.[295]

On the eastern side of the Balkan peninsula the second independent Kingdom of Bulgaria erected or took over and strengthened a number of frontier forts. Several Bulgarian mountain monasteries are also fortified, though few attempts appear to have been made to date their walls. Like those of Mount Athos in northern Greece, they probably date from many different periods, having been repaired or updated as and when the occasion and the money allowed. Bulgarian frontier defences were almost entirely Byzantine in style and there is no evidence of any architectural survivals from the Bulgars' now distant Turco-Mongol past, as had been seen in the Bulgar Khan's 8th–9th century citadel and palace at Pliska.[296] On the other hand more recent influence from the now Mongol-ruled steppes has been identified by some architectural historians,[297] eastern Bulgaria being under Mongol suzerainty for part of the 13th century.

North of the river Danube, the rising Rumanian principalities of Wallachia and Moldavia would develop their own styles of military architecture, again based firmly upon Byzantine traditions but with influences from Hungary, the steppes and perhaps Russia. Only the rulers seem to have been wealthy enough, or to have given permission, to erect stone or brick defences.[298] Those built by the nobility and perhaps by the Church relied on older traditions of earth and timber fortification. Even so, the earliest known stone examples in Wallachia date from the late 13th or early 14th century, while those in Moldavia had to await the second half of the 14th century.[299]

In contrast to the conservative nature of much Byzantine military architecture, at least until the later 12th century, that of the Armenian territories had a reputation for being both advanced and sometimes experimental, even before the arrival of the Turks and then the Crusaders altered the military circumstances in the Middle East.[300] The fortifications of the Cilician Kingdom of Lesser Armenia have been characterised as falling into three categories: the defended outpost or watchhouse, the 'baronial home' and the major garrison base. Several locations also served two of these functions.

Generally speaking the watchposts were small and appear to have been able to communicate with the nearest garrison base by beacon or by mounted courier down clearly identifiable roads or tracks. Their defences were passive, designed to provide a secure retreat in the face of a small enemy force which lacked siege equipment. Fortified baronial houses similarly had passive defences and were usually rectangular in layout, smaller than most Western European *donjons* or keeps but sometimes with small corner towers. They were located in or near agricultural land which formed the basis of wealth amongst the Armenian landed aristocracy. Armenian garrison forts varied considerably in size and are believed to have had garrisons ranging from some ten to thirty men. Their defences were often quite elaborate and included elements of active defence, meaning that their defenders could hit back rather than merely enduring behind their walls.[301] These occasionally impressive Armenian fortifications dated from the late 11th through the 12th and 13th centuries.[302]

In other respects, Cilician Armenian castles have been characterised as mostly small when compared to those of, for example, the Latin Crusader States in the Middle East. Most were sited in the mountains or at least in rugged coastal territory, relying to a considerable extent on precipitous locations. Otherwise their defences often incorporated multitiered series of walls built on steep slopes in which the defenders of each successive wall dominated the wall ahead of them. They were generally more compact and indeed vertical than those of the Crusader States, having half-round towers which protruded quite a long distance from the curtain walls. Few incorporated identifiable *donjon* keeps, though these were a feature of lowland Cilician castles which the Armenian rulers allowed the Crusading Military Orders to build or garrison. Some of the latter, dating from the later 13th century, also show elements of Western European architectural influence from the Lusignan-ruled Latin Kingdom of Cyprus.[303]

Where the elements that made up a system of fortification were concerned, the Byzantine Empire was primarily the heir of the Late Roman Empire. Roman fortification, though often massive and very impressive, was not the most sophisticated or scientific in the Ancient World. More complex military-architectural features could often be found in Iran, Central Asia, India and China. For example the bent entrance, which denied an enemy a direct assault or direct bombardment through a gate, also forced assault troops to expose their generally unshielded right side to defensive fire. It was apparently not incorporated within the main gatehouse or gate structure of early Byzantine fortifications. Instead early Byzantine gates, like those of the Romans, often constructed a 'bent' approach ahead of the gate itself but forming part of the *intervallum* of rampart and ditch.[304] Similar systems characterised early Islamic military architecture which was similarly heir to Later Rome,[305] but the Muslims then learned of the gate which incorporated a bent entrance in Central Asia and eastern Iran. Thereafter Byzantines adopted the idea from their Islamic neighbours in the 9th century.[306]

If Byzantine rural and frontier fortresses tended to be functional and only occasionally impressive, the Empire's major cities could be provided with massive defences. Those at Constantinople, Thessaloniki and Trebizond had multiple walls, some with ditches or moats ahead of them, plus doubled gates with 'killing zones' between them.[307] Some cities were also dominated by citadels, usually at their highest point, though several of these appear to be late additions. This was also true of the Armenian and Cilician frontier zones in the immediate pre-Crusader period.[308] A citadel was, for example, added to the huge walled area of Antioch in the mid-10th century.[309] This would then be enlarged during the Crusader occupation in the 12th and 13th centuries.

During the 12th century several of the Byzantine Empire's remaining urban fortifications were strengthened, as were frontier fortresses. A particularly clear example were the walls and towers of the Blachernae Palace which formed a massive bastion at the northern end of Constantinople's far older triple land-walls. They were added by the Emperor Manuel I Comnenus. Such mid-12th century defences differed from the older land-walls in several respects, their chambers having small loopholes rather than the large embrasures seen in other parts of Constantinople's walls. This may have reflected the Byzantine defenders' increasing use of crossbows and as such the Comnenid fortifications were closer in design and use to the fortifications of Western Europe. Another late 12th and 13th century feature was bulkier towers which are believed to have been designed as artillery bastions for the new counterweight *trebuchets* which seem to have been supplementing rather than replacing the earlier man-powered *mangonels* and mechanical *ballistae*.[310]

Such developments were taken further by the Lascarid rulers of the Empire of Nicaea in the first part of the 13th century. Their fortifications, largely in Anatolia, often incorporated traditional embrasures high up in the walls, perhaps for large frame-mounted stone- or arrow-shooting counter-siege weapons. Lower down such walls there were smaller loopholes, perhaps for crossbows. Meanwhile many existing towers were made sturdier and taller, probably to take the weight and considerable shooting forces of counterweight *trebuchets*.

Here it is interesting to note that Nicaea had previously only been exposed to Turkish raids, but with the fall of Constantinople to the Fourth Crusade it became much more threatened, not only by Crusaders from the west but from a now militarily sophisticated Seljuk Turkish Sultanate from the east. Hence it was really only now that the late Roman and early Byzantine fortifications of Nicaea were seriously strengthened.[311] Another large fortress that was substantially rebuilt and updated by the Lascarids was Ayasoluk (now more commonly known as Selçuk), overlooking the ruins of ancient Ephesus. Here the new Byzantine rulers detached the upper part of the ancient city to form a new citadel while the walls of the lower city were also repaired after a serious earthquake.[312]

SIEGE WARFARE

As heirs of Greece and Rome, the Byzantines inherited some very advanced and indeed scientific methods of siege warfare, both offensive and defensive. However, the Byzantine Empire was also heir to the centuries of economic and military decline that are summarised in Western Europe as 'The Fall of the Roman Empire' and 'The Dark Ages'. Neither term is strictly correct, for only the western half of the Roman Empire fell. The east survived and eventually flourished as what is widely, though again not strictly accurately, called the Byzantine Empire. The inhabitants of this state regarded themselves, quite correctly, as 'Romans' and continued to do so right down to the fall of Constantinople in the mid-15th century. Similarly there was no 'Dark Age' in the Near and Middle East, and even in Western Europe the term is coming to be seen as largely meaningless.

Where the technology of siege warfare was concerned, the Byzantines inherited a great deal but were not always in a position to make effective use of such knowledge. The Empire was often economically stagnant, its rulers barely able to pay for soldiers let alone for elaborate military technologies, many of which were in any case now seriously outdated. The Byzantines may, like so many Europeans in later centuries, have been in awe of their ancestors but their commanders had to deal with military circumstances as they were, not as they had once been.

Nevertheless this tendency to look back to a glorious past would have a profound effect upon Byzantine military technology and upon the military treatises which have survived in some numbers. For example, the well-known work on siege machines by Heron of Byzantium is actually a 10th century updating of earlier sources, plus a few new inventions.[313] Even the *Taktika* by Nikephoros Ouranos, written around 1010, tends to be couched in terms which sometimes appear archaic. At the same time it included a chapter on sieges which reflects practical experience of warfare against the Muslims in northern Syria.[314] Among its practical, though far from technologically sophisticated, recommendations were mantlets or large portable shields made of woven vine-branches covered with willow osiers, mulberry branches or wild brambles to be carried by troops when assaulting a fortress.[315]

These technical treatises suggest that Byzantine forces were confident in the effectiveness of their siege technology and its ability to capture Islamic cities during the 10th and early 11th centuries.[316] At the same time there was a new and more detailed focus on mining, rams and various methods of protecting engineers, miners or the men wielding such rams. This tends to reinforce the view that the Byzantine did not yet possess stone-throwing machines powerful enough to demolish any but the flimsiest fortified walls.[317] In other respects the course of a prolonged struggle for control of the mountainous frontiers show that the Byzantines did enjoy a superiority in siege warfare in mountainous regions. Whether this was a result of superior technology is very debatable, and is more likely to have reflected greater resources in men, materiel and logistical support at a time when the Islamic side of the frontier was deeply fragmented, both politically, militarily and culturally.[318]

The actual Byzantine siege techniques used during this and previous periods were not very sophisticated or indeed unusual.[319] Various forms of protective roofed timber *chelonai* 'tortoise' structures were used, usually with a steeply pitched roof to deflect missiles dropped on them from the walls. These tended to be heavy, perhaps rather cumbersome and essentially the same as those used in Roman times. During the 10th century, however, a new, significantly lighter and apparently portable structure was adopted. Known as the *laisa*, it is believed to have been of Slav origin and was one of very few military ideas that the Byzantines adopted from their Slav enemies or subjects. This *laisa* was used to protect miners attacking the base and foundations of an enemy wall and may have largely replaced the heavy old 'tortoises'.[320]

Similar devices were still being used in the mid-12th century when Byzantine miners attacked the base of the wall of Hungarian-held Semlin (Zemun) in 1165. Meanwhile their *mangonels* bombarded the upper parts of the wall – though presumably not too close to their own miners. The Hungarian defenders seemingly regarded the miners as the most immediate threat for, according to the chronicler Cinnamus: '*There was a stone of great size lying within the walls; girdling it with wooden beams they* (the defenders) *fastened their ropes to the timber and drew it up to a wooden turret which they had constructed projecting over the walls, to drop it on the Romans* (miners in their shed) *from there.*' But the weight was too much for the wooden wallhead structure which broke away from the wall.[321]

It is unclear how often Byzantine troops used wooden siege towers, though these continued to be described in some detail in their military treatises. Nor is it certain that the term *helepolis* always meant such a tower, and by the 11th century mining under the protection of *laisa* 'sheds' seems to have been the preferred technique, rather than attempting to attack the summit of the walls with moveable siege-towers.[322] Storming the walls might be attempted with ladders, especially if the walls were built on a shoreline where mining was impossible. This was tried during a Byzantine and Venetian attack on Sicilian–Norman-held Kerkyra in 1148, when the attackers apparently had to approach the walls in their ships. On this occasion the Byzantine *Dux* or commander, named Stephen, had an extremely long ladder constructed which extended far above the outer walls, but a great mass of stone thrown from the citadel struck this ladder. The stone itself also broke into pieces, one fragment killing Stephen.[323]

A more unusual method of scaling a wall was described in the 12th century Georgian epic poem, *The Man in the Panther's Skin*, where a hero did so with the help of a rope lassoo.[324] This almost certainly reflects an earlier Iranian heroic tradition, as described in the *Shanamah*. Furthermore, the lassoo was traditionally a Turkish or Mongol rather than a Georgian, Byzantine or indeed Iranian weapon (see volume II).

Byzantine terminology can be surprisingly imprecise where siege weapons are concerned. The word *magganika* or *manganika* was, for instance, used widely and could seemingly apply to mechanical weapons in general, including a torsion-powered stone- or bolt-shooting weapon as well as a stone-throwing beam-sling *mangonel*. The earliest identifiable Byzantine reference to a counterweight *mangonel* is in an account of the Byzantine siege of Semlin in Dalmatia in 1165.[325] This is virtually the same date as the earliest indisputable evidence in the Islamic world. Until further information comes to light, the credit for inventing this weapon seems to be shared between Byzantines, Muslims and perhaps Armenians, with a slight emphasis in favour of the latter.

Byzantine technical military treatises focus upon torsion-powered siege weapons and what might be described as 'giant crossbows' rather than beamsling weapons. This must surely reflect the deeply conservative nature of such writings rather than the current reality of siege warfare. Nevertheless, it also seems likely that torsion-powered siege weapons and giant crossbows of the types known and used in earlier Hellenistic and Roman times, continued to be used by Byzantine specialist troops to a greater extent than in technologically backward early medieval Western Europe or in the technologically advanced Islamic world.

The Hellenestic and Roman *carroballista* had been a torsion-powered, two-arm bolt- or stone-ball-shooting weapon. Knowledge of its sophisticated technology clearly survived, though whether such delicate and complex weapons were still used is more questionable.[326] The Byzantine *cheiroballista* may simply have been a smaller, more transportable *ballista* or torsion-powered version of the crossbow. As such it would have been essentially the same as the Islamic *ziyar* (see volume II) and the later Western European *espringal* (see volume II). In contrast the *onager*, though again torsion-powered, only had a single throwing arm. It may only have been widely used by the Romans in the 4th century, with the two-armed *ballista* remaining more popular and more effective, though also more complex and difficult to operate. All such torsion-power weapons were shot with a relatively flat trajectory which limited their range, usually being set up within 150 metres of an enemy fortification. They also shot relatively small or light missiles, though these could achieve considerable accuracy and impact.[327] Compared with even the early man-powered forms of beamsling traction-powered stone-throwing *mangonels*, their effectiveness was limited and their complexity a weakness.

Byzantine treatises and more general chronicles, like the written sources from other civilisations during this period, show that mechanical weapons were more important in defence than in attack. This was particularly the case where larger stone-throwing machines were concerned. According to one treatise: '*Trebuchets and arrow-shooting instruments are to be set up along the parapets, along with piles of stones, rocks, beams and logs, with which to bombard the attackers and their tortoises (*protective sheds*).*' At this stage the emphasis was still on keeping the enemy away from the base of the walls which were vulnerable to mining. There seemed to be no concern that the foe's stone-throwing artillery posed a significant threat to the walls themselves.[328]

Garrisons usually consisted of, or at least contained a significant proportion of, professional troops including specialists in defensive siege warfare such as engineers and artillerymen. Garrisons tended to be quite scattered and their numbers are likely to have been small. Evidence from the 13th century, for example, gives the impression that professional soldiers were separate from the local population, perhaps drawn from different regions or ethnic groups.[329] This is likely to have reflected a conscious policy on the part of Byzantine governments concerned to ensure that their garrisons remained loyal to the ruler rather than developing strong local connections. Within the territory of the Nicaean Empire, the commanders of fortresses and urban defences were called *kastrophylakes*, while beneath these officers the originally Turkish title of *tzaousios* was given to those in actual charge of garrison troops.[330]

One of the primary duties of garrisons was, of course, to man the walls and also to provide leadership and stiffening to local part-time militias. Various sometimes unexpected skills were demanded. For example, during the Norman attack on Durazzo (Dürres) in Albania in 1068, the enemy managed to bring a siege or assault tower with a drawbridge close to the wall. The Byzantine defenders then jammed the drawbridge with a large wooden beam before it could be lowered, rendering the tower virtually worthless. The garrison then burned it to the ground.[331]

During the 14th century the Turkish epic *Danishmandname* described Byzantine defensive measures which had probably been in use for at least a century. On one occasion the defended location was a fortified monastery of the type that dotted so much of the Orthodox Christian world and beyond. Here the garrison had *çarh* crossbows which had to be 'set up', perhaps indicating that they were the heavy types of weapon mounted on pedestals or frames. They or rather their operators were also protected by *meteris* mantlets.[332] In another part of the *Danishmandname* a description of the siege of Çorum appears to have been a later addition to the text, as the Christian defenders manning the walls not only used *naffad* Greek Fire, *naft oq* fire-arrows but also *tüfenkler* which are usually translated as an early form of handgun.[333]

Byzantine offensive siege warfare is described in useful detail in a treatise entitled *On Siege Warfare* which probably dates from the late 10th or 11th century. This makes it clear that the invaders' first major task was to harrass the surroundings of a fortified location, damaging crops to induce the surrender of a walled town. When a direct siege was to be conducted, the first thing was to send good cavalry around the site to inspect the exterior of its fortifications and identify weak points. Next the commander of the besiegers should place reliable units opposite the gates to prevent sorties by the defenders. He then set up camp about two bow-shots from the walls and beyond the range of *petroboloi* stone-throwing weapons.[334] Next: *'Battering rams must be prepared, tortoises, stone-throwing machines, ropes, wooden towers and ladders. A mound of earth is piled up to make a hill'*, this providing the attackers' siege artillery with a height advantage over the defences.[335] *'The stronger siege engines should be located and brought to bear on the more level section of the ditch dug by the enemy (*its least precipitous part*) and the more unsound part of the wall'.*[336]

This piling up of a ramp was clearly not merely a theory but was a practical aspect of siege warfare. A detailed Arab description of the Byzantine siege of Bikisra'il in the Syrian coastal mountains in 1032 stated that, after establishing a fortified siege-camp, the attackers bombarded the castle with *mangonels*. The curtain wall of Bikisra'il was built on top of steep rock which made mining virtually impossible,[337] so the Byzantines constructed a *mazlaqa* or slope with stones, tree trunks and earth 300 cubits (approximately 120 metres) long and 36 cubits (approximately 18 metres) wide leading up towards the castle walls. Siege machines were next mounted upon this so that they were better able to bombard Bikisra'il. It also enabled Byzantine archers to see their targets more clearly. Eventually part of the fortified wall facing this man-made slope collapsed and the place was taken.

Man-powered *mangonels* may have been able to destroy wall-head defences and perhaps even damage a weak wall such as that of the small hill-castle of Bikisra'il, but it was not until the widespread adoption of counterweight *mangonels* or *trebuchets* that strong walls could be seriously threatened by stone-throwing machines. Nevertheless, even the man-powered types could throw their missiles to a considerable height and range. During the Byzantine siege of Brindisi in southern Italy in 1156, according to Cinnamus, the city walls were too strong to break so the *mangonels* bombarded the city within the walls, dropping large stones which so demoralised the inhabitants that they turned against the garrison, obliging it to retreat into the citadel, whereupon the people opened their gates and let the Byzantine troops in.[338]

At the end of the earlier Byzantine siege of Bikisra'il in Syria, the attackers forced their way inside and found two hundred men of the garrison dead, mostly killed by stones thrown by Byzantine *mangonels*. The remaining five hundred defenders were taken prisoner.[339] Back at Brindisi it was eventually a combination of mining and *mangonel* bombardment which caused the collapse of one of the towers of the citadel. Unfortunately it fell so suddenly that many Byzantine soldiers were killed, most of them probably being miners, whereupon the besiegers retreated.[340]

Byzantine siege camps have already been mentioned several times. Surely one of the most strongly fortified siege positions was that recorded in an Arab account of the siege of Bikisra'il in 1032. The latter was defended by a particularly determined garrison, so the Byzantine commander ordered the construction of a wall of stones, wood and earth, five cubits high and four across, to protect his camp against sorties by the garrison and attack by any relief force which might approach.

PYROTECHNICS AND CHEMICAL WARFARE

The one area in which Byzantine armies are generally accepted to have been in advance of their rivals was that of pyrotechnics, with *Greek Fire* being the most famous example. However, the story is not quite as straightforward as it might seem. The petroleum-based incendiary material popularly known as *Greek Fire* is thought to have been invented in the 7th century and to have played a major part in 'saving' the Christian Byzantine Empire when it was under mortal threat from the newly risen power of Islam. Many experimental studies have been made in modern times in an effort to recreate a practical and effective Greek Fire but, until recently, few have proved very successful.[341]

This fearsome mixture of distilled mineral oil and other refined chemicals was in reality one step, though a large and dramatic one, in the history of oil-based incendiary materials that goes back way beyond Rome and Greece to ancient times, and almost certainly had its roots in the Middle East. Here, until the modern exploitation and extraction of mineral oil on a mass scale, oils and tars seeped to the surface of the earth in a number of places. The 12th century Byzantine Greek chronicler Cinnamus himself called the widely available and highly inflammable military incendiary liquid both *Greek Fire* and *Median Fire* Media being, to Greeks, what is now part of north-western Iran.

Contemporary chronicles highlight the huge moral impact that *Greek Fire*, or *naft* as it was known to the Arabs and other Muslims, had in early medieval warfare, particularly in sieges and even more notably in naval conflicts.[342] The most dramatic method of using this material would seem to have been in a medieval form of flame-thrower operated by a syphon pump. This is first illustrated in an 11th century Byzantine manuscript,[343] though it had clearly been known long before that date. It was also in current use, having helped Byzantine ships destroy a fleet of Russian or *Varangian* sea-raiders in the mid-11th century.[344] The Byzantine defenders of Durazzo (Dürres) in Albania are also said to have used smaller, apparently 'mouth-blown' fire-jets against the miners of besieging Normans from southern Italy in 1108.[345] *Naffad* operators or *Greek Fire* men were still numbered amongst the Byzantine defenders of Manquriya in the 14th century Turkish *Danishmandname* epic.[346]

The syphon flame-thrower was known amongst some of the Byzantines' foes, but does not seem to have become as popular as various forms of *Greek Fire* incendiary grenades. The latter were probably more reliable and almost certainly safer for their users, but might not have been as terrifying or as noisy as a roaring flame-thrower. Perhaps for this reason the Byzantines themselves used relatively simple incendiary grenades.

One example of their effectiveness was probably in 1052, during a Turkish siege of the strategic eastern frontier fortress of Manzikert. On this occasion a Frank or Western European mercenary emerged from the fortifications, rode right into the middle of the Turkish siege-lines and threw Greek Fire at the besiegers' stone-throwing *mangonel*, probably in the form of some sort of grenade. The *mangonel* was destroyed, the Frank escaped safely and the Turks abandoned their siege.[347] The fact that a Western mercenary rather than a native Byzantine specialist had been trained in the correct use of this advanced form of incendiary weapon is itself also worthy of note.

The Byzantine Empire's enemies probably had access to petroleum-based incendiary weapons such as *Greek Fire* at precisely the same time as the Byzantines themselves. Only the syphon-powered flame-thrower seems to have remained a Byzantine 'secret', and even that not for very long. So it is not surprising that the Byzantines, like these enemies, put considerable thought into methods of protection against Greek Fire. This came in various forms and usually seems to have relied on the wet hides of freshly slaughtered animals, or on absorbent material like felt that had been soaked in water, vinegar or a mixture of both.

A very different and indeed distinctive form of protection was described much later by the chronicler Cinnamus who again indicates his interest in the details of warfare and military technology. He described how, in the Byzantine army's siege of the fortress of Anazarva in 1136–7, the Cilician Armenian defenders; *'heated irons sufficiently in the fire and then by mechanisms (*shot them*) at the (*Byzantine*) stone throwers. Immediately when they came close they set afire the wooden uprights in front of them. This, which happened often, put the Emperor into a rage.'* The Emperor John Comnenus' son, the *Sebastokrator* Isaac, said, *'Come father, order the woodwork to be encased in brick'*. This was done and successfully stopped the siege machines being burned by the defenders' heated arrows, after which Anazarva surrendered at the end of an intensive siege lasting thirty-seven days.[348]

COMMUNICATION, TRANSPORT AND SUPPORT SERVICES

Remarkably little study has been undertaken into the support services of Byzantine armies. They were clearly the heirs of Rome in this regard, and were equally clearly capable of moving substantial forces, plus their supplies, around their sprawling empire efficiently and quickly. Beyond this, not much seems to be known. From the 11th to the early 14th century these capabilities remained good, or at least adequate, yet there is no real evidence to indicate that Byzantine military logistics, communications and other support services were any better than those of their neighbours. They may indeed have been inferior to those of the eastern Islamic states. The latter civilisation had inherited much the same bureaucratic and state structures as the Byzantines.

This was certainly the case where state munitions factories, stores or arsenals were concerned. Surprisingly, perhaps, more is known about these state military structures in the early medieval Islamic Caliphates and their increasingly fragmented successor states than in the Byzantine Empire. Yet it is clear that they existed in the imperial capital of Constantinople throughout this period and there is evidence for them in some, perhaps in reality all, major imperial cities. For example there was a large *zabareion* arsenal in Thessaloniki when the Normans attacked the city in 1185. It was located near the Vlattadon Monastery and was where arms and armour were both made and repaired.[349]

Other small pieces of information can be found embedded in chronicles of the Crusades. For example Tatikios, the senior officer of Turkish origin who commanded a small Byzantine force which accompanied the First Crusade on their march across Anatolia, also served as their military advisor and guide.[350] Or perhaps he should more correctly be regarded as the officer in charge of their guides. Beyond these duties, Tatikios had the discrete additional role of

Byzantine imperial representative and, one may assume, as the Emperor Alexios' 'spy', keeping an eye on political developments amongst the fractious Crusader leadership.

The vital role played by the Byzantine fleet in support of the First Crusade has only recently been recognised, having been consciously downplayed by Western European chroniclers.[351] Most of those ships which brought supplies to the First Crusaders when they regained the Mediterranean coast in Cilicia after a long, gruelling and bitterly contested march across Anatolia were Byzantine. They became even more important during the First Crusade's siege of Antioch and the Crusaders' defence of this city once they had taken it. A substantial naval squadron is already believed to have been based in the Byzantine-ruled island of Cyprus while the Anglo-Saxon ships and crews operating in the same area were under at least nominal Byzantine command. Their strength was such that they were never challenged by the Fatimid fleet from Egypt and the Palestine–Lebanon coast, this being the only effective Islamic navy currently operating in the eastern Mediterranean.[352]

Despite the Byzantine Empire's long and generally successful naval heritage, its technology seems to have been falling behind that of the Muslims even as early as the 10th century, and would soon be even more dramatically overtaken by that of the Italians. The ships used to transport horses were a case in point. Before the 11th century it appears that Byzantine armies were using a variety of available merchant ships to transport horses during long-range campaigns. There was no evidence of specialised horse-transports,[353] unlike those seen on the Islamic side,[354] and which would soon appear amongst the Normans of southern Italy. During the large, but ultimately unsuccessful, Byzantine invasion of Sicily in 1038 they clearly had some ships which carried horses. However, it is not clear that they were specialised vessels nor how many animals each carried. Almost exactly a generation later the Normans invaded Sicily, crossing the Straits of Messina with some twenty horses in each ship, these vessels almost certainly being drawn from ships that were already available in the area.[355]

The horses themselves were drawn from a variety of sources. Traditionally the high plains of central Anatolia had been a major horse-raising region for both the Late Roman and the Byzantine Empires. Here studs were maintained throughout the early medieval period, perhaps both by the imperial government and by the higher aristocracy. These had been the occasional targets of Islamic raids and major invasions, but with the loss of central Anatolia to the Turks in the late 11th century, other sources had to be found. Thrace in the south-eastern corner of the Balkan peninsula had similarly been a traditional horse-raising area, as were the plains of Thessaly in central Greece, but these were again vulnerable to invasion and would later be partially lost to central governmental control.

Small wonder that, at the start of his reign when Byzantine imperial territory had been reduced to little more than scattered enclaves, the Emperor Alexius sought cavalry mounts wherever they could be found. This included Islamic Syria, itself one of the best horse-raising regions of the Middle East as well as being home to the finest Arabian breeds.[356] The exchange of embassies between the Byzantine Emperor Isaac II Angelus and the Islamic Sultan Saladin in the wake of the latter's reconquest of Jerusalem has already been mentioned. In addition to arms and armour, horses were exchanged, though the numbers involved seem remarkably unbalanced as well as being suspect, the information coming from an unsympathetic Western European source. This anonymous letter or report from the Crusader East survived in a collection of documents transcribed a few years later in 1195. It claimed that Saladin sent one thousand and fifty Turkish warhorses, *dextrarios Turcos vel Turquimannos*, along with a hundred liberated Greek captives.[357] In return the Emperor's gift included no horses, while a second diplomatic gift from Saladin included a further twenty warhorses, this time captured from his Crusader foes. The numbers might be suspect, but the one-way delivery of cavalry horses certainly reflected the Byzantine army's serious shortages in this regard.

NAVAL AND RIVERINE WARFARE

Byzantine naval warfare and practice is in some respects very well recorded.[358] Byzantine fleets had played a predominant role in preserving the Empire during the dark days of the 7th and 8th centuries, after which they either led the way or played a vital supporting role in the reconquests of the late 9th and 10th centuries. Although the most abundant information comes from earlier glory days, it is clear that substantial Byzantine squadrons were still active along the northern Syrian coast in the mid-11th century.[359] They appear to have been operating from Cyprus and, perhaps to a lesser extent, from Cicilia and the coast of southern Anatolia. Meanwhile Constantinople naturally remained the main Byzantine naval base with the Sea of Marmara as a Byzantine 'lake', the Black and Aegean Seas similarly being almost entirely under the control of the Byzantine navy. Elsewhere, in the Adriatic and even in the Ionian Sea, Byzantine dominance was being challenged by various rising Italian naval powers while in the Tyrrhenian Sea and western Mediterranean Byzantine naval strength was already little more than a distant memory.

Even the catastrophic loss of virtually all of Anatolia to the Seljuk and other Turks in the later 11th century led to little more than a temporary setback at sea. Turkish invaders, raiders and adventurers reached the sea at numerous points and there were many cases of so-called 'Turkish piracy' during this period. But only one newly established Turkish local ruler seems to have taken to the sea with enthusiasm. This was Çaka who, known to Byzantine chroniclers as Tzachas, was, for a few years, the independent or autonomous *amir* of Smyrna (Izmir). Supposedly forming a strategic alliance with the Pechenegs who were currently threatening Byzantine authority in the Balkans, or in reality perhaps merely seizing a strategic opportunity, Çaka and his fleet attempted to blockade the imperial capital of Constantinople in 1090–1.

Çaka's navy did not, of course, suddenly emerge from nowhere. In reality it was more like a rebel Byzantine fleet, the vessels being ex-Byzantine or newly built by Greek shipwrights in what had been Byzantine yards while the sailors were almost entirely Greek. The only Turks, and perhaps the only Muslims, would have been soldiers now serving as marines and, of course, their commanders. Some of the latter are likely to have been new converts, or renegades in the eyes of the Byzantines.

The fleet that eventually defeated Çaka's daring maritime adventure in 1091, following the Byzantine army crushing of his Pecheneg allies, seems to have been largely manned by newly arrived Anglo-Saxon refugee recruits from England. This supposedly 'English' fleet was still present off the southern Anatolian and northern Syrian coasts at the time of the First Crusade.[360] A small squadron of Flemish 'pirates' was also moored in Tarsus in Cilicia when the Crusaders arrived in 1097. They were commanded by Guynemer de Boulogne who claimed to be a vassal of Count Eustace of Boulogne and had reportedly been operating in north-eastern Mediterranean waters for eight years. Some historians consider these Flemish ships to have formed part of the Anglo-Saxon fleet in Byzantine service which was also in this area by March 1098, and perhaps earlier.

Although direct navigation between the Byzantine Empire and northern Europe via the Straits of Gibraltar was unusual, it did take place. The ships that Guynemer de Boulogne and the Anglo-Saxon refugees under Edgar Atheling sailed from the English Channel to the eastern Mediterranean were, however, probably not warships. They are more likely to have been of the originally Scandinavian *knörr* or English *buss* type. Any real warships were probably Byzantine galleys. In March 1098 another fleet arrived at Saint-Symeon, the main port serving Antioch which was itself currently besieged by the First Crusade. It was again described as being English, but was not the Anglo-Saxon manned fleet that was operating under Byzantine command. The newcomers were, in fact, an independent and strictly 'Crusading' squadron.

The Byzantine navy was substantially rebuilt by the Comnenid Emperors during the 12th century and it was the remnants of this fleet which enabled the Lascarid rulers of the Byzantine successor Empire of Nicaea to maintain naval squadrons in the early 13th century Aegean and Sea of Marmara. These small but effective fleets were organised and largely manned in the same way as their Comnenid predecessors,[361] but it would soon become apparent that the shortage of suitable, trained and reliable naval personnel was growing serious. Or perhaps it was simply a matter of cost, with the Byzantines finding it cheaper to hire fleets than to maintain indigenous navies. For whatever reason, the naval alliance which developed between the subsequent Palaeolog Emperors of Byzantium and the powerful Italian naval republic of Genoa was vital.[362]

Almost the last Byzantine navy worthy of the name was a fleet of eighty ships which was sent to support a Byzantine army operating in Thessaly in 1283. Here the Emperor Michael Palaeologus had died the previous year, campaigning against a 'rebel', John the Bastard.[363] The new Emperor, Andronicus II, then virtually disbanded the fleet and relied on his Genoese allies. This was clearly because of the Empire's dire and declining financial situation, as Andronicus also tried to have an army on the cheap. Thereafter only small squadrons were maintained, their primary and perhaps only task being to control the Dardanelles, stopping Turkish raiders crossing from the Asian to the European shores and, as far as possible, stopping enemy ships passing through to threaten Constantinople. In fact the only sea which the Byzantines could now claim as their own was the tiny Sea of Marmara.

There was a clearer distinction between naval ships and merchant ships in the Byzantine Empire than in northern waters, and even perhaps in Italy. Byzantine warships were *dromon* galleys while larger, heavier and much less manoeuvrable vessels which primarily relied on the wind were merchant or transport ships. The latter would, of course, have needed to defend themselves, but offensive naval operations depended almost entirely upon galleys.

At one time there was considerable debate and disagreement about the design of these vessels, especially during the early medieval period. Now, however, it is generally accepted that during the 7th century there had been a change in Byzantine galley design, from having oars all at one level to having them in two levels. This was, of course, a period when the Mediterranean Sea changed from being in effect a Romano-Byzantine lake in which the only significant threats came from pirates, to an arena of mortal competition between the Byzantine Empire and the newly created naval power of the Arab-Islamic Caliphate. By the 10th century, when Byzantine fleets were reaching the peak of their power, large Byzantine *dromons* had their oars at two levels. Only the lower level were apparently provided with leather sleeves to keep out water which could slop into the hull in choppy weather.[364]

The 7th century saw another significant technological change in the design of Byzantine and other Mediterranean galleys, though this may already have been under way. It was the shift from hull-breaking rams to boarding beaks which were raised well above the waterline. This in turn must have been associated with an even more fundamental change in ship-building which would impact all large craft including both galleys and transports. It was the change from hull or skin-first to frame-first construction which used less timber, required less skill on the part of shipbuilders and also produced a stronger hull; indeed one that could rarely be damaged by a ram.

Here it is worth also noting that the ram had probably been designed to spring the planks of a ship constructed in the old hull-first style, and thus to cause leaks rather than to punch right through in the dramatic manner beloved by film-makers. This did not work with the stronger or perhaps more shock-absorbent frame-first construction.[365] Meanwhile the Arab *shini* galley similarly had two banks of oars and, like the Byzantine *dromon*, normally averaged about forty-two metres in length.[366] In fact the warships of the rival cultures, and perhaps their merchant vessels as well, shared virtually identical technologies throughout this period.

The crews of 11th century Byzantine warships, like those of the 10th and perhaps earlier centuries, consisted of sailors who normally did not fight, plus naval troops or marines who did. During the 11th century the fighting troops aboard ship included men from recognised regular units or *tagmata*. Some were archers, others spearmen or experts in the use of *Greek Fire*, but it was those equipped with adequate body armour who proved most effective in the close combat that characterised naval warfare of this period.[367] Perhaps some of these naval troops were indeed specialist marines, as suggested by Anna Comnena's comment that these men were good at sea but proved 'useless' on land in southern Italy.[368] Or it could simply be another of those ill-informed criticisms to which Anna was prone.

The cataclysmic events of the later 11th century clearly had an impact upon recruitment for the Byzantine fleet. In fact, the eagerness with which the Byzantine government accepted naval recruits from distant lands suggests a shortage of reliable personnel from within the Empire, despite the fact that coastal regions were fast becoming the only territories that the Byzantine state could control with much confidence. For many years the Byzantine navy, especially the most important and presumably élite part of it based in Constantinople, was said to be largely manned by specially hired foreigners. Whether this applied to the sailors or the marines or both is unclear.

Before the battle of Manzikert in 1071, the most notable such foreign recruits were *Varangians* and Russians, both groups being of largely Scandinavian origin who could be expected to bring with them vigorous traditions of naval warfare. After the disasters of the late 11th century the most important source of skilled foreign naval personnel was Western Europe and more especially Italians. By the late 12th century the situation was becoming so difficult that the Empire enlisted independent 'pirate' leaders, crews and ships which were already operating in the area. These included men from a great variety of origins, though most notably Genoese and Muslims.[369] Quite where the latter came from is unknown, as the nearest Islamic coasts were, at this time, in Egypt and North Africa. Perhaps they included some of the same ships and crews who fought for Saladin.

After the fall of Constantinople to the Fourth Crusade in 1204 the Nicaean and Palaeolog Emperors preferred locally recruited men, but it soon became clear that there were not enough of them. During the 13th century these locals included *Tzaconians* from south-eastern Greece, and those known as *Gasmoulis* who were of supposedly mixed Greek-Byzantine and Latin-Crusader parentage. When the Emperor Andronicus II disbanded most of the navy, some of these men sought service amongst the Latin States of Greece, though most apparently went over to the Turkish *amirs* who were establishing small states, and in many cases navies, along the Aegean coast of what is now Turkey.[370]

Nevertheless, the descendants of these *Gasmoulis*, still known by the same name, dominated what remained of the Byzantine navy during the 14th century. They then became the first sailors of the first Ottoman Turkish fleet based in Gallipoli during the second half of the 14th century.[371] Where possible the small fleets maintained by the Palaeolog Emperor in the second half of the 13th century recruited local Greeks,[372] but their most successful admiral was again an Italian. His name was Licario, a poor knight whose family came from the inland city of Verona. He had estates on the large, nominally Venetian-ruled Greek island of Evoia but fell out with his overlords and transferred to Byzantine service in 1271. There Licario was so successful that he regained several northern Aegean islands for the Empire and was nominated *Grand Constable*.[373]

The most common weapons aboard Byzantine ships, like those of other Mediterranean powers, were bows, later replaced to some degree by crossbows, plus javelins and close-combat weapons. When incendiary or other heavier weapons were used on board war-galleys, these were mounted on the *rostrum* or front part of the vessel, not amidships nor, apparently, in the stern.[374] The front of a galley had, throughout naval history, been the focus of its fighting potential, and would remain so until galleys finally fell out of use in the early 19th century.

Naval warfare was currently almost entirely a matter of defeating enemy crews rather than destroying their ships. The beak which had replaced the ram at the prow of a galley was no longer intended as a ship-destroying device, though it could still wreak havoc to an enemy's oars and oarsmen. Instead it primarily served as an aid to boarding an enemy vessel. Even the heavy wooden 'bombs' hurled from the crow's nests at the head of ships' mainmasts were primarily targeted at the crew, being spiked with nails that could injure the men's feet even if they did not hit them when first dropped.[375]

In fact the only real ship-destroying weapon available at this time was fire. *Greek Fire* had proved extremely effective in the hands of the Byzantine navy, though it could sometimes prove dangerous to its own side. Even so, the impact of *Greek Fire* seems to have been more moral than physical, with only a few cases of ships being consumed, but numerous instances of their crews retreating in haste when faced by such a terrifying weapon. The threat from *Greek Fire* and other incendiary devices also spurred the development of defensive countermeasures. According to Cinnamus, the Byzantines tried to use what he called *Median Fire* (another name for *Greek Fire*) against a Venetian fleet in 1171, but failed to have much impact because the Venetians had protected their ships with vinegar-soaked cloth. Some of the fire was also thrown too far, some too short or, when it hit, failed to set fire to the enemy ship, being *'repelled by the cloth and quenched in the water when it fell'*.[376] The weapons in question do, in fact, sound more like incendiary grenades than *Greek Fire* syphons.

In broader terms, the varied coasts of the eastern Mediterranean and neighbouring seas resulted in differing strategic circumstances. To the south the low-lying shores of Cilicia looks, on the map, highly vulnerable, but in reality their lack of good harbours and abundance of offshore shallows made this a dangerously exposed coast for shipping that came too close. Perhaps for this reason, the rulers of the Cilician Kingdom of Lesser Armenia largely left their coast to the Italians who dominated these neighbouring seas from the 12th century onwards.[377] On the other side of Anatolia lay the notoriously stormy Black Sea. This remained under effective Byzantine control long after the Empire's decline in the Mediterranean and even in the Aegean.

The Turks broke through to the coast in the final years of the 12th century, cutting off the Byzantine territory of Trebizond (Trabzon) from the rest of the Empire, but it was only with their capture of Sinope (Sinop) in 1214 that the Seljuks turned their attention to this northern sea. By now the Latin Fourth Crusade had seized Constantinople, resulting in rival Byzantine successor Empires being established at Nicaea in north-western Anatolia and Trebizond in north-eastern Anatolia. At around the same time that Sinope fell to the Turks, raising the spectre of a Turkish-Islamic challenge to the Byzantine monopoly of these waters, the Empire of Trebizond won control of the isolated Byzantine enclaves in the Crimea on the northern side of the Black Sea.

Only a few years later, in 1220, the new Seljuk governor of Sinop had sufficient ships and men at his command to send a fleet to ravage the Byzantine Crimea. The Venetians, as close allies of the newly established Latin Empire of Constantinople, were also active in this area while in 1221 the Seljuk Sultan used his new naval power to impose suzerainty on the newly established and nominally Genoese trading outpost at Sudak (Soldaia) in the Crimea where he installed a small garrison. Two years later a far more terrifying foe appeared on the scene, the Mongols who sacked Genoese Sudak, crushed a Russian–Kipchaq alliance at the battle of the Kalka River and, after returning some years later, conquered the entire region.

A new, complex and, for the Black Sea, entirely novel strategic situation had developed,[378] although the now dominant Mongol 'world empire' showed no interest in controlling the Black Sea, the Mongol Khans apparently being content to dominate virtually all the surrounding coasts of this virtually enclosed sea. Only when the Ottoman Turks finally conquered the Byzantine capital of Constantinople in 1453 did the Black Sea once again become the preserve of a single great naval power – this time the Ottomans themselves.

CHRISTIAN AFRICA

One significant culture that was directly involved in the struggle between Christendom and Islam during the 11th to 14th centuries has rarely received the attention which it deserves. This was the Christian civilisation of the Nubian kingdoms in large parts of what is now the Republic of Sudan and the Kingdom of Abyssinia in the northern part of what is today Ethiopia. Both regions were converted to Christianity by Coptic missionaries from Egypt in the pre-Islamic early Middle Ages. Thus their cultures, as well as their churches, were closely linked to the Coptic Church and culture of what was now the Islamic-ruled though perhaps not yet Muslim-majority land of Egypt.

Although there is no evidence of direct political and still less military links between the Crusader Kingdom of Jerusalem established in Palestine and the indigenous African Christian states, a number of Crusader naval raids in the Red Sea made Saladin and his successors realise that the Red Sea could no longer be regarded as an entirely secure Arab-Islamic lake. These Crusader naval operations, plus some associated incursions down the eastern coast of Arabia into the Islamic holy land of the Hijaz were instigated by Reynald de Châtillon, the Latin lord of Oultrejordain in the southern part of what is now Jordan. They also raised the fear, and perhaps the potential reality, of a strategic alliance between the Christian Crusader States and the ancient Christian kingdoms of Nubia and Abyssinia.[379]

In the event the feared alliance between east African Christendom and the Christian powers of Europe did not materialise until the 16th century when the Portuguese arrived, having sailed around the southern tip of Africa. They then forged a remarkable link with the Kingdom of Abyssinia, itself the only surviving indigenous Christian state in Africa. Yet the fact that it happened at all gives credibility to the concerns felt in Cairo in the 12th and 13th centuries.

The reality on the ground was, however, rather different from what Saladin and his successors feared. The rulers of the Christian states in Nubia, along the banks of the Nile and its branches in northern and central Sudan, had followed a policy of good relations with Cairo for centuries. Since the 7th century, when the first Arab-Islamic raids into Nubia had been unexpectedly defeated, a *baqt* or pact had been in force whereby the Muslim governors of Egypt and the kings of Nubia agreed to respect the territorial integrity of their mutual frontier.

Thereafter Nubian rulers almost always regarded an alliance with Egypt as the best guarantee of their own states' security and stability. In return the government in Cairo saw the effective dependence of the Christian churches in Nubia and Abyssinia upon the Coptic Church and hierarchy in Egypt as a means of exerting influence south of their border. These realms also had a shared interest in trade along the river Nile which still formed one of the most important links between the Mediterranean world and sub-Saharan Africa.

Despite occasional tensions and even a few skirmishes, this mutually beneficial relationship survived until the second half of the 13th century. Its decline then reflected major cultural and political changes within Egypt where a new Mamluk Sultanate had replaced the Ayyubid dynasty established by Saladin. Meanwhile the Nubian states had suffered a significant economic and political decline. Baybars ruled Egypt from 1260 until 1277, as the greatest of the early Mamluk Sultans. He also regarded the regions south of Egypt as vital security zones for the Mamluk state, to be kept subvervient or at least quiet and unthreatening while the Mamluk army focussed on a far more dangerous threat posed by the Mongols in the north.[380] However, the venerable *baqt* was still in operation, and Islamic law meant that Baybars could not simply attack another country without cause.

In 1272 an opportunity seemed to fall into Baybars' lap. During that year a Nubian force crossed the desert from the Nile valley and attacked an Egyptian outpost at Aydhab on the Red Sea coast. Here they robbed many Muslim pilgrims who were undertaking the *Haj* or Islamic pilgrimage to Mecca and Medina in Arabia. Another Nubian raiding force struck north, attacking the southern Egyptian frontier and garrison town of Aswan. The reasons for this sudden outbreak of fighting are unclear, but might have reflected the Nubians' wish to maintain access to the sea at a time when Egyptian Islamic power was spreading further down the Red Sea coast. It might also have been partially prompted by anti-Coptic actions by the new Mamluk government within Egypt itself. Traditionally the Nubian rulers had portrayed themselves as the protectors of Coptic interests, though their limited military power made this claim largely meaningless.[381] Or it may simply have been prompted by economic decline and increasing desperation within Nubia.

Whatever the causes, the results were devastating for the Nubian kingdoms, indeed ultimately fatal for Christianity in northern and central Sudan. The hugely powerful Mamluk Sultanate which now dominated Egypt and most of Syria responded with a series of raids. These were probably seen as little more than sideshows by the Mamluks who were far more concerned about the Mongol threat in Syria and by the remaining Crusader enclaves on the Syrian–Palestinian coast. For the Nubians they must have looked like major invasions which destroyed the ancient *baqt* system, toppled several Nubian kings and replaced them with puppet rulers who had no choice but to accept Mamluk overlordship.[382]

This was the general outline of a political and military relationship between Christian Nubia and its powerful Islamic neighbours to the north; a remarkably long-lasting and, until the last century or so, largely friendly relationship built upon shared economic interests. The slave trade had been vital to the economies of the Christian Nubian kingdoms for centuries, bringing African slaves from the south and selling them to the Mediterranean countries of the north. While Nubia remained prosperous, there had been some degree of military balance with Egypt, Nubian forces not only being able to raid Aswan at times of tension but even launching a remarkable attack across the Western Desert to pillage the western oases (al-Wahāt)in the 950s.[383]

Even as late as 1047 the Persian traveller Nasir-i Khusrau noted that Aswan was well fortified and had a proper garrison to defend the Fatimid Egyptian Caliphate's southern frontier against the Nubians.[384] He also noted that many soldiers were recruited into the Fatimid army from the lands of the *Masmuda* 'south of Nubia'. The location of *Masmuda* territory tended to be ill-defined in many medieval Islamic geographical texts, but in general terms the *Masmuda* seem to have come from the Sahel or semi-desert regions south of the Sahara. Nasir-i Khusrau reported, perhaps on the basis of conversation he had in Egypt, that the land of the *Masmuda* was a region of huge pastures and many warriors.[385]

Relations between the Christian kingdoms of Nubia and the Fatimid or Shi'ite Islamic Caliphate in Egypt had traditionally been good, but this situation deteriorated when the Fatimids were overthrown by Saladin. In 1172, only a year after the death of the last Fatimid Caliphate, a Nubian army again threatened southern Egypt. Here it was joined by Armenian soldiers who, having previously served the Fatimids, had been dismissed as politically unreliable by Saladin. Most of these men were, like the Nubians, Christians but they were joined by various other ex-Fatimid Islamic troops in an attempted siege of Aswan. Saladin sent reinforcements south, defeating the Nubian–rebel alliance which withdrew down the Nile.[386] In retaliation Saladin sent a raiding column into Nubia. This did not try to conquer territory but easily defeated the Nubian troops who, it was said, '*had no defence against arrows*'. Whether this indicated the Nubians' lack of armour or the superiority of Saladin's largely Turkish archers is unclear, but it was a sign of a fundamental shift in the military balance, and from now on the military advantage lay firmly with Islamic forces from Egypt.

With the exception of the Nubian frontier with Egypt south of Aswan, the borders of these medieval Christian states in the Sudan are virtually unknown. In many areas they probably did not extend much further than the narrow fertile strip along the river Nile. In other places the oases and the desert trade routes which ran through them were almost certainly under Nubian control, while various little-known desert and semi-desert tribes probably recognised Nubian overlordship during some periods but not at others. Archaeologists have even found evidence of Christian communities hundreds of kilometres west of the Nile in Darfur, between Darfur and Nubia, and in western Kordofan, apparently dating from the 8th to the end of the 12th century.[387] They are so distant from the Kingdom of Alwa and the centres of Nubian power that they are unlikely to have indicated Nubian rule in such regions, but they might have been Nubian trading outposts or islands of Christian culture that owed their origins to Nubian influence. Certainly some medieval Arab geographers noted the strong cultural similarity between those they called the *Ahadi* west of the Nile and the Nubians of the Nile valley itself.

By the late 13th century Nubian power and influence apparently extended no more than thirty kilometres west of the junction of the Blue and White Niles.[388] In fact the Sahel or sub-Saharan steppes known to medieval Muslims as *Bilad al-Sudan*, 'Land of the Blacks' but not to be confused with the huge modern state of Sudan, was rapidly being drawn into the wider Islamic world (see volume II). Meanwhile the Nubian kingdoms were now almost encircled by Islamic peoples or states to the east as well as the north. Territorial links with the still Christian Kingdom of Abyssinia were similarly becoming tenuous. Even the northernmost region of Nubia itself was dominated by the Banu Kanz and the Maris who were largely Arabised and now Muslim Nubians.[389]

The Mamluk Sultanate in Egypt had demonstrated its superiority on the battlefield but does not yet seem to have wanted the political and military distraction of conquest. Instead the late 13th and early 14th century Mamluk Sultans preferred a stable relationship, with Nubia paying tribute and not causing problems, and it is unclear how much direct Mamluk influence there was over Nubia during this later period.[390]

THE ARMIES OF ALWA AND MAKKURIA

Nubia itself had originally been divided into three kingdoms. The southernmost and largest was Alwa, centred upon the region where the Blue and White Niles meet in the vicinity of the modern Sudanese capital of Khartoum. Soba, the capital of Alwa, was, in fact, not far from present-day Khartoum. It covered a substantial area, had a large cathedral and enjoyed a prolonged golden age from the 9th to the 12th century.[391] Unfortunately virtually nothing is known about its armies, though excavations at Soba have uncovered the usual variety of spear- and arrowheads, but as yet no swords. A decline then set in and Alwa divided into two states. Much of its territory fell under the domination of the once pagan but now increasingly Islamic Baja nomads who had inhabited the semi-desert mountains between the Nile and the Red Sea. The story of the Sudanese Christian realm of Alwa finally came to an end in the late 15th century when it was conquered by the Funj, a Sudanese tribe which established an Islamic state.[392]

Considerably more is known about the government and the military systems of the northern Nubian Kingdom of Makkuria which had by now absorbed the third and smallest Nubian state of Nobatia. Egyptian influence had been strong in all these regions since ancient times, being followed by Greek or Graeco-Roman influence. This Greek influence remained remarkably strong in Nobatia and Makkuria, and to a lesser extent in Alwa, throughout the Middle Ages, being constantly reinforced in a rather roundabout way via the Coptic Church in Egypt. It could be found in military and administrative terminology as well as Christian art and architecture.

Nobatia had been the frontier kingdom, stretching from the Egyptian border along that part of the Nile valley which now lies beneath the waters of man-made Lake Nasser to just north of the great bend in the Nile in what is now northern Sudan. Its rulers remained as sub-kings or governors and became known as the '*Lords of Horses*'.[393] Their primary function does, in fact, seem to have been military, as guardians of the northern frontier. In earlier times, before the large-scale introduction of camels into Egypt, North Africa and the Sahara Desert during the early medieval centuries and before the first wave of Arab-Islamic conquests, crossing the Sahara had been immensely difficult. The Nile valley provided the easiest link between the Mediterranean and sub-Saharan world, was relatively easy to defend and could be closed almost like a door. This inevitably brought great wealth and strategic importance to Nubia.

However, the camel gradually changed almost everything. Long and waterless routes between oases and sources of water which stood like islands in the Sahara's vast 'sea' of gravel, rock, sand and scrub could now be 'navigated'. The desert remained difficult and expensive to cross, but the camel-owning and camel-raiding nomadic tribes who dominated oases and caravan routes now became powerful players in international trade and international politics.

Nubia was gradually becoming little more than just one in a series of north–south links. Furthermore its own desert and semi-desert flanks became increasingly vulnerable to pressure from neighbouring tribes. The Nubian social and economic system was further disrupted after 1200 by an influx of Arab bedouin tribes from Egypt. Since the Arab-Islamic conquest of Egypt in the 7th century these tribes had, despite ups and downs in their fortunes, been a privileged and powerful community within Egypt; almost a state within a state. This was particularly true during the period of the Fatimid Caliphate which they had generally supported with enthusiasm.

Saladin's seizure of control saw the start of a steady decline in the status and fortunes of the distinctive bedouin tribes of Egypt, and a migration southwards by those who would not or could not accept the new situation. This flow became even more pronounced in the 14th century when the new Mamluk Sultans of Egypt adopted a policy hostile towards the bedouin. Once again camels played a part, enabling these new communities to cross the bone dry, virtually uninhabitable desert of sand and rock which lay north of the great bend in the Nile. This also meant that they did not have to fight their way down the northernmost stretch of the Nubian Nile valley known as *Batn al-Haja* or 'Belly of Stones'. Lying between the Second Cataract and Akasha, this had for centuries served as Nubia's first and most effective line of defence against threats from Egypt.

The Nubians themselves were unable or unwilling to adopt these new forms of desert warfare, at least not to a degree which would have enabled them to continue to face their northern rivals on equal terms. Back in the 7th century the Nubians earned themselves the title of 'A Nations of Archers' by defeating the first Arab-Islamic invasion, then defeating a second assault which included cavalry whose horse armour was intended to resist Nubian archery.[394] Clearly Nubian archery then declined, at least in relative terms, and in 1172 the defenders of fortified Qasr Ibrim could not resist the bows and other weapons used by Saladin's raiders.[395] The fact that the Nubians were now increasingly forced onto the defensive while being threatened from several directions, must account for the large castles and other fortifications which became a feature of later medieval Nubia.[396]

The famous Nubian archers of the early medieval period were almost certainly infantry, but Nubian forces had also been known for their cavalry. Not that their horses were particularly impressive, as the great Islamic chronicler and geographer Mas'udi wrote in the 10th century, quoting a Coptic Egyptian source: '*Their king rides a fine bred horse but the people are mounted on mares of small size*'.[397] By the late 13th century, during their clashes with Mamluk punitive raids, the Nubians had few horses but had clearly adopted camels. The latter were good for crossing deserts and as riding beasts, but even the Arab bedouin rarely attempted to fight on camel-back. In battle outside Dongola, the capital of the northern Kingdom of Makkuria in 1276, the camel-riding Nubians were armed with spears and used large black felt cloaks as a defence against arrows. They were, perhaps not surprisingly, utterly routed.[398]

The 10th century geographer Mas'udi's quote from a Coptic source also sheds interesting light on the bows which had at one time made Nubian archers so respected. He wrote that: '*they fight with curiously shaped bows (*shooting *nabl* arrows*) and it is from them that the tribes of the Hijaz, of Yemen and the other Arab tribes have adopted the use of the bow. The Arabs called them the habitual archers*'.[399] This and other evidence seems to indicate that the traditional Nubian bow was of simple, that is one-piece, wooden construction, probably carved from acacia and having the curved ends which had characterised bows used in Ancient Egypt. Indeed it may have been essentially the same weapon.[400] The medieval arrowheads excavated in the city of Soba were also of tanged rather than socket form, which puts them in the Middle Eastern and Asian rather than Western European tradition.[401]

A remarkable *chamfron* or headpiece from a horse-armour was excavated in Soba, but this was almost certainly imported from Egypt and will be discussed in the context of Islamic horse-armour (see volume II). The only other piece of armour which is known to come from Nubia during this period is a helmet made of crocodile skin. It was excavated in what was Egyptian Nubia, now lying beneath Lake Nasser, but without a dateable archaeological context. No carbon-dating tests are known to have been carried out on this unique helmet, but its lamellar neckpiece looks more medieval than ancient.[402]

On or beyond the fringes of medieval Nubia were other, perhaps culturally related peoples whose military traditions are distantly recorded in some Islamic chronicles or geographical works. Of *Masmuda* territory *'south of Nubia'*, the mid-11th century Central Asian Persian traveller Nasir-i Khusrau wrote that its warriors fought with *shamshir* sword and *nizah* spear, but used no other weapons. This would indicate that the Nubians' famous archery skills had not yet been copied by their pagan southern neighbours.[403] Of the Christian *Ahadi* people whose territory lay *'five days' march west'* of Nubian Alwa, the late 10th century Arab geographer wrote that their warriors had shields like the *Maghribi* (North African) *lamt* which was large and traditionally made of antelope hide. These *Ahadi* also had poor quality swords and quilted soft armour.[404]

The biggest and most powerful of the medieval Christian states in East Africa was also the most distant and is today the only one to survive. This was Abyssinia (today officially known as Ethiopia). Building upon a tradition of friendly relations with Islam that dated back to the life of the Prophet Muhammad himself, and despite a number of quite serious clashes during the first century of Arab-Islamic expansion, the first Christian Abyssinian Kingdom of Axum developed close trading links with Islamic communities around the Red Sea. By the start of the 10th century the Dahlak Islands and the mainland port of Massawa (both now part of independent Eritrea) were firmly in Islamic hands, though their governor paid tribute to the neighbouring *Negus* or Abyssinian ruler in Axum. This was also the case with the Islamic coastal state of Zayla, close to the vital Bab al-Mandab straits linking the Red Sea and Indian Ocean.[405]

After 975, however, the power of the Abyssinian Kingdom of Axum suddenly collapsed while the armies of a 'pagan queen' known as Gudit or Judith ravaged the country. These Agau-speaking non-Christians may have largely consisted of pagan tribes from the Damot area, in a loop of the Abai river, but may also have included or been led by the ancient Jewish community in Ethiopia, the partly Agau-speaking ancestors of the present-day Falashas. Whoever they were, their overthrow of Axum had a profound impact upon Ethiopian history. Christianity declined in the north and along the Red Sea coasts where it was substantially replaced by Islam, but would subsequently spread southward.[406] Over a century of apparent chaos ensued, about which Arab and Ethiopian sources say very little. This was, for probably unconnected reasons, also a period of acute political fragmentation within the Islamic world.

Then, in the early 12th century, a new Christian ruling dynasty of Abyssinian *Negus* kings emerged to establish a powerful kingdom to the south of what had been the Axumite heartland. Though descended from fiercely anti-Christian Gudit, these rulers became emphatically Christian and, adopting the dynastic name of Zagwé in 1137, were responsible for the astonishing late 12th and 13th century rock-cut churches of Lalibela which are today one of the glories of Ethiopia. The centre of Zagwé power was no longer in the strongly Semitic-influenced northern mountains with their cultural links to Yemen, but in the non-Semitic highlands of central Ethiopia. Though still ecclesiastically dependent upon the Coptic Church in Cairo, their links with Egypt were much more tenuous than Axum's had been. Furthermore, the balance of power between Muslim Egypt and Christian Abyssinia in the Red Sea region had now shifted firmly in favour of Egypt.[407]

Some time around 1268 the last king of the Zagwé dynasty was overthrown by another *Negus* who claimed to be a descendant of Axumite rulers who themselves had claimed descent from King Solomon and the Queen of Sheba. This further dynastic change resulted in another shift southwards in the centre of Ethiopian power and a series of major conflicts with surrounding states. Meanwhile, the only proven links between Abyssinia and the Latin Crusader Kingdom of Jerusalem were ecclesiastical, the Abyssinians having a presence in the Church of the Holy Sepulchre in Jerusalem, though essentially as an offshoot of the Coptic Church of Egypt. The Pope in Rome is also known to have sent missionaries to Nubia and perhaps to Abyssinia in the mid-13th century.[408]

In the Middle Ages religion and politics were inextricably entwined and Latin or Catholic missionary work, or even the establishing of contacts with other churches, was itself also a political act. So it is hardly surprising that the Mamluk Sultans in Cairo viewed these activities with suspicion. Yet it is unlikely that such concerns played a major part in a serious deterioration in relations between Mamluk Egypt and Abyssinia during the latter part of the reign of the *Negus* Yikunno-'Almak (1270–85). There was already a substantial Islamic population in the Kingdom of Abyssinia,[409] and the late 13th century *Negus* Yabga-Siyon claimed to be protector of Muslims within his territory just as the Mamluk Sultan was protector of Christians within his. In reality it was a lopsided relationship, with Abyssinia as a very junior partner. The stability of the Abyssinian church and state were now virtually in the hands of whoever ruled in Cairo.[410]

Despite Abyssinia's decline as a military power, it still had considerable regional significance and its armies attracted the attention of several later medieval Arab geographers and historians. Al-Maqrizi, for example, wrote that the late 13th and 14th century Abyssinian government did not have a *diwan* or special department dealing with military affairs as did most Islamic states. Instead the army resembled a *jund* or local militia and its numbers were checked by the use of 'special stones'.[411] Presumably each man who attended muster dropped a stone into a container so that they could later be counted.

Ibn Fadl Allah al-Umari, writing in the mid-14th century, mentioned the numerous cavalry of Awfat which was by now a largely Islamic area between Christian central Ethiopia and the Islamic sultanate of Zayla on the coast. These horsemen rode '*without wood framed saddles*', which probably meant that they used the simple padded and unframed saddles that had been used by Arabs and many other peoples in the Middle East before and during the very early Islamic period. This is also likely to have meant that they did not use stirrups.[412] Furthermore, according to al-Umari, the warriors of the Christian part of Abyssinia fought with the bow, using large *nushshab* arrows, plus swords, javelins, spears and long narrow shields, though their most common weapon was the javelin.

Several types of bow seem to have been used, one of which was a notably long weapon called a *qaws al-qutn* or 'cotton bow' which meant, of course, that its string was made of cotton thread. It was said to resemble a crossbow, though it is not clear how, and shot short arrows. Perhaps this meant that Abyssinian troops had adopted the arrow-guide, known to the Arabs as a *majra* (see volume II) and to the Byzantines as a *solenarion*. Finally, al-Umari noted that Abyssinian armies made use of horns made of bamboo and cow-horn to rally or encourage their troops.[413] Clearly these were quite sophisticated forces which, though perhaps rather old-fashioned and ill-equipped by the standards of their Islamic neighbours in Egypt and Arabia, were nevertheless not the 'black hordes' of the 'Dark Continent' that they were too often been assumed to be by nineteenth and twentieth century Western historians.

3

The Military Heritage and Impact of Crusading Warfare on the Christian World

The cultural and political impact of the Crusades on those peoples involved, and in a broader sense upon the cultures that were drawn into these conflicts, has been widely discussed for many years. The more specific military impact has received less attention. Nevertheless it was profound. The most obvious flow of new or more advanced military ideas was from the medieval Islamic world to medieval Western, Latin or Catholic Europe. This could be seen in new forms of armour, though less so in weapons, with the possible exception of incendiaries and gunpowder. A possible Mongol role in the transmission of the latter technology cannot be ignored. There was similarly a flow or, more correctly perhaps, a mutual exchange of ideas in the design of fortification[1] and of increasingly powerful siege weapons.

This exchange of ideas was not, of course, the only stimulus to change. There was also the pressure of warfare itself. The period of the Crusades witnessed some remarkable advances in, for example, the design, power and size of stone-throwing *trebuchets*. Their larger and more accurate missiles had a profound impact on the design of fortifications and on defensive planning. On the other hand, it should never be forgotten that, at least in the initial period, the major impact of the counterweight *trebuchet* was in defence rather than in attack.[2] The role of warfare, and of the injuries as well as the disease it caused, in the spread of Islamic medical knowledge to Western Europe is less obvious. However, it is interesting to note that the influence of this much more advanced knowledge was at first upon the practical rather than the theoretical side of medieval European medicine.[3] This was especially apparent during the second half of the 12th century which was, in many respects, the most dramatic period of such transmission.

The effect of the Crusades upon the indigenous Christian peoples of the Middle East, upon those whom the Crusades were in part launched to 'save' from supposed Islamic oppression, was entirely negative. Indeed in many areas it was catastrophic.[4] Even so, this catastrophe was not solely a result of the Crusades. The way in which several local Christian communities either rallied to, or were thought to be sympathetic to, the Mongol invaders may have been more important. Nevertheless, the modus vivendi which had characterised relations between Christians, Muslims and others had been gravely undermined by the Crusades well before the Mongols appeared on the scene.

The breaking of the old *convivencia* in the Iberian peninsula similarly resulted from Christian aggression, though this was at first localised. The sudden collapse of al-Andalus in the mid- to late 13th century, leaving Granada as the only surviving bastion of Iberian Islam, had a much more profound impact in the rest of the Islamic world. Here there was a notable increase in anti-Christian feelings, not least in the Mamluk Sultanate of Egypt and Syria where the position of indigenous Christian *dhimmis* or Christians under Islamic rule was gravely undermined.[5] Coptic Egyptian conversion to Islam, which had previously been a trickle, became a flood in the 14th century, even in Upper Egypt where Christians had remained a majority and had been supported by strong links with the Christian kingdoms of Nubia. Jews, meanwhile, were not seen as a threat and therefore avoided the most fanatical elements of the persecution which scarred this period of Mamluk history.[6]

Far more positive was the effect both the Crusades and the Mongol conquests had upon long-distance trade and patterns of trade, though even here there were losers as well as winners. From the 13th to the end of the 15th century the Black Sea became a more important hub of north–south and east–west trade than it had been. This was largely because of the stability established by the Mongol Golden Horde and maintained, more or less, by its successor *Khanates*. Meanwhile east–west trade seems largely to have consisted of luxury or exotic goods. North–south trade largely consisted of bulk goods such as grain or leather and a distinctive slave trade which shipped new *mamluk* recruits from north or east of the Black Sea to the Mamluk Sultanate in Egypt and Syria. Constantinople and Trebizond, the capitals of two rival Byzantine 'successor-empires', were hubs of this north–south and, to a lesser extent, east–west trade. Both remained wealthy as a result and consequently became targets for future Ottoman Turkish aggression.

Terminology

Ara = Arabic; Arm = Armenian; Ber = Berber; Cat = Catalan; Far = Farsi; Fle = Flemish; Geo = Georgian; Gr = Greek; Lat = Latin, including medieval Latin; ME = medieval English; MF = medieval French; MG = medieval German; MI = medieval Italian; Mon = Mongol; MS = medieval Spanish; Occ = Occitan; Por = Portuguese; Sl = Slavic (various); Tur = Turkish;

a la brida (Spanish)	riding technique with long stirrup leathers
a la jinete (Spanish)	riding technique with short stirrup leathers
adalid (MS)	cavalry commander: 37
afelter (MF)	to arm oneself: 98
agulani (Lat)	from *ghulam*, Islamic soldier of slave-recruited origin
aketon (MF)	quilted soft armour: 96, 99
akontion (Gr)	spear: 199
akritoi (Gr)	Byzantine frontier troops: 161, 168, 183, 185, 206
albarrana (MS)	freestanding external towers attached to main fortification by a bridge
alberc (MF)	mail hauberk (body armour)
alcalde (MS)	person responsible for administrative aspects of a militia: 37, 59
alcazaba (MS)	citadel
alferes mor (Por)	head of the Portuguese army, beneath the ruler himself: 37
algara (MP)	that part of an urban militia carrying out raids: 58
algarrada (MP)	stone-throwing siege machine, from Arabic *al-'arrada*: 120
alla sensile (MI)	literally 'in simple fashion', method of manning the oars of a galley: 142
allagator (Gr)	officer in command of an *allagion* military unit: 178
allagion (Gr)	Byzantine military unit: 178–80, 183
almenara (MS)	small frontier tower: 112
almocadén (MS)	infantry commander: 37
almogávares, almugavars (MS)	Iberian light infantry of Moorish origin: 26–7, 74, 148
amirate (Ara)	small state ruled by an *amir*
amis (MF)	band of comrades, 'friends': 78
anubda (MS)	frontier guard duty: 26
apellido (MS)	defensive action by an urban militia: 26
arbalete à tour (MF)	large form of crossbow: 91, 122
archontes, archons (Gr)	member of local or lower Byzantine aristocracy: 10, 19, 162, 177
archontopouloi (Gr)	one of the Byzantine regiments, literally 'sons of *archontes*': 176
aretueil (MF)	butt of spear: 69
arevordik (Arm)	Armenian non-Christian or 'heretical' community
armigeri (MI)	military servant or squire: 30

ʻarrada (Ara)	beamsling stonethrowing siege weapon, usually manpowered: 120
arróbda (MS)	frontier guard duty: 26
ars de cor (MF)	bow of composite construction
asagai	short-hafted spear widely used in pre-modern sub-Saharan Africa: 83
atalaya (MS)	small frontier tower or watchtower: 112
atalayero (MS)	scout: 26
aubers conugut (MF)	probably a hauberk with a surcoat over it: 80
auqueton (MF)	quilted soft armour (see *aketon*)
ausberc doblier (MF)	doubled or double-layer mail hauberk: 80
auscona (MS)	javelin: 83
avak baron (Arm)	senior baron: 182
azaga (MS)	part of urban militia used to protect a base-camp: 58
azatk' (Arm)	those holding land in return for military service: 182
azcona (MS)	javelin: 83
bacinets de cuero (MI)	helmets of, or partly of, leather: 101
badelaire (MF)	possibly a cutlass: 84
bailli (MF)	senior local authority: 31, 34
balista (MI)	crossbow: 90
balista de cornu (MF)	crossbow with composite bowstave: 90
balista de torno (MF)	large form of crossbow: 90
baliste ad duas pedes (MI)	crossbow spanned with both feet: 91
baliste ad estrif (MI)	crossbow with spanning stirrup: 91
baliste ad tornum (MI)	large form of crossbow: 146
ballesta (MS)	crossbow: 72
ban (MF)	military summons: 13
bandoliere (MI)	possibly a shoulder belt to span a crossbow: 91
baqt (Ara from Gk)	treaty or 'pact': 229–30
barbacana (MF)	additional fortified wall or barbican
barbuta (MI)	open-faced helmet: 72
barkil (Ara)	term sometimes used for turcopoles in Crusader service: 14, 50
bascinet (MF)	light form of helmet: 101
bataille (MF)	division of an army: 31, 66, 69
bayl (Arm)	local authority or governor, from French *bailli*: 182
bazineto (MI)	light form of helmet
belesin (Gr)	javelin: 197
belfry (MF)	wooden siege tower: 118
bellatorum (Lat)	stern castle of a ship: 142
benefice (MF)	fief: 37
berrovieri (MI)	light cavalry: 72
besague (MF)	form of infantry staff weapon: 85
bevor (MF)	chin and throat protection: 102
beylik (Tur)	small state ruled by a *bey* or *beg*: 157, 171
bible (MF)	perhaps a traversable *mangonel*: 121
biblieta (MI)	perhaps a traversable *mangonel*: 121
biffa, biffe (MF)	large *trebuchet*: 119
birka (Ara)	water cistern: 122
biscoti (MI)	ship's biscuit: 145
bouzon, bozon (MF)	large arrow or bolt shot from a large crossbow

braoneras (Cat)	arm defences: 97
brassonieras (MS)	arm defences: 97
bricola, brigola (MI)	perhaps a traversable *mangonel*: 121
brofuneras (MS)	leg protections: 81
broine (MF)	mail hauberk, body armour: 97
budluq (Tk)	armour for the thighs: 204
buffa (MI)	large *trebuchet*: 119
buisine (MF)	trumpet: 132
bull (Lat)	Papal edict or law: 40
burgess (ME)	member of middle class, usually urban: 16, 21, 86, 123, 134
buss (MF)	sailing ship: 223
caable (MF)	stone-throwing siege engine, probably of traction type
cabalgada (MS)	offensive raid led by the king or senior aristocrat: 26
caballer, caballeria (MS)	cavalryman, cavalry: 26, 81
caballeros villanos (MS)	middle-class cavalry: 26, 29
calcar (MI)	beak or boarding prow on a galley: 142
calthrop (ME)	spikes scattered to injure horses' feet: 194
cambays (MF)	quilted soft armour: 99
caparison (ME)	protective covering for horse: 39, 103, 206
capellina (MS)	mail *coif*
cappa clausa (Lat)	monastic costume: 40
caravan (MF)	cavalry raid: 133
caravel (MS)	type of sailing ship: 143
caravo (MS)	type of sailing ship: 143
çarh (Tk)	crossbow: 217
carpentarius bridarum (Lat)	builder of large stone-throwing engine: 128
carrel (MF)	arrow or bolt shot by a crossbow
carroballista (Lat)	torsion-powered, two-arm bolt- or ball-shooting weapon: 215
carroccio (MI)	waggon displaying flags or banners: 40–1, 79, 192
casales (MF)	farm-estates: 138, 208
casa-torre (MI)	fortified tower-house: 177
castra (Lat)	fortified village: 109
cauces ploieïces (MF)	pliable *chausses*, leg armour
çauş (Tur)	official or officer: 182
caussas de ferre (MF)	mail leg armour: 98
cavaleiros (Por)	knights: 37–8
cavalleriae (MS)	knight: 30
cebe (Tur)	mail-lined armour or hauberk: 201
cendal (MF)	fine cloth: 103
cerveliere (MF)	small helmet: 100
cestrosphendone (Gk)	sling to throw a javelin
chaablum, chaable, chadable, chadabula (Lat, MF & MI)	stone-throwing siege engine, probably of traction type: 121
chalumiaux (MF)	perhaps bagpipes: 132
chamfron (MF)	armour for horse's head: 234
chantsler (Arm)	senior government figure, chancellor: 182
chapeau de fer, chapel de fer (MF)	brimmed form of helmet: 80, 101
charcloie (MF)	moveable protective roof or shed: 119
chastiaus (MF)	fighting castle on stern or forecastle of a ship
chatelain (MF)	castle commander: 31–2, 34

chausses (MF)	mail leg armour: 80, 98, 203
cheiroballista (Gr)	perhaps a small ballista or torsion-powered crossbow: 215–16
cheirotoxobolistra (Gr)	crossbow: 201
chelandion (Gr)	galley, perhaps landing craft or horse-transport: 135, 151, 214
chelandre, chellande (MF)	specialised horse-transporting galley: 135, 151, 214
chelonai (Gr)	defensive shed or roof, literally 'tortoise': 214
chevalier (MF)	knight: 183
chevaucher (MF)	raid or order of march: 64
cirit (Tur)	mounted combat game using blunted javelins
cirujanos (MS)	surgeons: 140
cistarelle (MI)	unclear item made of wood; either a helmet or leg protection: 98, 101
clavain, claviere (MF)	throat protection: 102
coat-of-plates (modern term)	armour of iron plates riveted to a cloth covering: 96–7
cog (ME)	sailing ship: 148
coif (ME)	head-covering of cloth or mail, civilian or military: 101
coife fort et turcoise (MF)	strong mail-lined, cloth-covered *coif*
coirassas (MS)	coat-of-plates form of body armour: 96
coivre (MF)	quiver: 150
colerias (MS)	neck protection: 102
collación (MS)	quarter of a town: 37
coltellaccio, coltello (MI)	large dagger, short sword or cutlass: 72
compagnie (MF)	group of knights, later an association of mercenaries: 78
compline (Lat)	evening prayer and mass: 122
concejo (MS)	blessing of standards and flags: 40
condotte (MI)	contract, often military: 74
connaissance (MF)	heraldic device: 39
connetable (MF)	chief of the army after the ruler himself: 31, 182
conrois (MF)	small, closely packed cavalry formation: 66–8
contado (MI)	immediate surroundings of a city: 24, 82
convent (MF)	headquarters of a Military Order: 116
convivencia (MS)	co-existence, living in peace or respect, toleration: 6, 238
corazas (MS)	coat-of-plates, plate-lined cuirass: 95–6
corettum (Lat)	cuirass
couched lance (modern term)	method of holding a cavalry lance tucked beneath the armpit: 66, 70–71, 75, 102, 156, 187
couteau d'armes (MF)	fighting knife or dagger: 84
couter (ME)	elbow protection: 94, 97
couverture (MF)	covering for a horse: 103
croc (MF)	hook: 91
cuchiello serranil (MS)	long knife: 73
cuir bouilli (MF)	hardened leather: 93
cuirie (MF)	leather body-armour: 96–7
cuisse, cuissot, cuixa, cuja, cuxa (MF, MS)	thigh armour: 98
cursores et defensores (Lat)	method of repeated cavalry attack and withdrawal: 65
dapifer regis (MF)	alternative title for Senechal: 31
dard, dardos (MF, MS)	small javelin or dart: 75
dardiers (MF)	javelin or dart throwers: 75
decine (MI)	militia units of ten: 37
devsirme (Tur)	forcible recruitment of children: 167

dezanvana (MF)	parapet
diwan (Ara)	government department or office: 236
donjon (MF)	keep or main tower of a castle: 110, 112, 211
dromon (Gr)	galley: 224–5
dux (Lat & Gr)	duke: 176–8, 180, 215
enbuschement (MF)	ambush: 67
enceinte (MF)	curtain-walls or walled enclosure of castle or city: 112
eparch (Gr)	senior military commander in Nubian kingdoms
epilorikon (Gr)	quilted soft armour or surcoat: 203, 205
escalus (Lat)	squadron: 67
eschiele (MF)	squadron: 67
escudeiros (Por)	squires: 38
esculca (MS)	guard of migrating flocks: 59
espalier, espalliere (MF)	shoulder protection: 97, 102
espringal (MF)	torsion-powered siege weapon: 122, 146, 216
exeas (Lat)	official responsible for exchange or release of military prisoners: 50
fabricae (Lat)	factory, workshop: 207
falchion (ME & MF)	broad, single-edged sword: 76, 84, 86
famuli (Lat)	palace retainers: 20
faqi (Ara)	Islamic religious scholar: 22
faubourg (MF)	suburb or new town: 116
fauchart, fauchon (MF)	single-edged weapons, either on short haft or with sword-like hilt: 76, 86
faussart (MF)	single-edged weapons, either on short haft or with sword-like hilt: 86
faussó (MS)	single-edged weapons, either on short haft or with sword-like hilt: 86
ferrarii (Lat)	ironworkers: 105
feu grejois (MF)	Greek Fire: 119, 129
fojas (MS)	scale armour: 95
fonsadera (MS)	fine imposed for non-attendance in militia, later a form of payment instead of military service: 26
fonsado (MS)	service in major expedition: 26
fossator (MF)	miner: 128
frestiax (MF)	form of multiple flute: 132
frontera (MS)	frontier zone
fueros (MS)	laws of a Spanish town: 49
funde (MF)	sling: 123
galea (Lat)	helmet: 100
galeas dublices (Lat)	doubled helmet: 100
galleon (MS)	in medieval period a small ship using sails and oars: 29, 144
gambais, gambaisel, gambeson (MF)	quilted soft armour: 75, 205
gambax (MF)	quilted soft armour
gamberas (MI)	limb protections: 107
gamboisées (MF)	quilted or stuffed: 102
gamboison d'estoupes (MF)	quilted soft armour
gasmouli (MI)	supposedly descendants of mixed Greek–Latin marriages: 179, 185, 226
gastaldate (MI)	pre-feudal territorial and aristocratic territorial division: 35

genellieres (MF)	knee protections: 98
ghulam (Ara)	slave recruited to be trained as a soldier: 13, 166
gibelline	pro-Imperial faction in Italy: 70
gisarme (MF)	infantry staff weapon: 85
goedendag (Fle)	large infantry mace
gonfanon (MF)	small pennon or flag: 39
gonfanonier (MF)	standard-bearer: 61, 67, 102, 133
gorgerette (MF)	quilted neck protection, perhaps mail-lined: 102
gorget, gorgiere (MF)	neck armour: 95, 102
goulabios (Gr)	retainers, military followers: 166
gran maza (Occ)	large mace: 84
grand archon (Gr)	senior official responsible for the imperial retinue: 178
grand domestic (Gr)	most senior official in the Byzantine government after the Emperor: 178
grand primmikerios (Gr)	official in charge of the imperial retinue: 178
grand stratopedarch (Gr)	head of the commissariat: 178
grand turcoplier (MF)	officer in command of *turcopoles*: 31
grand tzaousios (Gr)	officer commanding garrison troops: 178
granz gisarmes (MF)	large infantry pole-arms: 86
great helm (modern term)	fully enclosing form of helmet: 100–1
guardadors (MS)	men guarding prisoners: 140
guasarma (MS)	infantry pole-arm
guastatori (MI)	infantry ravagers or devastators: 23
guelph	pro-Papal faction in Italy: 70
guige (MF)	shoulder-strap for shield: 93
guisarma (MI)	infantry pole-arm: 86
guisarme (MF)	infantry pole-arm: 77, 86
gyula (Magyar)	autonomous governor of Transylvania under early Hungarian rule: 38
haj (Ara)	Islamic pilgrimage to Mecca: 229
hasegaies (ME)	short spear or javelin: 86
haubergeon (MF)	smaller or more limited form of mail *hauberk*: 72
hauberk (MF)	mail armour for body and usually arms: 73, 82, 94, 97, 203
haute cour (MF)	High Court of a kingdom: 14
helepolis (Gr)	siege tower: 215
helm (ME)	helmet
hourdeis (MF)	fence or bulwark
hueste (MS)	major campaign: 26, 49
infanções (Por)	knights: 38
ingenui (Por)	ancient senior families of free status: 38
intervallum (Lat)	space between fortified ditches or moats: 212
ʻiqta (Ara)	sources of revenue, usually in form of land allocation: 36
ispahbadh (Far)	senior officer: 181
iubba (MI)	quilted soft-armour: 72, 100
jaserant, jazerant, jaseran (MF)	cloth-covered, lined and padded mail *hauberk*: 95
jawshan (Ara)	lamellar cuirass: 204
jazrain hauberk (MF)	cloth-covered, lined and padded mail *hauberk*: 95
jeunes (MF)	young or adolescent members of cavalry élite: 78
jiavors (Arm)	warrior class, comparable to European knights: 182
Jihad (Ara)	religious struggle, the Greater Jihad being spiritual and the Lesser Jihad being physical: xii, 51

jubba (MI)	quilted soft armour: 72, 99
jund (Ara)	regional forces: 22, 236
jupau (MF)	quilted jacket: 99
jupeau d'armer (MF)	quilted soft-armour: 100
jupon (MF)	quilted jacket: 40
jusarme (MF)	infantry pole-arm: 86
kabadion (Gr)	quilted soft-armour: 99, 204–5
kamilaukitzin (Gr)	hat or hood: 203
karib (Ara)	sailing ship: 143
karr wa farr (Ara)	cavalry tactic of repeated attack and withdrawal: 65
kastron (Gr)	fortified town or fortress: 181, 210
kastrophylax (Gr)	officer in command of a *kastron*: 180, 210, 216
kavallarioi (Gr)	fief- or *pronoia*-holding cavalry: 183
kentouklon, kentouklion (Gr)	soft armour: 205–6
kephales (Gr)	commander of local forces: 180
kestros (Gr)	dart-throwing sling
khan (Tur & Mon)	ruler: 175
khanate (Tur & Mon)	state ruled by a khan: 158
klibanion (Gr)	lamellar cuirass: 204
knezat (Sla)	governorate: 163
knörr (Danish)	sailing ship: 223
kombarion (Gr)	sailing ship
kontarion (Gr)	lance: 198
laisa (Gr & Sl)	portable defensive structure: 214–15
lamt (Ara)	large shield made of leather: 93, 234
lance (MF)	heavy cavalry spear: 83, 197–8, 208
launas (Cat)	metal scales: 95
lavra (Gr)	Byzantine monastic hermitage: 54, 115
linothorax (Gr)	probably *surcoat*: 205
lorica (Lat)	mail hauberk: 208
loricas duplices (Lat)	doubled mail *hauberk*: 94
loriga (MS)	mail *hauberk*: 81, 95
loriga de cavallo (MS)	horse-armour: 103–4
lorigas dobladas (MS)	doubled mail *hauberk*: 94
lourikin (Gr)	mail *hauberk*: 203
machicolated galleries (modern term)	*machicolation* extended along the length of a fortified wall: 114
machicolation (MF)	architectural addition to the exterior of a wall, enabling missiles to be shot or dropped vertically: 114–15
maçue (MF)	mace: 76, 82, 84
magganika (Gr)	mechanical weapon, machine: 215
magister balistarius (Lat)	master crossbowman or commander of crossbowmen
magnus archonte (Gr)	senior *archon* or regional authority: 162
mahonesi (MI)	governing authorities in Genoese colonial possessions: 11
maisnie (MF)	group of knights, military following: 78
majra (Ara)	arrow-guide: 236
mamluk (Ara)	soldier of slave-recruited origin: 13, 238
manganika (Gr)	mechanical weapon, machine: 215
mangonel (MF)	traction-powered beamsling stone-throwing siege weapon: 118–20, 124, 127–8, 143, 150, 209, 214–19
manguanel (MS)	traction-powered beamsling stone-throwing siege weapon: 120

manicle de fer (MF)	mail protection for hand: 97
manjaniq (Ara)	beamsling stone-throwing siege weapon, also used for stone-throwing siege weapons in general: 118
marachakhd (Arm)	senior military official, from the French *marshal*: 182
maravedís (MS)	Castilian currency: 81
marechal (MF)	senior military official: 31–2
maréchal d'Albanie (MF)	military governor of Angevin Albania: 34
marshal (MF)	senior military official: 63, 68, 133, 138, 159
masnadas reales (MS)	ruler's own immediately available military force: 37
masnadieri (MI)	member of a *masnata* military following: 36
masnata (MI)	military following or retinue: 36
masses (MF)	maces: 84
masseta (Occ)	small mace: 84
materas (MF)	large crossbow *bolt*: 92
mauri pacis (MS)	'pacified Moors', recruited as soldiers: 27
maza (MS)	mace: 76, 84
mazlaqa (Ara)	artificial slope of earth, rocks, etc., constructed during siege operations: 217
megaloallagitai (Gr)	large military force based in a city: 179
melée (MF)	close combat between groups of units: 46, 66, 70, 78
mesnada (MS)	military following or retinue: 37
mesnie (MF)	military following or retinue: 37
milites (Lat)	cavalrymen or knights: 20–1, 25, 108
ministeriales (Lat)	élite German cavalrymen of theoretically slave or serf status: 13, 27–8, 43, 133
mitrad (Ara)	small spear or javelin: 92
mixobarbaroi (Gr)	semi-barbarians: 159
mizraq (Ara)	javelin: 83
money fief (modern term)	source of revenue as a *fief*, instead of a piece of land as a *fief*
monokaballoi (Gr)	regiment, probably of cavalry: 178
monoprosopon (Gr)	officer in charge of munitions while on the march: 193
motte (MF)	small artificial hill with a castle on top: 109, 115
mourtatoi (Gr)	ex-Muslims, as soldiers: 170, 178
mozarabs (MS)	Arabised Christians from Islamic-ruled al-Andalus: 25, 112
mudejar (MS)	Muslims under Christian rule
mufflers (ME, MF)	mail mittens, intregral extension of the sleeves: 97
murtat (Tur)	renegade: 170
murtidd (Ara)	renegade: 170
múserat (MF)	javelin: 83
myrtaïtai (Gr)	Byzantine military group or Turkish origin: 170
nacharak' (Arm)	baron: 182
naffad (Tur)	naft, Greek Fire: 217, 219
naft (Ara)	petroleum-based incendiary mixture, Greek Fire: 219
naft oq (Tur)	fire-arrows: 217
naqar (Ara)	drum: 184
nefir (Tur)	trumpet: 184
negus (Lat & Ara)	Abyssinian ruler: 234–5
novitiate (Lat)	new or 'trainee' member of a monastic order: 17
nushab (Far)	arrow: 236
onager (Lat)	torsion-powered stone-throwing machine with a single throwing arm: 216

onagros (Gr)	torsion-powered stone-throwing machine with a single throwing arm
opathobakion (Gr)	possibly a mace or club: 200
opathorrabdin (Gr)	mace, club or heavy staff-weapon: 200
organa (Gk)	organ, musical instrument, sometimes portable: 184
paidopoula (Gr)	page or personal servant: 178
paile d'auqueton (MF)	quilted mantle: 99
pair-of-plates (modern term)	early form of scale-lined coat-of-plates body armour: 96
palash (Sl & Hungarian)	single-edged straight sword
palatinate (MF)	virtually autonomous principality: 33
pales (MF)	possibly the iron elements in an early *coat-of-plates* body armour: 96
palvesari (MI)	shield bearers: 70
panceriam (Lat)	a form of mail *hauberk* or body armour: 95
panthera (MI)	specialised battlefield waggons: 65
panzere (MI)	a form of mail *hauberk* or body armour: 72
pastores (MS)	those who guard the militias' animal herds: 140
pavensibus (Lat)	large shield or mantlet
pavise, pavois (MF)	large shield or mantlet: 93, 143
payk (Tur)	court page: 178
pedites (Lat)	infantry: 23
peones, peonias (MS)	infantry: 26
peregrini (Lat)	pilgrims: 134
perpunt (MF)	quilted soft armour: 81
perriere (MF)	beamsling stone-throwing siege machine
petraria turquesa (Lat)	beamsling stone-throwing siege weapon: 120
petroboloi (Gr)	beamsling stone-throwing siege weapon: 217
peytral (MF)	broad breast-strap of horse-harness: 80, 103
picois (MF)	long spear or pike: 86
piratae (Lat)	sailors also trained to fight: 144
pius (Lat)	long spear or pike: 86
plaustrella (MI)	specialised battlefield waggons: 65
plumée (MF)	perhaps a lead-weighted javelin: 123
poitrail, poitral (MF)	front part of horse-armour: 103
poitrine (MF)	front part of horse-armour or a broad breast-strap: 102
poleyn (MF)	knee protection: 94, 98
portcullis (modern term)	large grill to be raised and lowered within a fortified gate system: 115
postern (modern term)	small external door in a fortified place: 115
poulains (MF)	those of mixed parentage or origin: 8, 17
pourpoint, perpon (MF)	quilted soft armour: 99
primmikerios (Gr)	commander of Vardariot troops: 178
prokathemenoi (Gr)	senior civil officials: 180
pronoia (Gr)	allocation of land or source of revenue: 34, 176–7, 180, 183
prosalentai (Gr)	those supported by small allocations of land: 179
protostrator (Gr)	deputy to the grand domestic: 178, 181
proximos (Gr)	a military rank: 182
pugils (ME)	those who taught the art of boxing: 79
qa'id (Ara)	officer rank: 22
qaws al-lawlab (Ara)	large form of crossbow spanned with a windlass or winch: 91
qaws al-qutn (Ara)	bow having a cotton bowstring: 236

quadrillero (MS)	official to divide booty: 49
quarel, quadrel, quarrel (MF)	arrow or *bolt* shot from a crossbow: 92
quintain (MF)	training target for lance-wielding cavalrymen: 78
quir boli (MF)	hardened leather, *cuir bouilli*
rabdin (Gr)	club: 200
rafala (MS)	military escort for migrating herds of pigs: 59
rafalero (MS)	mounted guard, part of a *rafala*: 59
ra'is (Ara)	headman: 16
rastrillo (MS)	portcullis
razzia (Ara)	raiding style of warfare: 53
regius marescalus (Lat)	marshal or *marechal*: 31
regni constabularius (Lat)	constable or *connetable*: 31
restor (MF)	replacement cost of lost warhorse: 138
rhomphaion (Gr)	single-edged sword: 199
ricos-homens (Por)	head of ancient senior families of free status: 38
rochet (MI)	long-hafted axe to cut the enemy's rigging: 146
rostrum (Lat)	front part of a galley: 226
rotelle (MF)	small round shield: 74
sagenae (Lat)	lateen rigged sailing vessel: 142
sagita, sagittiae (MI)	small ship: 149
salandria (MI)	specialised form of sailing ship: 135
saraceno (MI)	coastal watch-towers: 150
satellites (Lat)	ruler's close companion: 20
scurzatae (MI)	small ship, probably galley: 149
scutiferi (MI)	squires or shield-bearers: 30
scutum (Lat)	large shield: 72
sebastius (Gr)	commander of foreign troops: 176
sebastokrator (Gr)	senior commander: 220
sebastos (Arm)	senior officer: 182
selle d'arme (MF)	war saddle
selle de croce, selle de cronce (MF)	Western European style war saddle
senechal (MF)	senior military title: 15, 31
seréement (MF)	in more than one row: 66
sergeant (MF)	soldier of non-knightly rank: 67, 111, 123, 132, 140, 192
serjanz (MF)	*sergeant*, non-noble soldier: 124
serviens (MF)	servants: 30
shabraqan (Ara)	hard 'male iron'
shaykh (Ara)	respected elder figure, leader: 22
sheld (ME)	shield: 72
shini (Ara)	galley: 225
slot machicolation (modern term)	grooves in fortification, plus overhanging element permitting missiles to be dropped or shot vertically downwards: 115
socii (Lat)	ruler's closest companions in arms, or people travelling as a group: 20
sodoiers (MI)	poor men hired as soldiers by the richer to take their place in a communal militia: 24
solenarion (Gr)	arrow-guide: 200, 236
spasalar (Arm)	army commander: 182
spaspeti (Geo)	commander-in-chief: 181
springald, springallis (ME)	torsion-powered siege weapon, *espringal*: 122

stolos (Gr)	convoy
stradioti, strateoiti (Gr)	provincial troops of middle rank: 175, 177, 180, 183
strategios (Gr)	senior officer rank: 165
strateia, stratior (Gr)	soldier of the *stradioti*: 175, 180
stratopedarch (Gr)	commander of a formation: 177–8
superstites (MI)	guards at gate of a city: 107
surcoat (modern term)	garment worn over armour, often in heraldic colours and pattern: 96, 205
tabor, tabour (MF)	drum: 132
tagmata (Gr)	central or metropolitan military units: 177, 225
ta'ifa (Ara)	faction or party, also name given to fragmented states of al-Andalus: 38, 72
talamaccium (Lat)	large shield: 72
talayeros (MS)	scouts: 26
talevas (MF)	large shield: 72, 93
talus (Lat)	sloping base of a fortified wall as defence against mining: 114
tang (modern term)	extension of a blade to go inside a sword-hilt or inside an arrow-shaft: 3, 198, 234
tapia (MS)	tamped earth method of construction
tarchais (MF)	bowcase or quiver, from Persian tarkash: 150
targe (MF)	large shield: 93
taride (MF)	specialised galley as horse-transport or landing-craft: 135–6, 142, 149–50
tarite (MI)	specialised galley as horse-transport or landing-craft: 149
testinia (MS)	armour for horse's head, *chamfron*
testudo (Lat)	infantry formation with interlocked shields: 126
thegns (ME)	Anglo-Saxon aristocracy: 172
thelematarioi (Gr)	troops living around Constantinople: 179
theme (Gr)	military province and its associated regional forces: 20, 153–154, 158, 165, 175, 177, 181
thorak (Gr)	cuirass: 204
torno fuya (MS)	cavalry tactic of repeated attack and withdrawal: 65
torre (MI)	tower: 117
tourkopouli (Gr)	ex-Turkish troops or descendants of Turkish troops: 171, 180
toxobolistrai (Gr)	large crossbow: 201
trabuquetz (MS)	counterweight *trebuchet* stone-throwing siege machine: 1120
trebuchel (MF)	early *trebuchet*: 120
trebuchet (MF)	counterweight beamsling stone-throwing siege machine: 109, 119–21, 125, 129, 135, 212–13, 216, 218, 237
treuil (MF)	large crossbow: 122
triboli (MI)	calthrops: 146
tripantum (Lat)	large *trebuchet*: 120
troynnes (MF)	trumpet: 132
truble (MF)	infantry staff weapon: 85–6
tüfenkler (Tur)	men armed with early form of handgun: 217
turcopole (MF)	horse-archer, light cavalryman, of supposed Turkish-Islamic origin in Christian service: 13–14, 18, 31, 33, 50, 68, 72, 108, 123, 132
turcopolier (MF)	commander of *turcopoles*: 33, 67
turcorum more (MF)	large stone-throwing *mangonel* of supposed Turkish type: 120

tzaggatores (Gr)	crossbowmen: 178
tzagrai, tzanggra, tzangra (Gr)	hand-held crossbow: 201
tzakones (Gr)	regional force from southern Greece: 178–9, 226
tzaousios (Gr)	officer in command of garrison troops: 178, 182, 216
tzouloukonai (Gr)	servants or camp-followers: 178
upokonta rabdia (Gr)	mace, club or heavy staff-weapon: 200
upolorikon (Gr)	perhaps a padded surcoat: 203
valetti (MI)	servant: 30
varangian (Gr)	élite soldier of Scandinavian, Russian or Anglo-Saxon origin: 164, 172–3, 178, 196, 199, 202–3, 205–7, 219, 225
vardariot (Gr)	Byzantine regiment: 178
vasmuli (Gr)	naval troops of supposed mixed Greek and Latin parentage
vavasseur (MF)	feudal vassal: 47
venablo (MS)	javelin or staff weapon: 83
venticinquine (MI)	militia unit of twenty-five: 37
vicar (Lat)	provincial governor with viceregal authority: 34
voivod, vojvod (Sl)	military governor: 38
voivodates (Sl)	territory governed by a *voivod*: 163
vucomity (Gr)	local government territory, from Italian *vicomte*: 159
wambeis (MF)	quilted soft armour: 99
ward (ME)	enclosed area inside a castle
xamete (MS)	decorative fabric covering: 96
xebec (Spanish)	sailing ship also using oars, of North African origin
zabareion (Gr)	arsenal: 220
zagaya, zaghaya (Ber)	javelin or short spear: 83, 86
zarad (Ara)	mail: 103
zeugelateion (Gr)	*pronoia* granted in perpetuity: 177
ziyar (Ara)	torsion-powered siege weapons: 216
zorovar (Arm)	general: 165
zupan (Sl)	nobleman: 134
zurna (Tur)	large form of clarinet: 184

Notes

Notes to Introduction

1 Riley-Smith, J. (1978) p. 87.
2 Russell, J.C., pp. 52–5.
3 For the Papacy's enthusiasm for a 'great battle' between Castile and the Muwahhidun (Almohades) in Spain, see García Fitz (1996) p. 274 n.22.
4 Gillingham, J. (1984) p. 91; Bennett, M. (1998); Morillo, S. (1999).
5 Guest, K., pp. 28–9.
6 Morillo, S. (2002) p. 41.

Notes to Chapter 1: Western Europe and the Crusader States

1 Whitney, E., pp. 150, 154–6.
2 Sebestyén, K. Cs., p. 254.
3 Bartha, A., pp. 118–120.
4 Kosztolnyik, pp. 15, 30–2.
5 Glassl, H., pp. 40–2.
6 Cowdrey, H.E.J., pp. 21–2.
7 Bragadin, M.-A., pp. 29–34.
8 Bishko, C.J., p. 54.
9 Burns, R.I. (1961) p. 436.
10 Kreutz, B.M. (1991) pp. 149–151.
11 Riley-Smith, J. (1999).
12 Riley-Smith, J. (1986) p. 63.
13 Favreau-Lilie, M.-L., pp. 220–1.
14 'Mercantile relations continued undisturbed, including the sale of war material to the Mamluks', Friedman, Y. (2002) p. 102.
15 Balard, M. (1989) pp. 161–2, 171.
16 Burns, R.I. (1976) pp. 106–8.
17 Bisson, T.N. (1986) pp. 17–18.
18 For a detailed study of Godfrey de Bouillon's contingent on the First Crusade see Murray, A.V.
19 Riley-Smith, J. (1986) p. 43.
20 Krey, A.C., p. 116, Raymond d'Aguilers, p. 135.
21 Powell, J.M. (1992) pp. 296–301.
22 La Monte, J.L. (1932) p. 159.
23 Vryonis, S. (1975) pp. 133–4.
24 Richard, J. (1986) pp. 262–6.
25 Holt, P.M. (1985) p. 243.
26 La Monte, J.L. (1932) pp. 160–1, 162 n.2.
27 La Monte, J.L. (1932) pp. 141–4.
28 Mayer, H.E. (1985) pp. 108–21.
29 Mayer, H.E. (1985) p. 131.
30 Bennett, M. (1986) p. 7.
31 Marshall, C.J. (1989) pp. 301–6.
32 Abulafia, D. (1986) p. 543.
33 Prawer, J. (1952) pp. 495–7; the mosaic floors of largely ruined Christian churches and monasteries uncovered by archaeologists in and around Madaba remain one of the cultural glories of Jordan.
34 Salibi, K.S. (1957) pp. 291–2.
35 Jacoby, D. (1986) p. 176.
36 Amououx-Mourad, M., pp. 120–5.
37 Forey, A. (1984) pp. 79, 82–6, 88–9.
38 Bennett, M. (1989) pp. 7–8.
39 Marcombe, D., p. 11.
40 Richard, J. (1979a) pp. 166–7.
41 Jacoby, D. (1973) pp. 888–9.
42 La Monte, J.L. (1932) p. 142.

43 La Monte, J.L. (1932) p. 152 n.1.
44 Lock, P.W. (1994) p. 334.
45 Hendrickx, B., pp. 217–18.
46 Jacoby, D. (1973) pp. 892–3.
47 Vasiliev, A.A. (1952) p. 595.
48 Ducellier, A., pp. 256–7.
49 Dunbabin, J., p. 171.
50 Epstein, S.A., p. 99.
51 Jacoby, D. (1976) pp. 29–30.
52 Taviani-Carozzi, H., pp. 469–75.
53 Loud, G.A. (1983) pp. 32–4.
54 Guillou, A. (1974) pp. 174–5.
55 Loud, G.A. (1981) pp. 19–20.
56 Matheson, L.S.G., p. 273 n.1.
57 Curtis, E., pp. 356–8.
58 Abulafia, D. (1990) p. 108.
59 Bresc, H., pp. 53–4.
60 Ahmad, Aziz (1975) p. 64.
61 Jamison, E. (1957) pp. 39, 114; Waley, D.P. (1954) p. 121.
62 Kantorowixz, E., pp. 130–1
63 Kantorowixz, E., p. 288.
64 Abulafia, D. (1990) p. 130.
65 Dunbabin, J., pp. 153–4.
66 Abulafia, D. (1975) p. 112.
67 Tabacco, G., pp. 788–9.
68 Ancona, C., pp. 647–8.
69 *Ibid.*
70 Herlihy, D., pp. 140–6.
71 Lansing, C.L., p. 188.
72 Hodgson, F.C., p. 168.
73 Bianchi, L.G. and Poleggi, E., pp. 157–8.
74 Airaldi, G., p. 279.
75 Balbi, G.P., p. 104.
76 Hyde, J.K., pp. 102–3.
77 Kantorowixz, E., pp. 463–4.
78 Abulafia, D. (1993) pp. 24, 29.
79 Lacarra, J.M. (1963) p. 212.
80 Powers, J.F. (1970) pp. 91–7, Lomax, D.W., p. 100.
81 *Ibid.*
82 Burns, R.I. (1976) p. 123.
83 Burns, R.I. (2004) p. 162.
84 Powers, J.F. (1971) pp. 652–3.
85 Lacarra, J.M. (1963) p. 213.
86 García Fitz, F. (1995) pp. 179–80.
87 De Oliveiro-Marques, A.H., pp. 78–9.
88 Boussard, J., pp. 165–6; Hallam, E.M., p. 163.
89 Gillingham, J. (1984) p. 91.
90 Arnold, B., p. 66.
91 Pálóczi Horváth, A., *passim.*
92 Pamlényi, E., pp. 67–8.
93 Tyerman, C., p. 24.
94 Ashtor, E. (1969) p. 536.
95 Constable, G., p. 65, *passim.*
96 Barber, M. (1989) p. 123.
97 Schneidman, J.L., p. 361.
98 Kantorowixz, E., p. 540.
99 Robbert, L.B. (1994) p. 387.
100 Audouin, E., pp. 37, 55, 67, 75, 84.
101 Audouin, E., pp. 98–100.
102 Walker, R.F., pp. 82–90.
103 Arnold, B., p. 158.
104 Bennett, M. (1986) pp. 2–3, 9.
105 La Monte, J.L. (1932) pp. 140–1.
106 Chehab, M.H., p. 21; Dodu, G., pp. 156–7.
107 Chehab, M.H., pp. 21–2; Dodu, G., pp. 177–9.
108 Dodu, G., p. 159.
109 Chehab, M.H., p. 20.
110 Amououx-Mourad, M., pp. 114–20.
111 Riley-Smith, J. (1986) p. 42.
112 Chehab, M.H., pp. 25–8.
113 Chehab, M.H., p. 29.
114 La Monte, J.L. (1932) p. 139.
115 Richard, J. (1945) p. 52.
116 Riley-Smith, J. (1967) pp. 313–15.
117 Forey, A. (1992) pp. 54–5.
118 Forey, A. (1992) pp. 50, 57, 71, 73.
119 Kennedy, H., pp. 147–8.
120 Riley-Smith, J. (1967) p. 325.
121 Forey, A. (1992) p. 69.
122 Elisseeff, N. (1967) p. 725.
123 Edbury, P.W., pp. 180–3.
124 Richard, J. (1979a) p. 161.
125 *Ibid.*
126 Jacoby, D. (1967) p. 443.
127 Bon, A. (1969) pp. 87–9.
128 Miller, W. (1908) p. 65.
129 Bon, A. (1969) p. 103.
130 Bon, A. (1969) pp. 153–4.
131 Ducellier, A., p. 265.
132 Ducellier, A., pp. 241–4.

133 Jacoby, D. (1989) pp. 3–5.
134 Morris, J. (1980) pp. 73–4.
135 Pistarino, G., pp. 47–8.
136 Byrne, E.H. (1928) p. 182.
137 Kreutz, B.M. (1991) p. 155.
138 Jamison, E. (1913) p. 292.
139 Johns, J. (1993) p. 135.
140 Ancona, C., pp. 651–3.
141 Oerter, H.L., p. 433 n.18.
142 Becker, M.B., p. 177.
143 Ancona, C., pp. 651–3.
144 Coelho, E.T., p. 100.
145 Lomax, D.W., p. 99.
146 Burns, R.I. (1976) p. 117.
147 García Fitz, F. (1995) p. 165.
148 Lourie, L., pp. 55–7.
149 Powers, J.F. (1971) p. 652; García Fitz, F. (1995) p. 183.
150 Powers, J.F. (1971) p. 642.
151 De Oliveiro-Marques, A.H., p. 55.
152 Contamine, P. (1982).
153 Bosson, C., p. 2.
154 Kantorowixz, E., pp. 427–8.
155 Pamlényi, E., pp. 52–3, 60–1.
156 Erdmann, C., pp. 42–3, 51–2, 86–7.
157 Braibant, C., pp. 40–1.
158 Adam, P., pp. 172–3.
159 Siberry, E., pp. 104–5.
160 Baha' al-Din Ibn Shaddad (1897b) pp. 226–7.
161 King, E.J. (1931) pp. 278–9.
162 Riley-Smith, J. (1967) pp. 238–9.
163 Anon., *Cartulaire Général de l'Ordre des Hospitaliers de St. Jean de Jérusalem*, p. 64.
164 Verbruggen, J.F. (1977b) p. 125.
165 Galletti, A.I., p. 48.
166 Abulafia, D. (1984) p. 201.
167 Adam, P., p. 169.
168 *Ibid.*
169 Verse 6722, in Adam, P., p. 169.
170 Adam, P., p. 172.
171 Moravcsik, G., p. 85.
172 Tyerman, C., pp. 18–21.
173 Munro, D.C., pp. 330–1.
174 Munro, D.C., p. 334.
175 Wasserstein, D., pp. 276–7.
176 Riley-Smith, J. (1986) pp. 108–110.
177 Richard, J. (1979c) p. 378.
178 Riley-Smith, J. (1978) pp. 93–9.
179 Bresc, H., pp. 54–6.
180 Lomax, D.W., p. 8.
181 Alexander, J.J.G., p. 19 n.60.
182 Jackson, W.H., p. 193.
183 Bisson, T.N. (1989) p. 233.
184 Forey, A. (1992) p. 83.
185 Hamblin, W.J. (1992) pp. 237–8.
186 Forey, A. (1992) p. 38.
187 Forey, A. (1986) pp. 141–3.
188 Forey, A. (1992) p. 100.
189 Forey, A. (1992) pp. 207–12; Nicholson, H., pp. 68–9.
190 Forey, A. (1992) p. 51.
191 Gillingham, J. (1989) pp. 256–9, 261–2
192 La Monte, J.L. (1937) pp. 420–1.
193 Keen, M.H. (1968) pp. 212–14.
194 Jacoby, D. (1984) pp. 622–3.
195 Keen, M. (1987) p. 100.
196 Evans, M.R. (2000) *passim.*
197 Lloyd, S., *passim.*
198 Hatto, A.T., p. 49.
199 For a detailed look at lower status participants in the Crusades from the English Midlands, see Evans, M.R. (1996).
200 Morris, J. (1961) pp. 14–15, 87, 242.
201 Tabacco, G., pp. 788–90.
202 Siberry, E., p. 99.
203 Langlois, C.-V., p. 62.
204 Molin, B.K., p. 135.
205 Richard, J. (1979c) p. 210.
206 Favreau-Lilie, M.-L., pp. 212–13.
207 Ahmad, Aziz (1977) pp. 203–4.
208 Williams, J., p. 29.
209 Williams, J., p. 34.
210 Hiestand, R.
211 Jackson, P. (1991) pp. 7–9.
212 Goitein, S.D. (1952) p. 170.
213 Mitchison, R., pp. 124–36.
214 Usamah Ibn Munqidh (1929) p. 95; Usamah Ibn Munqidh (1930) p. 66.
215 Mayer, H.E. (1978) p. 187.
216 Richard, J. (1998a) p. 72.
217 Forey, A. (1991) pp. 274–5.
218 Jackson, P. (1980) p. 490.
219 Forey, A. (1991) p. 275.

220 Riley-Smith, J. (1973) p. 63.
221 Powers, J.F. (1971) p. 652.
222 Edwards, J., p. 19.
223 Brodman, J.W., pp. 7–10.
224 Edwards, J., p. 20; Brodman, J.W., pp. 15–16.
225 Friedman, Y. (1996) pp. 178–80.
226 Pirie Gordon, C.H., pp. 458–9.
227 Friedman, Y. (1996) pp. 184–7.
228 Friedman, Y. (2001) p. 103.
229 Granara, W.E., pp. 118–20.
230 Riley-Smith, J. (1978) pp. 88–9.
231 Boussard, J., pp. 206–7.
232 Barlozzetti, U. and Giuliani, M., *passim.*
233 Hackett, J.W., pp. 28–31.
234 Ellenblum, R. (2003) p. 97.
235 Eydoux, H.-P., pp. 61–3.
236 Brooker, C.H. and Knauf, E.A., p. 187.
237 Forey, A. (1992) pp. 87–8.
238 Prawer, J. (1980) pp. 477–8.
239 Prawer, J. (1980) pp. 481–2.
240 Gillingham, J. (1984) pp. 81–4.
241 Gillingham, J. (1984) p. 89.
242 Molin, B.K., p. 110.
243 Kedar, B.Z. (1979) p. 212.
244 Molin, B.K., pp. 85, 167–71
245 Lock, P.W. (1998) pp. 175–7.
246 Burridge, P.
247 Lock, P.W. (1998) pp. 179–81.
248 Lock, P.W. (1989) pp. 138–40.
249 Airaldi, G., p. 276.
250 Vann, T.M., *passim.*
251 Lacarra, J.M. (1963) pp. 209–10.
252 Bishko, C.J., p. 51
253 Lomax, D.W., pp. 94–5.
254 Durand, R., pp. 185–6.
255 Lomax, D.W., p. 97.
256 Bishko, C.J., p. 50.
257 Lomax, D.W., p. 101.
258 Bishko, C.J., pp. 57–8.
259 Bishko, C.J., p. 28.
260 García Fitz, F. (1999).
261 Soler del Campo, A. (1986b) p. 7.
262 Marvin, L.W., p. 5.
263 Marvin, L.W., pp. 6–7.
264 Marvin, L.W., pp. 7–11.
265 Baldwin, M.W., p. 11.
266 Bennett, M. (1986) pp. 4–6.
267 Forey, A. (1992) p. 89.
268 Peal, A., pp. 118–19.
269 A rather extreme version of this approach was published in Berlin in 1940, and included attempts to differentiate the archtetypal battlefield tactics of various medieval Middle Eastern 'races', including the supposed early Crusader and later Crusader systems (Von Pawlikowski-Cholewa, A., pp. 266–8).
270 Sumption, J., p. 167.
271 Dieulafoy, M.M., p. 125.
272 Smail, R.C. (1956) pp. 156–7.
273 Nicholson, R.L. (1940) pp. 142–3.
274 Oerter, H.L., p. 447.
275 Bono Giamboni, p. 104.
276 Legge, M.D., p. 264.
277 Benn, W., pp. 247–8.
278 Powers, J.F. (1985) p. 102.
279 Bennett, M. (1989) pp. 15–18.
280 Nesbitt, J.W., pp. 179–80.
281 Bennett, M. (2000) p. 22.
282 Bennett, M. (1989) p. 14.
283 King, E.J. (1934) p. 68.
284 Bennett, M. (1989) p. 14.
285 Bachrach, B.S. (1993) p. 41.
286 Contamine, P. (1980) p. 113.
287 Settia, A.A., pp. 119–21.
288 Bennett, M. (1989) pp. 13–14.
289 Hendrix, W.S., p. 46.
290 Lourie, L., p. 73.
291 Verbruggen, J.F. (1977b) p. 8.
292 Verbruggen, J.F. (1977b) p. 39.
293 Verbruggen, J.F. (1977b) p. 75.
294 Verbruggen, J.F. (1947); Verbruggen, J.F. (2005) *passim.*
295 France, J. (1996) pp. 167–8.
296 Bennett, M. (1989) p. 15.
297 Bennett, M. (1989) p. 17.
298 Anon., *The Third Crusade, Itinerarium Peregrinorum*, pp. 131–2
299 Bennett, M. (1992) p. 245.
300 Barlozzetti, U. and Giuliani, M., *passim.*
301 Bennett, M. (1989) p. 17.
302 Bennett, M. (1989) p. 15.

303 Anon., *La Chanson de Rolan*, l. p. 1034.
304 Bennett, M. (1989) p. 14.
305 Nelli, R. and Lavaud, R., p. 366.
306 Lourie, L., p. 70.
307 Marshall, C.J. (1990) pp. 222–4.
308 Gabrieli, F., p. 58.
309 Marshall, C.J. (1990) pp. 225–6.
310 Baha' al-Din Ibn Shaddad (1897a) p. 232; Baha' al-Din Ibn Shaddad (1897b) p. 380.
311 Baha' al-Din Ibn Shaddad (1897b) p. 343.
312 Villehardouin (1952) p. 180; Villehardouin (1921) p. 116.
313 Bennett, M. (1992) p. 242.
314 Bennett, M. (1992) p. 249.
315 Boussard, J., pp. 220–2.
316 Bennett, M. (1992) pp. 249–50.
317 Anon., *La Siège de Barbastre*, l. p. 1870.
318 Usamah Ibn Munqidh (1929) p. 75.
319 Lyon, B.D., p. 301.
320 Anon., *The Third Crusade, Itinerarium Peregrinorum*, p. 151.
321 Barlozzetti, U. and Giuliani, M., *passim*.
322 *Ibid.*
323 Pieri, P. (1953) *passim*; Pieri, P. (1966) pp. 67–70; Amatuccio, G., *passim*.
324 Peel, C., pp. 399–400.
325 Soler Del Campo, A. (1986c) p. 74.
326 The Alexiad by Anna Comnena, confirms that the Crusaders or 'Franks' used very long lances (Comnena, Anna, LXI).
327 Prawer, J. (1980) pp. 491–2.
328 Anon., *Two Old French Gauvain Romances, Le Chevalier à l'Épée and La Mule sans Frein*, ll. pp. 735–9
329 Waley, D.P. (1975) pp. 341, 364, *passim*.
330 Bennett, M. (1994) p. 39.
331 Usamah Ibn Munqidh (1929) p. 68.
332 Subrenat, J., p. 357.
333 Settia, A.A., pp. 71–2, *passim*.
334 Settia, A.A., pp. 83–4.
335 Anon., *The Lay of Havelock the Dane*, ll. pp. 2322–3.
336 Bennett, M. (1989) p. 10.
337 Powers, J.F. (1971) p. 654.
338 Powers, J.F. (1985) p. 109.
339 Comnena, Anna, p. lxxxix.
340 Paterson, L.M. (1984) p. 116.
341 Bradbury, J., p. 3.
342 Jones, P.N., p. 111.
343 Bradbury, J., pp. 1–2.
344 Hatto, A.T., p. 44.
345 Hatto, A.T., p. 47 n.1.
346 Audouin, E., p. 82.
347 Walker, R.F., pp. 29–31.
348 Minieri Riccio, C., pp. 87, 278–9.
349 Salibi, K.S. (1957) p. 291.
350 Bachrach, B.S. (1993) p. 41, *passim*.
351 Soler del Campo, A. (1993) pp. 66–75; Alm, J. (1947) pp. 124–6.
352 Alm, J. (1947) p. 127.
353 Waley, D.P. (1975) p. 343, *passim*; Minieri Riccio, C., pp. 98–9.
354 Barlozzetti, U. and Giuliani, M., pp. 56, 63 n.28.
355 Sumption, J., pp. 85, 203.
356 Flori, J., *passim*.
357 Usamah Ibn Munqidh (1929) p. 88.
358 Buttin, F. (1965) pp. 79–80.
359 Anon., *Le Roman de Renart*, ll. pp. 8151–60, *passim*.
360 Aylward, J.D., p. 2.
361 Anon., *Aucassin et Nicolette, chantefable du XIIIe siècle*, p. 10.
362 De Joinville (1921) p. 190.
363 De Joinville (1952) p. 226; De Joinville (1921) p. 165.
364 De Riquer, M. (1969b) p. 224.
365 De Riquer, M. (1980) pp. 350–1.
366 De Riquer, M. (1948) p. 91.
367 Peel, C., p. 397; Anon., *Le Roman de Renart*, p. 1562.
368 Subrenat, J., p. 358.
369 Anon., *Two Old French Gauvain Romances, Le Chevalier à l'Épée and La Mule sans Frein*, ll. pp. 512, 576, 588–92.
370 Boit, B.A. (1991a) pp. 39–40.
371 Boit, B.A. (1991a) p. 38.
372 Edgington, S. (1994) p. 321.
373 Anon., *La Chanson de Roland*, l. p. 113.
374 Crouch, D. (1988).
375 Bennett, M. (1992) pp. 244–5.

376 Mayer, H.E. (1982) p. 104.
377 Duby, G., pp. 837–9.
378 Anon., *The Old French Crusade Cycle, vol. I: La Naissance du Chevalier au Cygne: Elioxe*, l. p. 441.
379 Anon., *The Nibelungenlied*, p. 31.
380 Anglo, S., pp. 248–50.
381 Anglo, S., pp. 251–4.
382 King, E.J. (1934) pp. 145–6.
383 Bennett, M. (1989) p. 12.
384 Settia, A.A., pp. 29–44.
385 Ancona, C., p. 651.
386 Bianchi, L.G. and Poleggi, E., pp. 158–60.
387 Bianchi, L.G. and Poleggi, E., p. 190.
388 Aylward, J.D., p. 8.
389 Aylward, J.D., pp. 1–2, 9–10.
390 Paterson, L.M. (1986) pp. 146–7.
391 Anon., *The Rule of the Templars*, pp. 12–13.
392 Anon., *The Rule of the Templars*, *passim.*
393 For the military equipment mentioned in the series of epic poems known as the Old French Crusade Cycle, see D.C. Nicolle, 'Armes et Armures dans les Épopées des Croisades', in K.H. Bender (ed.), *Les Épopées des Croisades: Zeitschrift für französische Sprache und Literatur*, 11 (Trier 1987) pp. 17–34.
394 Babuin, A. (1996) *passim.*
395 Soler Del Campo, A. (1986c) p. 73; Mann, J., *passim.*
396 Powers, J.F. (1985) p. 105.
397 Powers, J.F. (1985) *passim.*
398 Hackett, J.W., p. 70.
399 Flutre, L.F., p. 316.
400 Galletti, A.I., pp. 41–2.
401 Brown, R.A., p. 138.
402 Riley-Smith, J. (1967) p. 318.
403 Peel, C., p. 393.
404 Anon., *The Old French Crusade Cycle, vol. I: La Naissance du Chevalier au Cygne: Elioxe*, l. p. 3165.
405 Anon., *La Chanson de Rolan*, ll. pp. 2075, 2156.
406 Bucher, F., p. 131.
407 De Riquer, M. (1969a) pp. 469–73.
408 Greimas, A.J., p. 57.
409 Blair, C. (1959) pp. 42–3; Collin, B., pp. 3–15.
410 Anstee, J.W. and Biek, L., p. 83.
411 Melville, M., p. 110.
412 Minieri Riccio, C., pp. 86–7, *passim.*
413 Graindor de Douai, l. p. 8263, addit l. p. 91.
414 Nelli, R. and Lavaud, R., pp. 466, 540, 554.
415 De Riquer, M. (1980) pp. 350–1.
416 Anon., *The Nibelungenlied*, p. 71.
417 Minieri Riccio, C., *passim.*
418 Bennett, M. (1992) p. 243.
419 A gallant effort to do just this was made by Troso, M., *Le Armi in Asta delle Fanterie Europeen (1000–1500)* (Novara 1988).
420 Anon., *The Old French Crusade Cycle, vol. I: La Naissance du Chevalier au Cygne: Beatrix, passim.*
421 Greimas, A.J., p. 314.
422 Anon., *Le Roman de Thèbes*, l. p. 4304.
423 Graindor de Douai, l. 8263, addit l. p. 91.
424 Anon., *Two Old French Gauvain Romances, Le Chevalier à l'Épée and La Mule sans Frein*, ll. pp. 512, 576, ll. pp. 588–92.
425 Coelho, E.T., p. 99.
426 Borg, A., p. 338.
427 Bennett, M. (1992) p. 243.
428 De Riquer, M. (1969b) p. 225.
429 Greimas, A.J., p. 278.
430 Subrenat, J., pp. 357–8.
431 Miller, R. (1985a).
432 Anon., *Gesta Francorum, The Deeds of the Franks and other Pilgrims to Jerusalem*, p. 51.
433 Walker, R.F., p. 27.
434 Soler del Campo, A. (1993) pp. 63–6.
435 Coelho, E.T., p. 100.
436 Walker, R.F., pp. 27–8, 31–2.
437 Soler del Campo, A. (1986a) pp. 327–8.
438 Bradbury, J., pp. 80–2.
439 Alm, J. (1994) *passim.*
440 Longworth, P., p. 47.
441 Molmenti, P.G., p. 88.

442 Renn, D.F. (1971) pp. 72–4.
443 Alm, J. (1947) pp. 117–18.
444 Richter, H., *passim*.
445 Alm, J. (1947) p. 119.
446 Flutre, L.F., pp. 309–10.
447 Audouin, E., pp. 187–9, 194, 196.
448 Alm, J. (1947) p. 127.
449 Minieri Riccio, C., *passim*.
450 *Beatus Commentaries* (Cathedal Library, Burgo de Osma): 'And I saw, and behold a white horse; and he that sat upon him had a bow; and a crown was given unto him: and he went forth conquering, and to conquer.' (Revelations 6:2).
451 Wolff, P., p. 397.
452 Airaldi, G., p. 279.
453 Colardelle, R.M., p. 195.
454 Alm, J. (1947) *passim*.
455 Minieri Riccio, C., p. 90.
456 Audouin, E., p. 82.
457 Dozy, R., vol. 2, p. 460.
458 Paterson, W.F. (1990) pp. 49–50.
459 Alm, J. (1947) pp. 124–6; Audouin, E., pp. 187–9, 194, 196.
460 Minieri Riccio, C., p. 86.
461 Greimas, A.J., p. 521; Anon., *La Chanson de Rolan*, l. p. 2265.
462 Audouin, E., p. 102 n.7.
463 Serdon, V., *passim*.
464 Greimas, A.J., p. 399.
465 Walker, R.F., p. 32.
466 Tempany, T.W., pp. 443–4.
467 Greimas, A.J., pp. 358, 362.
468 Denkstein, V., p. 168.
469 Anon., *The Old French Crusade Cycle, vol. I: La Naissance du Chevalier au Cygne: Beatrix*, l. p. 1076.
470 Bennett, M. (1992) p. 243; Greimas, A.J., p. 618.
471 Denkstein, V., pp. 155–6.
472 Baart, J.M., p. 58.
473 Anon., *The Nibelungenlied*, p. 220.
474 Blair, C. (1958) p. 37.
475 Blair, C. (1958) p. 39.
476 Anon., *La Chanson de Rolan*, l. p. 3425.
477 Anon., *La Chanson de Rolan*, ll. pp. 994–5.
478 De Riquer, M. (1969b) p. 231.
479 Anon., *Aucassin et Nicolette, chantefable du XIIIe siècle*, p. 9.
480 Audouin, E., p. 188.
481 De Riquer, M. (1969a) p. 480.
482 Morris, W.S., p. 197.
483 Anon., *La Chanson de Rolan*, l. p. 164.
484 Anon., *Le Charroi de Nimes*, 45, l. p. 1425; Anon., *The Old French Crusade Cycle, vol. I: La Naissance du Chevalier au Cygne: Beatrix*, ll. pp. 2449, 3038, 3087–8.
485 Greimas, A.J., p. 346; Anon., *The Old French Crusade Cycle, vol. V: Les Chétifs, passim*.
486 De Riquer, M. (1980) pp. 333–4, 392–5.
487 De Hoffmeyer, A.B. (1982) p. 232.
488 Rocca, E.N., pp. 81–5.
489 Scalini, M., pp. 83–5.
490 Colardelle, M. (et al.) pp. 107–10.
491 Nicolle, D.C. (2004c) pp. 184–7.
492 Blair, C. (1958) pp. 38–9.
493 De Riquer, M. (1980) pp. 391–2.
494 *Ibid.*
495 Settia, A.A., p. 43.
496 Freeman, A.Z., pp. 6–7.
497 Norman, A.V.B., pp. 38–9; the Bibliothèque Nationale considers this manuscript to date from the very late 12th or very early 13th century.
498 Lacy, M.S., p. 7.
499 Kelly, F.M., p. 105.
500 De Joinville (1921) p. 213.
501 Blair, C. (1958) pp. 39–40.
502 Nicolle, D.C. (2002a) *passim*.
503 De Riquer, M. (1969b) p. 237.
504 Blair, C. (1958) p. 29.
505 Anon., *The Old French Crusade Cycle, vol. V: Les Chétifs*, l. p. 1109.
506 Blair, C. (1958) p. 41.
507 Anon., *La Siège de Barbastre, passim*.
508 Greimas, A.J., p. 257.
509 Anon., *La règle du Temple*, pp. 109–11.
510 Nicolle, D.C. (2005a) pp. 27–9.
511 De Riquer, M. (1969b) p. 236.
512 Bennett, M. (1989) p. 9.
513 De Riquer, M. (1980) p. 398.

514 Anon., *The Old French Crusade Cycle, vol. I: La Naissance du Chevalier au Cygne: Elioxe*, l. p. 790.
515 Greimas, A.J., p. 12.
516 De Riquer, M. (1969b) p. 238; Chambers, F.M., pp. 44–5.
517 Piel, C. and Bédat, I., *passim*.
518 Blair, C. (1958) pp. 32–3.
519 Greimas, A.J., p. 307.
520 De Riquer, M. (1969b) p. 235; De Riquer, M. (1980) pp. 400–1; De Riquer, M. (1969a) pp. 488–9.
521 Graindor de Douai, ll. pp. 7455–6.
522 Anon., *La règle du Temple*, pp. 109–11.
523 Piponnier, F., *passim*.
524 Audouin, E., pp. 187–9.
525 Anon., *Le Roman de Thèbes*, l. p. 5875.
526 Anon., *The Old French Crusade Cycle, vol. I: La Naissance du Chevalier au Cygne: Elioxe, passim*; Nicolle, D.C. (1987) pp. 17–34.
527 Blair, C. (1958) pp. 31–2.
528 Scalini, M., p. 87.
529 De Hoffmeyer, A.B. (1982) p. 151.
530 Settia, A.A., pp. 147–8.
531 Scalini, M., p. 89 n.6.
532 Anon., *The Old French Crusade Cycle, vol. I: La Naissance du Chevalier au Cygne: Beatrix*, ll. pp. 1041, 1273.
533 *The Old French Crusade Cycle, vol. I: La Naissance du Chevalier au Cygne: Elioxe, passim*.
534 Greimas, A.J., p. 117.
535 Audouin, E., p. 91.
536 Now mostly in the Pierpont Morgan Library, New York.
537 Greimas, A.J., p. 317.
538 Wolff, P., p. 396.
539 Bachrach, B.S. (1969) pp. 168, 168 n.9.
540 Greimas, A.J., p. 499.
541 Greimas, A.J., p. 500.
542 De Riquer, M. (1969b) p. 226.
543 Radulfus Niger, p. 105.
544 Anon., *Le Roman de Thèbes*, pp. 6299–6302.
545 Anon., *The Old French Crusade Cycle, vol. I: La Naissance du Chevalier au Cygne: Beatrix*, l. p. 1293.
546 Baha' al-Din Ibn Shaddad (1897a) p. 135.
547 Moravcsik, G., p. 85.
548 Robert de Clari, p. 39.
549 Barber, M. (1992) p. 316.
550 Powers, J.F. (1985) p. 107.
551 Ibn Abi Zar', p. 454.
552 Guillou, A. (1974) pp. 166–7, 170.
553 Anstee, J.W. and Biek, L., pp. 83–8.
554 Ashtor, E. (1983) pp. 298–9, 399.
555 Dobson, C., *passim*.
556 Epstein, S.A., pp. 99–100.
557 Airaldi, G., p. 279.
558 Bachrach, D., p. 84; Rausing, E., p. 160.
559 Bachrach, D., pp. 85–6.
560 Walker, R.F., pp. 32–3.
561 Audouin, E., p. 102.
562 Audouin, E., p. 103 n.6.
563 Audouin, E., pp. 102–4.
564 Anon., *The Old French Crusade Cycle, vol. I: La Naissance du Chevalier au Cygne: Beatrix*, l. p. 1271.
565 Burns, R.I. (2004) p. 161.
566 Ahmad, Aziz (1977) p. 203.
567 De Joinville (1921) p. 246.
568 Jackson, P. (1987) pp. 42–3.
569 Abulafia, D. (1977) pp. 121, 184–5, 205, 280.
570 Bachrach, D., p. 82.
571 Byrne, E.H. (1920) p. 218 n.109.
572 Byrne, E.H. (1920) p. 218.
573 Walker, R.F., pp. 32–3.
574 Powers, J.F. (1985) p. 102.
575 Galletti, A.I., pp. 46–7.
576 Giles, K.R., p. 69.
577 Anon., *La règle du Temple*, pp. 109–10, *passim*.
578 Anon., *Cartulaire Général de l'Ordre des Hospitaliers de St. Jean de Jérusalem*, p. 64.
579 Bennett, M. (1992) p. 235.
580 Bennett, M. (1992) pp. 230–5.
581 Lewis, A.R. (1964) pp. 256–9.
582 Taylor, A. (1974) pp. 209–10.
583 Loud, G.A. (1983) p. 39.
584 Ellenblum, R. (2001) pp. 188, 198; for a detailed study of the stages in the development of Crusader castle

building, and the reasons for it, see Ellenblum, R. (1996) *passim.*
585 Kennedy, H., pp. 57–9.
586 Hackett, J.W., p. 56.
587 Müller-Wiener, W., p. 36.
588 For an architectural study see Bon, A. (1937) *passim.*
589 Lock, P.W. (1998) p. 181.
590 Bon, A. (1969) pp. 680–3.
591 Bon, A. (1969) p. 601.
592 Bon, A. (1969) p. 680.
593 Lock, P.W. (1998) pp. 182–4; Lock, P.W. (1986) pp. 102–8.
594 Anghel, G. (1977) pp. 14–15.
595 Anderson, W., pp. 233, 237.
596 Bazzana, A. (1977) *passim.*
597 Glick, T.F. (1979) pp. 61–2.
598 Pringle, R.D. (1980) *passim.*
599 Cohen, M., *passim.*
600 Kennedy, H., p. 55.
601 Pringle, R.D. (1994a) pp. 336–9.
602 Prawer, J. (1977) p. 180.
603 Marino, L. (1997b) *passim.*
604 Barber, M. (1998) *passim.*
605 Ellenblum, R. (2003) pp. 91–6.
606 Fedden, R. and Thomson, J., pp. 82–3.
607 Eydoux, H.-P., pp. 70–2.
608 Müller-Wiener, W., p. 27.
609 Pringle, R.D. (1998) pp. 189–90.
610 Nicolle, D.C. (1988) *passim*; Nicolle, D.C. (1989a) *passim.*
611 Usamah Ibn Munqidh (1929) p. 106.
612 Salibi, K.S. (1957) p. 294.
613 Pringle, R.D. (1997) p. 3.
614 Molin, B.K., pp. 51–4.
615 Molin, B.K., p. 63.
616 Jacoby, D. (1979) pp. 7, 25–9.
617 Lansing, C.L., pp. 104–5.
618 Rogers, R., pp. 113, 115.
619 Rogers, R., pp. 130–1.
620 Subotic, V., pp. 116–17.
621 Rogers, R., p. 139.
622 Ibn al-Qalanisi (1908) pp. 167–8.
623 Ibn al-Qalanisi (1908) p. 171.
624 Ibn al-Qalanisi (1908) p. 179.
625 Ibn al-Qalanisi (1908) p. 180.
626 Rogers, R., pp. 166–8.
627 Rogers, R., pp. 138–9.
628 Rogers, R., p. 157.
629 Rogers, R., pp. 233–4.
630 Anon., *Le Roman de Thèbes*, l. p. 3161, *passim.*
631 Rogers, R., p. 223.
632 Rogers, R., p. 114.
633 Walker, R.F., pp. 33–4.
634 De Poerck, G., *passim.*
635 Cathcart King, D.J. (1982) p. 463.
636 Nelli, R. and Lavaud, R., p. 598.
637 Cathcart King, D.J. (1982) p. 460.
638 Liebel, J. (1980) p. 5; Liebel, J. (1998) p. 3; Audouin, E., p. 191.
639 Guillaume le Breton, liber II, l. p. 350.
640 Anon., *La Chanson de Rolan*, l. p. 1971.
641 Greimas, A.J., p. 639.
642 Cathcart King, D.J. (1982) p. 461.
643 Rogers, R., pp. 226–7.
644 De Vries, K., p. 139.
645 Hill, D.R. (1993) p. 118.
646 Needham, J. (1976) p. 110.
647 Hanawalt, B.A., pp. 14–16.
648 Mot, G.J., p. 414.
649 Freeman, A.Z., p. 7.
650 De Vries, K., p. 139.
651 Nicolle, D.C. (2004c) pp. 170–3.
652 De Poerck, G., *passim.*
653 Anon., *La Chanson de Roland*, ll. pp. 98, 237.
654 Audouin, E., pp. 101–2.
655 Liebel, J. (1980) pp. 5–6; Liebel, J. (1998) pp. 2–22.
656 Mot, G.J., pp. 411–3, 415.
657 Freeman, A.Z., pp. 5–6.
658 Molin, B.K., pp. 79–80.
659 Fedden, R. and Thomson, J., p. 66.
660 Alm, J. (1947) p. 128.
661 Brett, M. (1997); an important study of siege warfare by Castile-Leon in the 11th to 13th centuries shows a similar approach, see García Fitz, F. (1997) *passim.*
662 Eydoux, H.-P., p. 63.
663 Elisseeff, N. (1991) p. 581.
664 Anon., *De Expugnatione Terrae Sanctae per Saladinum, Libellus*, p. 197.
665 Riley-Smith, J. (1967) p. 323.
666 Hackett, J.W., pp. 63–5.

667 Pringle, R.D. (1985) p. 139.
668 Elisseeff, N. (1991) p. 599.
669 Favreau-Lilie, M.-L., p. 202.
670 Bennett, M. (1992) p. 243.
671 Anon., *Aucassin et Nicolette, chantefable du XIIIe siècle*, pp. 7–8.
672 Anon., *The Nibelungenlied, passim.*
673 Anon., *The Third Crusade, Itinerarium Peregrinorum*, p. 35.
674 Chambers, F.M., pp. 48–50.
675 Anon., *Le Roman de Thèbes*, ll. pp. 3465–70.
676 Balard, M. (1973) *passim.*
677 Rosser, J. (1986) p. 47; Rosser, J. (1985) p. 89.
678 Jones, P.N. and Renn, D., pp. 445–6.
679 *Ibid.*
680 Jones, P.N. and Renn, D., pp. 450–1.
681 Benton, J.F. (ed.), C.C. Swinton Bland (tr.) pp. 205–6.
682 Baudry, M.-P.
683 Beech, G.T., p. 36.
684 García Fitz, F. (1998a) *passim.*
685 Fowler, G.H.; for a more recent study of the siege of Bedford in 1224 see Amt, E., *passim.*
686 Powers, J.F. (1971) pp. 641–2.
687 Bradbury, J., pp. 4–5.
688 Walter the Chancellor, p. 94.
689 Nicholson, R.L. (1940) p. 221.
690 Rogers, R., p. 209.
691 Anon., *Gesta Francorum, The Deeds of the Franks and other Pilgrims to Jerusalem*, p. 14.
692 Anon., *Gesta Francorum, The Deeds of the Franks and other Pilgrims to Jerusalem*, p. 78.
693 Rogers, R., p. 60.
694 Rogers, R., p. 59.
695 Rogers, R., p. 75.
696 Rogers, R., p. 135.
697 Rogers, R., p. 234.
698 Prouteau, N., *passim.*
699 Sumption, J., pp. 116–17.
700 Rogers, R., p. 19.
701 Airaldi, G., pp. 271–2.
702 Rogers, R., pp. 173–9.
703 Bennett, M. (2001) p. 81.
704 Riley-Smith, J. (1967) p. 326.
705 Rogers, R., p. 83.
706 Kantorowixz, E., pp. 464–5.
707 Amari, M. (1933) vol. III, pp. 706–7.
708 *Ibid.*
709 Anderson, W., pp. 71–2.
710 Renn, D.F. (2004) *passim.*
711 Taylor, A. (1989) *passim.*
712 Vale, M.G.A., p. 141 n.61.
713 Bennett, M. (2001) p. 81.
714 Rogers, R., pp. 96–7.
715 Amari, M. (1876) *passim.*
716 Brooks, F.W., p. 131.
717 Rogers, R., p. 168.
718 Sumption, J., p. 117.
719 Robert, E., p. 14.
720 Anon., *Le Roman de Thèbes*, l. p. 3161, *passim*
721 Brooks, F.W., p. 116.
722 Barlozzetti, U. and Giuliani, M., p. 67 n.33.
723 Gravett, C., pp. 28–9.
724 Gravett, C., p. 30.
725 Nesbitt, J.W., pp. 173–80.
726 Anon., *Gesta Francorum, The Deeds of the Franks and other Pilgrims to Jerusalem*, p. 14.
727 Peirce, I., p. 152.
728 Tyerman, C., p. 23.
729 Gillingham, J. (1978) p. 131.
730 Barber, M. (1992) pp. 314–15.
731 Bon, A. (1969) p. 155; Barber, M. (1989) pp. 120–1.
732 For a recent study of the significance of these maritime links see Richard, J., (1995) *passim.*
733 Menache, S., pp. 294–303.
734 Menache, S., pp. 308–9.
735 *Ibid.*
736 Edgington, S. (1967) pp. 170–3.
737 Melville, M., p. 99.
738 Anon., *Le Roman de Thèbes, passim.*
739 For the importance of the ancient road system in the Hattin campaign, see Kedar, B.Z. (1991) p. 191.
740 Audouin, E., p. 94.
741 Amari, M. (1933) vol. III, p. 190.
742 Arnold, B., pp. 23–4.

743 Anon., *The Nibelungenlied*, pp. 25, 200.
744 Bennett, M. (1989) p. 13.
745 Goitein, S.D. (1970) p. 58.
746 Barber, M. (1992) p. 325.
747 Riley-Smith, J. (1967) p. 329.
748 Balard M. (1966) pp. 484–5.
749 Mollat, M., p. 352.
750 *Ibid.*
751 Kedar, B.Z. (1972) pp. 267–78.
752 Riley-Smith, J. (1973) pp. 63–4.
753 Fotheringham, J.K., p. 46.
754 Walker, R.F., pp. 33–4.
755 Pryor, J.H. (1982) p. 12.
756 *Ibid.*
757 Pryor, J.H. (1982) p. 13.
758 Bennett, M. (1993) p. 49.
759 Pryor, J.H. (1982) pp. 14–15.
760 *Ibid.*
761 Pryor, J.H. (1982) pp. 20–1.
762 Pryor, J.H. (1992) pp. 125–6.
763 Dotson, J.E., *passim*; Pryor, J.H. (1983a) *passim*; Pryor, J.H. (1990) *passim*.
764 Tucci, U., pp. 834–5.
765 Pryor, J.H. (1990) pp. 252–5.
766 Nicolle, D.C. (1994c) p. 45.
767 Pryor, J.H. (1993) *passim*.
768 For a significant and detailed study of documentary records dealing with the medieval arsenal of Pisa from the 11th to the start of the 15th century see Garzella, G., *passim*.
769 Pryor, J.H. (1992) pp. 117–19.
770 Pryor, J.H. (1982) p. 13.
771 Pringle, R.D. (1997) p. 6.
772 Gertwagen, R. (1996) *passim*; Gertwagen, R. (2006) *passim*.
773 Lock, P.W. (1994) p. 333.
774 Minieri Riccio, C., *passim*.
775 Bartusis, M.C., p. 63.
776 Walker, R.F., p. 20.
777 For a realistic look at the size, training, role, cost, etc. of the medieval warhorse, see Bennett, M. (1994) *passim*.
778 Rackham, D.J., pp. 169–74.
779 France, J. (1996) pp. 165–6.
780 Riley-Smith, J. (1986) pp. 64–5.
781 Richard, J. (1979c) pp. 16–17.
782 La Monte, J.L. (1932) p. 152.
783 Bennett, M. (1989) p. 11.
784 Ashtor, E. (1969) p. 463.
785 Ashtor, E. (1969) p. 504.
786 Audouin, E., p. 65.
787 Ashtor, E. (1969) pp. 507–8.
788 *Ibid.*
789 Pamlényi, E., pp. 37–8, 50.
790 Kantorowixz, E., p. 288.
791 Galletti, A.I., pp. 41–2.
792 For a discussion of the medical aspects of Western warfare during this period, see Paterson, L.M. (1988) *passim*.
793 For archaeological evidence for wounds during the medieval period, particularly the Crusader states, see Mitchell, P.D. (2004b) pp. 108–23.
794 Mitchell, P.D. (2004a); Mitchell, P.D., Nagar, Y. and Ellenblum, R., *passim*.
795 Mitchell, P.D. (1999) p. 335.
796 Mitchell, P.D. (1999) p. 336.
797 Paterson, L.M. (1988) p. 119.
798 Amari, M. (1933) vol. III, pp. 706–7
799 Paterson, L.M. (1988) p. 132.
800 Hunt, T., pp. 13, 14, 41.
801 Paterson, L.M. (1988) p. 125.
802 Paterson, L.M. (1988) pp. 125–7.
803 Powers, J.F. (1971) p. 653.
804 Mitchell, P.D. (2004b) pp. 11–45, 220–31.
805 Edgington, S. (1994) p. 326; Mitchell, P.D. (2004b) pp. 184–219.
806 Kohlberg, E. and Kedar, B.Z., pp. 117–18.
807 Mitchell, P.D. (2004b) pp. 46–107.
808 Forey, A. (1992) p. 97.
809 Bragadin, M.-A., pp. 20–7.
810 Halphen, L., pp. 178–9.
811 Byrne, E.H. (1920) p. 195.
812 Luttrell, A.T., p. 147.
813 Mollat du Jourdain, M., *passim*.
814 Kreutz, B.M. (1976) pp. 107–8.
815 Kreutz, B.M. (1976) p. 107 n.132.
816 Brooks, F.W., p. 127.
817 Kreutz, B.M. (1976) p. 102.
818 Bennett, M. (1993) pp. 55–6.
819 Anderson, R.C., p. 52.

820 Pryor, J.H. (1983b) p. 193.
821 Balard, M. (1986) p. 148.
822 Hamilton, B., pp. 103–4.
823 Lonchambon, C, pp. 64–70.
824 Rule, M. and Monaghan, J., *passim.*
825 Nicolle, D.C. (2002b) *passim.*
826 De Oliveiro-Marques, A.H., pp. 89, 134–6.
827 Bennett, M. (1993) p. 53.
828 Barlow, F., p. 74 n.99.
829 Abulafia, D. (1975) p. 120.
830 Lane, F.C. (1973b) pp. 48–9.
831 Robbert, L.B. (1969) pp. 141–8.
832 Lane, F.C. (1969) p. 162, *passim.*
833 Lane, F.C. (1973a) p. 415.
834 Lane, F.C. (1973a) p. 408.
835 Lane, F.C. (1969) pp. 163–4.
836 Balard, M. (1986) pp. 148, 165.
837 Pryor, J.H. (1983b) p. 186.
838 Bachrach, B.S. (2002) p. 95.
839 Pryor, J.H. (2001) pp. 22, 28.
840 Abulafia, D. (1975) p. 115.
841 Pryor, J.H. (1983b) p. 185.
842 Bennett, M. (1993) p. 57.
843 Pryor, J.H. (1983b) pp. 179, 188.
844 Mott, L.V., p. 171.
845 Latimer, J., p. 46.
846 Pryor, J.H. (1983b) p. 185.
847 Brooks, F.W., pp. 121–5, *passim.*
848 Liebel, J. (1980) p. 22; see also Liebel, J. (1998) pp. 2–22.
849 Robbert, L.B. (1969) pp. 141–8.
850 Brooks, F.W., pp. 126–7; Gillingham, J. (1989) p. 260.
851 Brooks, F.W., p. 115.
852 Brooks, F.W., pp. 119–20.
853 Bennett, M. (1993) p. 57.
854 Brooks, F.W., p. 119.
855 Amari, M. (1880–1) vol. II, p. 70.
856 Yarrison, J.L., pp. 249–51.
857 Yarrison, J.L., pp. 98, 118.
858 Lane, F.C. (1973b) pp. 28–9.
859 Brooks, F.W., p. 127.
860 Bennett, M. (1993) pp. 56–7.
861 Gillingham, J. (1989) p. 260.
862 Pryor, J.H. (1983b) p. 188.
863 Krueger, H.C., p. 118.
864 Williams, J., p. 34.
865 Krueger, H.C., p. 123.
866 Curtis, E., p. 362.
867 Douglas, D.C., p. 55.
868 Clements, J., p. 343.
869 Clementi, D.R., pp. 336–40.
870 Dodu, G., p. 220.
871 Richard, J. (1945) p. 54.
872 Forey, A. (1992) pp. 95–6.
873 Hackett, J.W., p. 40.
874 Abu'l-Fida, 17; Little, D.P., p. 173.
875 Tamari, S., pp. 32–41.
876 Jackson, P. (1987) p. 53.
877 Lane, F.C. (1973b) pp. 40–1.
878 Lyon, B.D., p. 76.
879 Pryor, J.H. (1982) p. 19.
880 Bennett, M. (1992) pp. 238–9.
881 Gillingham, J. (1978) pp. 212–13.
882 Pryor, J.H. (1982) p. 17.
883 Ahrweiler, H. (1966b) p. 295.
884 Pryor, J.H. (1992) pp. 114–15.
885 Giles, K.R., p. 85.

Notes to Chapter 2: Byzantium and the Orthodox Christian States

1 Kazhdan, A. (1997) *passim.*
2 Howard-Johnson, J.D., pp. 113–15.
3 Kollias, T. (1984) p. 135; Nicolle, D.C. (1992) *passim.*; Nicolle, D.C. (1995) *passim.*
4 Nicholson, R.L. (1940) p. 24.
5 Mullett, M., pp. 240–1.
6 The 11th and 12th century Byzantine campaigns of 'Collapse and Recovery' have been studied and described in detail in Haldon, J.F. (2001) pp. 109–44.
7 Lindner, R.P. (1982) *passim.*
8 Lilie, R-J., p. 257.
9 Jacoby, D. (1989) p. 2.
10 Whittow, M., p. 67.
11 Nicol, D.M. (1979) p. 19.
12 Kaegi, W.E. (1964) p. 3.
13 Toumanoff, C., p. 620.
14 Dachkévytch, pp. 306, 355–6.
15 Şesan, M., p. 48.
16 Wozniak, F.E., p. 66.
17 Obolensky, D. (1978) p. 132.

18 Miller, W. (1969) pp. 29–30.
19 Obolensky, D. (1974) p. 312.
20 Mullett, M., pp. 244–7.
21 Magdalino, P. (1989) p. 88.
22 Nicol, D.M. (1979) pp. 19–20.
23 Magdalino, P. (1989) p. 91.
24 Yarnley, C.J., p. 82.
25 Laurent, J. (1971) p. 81.
26 Toumanoff, C., pp. 628–9.
27 Kazhdan, A. (1984) pp. 448–9.
28 Dadoyan, S.B., pp. 75–80.
29 Laurent, J. (1928) pp. 67–72.
30 Gilet, J., *passim*.
31 Housley, N., pp. 178–80.
32 Boase, T.S.R., p. 28.
33 Housley, N., pp. 179–80.
34 Northrup, L.S., p. 81.
35 Shot'ha Rust'haveli, p. viii.
36 Pollo, S. and Puto, A., pp. 43–4.
37 Ştefanescu, Ş., pp. 41–2.
38 Ştefanescu, Ş., pp. 43–4.
39 Whittow, M., pp. 57–9.
40 Shepard, J. (1993) pp. 276, 287.
41 Kaegi, W.E. (1971) p. 9.
42 Guillou, A. (1963) pp. 63–4.
43 Whittow, M., pp. 61–2.
44 Abulafia, D. (1984) pp. 196, 214.
45 Miller, W. (1969) p. 31.
46 Angold, M. (1984) pp. 15–16.
47 Diaconu, P. (1970) pp. 34–8.
48 Oikonomides, N. (1974) pp. 296–7.
49 Lev, Y. (1995) p. 204.
50 Kazhdan, A. (1984) pp. 443–5.
51 *Ibid.*
52 Kyrris, C.P., pp. 160–1.
53 Anon., *Digenes Akritas*, l. p. 47.
54 Zakkar, S., pp. 50–4.
55 Kyrris, C.P., p. 177.
56 Chaladon, F., pp. 278–9.
57 Zakythinos, D.A., p. 133.
58 Ducellier, A., pp. 994–5, 171.
59 Cahen, C. (1970) pp. 215–16.
60 Cheetham, N., pp. 115–16.
61 Ducellier, A., p. 516.
62 Angold, M. (1975) p. 284; Magdalino, P. (1976) pp. 15, 110.
63 Diaconu, P. (1978) p. 103.
64 Angold, M. (1975) p. 185.
65 Angold, M. (1975) pp. 190–1.
66 Nicol, D.M. (1972) p. 131.
67 Angold, M. (1984) pp. 15–16, 109–11.
68 Comnena, Anna, p. liv.
69 Bartusis, M.C., pp. 26–7.
70 Vryonis, S. (1975) p. 131.
71 Ahrweiler, H. (1966b) p. 214.
72 Angold, M. (1975) p. 189.
73 Bartu, p. 53
74 Bartusis, M.C., pp. 61–2.
75 Janin, R., p. 69.
76 Janin, R., pp. 69–70.
77 Angold, M. (1975) p. 182.
78 Shepard, J. (1973) pp. 55–9.
79 Shepard, J. (1973) pp. 72–3.
80 Shepard, J. (1973) pp. 77–8.
81 Godfrey, J., pp. 69–70.
82 Dawkins, R.M., pp. 39–41.
83 Blondal, S. and Beneditz, B.S., p. 158.
84 Schlumberger, G., p. 291.
85 Janin, R., pp. 68–9.
86 Ciggaar, K., pp. 45–7.
87 Comnena, Anna, vol. 1, p. 92.
88 Chaladon, F., pp. 614–16.
89 Comnena, Anna, p. liv.
90 Fotheringham, J.K., p. 33.
91 Cahen, C. (1951) p. 104.
92 Geanakoplos, D.J. (1959) p. 297.
93 Geanakoplos, D.J. (1959) p. 296.
94 Chaladon, F., pp. 614–16.
95 Angold, M. (1975) pp. 187–8.
96 Bryer, A., p. 3.
97 Miller, W. (1969) p. 17.
98 Toumanoff, C., pp. 622–3.
99 Hazai, G., pp. 125–6.
100 Angold, M. (1975) pp. 195–6.
101 Laurent, J. (1913) pp. 33, 53–4.
102 Laurent, J. (1971) pp. 72–3.
103 Laurent, J. (1913) pp. 33, 53–4.
104 Angold, M. (1975) p. 177.
105 Ahrweiler, H. (1966a) pp. 34–8.
106 Bartusis, M.C., pp. 5–6.
107 Angold, M. (1975) pp. 193–4, 256.
108 Brand, C.M. (1968) p. 148.
109 Jacoby, D. (1989) pp. 3–4.
110 Angold, M. (1975) p. 182.
111 Angold, M. (1975) p. 126.
112 Ahrweiler, H. (1959) pp. 52, 57–9.

113 Angold, M. (1975) pp. 192–3.
114 Bartusis, M.C., pp. 29–30.
115 Angold, M. (1975) pp. 182–5.
116 Angold, M. (1975) pp. 185–6.
117 Bartusis, M.C., p. 194.
118 Oikonomides, N. (1964) p. 162.
119 Angold, M. (1975) p. 187.
120 Angold, M. (1975) pp. 176–7.
121 Angold, M. (1975) p. 193.
122 Angold, M. (1975) pp. 188–9.
123 Angold, M. (1975) pp. 189–90.
124 Ahrweiler, H. (1966b) p. 333.
125 Bartusis, M.C., pp. 43–4.
126 Angold, M. (1975) p. 191.
127 Zakythinos, D.A., p. 133.
128 Zakythinos, D.A., p. 139.
129 Angold, M. (1975) p. 194.
130 Angold, M. (1975) pp. 142–3.
131 Jacoby, D. (1973) p. 902.
132 Oikonomides, N. (1964) pp. 158–61.
133 Jacoby, D. (1973) p. 877.
134 Angold, M. (1975) pp. 195–6.
135 Miller, W. (1969) p. 25.
136 Bryer, A., pp. 3–4.
137 Nicol, D.M. (1984) pp. 217–9.
138 Magdalino, P. (1976) introduction, pp. 14, 126.
139 Bosworth, C.E. (1978a) p. 28.
140 Laurent, J. (1971) pp. 121–2.
141 Yarnley, C.J., pp. 79–80.
142 Der Nersessian, S. (1969) pp. 650–1.
143 Edwards, R.W., p. 47.
144 Magdalino, P. (1989) pp. 101–2.
145 Angold, M. (1975) pp. 187–8.
146 Angold, M. (1975) p. 193.
147 Angold, M. (1975) pp. 131, 195–6.
148 Comnena, Anna, pp. lv–lvi.
149 Angold, M. (1975) p. 191.
150 Anon., *Digenes Akritas*, ll. pp. 3012–7.
151 Anon., *Digenes Akritas*, ll. pp. 1876–7 and l. 1927.
152 Buckler, G., p. 210.
153 Comnena, Anna, pp. lv–lvi.
154 'Arif 'Ali of Toqat, *passim*.
155 Kazhdan, A. (1984) pp. 447–8.
156 *Ibid.*
157 Hendrickx, B., pp. 219–221.
158 Angelov, D., *passim*.
159 Nicol, D.M. (1972) pp. 88–90.
160 Miller, W. (1908) p. 121 n. 1, 148.
161 Vryonis, S. (1967) p. 154.
162 Bianquis, T. (1983) p. 310, *passim*.
163 Richard, J. (1998a) p. 63.
164 Ahrweiler, H. (1974) pp. 223–5.
165 Dain, A., pp. 107–8.
166 McGeer, E. (1991) p. 131.
167 McGeer, E. (1991) p. 134.
168 McGeer, E. (1994) p. 124.
169 Savvides, A.G.C. (2000a) pp. 133–4.
170 For an up-to-date and in-depth study of the Byzantine campaigns during the later 11th century see Haldon, J.F. (2001) pp. 109–37.
171 Ross, D.J.A., *passim*.
172 Bianquis, T. (1983) p. 478.
173 Hussey, J.M., pp. 213–4.
174 For these Comnenian campaigns see Haldon, J.F. (2001) pp. 137–44.
175 Bartusis, M.C., pp. 25–6.
176 Geanakoplos, D.J. (1953) *passim*.
177 Ducellier, A., pp. 254–5.
178 Haldon, J.F. (2001) pp. 18–19.
179 Foss, C. (1979b) pp. 121–3.
180 Ahrweiler, H. (1960) pp. 182–9.
181 Miller, W. (1969) pp. 21–2.
182 Edwards, R.W., p. 38.
183 Der Nersessian, S. (1959) p. 153.
184 Smbat (G. Dédéyan tr.) p. 110.
185 Haldon, J.F. (2001) pp. 110–37.
186 Howard-Johnson, J.D., pp. 102–4.
187 Comnena, Anna, p. lxxv.
188 Moravcsik, G., p. 85; this battle is also discussed in detail in Haldon, J.F. (2001) pp. 138–9.
189 Villehardouin (1952) p. 122; Villehardouin (1921) p. 34.
190 Geanakoplos, D.J. (1953) p. 129.
191 Geanakoplos, D.J. (1953) p. 127.
192 Geanakoplos, D.J. (1959) p. 332.
193 Dennis, G.T. (1985) p. 325 n.1.
194 Dennis, G.T. (1985) p. 279.
195 Dennis, G.T. (1985) p. 281.
196 Dennis, G.T. (1985) p. 295.
197 Dennis, G.T. (1985) p. 301.
198 Lilie, R-J., p. 265; Haldon, J.F. (2001) pp. 139–45.

199 Dennis, G.T. (1985) pp. 241–2.
200 Dennis, G.T. (1985) p. 263.
201 *Ibid.*
202 Dennis, G.T. (1985) p. 271.
203 De Foucault, J.-A., pp. 298–300.
204 Zakkar, S., pp. 116–22.
205 Bianquis, T. (1983) p. 474.
206 Buckler, G., p. 377.
207 Comnena, Anna, vol. 1, p. 114.
208 Chaladon, F., pp. 618–20.
209 Moravcsik, G., p. 85.
210 Cheetham, N., p. 58.
211 Dennis, G.T. (1985) p. 283.
212 Blondal, S. and Beneditz, B.S., p. 47.
213 Blondal, S. and Beneditz, B.S., pp. 108, 183–4.
214 Blondal, S. and Beneditz, B.S., p. 212.
215 Kaegi, W.E. (1964) p. 105.
216 Buckler, G., p. 395.
217 Anon., *The Third Crusade, Itinerarium Peregrinorum*, pp. 47, 53.
218 'Arif 'Ali of Toqat, *passim.*
219 Marco Polo, p. 31.
220 Anon., *Digenes Akritas, passim.*
221 Buckler, G., pp. 363–4.
222 Comnena, Anna, vol. 1, pp. 34–5.
223 Smbat (G. Dédéyan tr.) p. 104.
224 Kaegi, W.E. (1964) p. 102.
225 Anon., *Digenes Akritas*, l. p. 3150.
226 Psellus, M., p. 36.
227 Kaegi, W.E. (1964) p. 101.
228 Buckler, G., pp. 181–3.
229 Miller, W. (1969) p. 25.
230 Ferrard, C.G., pp. 96–7.
231 Brett, G., pp. 98–9.
232 This might be seen in the military equipment from an 8th–9th century grave-site at Gelendjik on the north-eastern shore of the Black Sea, though the items in question could be as much Byzantine as Khazar Turkish; see Gorelik, M.V. (2002a) pp. 132–47, plates XI–3 to XI–10.
233 Nicolle, D.C. (1995) *passim.*; Nicolle, D.C. (1992) *passim.*
234 Anon., *Digenes Akritas*, ll. pp. 147–8.
235 Anon., *Digenes Akritas*, ll. pp. 1230–1.
236 Anon., *Digenes Akritas*, l. p. 1990.
237 Anon., *Digenes Akritas*, ll. pp. 3380–5.
238 Psellus, M., p. 156.
239 Psellus, M., p. 359.
240 Two examples from Lake Sigridsholm in Sweden (National Museum Stockholm) and from Iceland (National Museum Reykjavik), dated to the 10th and 11th centuries respectively, are both distinguished by almost conical pommels, unlike those normally found on Scandinavian swords of this period.
241 Djanpoladian, R. and Kirpicnikov, A., pp. 17–23.
242 Anon., *Digenes Akritas, passim.*
243 Nishimura, D., 422, *passim*; Dennis, G.T. (1981) p. 1.
244 Dennis, G.T. (1981) pp. 1–3.
245 Haldon, J.F. (1999) p. 135.
246 Haldon, J.F. (1999) p. 136.
247 Buckler, G., p. 369.
248 Kollias, T. (1988) pp. 245–6.
249 De Joinville (1921) p. 284.
250 Nikolova, J., p. 390.
251 Now in the National Museum, inv. nr. 1/64, Aleppo; Nicolle, D.C. (1995) pp. 226–30, pl. 1, figs. 1, 8.
252 Blondal, S. and Beneditz, B.S., p. 207.
253 Gaier, C., *passim.*
254 Nikolova, J., p. 390.
255 Amongst the first serious studies was the Doctoral thesis by Kolias, T. (1980b), later revised and extended as a book, Kollias, T. (1988); more recently a detailed study of Byzantine armour of the mid-10th to the start of the 13th century with particular reference to the use of lamellar and quilted soft armour was published by Dawson, T. (2002) while a huge survey of Byzantine arms and armour based upon a careful interpretation of the pictorial record was completed by Babuin, A. as a Doctoral thesis (2003), but has yet to be published.
256 Bartlett-Wells, H.
257 Psellus, M., p. 211.
258 Anon., *Digenes Akritas*, ll. 1094–99.

259 Blondal, S. and Beneditz, B.S., p. 108.
260 Blondal, S. and Beneditz, B.S., p. 184.
261 ʻArif ʻAli of Toqat, vol. I, pp. 224, 352, vol. II, pp. 38, 167.
262 Dagron, G. and Mihaescu, H., p. 189 n.35.
263 This is the view of Dr. M.V. Gorelik (2002a) *passim.*
264 Arendt, W. (1936) pp. 31–2.
265 ʻArif ʻAli of Toqat, vol. I, p. 352, vol. II, p. 167.
266 Kollias, T. (1980b) pp. 65–6.
267 *Ibid.*
268 Anon., *Digenes Akritas*, ll. pp. 895–7.
269 Kollias, T. (1980b) pp. 69–70.
270 Blondal, S. and Beneditz, B.S., p. 207.
271 Moravcsik, G., p. 81.
272 Vasiliev, A.A. (1934–50) vol. II, p. 333.
273 Kollias, T. (1980b) p. 65.
274 ʻArif ʻAli of Toqat, vol. I, p. 224, vol. II, p. 38.
275 Vryonis, S. (1971) p. 282.
276 Blondal, S. and Beneditz, B.S., p. 207.
277 Anon., *The Third Crusade, Itinerarium Peregrinorum*, p. 47.
278 Anon., *The Book of Dede Korkut*, p. 91.
279 Vryonis, S. (1971) pp. 6, 6 n.16.
280 Nikolova, J., p. 390.
281 Blondal, S. and Beneditz, B.S., p. 203.
282 King, E.J. (1931) p. 235.
283 Bartusis, M.C., p. 39.
284 Ducellier, A., p. 187.
285 Anon., ʻChronica collecta a Magno presbytero – 1195ʼ, pp. 511–12; Brand, C.M. (1962) pp. 170–1.
286 Ebersolt, J., pp. 105–6.
287 Specialists in this field, such as C. Foss, nevertheless point to the need for considerably more study to fully understand the siting and specific purposes of many of these increasingly impressive fortifications; Foss, C. (1982) p. 201.
288 For Nicaean and later 13th century Palaeolog fortifications, especially those in Lydia, see Foss, C. (1979a) *passim.*
289 Foss, C. and Winfield, D., p. 166.
290 Sinclair, T., p. 314.
291 Faucherre, N.
292 For a recent study of Shayzar see Tonghini, C. and Montevecchi, *passim.*
293 Bianquis, T. (1983) p. 418.
294 Nicol, D.M. (1984) p. 222.
295 Ducellier, A., p. 43.
296 Lang, D.M., pp. 79, 81–2.
297 Lang, D.M., pp. 83–5.
298 Anghel, G. (1983) p. 274.
299 Anghel, G. (1983) p. 275.
300 Bianquis, T. (1983) p. 478.
301 Edwards, R.W., pp. 24–6.
302 Edwards, R.W., p. 37.
303 Müller-Wiener, W., p. 30.
304 Creswell, K.A.C. (1952) pp. 100–3.
305 Creswell, K.A.C. (1952) pp. 108–9.
306 Creswell, K.A.C. (1960) p. 107.
307 Ebersolt, J., p. 104.
308 Bianquis, T. (1983) p. 478.
309 Sinclair, T., p. 313.
310 Foss, C. and Winfield, D., p. 48.
311 Foss, C. and Winfield, D., p. 115.
312 Foss, C. (1979b) p. 135.
313 Sullivan, D., pp. 196–9.
314 McGeer, E. (1994) p. 124.
315 De Foucault, J.-A., pp. 298–300.
316 McGeer, E. (1994) pp. 124–5.
317 McGeer, E. (1994) pp. 125–6.
318 Bianquis, T. (1983) pp. 484–5.
319 For a broad study of Byzantine offensive siege warfare in the 10th century see Sullivan, D., *passim.* He notes a revival of military science in Byzantium, both in written theory and in practice as described by both Byzantine and Islamic sources, Sullivan, D., p. 180, *passim.* Unfortunately he does not look at the Islamic military texts from a similar period.
320 Haldon, J.F. (1999) pp. 184–7.
321 Kinnamos, John, pp. 181–4.
322 Haldon, J.F. (1999) pp. 186–8.
323 Kinnamos, John, p. 79.
324 Shot'ha Rust'haveli, verse 1371.
325 De Vries, K., p. 138.
326 Cathcart King, D.J. (1982) pp. 458–9.

327 De Vries, K., pp. 130–2.
328 McGeer, E. (1994) pp. 126–7.
329 Angold, M. (1975) p. 288.
330 Angold, M. (1975) p. 194.
331 Rogers, R., p. 102.
332 'Arif 'Ali of Toqat, where vol. I, p. 266, vol. II, p. 80, are wrongly translated but have here been corrected.
333 'Arif 'Ali of Toqat, vol. I, p. 415 and 415 note 1.
334 Dennis, G.T. (1985) p. 302.
335 Dennis, G.T. (1985) pp. 317–19.
336 *Ibid.*
337 Vachon, V., pp. 219–41.
338 Kinnamos, John, pp. 123–4.
339 Bianquis, T. (1983) pp. 493–4.
340 Kinnamos, John, pp. 126–7.
341 For one of the more likely explanations of how Greek Fire really worked, see Haldon, J.F. and Byrne, M., *passim.*
342 Ellis Davidson, H.R., pp. 73–4.
343 Partington, J.R., p. 15.
344 Psellus, M., p. 202.
345 Partington, J.R., pp. 19–20.
346 'Arif 'Ali of Toqat, vol. I, p. 366–7, vol. II, p. 181.
347 Janin, R., p. 64.
348 Kinnamos, John, p. 23.
349 Kollias, T. (1980a) p. 31.
350 France, J. (1971) pp. 139–45.
351 Bachrach, B.S. (2002) p. 83.
352 France, J. (1996) p. 164.
353 Pryor, J.H. (1982) pp. 12–13.
354 By the late 10th century the Arab *tarida* could carry forty horses; Bennett, M. (1993) p. 49.
355 Bennett, M. (1993) p. 49.
356 Chaladon, F., p. 279.
357 Brand, C.M. (1962) pp. 170–1; Anon., 'Chronica collecta a Magno presbytero – 1195', p. 511.
358 For the organisation of the Byzantine fleet during the late 11th and 12th centuries see Şesan, M., pp. 51–2.
359 Bianquis, T. (1983) p. 567.
360 Shepard, J. (1973) p. 82.
361 Angold, M. (1975) p. 197.
362 Ahrweiler, H. (1966b) p. 339.
363 Nicol, D.M. (1972) pp. 114–15.
364 Makrypoulias, C.G. (1995) p. 164; this source also provides further detailed information about the ships, their crews and the marines who served aboard them.
365 Makrypoulias, C.G. (1997) *passim.*
366 *Ibid.*
367 Ahrweiler, H. (1966b) pp. 160, 215.
368 Comnena, Anna, p. lxiii.
369 Ahrweiler, H. (1966b) p. 362.
370 Oikonomides, N. (1979) p. 86.
371 Ahrweiler, H. (1966b) p. 405.
372 Ahrweiler, H. (1966b) pp. 344–5.
373 Norwich, J.J., pp. 239–40; Cheetham, N., pp. 103–4.
374 Brooks, F.W., p. 116.
375 Bennett, M. (1993) p. 54.
376 Kinnamos, John, p. 212.
377 Edwards, R.W., p. 38.
378 Miller, W. (1969) pp. 18–20.
379 Cuoq, J., pp. 71–2.
380 Cuoq, J., pp. 69–70.
381 Cuoq, J., pp. 72–3.
382 Cuoq, J., pp. 76–9.
383 Bianquis, T. (1983) p. 19.
384 Nasir-i Khusrau (1881) p. 175.
385 Nasir-i Khusrau (1881) p. 124.
386 Lyon, B.D., pp. 59–61.
387 Arkell, A.J., p. 119.
388 Northrup, L.S., p. 108.
389 Cuoq, J., p. 70.
390 Northrup, L.S., p. 108.
391 Welsby, D.A., pp. 166–7.
392 Welsby, D.A., pp. 168–9.
393 Adams, W.Y., p. 464.
394 Adams, W.Y., pp. 450–1.
395 Ayalon, D. (1976) p. 201.
396 Adams, W.Y., pp. 516–17.
397 Mas'udi, al-, vol. II, pp. 382–3.
398 Thorau, P., p. 224.
399 Mas'udi, al-, vol. II, pp. 382–3.
400 Paterson, W.F. (1983) *passim.*
401 Allason-Jones, L., *passim.*
402 Schröder, B., *passim.*
403 Nasir-i Khusrau (1881) p. 124.
404 Ibn Hauqal (1939) p. 58; Ibn Hauqal (1964) pp. 55–6.

405 Jones, A.H.M. and Monro, E., p. 46.
406 Jones, A.H.M. and Monro, E., pp. 46–9.
407 Jones, A.H.M. and Monro, E., pp. 48–50.
408 Richard, J. (1960) pp. 324–7, 335; Richard, J. (1998b) p. 65.
409 Northrup, L.S., pp. 105–6.
410 Northrup, L.S., pp. 103–4; for a detailed study of Abyssinian–Mamluk relations during this period, but largely focussing upon ecclesiastical matters, see Wiet, G., pp. 117–22
411 Umari, Ibn Fadl Allah al-, pp. 35–6.
412 Umari, Ibn Fadl Allah al-, p. 6.
413 Umari, Ibn Fadl Allah al-, pp. 25–6.

Notes to Chapter 3: The Military Heritage and Impact of Crusading Warfare on the Christian World

1 Voisin, J-C., *passim.*
2 Chevedden, P.E. (1999) *passim.*
3 Paterson, L.M. (1988) pp. 118–19.
4 Hitti, P.K., *passim.*
5 Bosworth, C.E. (1972) p. 65.
6 Bosworth, C.E. (1972) pp. 65–6.

Bibliography

Abulafia, D., (1975) 'Count Henry of Malta and his Mediterranean activities: 1203–1230', in A.T. Luttrell (ed.), *Medieval Malta: Studies in Malta before the Knights* (London 1975) pp. 104–25.

Abulafia, D., (1977) *The Two Italies: Economic Relations between the Norman Kingdom of Sicily and the Northern Communes* (Cambridge 1977).

Abulafia, D., (1984) 'Ancona, Byzantium and the Adriatic, 1155–1173', *Papers of the British School at Rome*, 52 (1984) pp. 195–216.

Abulafia, D., (1986) 'The Anconitan privileges in the Kingdom of Jerusalem and the Levant trade of Ancona', in G. Airaldi & B.Z. Kedar (eds.), *I Comuni Italiani nel Regno Crociato di Gerusalemme* (Genoa 1986) pp. 523–59.

Abulafia, D., (1990) 'The end of Muslim Sicily', in J.M. Powell (ed.), *Muslims under Latin Rule, 1100–1300* (Princeton 1990) pp. 103–33.

Abulafia, D., (1993) 'Southern Italy, Sicily and Sardinia in the medieval Mediterranean economy', in D. Abufalia (ed.), *Commerce and Conquest in the Mediterranean, 1100–1500* (London 1993) pp. 1–32.

Abu'l-Fida, (P.M. Holt tr.), *The Memoirs of a Syrian Prince: Abu'l Fida, Sultan of Hamah (672–737/1273–1331)* (Wiesbaden 1983).

Adam, P., 'Les enseignes militaires du Moyen Age et leur influence sur l'héraldique', in *Ve Congrès international des sciences généologiques et héraldiques* (Stockholm 1961) pp. 167–94.

Adams, W.Y., *Nubia, Corridor to Africa* (London 1977).

Ahmad, Aziz, (1975) *A History of Islamic Sicily* (Edinburgh 1975).

Ahmad, Aziz, (1977) *Storia della Sicilia islamica* (Catania 1977).

Ahrweiler, H., (1959) 'La politique agraire des empereurs de Nicée', *Byzantion*, 28 (1959) pp. 51–66, 135–6.

Ahrweiler, H., (1960) 'Les forteresses construites en Asie Mineure face à l'invasion seldjoucide', *Akten des XI. internationalen Byzantinist Kongresses* (Munich 1960) pp. 182–9.

Ahrweiler, H., (1966a) 'Le sébaste, chef des groupes ethniques', in *Polychronicion (Festschrift für F. Dölger)* (Munich 1966) pp. 34–8.

Ahrweiler, H., (1966b) *Byzance et la mer: la marine de guerre, la politique et les institutions maritimes de Byzance aux VIIe–XVe siècles* (Paris 1966).

Ahrweiler, H., (1974) 'La frontière et les frontières de Byzance en Orient', in *Actes du XIVe Congrès International des Études Byzantines, Bucarest, 6–12 Septembre, 1971, vol. I* (Bucharest 1974) pp. 209–30.

Airaldi, G., 'The Genoese art of warfare', in D.A. Agius & I.R. Netton (eds.), *Across the Mediterranean Frontiers: Trade, Politics and Religion, 650–1450* (Turnhout 1997) pp. 269–82.

Alexander, J.J.G., 'Ideological representation of military combat in Anglo-Norman art', *Anglo-Norman Studies*, 15 (1993) pp. 1–24.

Allason-Jones, L., 'Catalogue of weaponry from Soba excavations, 8–14 cents.' (unpublished 1992).

Allouche, I.S., 'Une texte relatif aux premiers canons', *Hespéris*, 32 (1945) pp. 81–4.

Alm, J., (1947) 'Europeiska armborst: en översickt', *Vaaben-historisk Aarboger*, 5/b (1947) pp. 107–255.

Alm, J., (1994) (H. Bartlett Wells & G.M. Wilson trs.), *European Crossbows: A Survey by Josef Alm* (Leeds 1994).

Amari, M., (1876) 'Su i fuochi da guerra usati nel Mediterraneo nell'XI e XII secolo', *Atti della Reale Academia dei Lincei* (1876) pp. 3–16.

Amari, M., (1880–1) *Biblioteca Arabo-Sicula* (Turin & Rome 1880–1).

Amari, M., (1933) *Storia dei Musulmani di Sicilia* (Catania 1933).

Amatuccio, G., 'Saracen archers in southern Italy', *De Re Militari website* (2004).

Amououx-Mourad, M., *Le Comté d'Edesse* (Beirut 1988).

Amt, E., 'Besieging Bedford: military logistics in 1224', *The Journal of Medieval Military History*, 1 (2002) pp. 101–24.

Anastasijevic, D. and Ostrogorsky, G., 'Les Koumanes Pronoïaires', *Annuaire de l'Institut de philologie et d'histoire Orientales et Slaves*, 11 (1951) pp. 19–29.

Ancona, C., 'Milizie e condottieri', in G. Einaudi (ed.), *Storia d'Italia, volume quinto, I documenti* (Turin 1973) pp. 642–65.

Anderson, R.C., *Oared Fighting Ships* (Kings Langley 1976).

Anderson, W., *Castles of Europe from Charlemagne to the Renaissance* (London 1970).

Angelov, D., 'Le mouvement bogomile dans les pays slaves balkaniques et dans Byzance', *Academia Nazionale dei Lincei, Quaderno*, 62 (1964) pp. 607–16.

Anghel, G., (1977) 'Les premiers donjons de Pierre de Transylvanie (Roumanie)', *Château Gaillard 1976*, 8 (1977) pp. 7–20.

Anghel, G., (1983) 'Quelques considérations concernant le développement de l'architecture des fortifications médiévales de Roumanie du XIIIe siècle au début du XVIe siècle', *Château Gaillard, 1982*, 9–10 (1983) pp. 273–92.

Anglo, S., 'How to win at tournaments: the technique of chivalric combat', *The Antiquaries Journal*, 68 (1988) pp. 248–64.

Angold, M., (1975) *A Byzantine Government in Exile* (Oxford 1975).

Angold, M., (1984) *The Byzantine Empire 1025–1204* (London 1984).

Anon., *Aucassin et Nicolette, chantefable du XIIIe siècle,* (M. Roques ed.) (Paris 1936).

Anon., *Cartulaire Général de l'Ordre des Hospitaliers de St. Jean de Jérusalem,* (J. Delaville Le Roulx, ed.) (Paris 1894–1906)

Anon., 'Chronica collecta a Magno presbytero – 1195', (W. Wattenbach ed.) in G.H. Pertz ed., *Monumenta Germaniae Historica, Scriptorum, vol. XVII* (Hanover 1861; reprinted New York 1963).

Anon., *David of Sassoun: The Armenian Folk Epic in Four Cycles,* (A.K. Shalian tr.) (Athens Ohio 1964).

Anon., *De Expugnatione Terrae Sanctae per Saladinum, Libellus: Rolls Serie; vol. 66,* (J. Stevenson ed.) (London 1875).

Anon., *Digenes Akritas,* (J. Mavrogordato tr.) (Oxford 1956).

Anon., *Gesta Francorum, The Deeds of the Franks and other Pilgrims to Jerusalem,* (R. Hill ed. & tr.) (London 1962).

Anon., *La Chanson de Roland,* (T.A. Jenkins ed.) (London 1924).

Anon., *La Continuation de Guillaume de Tyr (1184–1197),* (M.R. Morgan ed.) (Paris 1982).

Anon., *La règle du Temple. Société de l'Histoire de France*, 228, (H. De Curzon, ed.) (1886).

Anon., *La Siège de Barbastre,* (J.-L. Perrier ed.) (Paris 1926).

Anon., *Le Charroi de Nimes,* (J-L. Perrier ed.) (Paris 1963).

Anon., *Le Roman de Renart,* (M. Roques ed.) (Paris 1955–68).
Anon., *Le Roman de Thèbes,* (G.R. De Lage ed.) (Paris 1966).
Anon., *Sassountzy David, Haykakan Zhoghovrdakan Epos,* (anon. ed.) (Erevan 1939).
Anon., *The Lay of Havelock the Dane,* (K. Sisam & W.W. Skeats eds.) (Oxford 1973).
Anon., *The Nibelungenlied,* (A.T. Hatto tr.) (London 1965).
Anon., *The Old French Crusade Cycle, vol. I: La Naissance du Chevalier au Cygne: Elioxe,* (E.J. Mickel ed.) (Alabama 1977).
Anon., *The Old French Crusade Cycle, vol. I: La Naissance du Chevalier au Cygne: Beatrix,* (J.A. Nelson ed.) (Alabama 1977).
Anon., *The Old French Crusade Cycle, vol. V: Les Chétifs,* (G.M. Myers ed.) (Alabama 1981).
Anon., *The Rule of the Templars,* (J.M. Upton-Ward tr.) (Woodbridge 1992).
Anon., *The Song of Roland,* (D.L. Sayers tr.) (London 1957).
Anon., *The 'Templar of Tyre': part III of the 'Deeds of the Cypriots',* (P. Crawford tr.) (Aldershot 2003).
Anon., *The Third Crusade, Itinerarium Peregrinorum,* (K. Fenwick tr.) (London 1958).
Anon., *Two Old French Gauvain Romances, Le Chevalier à l'Épée and La Mule sans Frein,* (R.C. Johnston & D.D.R. Owen eds.) (Edinburgh 1972).
Anstee, J.W. and Biek, L., 'A study in pattern-welding', *Medieval Archaeology,* 5 (1961) pp. 71–93.
Arendt, W., (1932–4) 'Sirgeron-Kubetschi', *Zeitschrift für Historische Waffen- und Kostümkunde,* n.s. 4 (1932–4).
Arendt, W., (1936) 'Der Nomadenhelm des Frühen Mittelalters in Osteuropa', *Zeitschrift für Historische Waffen- und Kostümkunde,* n.s. 5 (1936) pp. 26–34.
'Arif 'Ali of Toqat ('Arif 'Ali de Tokat), (I. Melikoff ed. & tr.), *Danishmandname: la geste de Melik Danişment* (Paris 1960).
Arkell, A.J., 'A Christian church and monastery at Ain Farah, Darfur', *Kush,* 8 (1959) pp. 115–19.
Arnold, B., *German Knighthood 1050–1300* (Oxford 1985).
Ashtor, E., (1969) *Histoire des prix et des salaires dans l'orient médiévale* (Paris 1969).
Ashtor, E., (1976) *A Social and Economic History of the Near East in the Middle Ages* (London 1976).
Ashtor, E., (1983) 'L'ascendant technologique de l'Occident médiévale', *Revue Suisse d'Histoire,* 33 (1983) pp. 385–413.
Atiya, A.S., *The Crusade in the Later Middle Ages* (London 1938).
Audouin, E., *Essai sur l'Armée Royale au Temps de Philippe Auguste* (Paris 1913).
Aylward, J.D., *The English Master of Arms from the Twelfth to the Twentieth Century* (London 1956).
Baart, J.M., 'Mittelalterliche Holzfunde aus Amsterdam. Der Zusammenhang zwischen Holzart und Gerätform', *Zeitschrift für Archäologie des Mittelalters,* 10 (1982) pp. 51–62.
Babuin, A., (1996) 'Armi e armature nel Codice Matritense di Skylitzes', *Quaterni Utinensi* (1996) pp. 301–12.
Babuin, A., (2003) 'O Exoplismos tou Stratou kata tin Isteri bizantini periodo 1204–1453 (Graptes kai ikonografikes piges)' (The equipment of the Army during the late-Byzantine period 1204–1453, written and iconographic sources), in Greek (PhD thesis, University of Ioannina 2003).
Bacharach, J.L., 'African military slaves in the medieval Middle East', *International Journal of Middle East Studies,* 13 (1981) pp. 471–95.
Bachrach, B.S., (1969) 'The origins of Armorican chivalry', *Technology and Culture,* 10 (1969) pp. 166–71.

Bachrach, B.S., (1993) *Fulk Nerra, the Neo-Roman Consul, 987–1040: A Political Biography of the Angevin Count* (Berkeley 1993).
Bachrach, B.S., (2002) 'Some observations on the role of the Byzantine navy in the success of the First Crusade', *The Journal of Medieval Military History*, 1 (2002) pp. 83–100.
Bachrach, D., 'Origins of the crossbow industry in England', *The Journal of Medieval Military History*, 2 (2004) pp. 73–88.
Baha' al-Din Ibn Shaddad, (1897a) (Yusuf Ibn Rafi' ed.), *Al-Nawadir al-Sultaniyah* (Cairo 1897).
Baha' al-Din Ibn Shaddad, (1897b) (C.W. Wilson tr.), *Saladin, what befell Sultan Yusuf: Palestine Pilgrim's Text Society* (London 1997).
Baha' al-Din Ibn Shaddad, (2002) (D.C. Richards tr.), *The Rare and Excellent History of Saladin* (Aldershot 2002).
Balard M., (1966) 'Les Génois en Romanie entre 1204 et 1261, recherches dans les minutiers notariaux génois', *Mélanges d'Archéologie et d'Histoire publiés par l'Ecole Française de Rome*, 78 (1966) pp. 467–502.
Balard, M., (1973) *Gênes et l'Outre-Mer, vol. I. Les Actes de Caffa du notaire Lamberto di Sambuceto 1289–1290* (Paris 1973).
Balard, M., (1983) 'Gênes et la Mer Noire (XIIIe–XVe siècle)', *Revue Historiques* 270 (1983) pp. 31–54.
Balard, M., (1986) 'Les transports maritimes Génois vers la Terra Sainte', in G. Airaldi & B.Z. Kedar (eds.), *I Comuni Italiani nel Regno Crociato di Gerusalemme* (Genoa 1986) pp. 141–74.
Balard, M., (1989) 'The Genoese in the Aegean (1204–1566)', in B. Arbel, B. Hamilton & D. Jacoby (ed.), *Latins and Greeks in the Eastern Mediterranean after 1204* (London 1989) pp. 158–74.
Balbi, G.P., *Una città e il suo mare, Genova nel Medioevo* (Bologna 1991).
Baldwin, M.W., *Raymond III of Tripoli and the Fall of Jerusalem (1140–1187)* (Princeton 1936).
Barber, M., (1989) 'Western attitudes to Frankish Greece in the thirteenth century', in B. Arbel, B. Hamilton & D. Jacoby (eds.), *Latins and Greeks in the Eastern Mediterranean after 1204* (London 1989) pp. 111–28.
Barber, M., (1992) 'Supplying the Crusader States: the role of the Templars', in B.Z. Kedar (ed.), *The Horns of Hattin* (Jerusalem & London 1992) pp. 314–26.
Barber, M., (1998) 'Frontier warfare in the Latin Kingdom of Jerusalem: the campaign at Jacob's Ford, 1178–79', in J. France & W.G. Zajac (eds.), *The Crusades and their Sources: Essays Presented to Bernard Hamilton* (Aldershot 1998) pp. 9–22.
Barker, P., correspondence on Byzantine 'shoulder tufts' (8 July 1983).
Barlow, F., *William Rufus* (London 1983).
Barlozzetti, U. and Giuliani, M., 'La Prassi Guerresca in Toscana', in L.G. Boccia & M. Scalini (eds.), *Guerre e assoldati in Toscana, 1260–1364* (Florence 1982) pp. 51–67.
Bartha, A., *Hungarian Society in the 9th and 10th Centuries* (Budapest 1975).
Bartlett-Wells, H., correspondence on Byzantine steel (12 February 1983).
Bartusis, M.C., *The Late Byzantine Army: Arms and Society 1204–1453* (Philadelphia 1992).
Baudry, M.-P., conversation on the 'trench' in the summit of the main solid tower in the castle of Bressuire (26 September 2002).
Becker, M.B., 'Some common features of Italian urban experience (c.1200–1500)', *Medievalia et Humanistica*, 1 (1970) pp. 175–201.
Beech, G.T., 'A Norman-Italian adventurer in the East: Richard of Salerno 1097–1112', *Anglo-Norman Studies*, 15 (1993) pp. 25–40.
Beeler, J., *Warfare in Feudal Europe, 730–1200* (Ithaca 1971).

Bellafiore, G., 'The Cathedral of Monreale', *Connoisseur* (March 1975) pp. 216–22.

Ben-Ami, A., *Social Change in a Hostile Environment: The Crusaders' Kingdom of Jerusalem* (Princeton 1969).

Bennett, M., (1986) 'The status of the squire: the northern evidence', in C. Harper-Bill & R. Harvey (eds.), *The Ideals and Practice of Medieval Knighthood (Papers from the first and second Strawberry Hill Conferences)* (Bury St. Edmunds 1986) pp. 1–11.

Bennett, M., (1989) 'La Règle du Temple as a military manual, or how to deliver a cavalry charge', in C. Harper-Bill (et al. eds.), *Studies in Medieval History Presented to R. Allen Brown* (Woodbridge 1989) 7–19; also in J.M. Upton-Ward (ed.), *The Rule of the Templars* (Woodbridge 1992) pp. 175–88.

Bennett, M., (1992) 'Wace and warfare', *Anglo-Norman Studies*, 11 (1989) pp. 37–58; also in M. Strickland (ed.), *Anglo-Norman Warfare* (Woodbridge 1992) pp. 230–50.

Bennett, M., (1993) 'Norman naval activity in the Mediterranean c.1060–1108', *Anglo-Norman Studies*, 15 (Woodbridge 1993) pp. 41–58.

Bennett, M., (1994) 'The medieval warhorse reconsidered', in S. Church & R. Harvey (eds.), *Medieval Knighthood vol. V* (Woodbridge 1994) pp. 19–40.

Bennett, M., (1998) 'The myth of the military supremacy of knightly cavalry', in M. Strickland (ed.), *Armies, Chivalry and Warfare of Medieval Britain and France, Harlaxton Medieval Studies VII* (London 1998) pp. 304–16.

Bennett, M., (2000) 'The Crusader fighting march revisited', pre-publication draft (April 2000).

Bennett, M., (2001) 'Military aspects of the conquest of Lisbon, 1147', in J. Phillips & M. Hoch (eds.), *The Second Crusade: Scope and Consequences* (Manchester 2001) pp. 71–89.

Benton, J.F., (ed.) and Swinton Bland, C.C., (tr.), *Self and Society in Medieval France: The Memoirs of Abbot Guibert of Nogent (1064?–c.1125)* (New York 1970).

Bianchi, L.G. and Poleggi, E., *Una Citta Portuale del Medioeva, Genova nei secoli X–XVI* (Genoa 1987).

Bishko, C.J., 'The Castilian as plainsman: the medieval ranching frontier in La Mancha and Extremadura', in A. Lewis & T. McGunn (eds.), *The New World Looks at its History* (Austin 1963) pp. 46–69.

Bisson, T.N., (1986) *The Medieval Crown of Aragon* (Oxford 1986).

Bisson, T.N., (1989) *Medieval France and her Pyrenean Neighbours* (London 1989).

Blair, C., (1958) *European Armour* (London 1958).

Blair, C., (1959) 'Medieval swords and spurs in Toledo Cathedral', *Journal of the Arms and Armour Society*, 3 (1959) pp. 41–52.

Blondal, S. and Beneditz, B.S., *The Varangians of Byzantium* (Cambridge 1978).

Boase, T.S.R., (ed.), *The Cilician Kingdom of Armenia* (New York & Edinburgh 1978).

Bon, A., (1937) 'Forteresses médiévales de la Grèce Centrale', *Bulletin de Correspondence Hellénique*, 61 (1937) pp. 136–208.

Bon, A., (1969) *La Morée Franque* (Paris 1969).

Bono Giamboni, 'Dal volgarizzamento dell'arte della guerra di Flavio Vegezio', in E. Grillo (intro. & ed.), *Early Italian Literature, volume II, The Dawn of Italian Prose* (London 1920) pp. 101–07.

Borg, A., 'Gisarmes and great axes', *Journal of the Arms and Armour Society*, 8 (1974–6) pp. 337–42.

Bosson, C., 'L'Arbalète', *Les Musées de Genève* (February 1956) 2.

Boussard, J., 'Les mercenaires au XIIIe siècle', *Bibliothèque de l'Ecole des Chartres*, 106 (1945–6) pp. 189–224.

Bowlus, C.R., 'Tactical and strategic weaknesses of horse-archers on the eve of the First Crusade', in M. Balard (ed.), *Autour de la Première Croisade* (Paris 1996) pp. 159–66.

Bradbury, J., *The Medieval Archer* (Woodbridge 1985).

Bragadin, M.-A., *Histoire des Républiques Maritimes Italiennes: Venise-Amalfi-Pise-Gênes* (Paris 1955).

Braibant, C., *Les Blasons et les Sceaux* (Paris 1950).

Brand, C.M., (1962) 'The Byzantines and Saladin, 1185–1192: Opponents of the Third Crusade', *Speculum*, 37 (1962) pp. 167–81.

Brand, C.M., (1968) *Byzantium Confronts the West: 1180–1204* (Cambridge Massachusetts 1968).

Bresc, H., 'Mudejars des Pays de la Couronne d'Aragon et Sarrasins de la Sicile Normande: Le Problème d'Acculturation', in *X Congreso de Historia de la Corona de Aragon: Jaime I y su Epoca (Zaragoza, 1975), t. III* (Saragossa 1980) pp. 51–60.

Brett, G., 'Small finds', in G. Brett (ed.), *The Great Palace of the Byzantine Emperors (First Report)* (London 1947) pp. 98–100.

Brodman, J.W., *Ransoming Captives in Crusader Spain* (Philadelphia 1986).

Brooker, C.H. and Knauf, E.A., 'Notes on Crusader Transjordan', *Zeitschrift des Deutschen Palaestina-vereins*, 104 (1988) pp. 185–8.

Brooks, F.W., 'Naval armament in the thirteenth century', *Mariner's Mirror*, 14 (1928) pp. 115–31.

Brown, R.A., 'The status of the Norman knight', in J. Gillingham & J.C. Holt (eds.) *War and Government in the Middle Ages* (Woodbridge 1984) 18–32; also in M. Strickland (ed.), *Anglo-Norman Warfare* (Woodbridge 1992) pp. 92–127.

Bryer, A., 'Shipping on the Empire of Trebizond', *Mariner's Mirror*, 52 (1966) pp. 3–12.

Bucher, F., *The Pamplona Bibles, 1197–1200 AD* (New Haven 1970).

Buckler, G., *Anna Comnena, a Study* (London 1929).

Bulliet, R.W., *The Camel and the Wheel* (Cambridge Massachusetts 1975).

Burns, R.I., (1961) 'The Friars of the Sack in Valencia', *Speculum*, 36 (1961) pp. 435–8.

Burns, R.I., (1976) 'The Muslim in the Christian feudal order: the Kingdom of Valencia, 1240–1280', *Studies in Medieval Culture*, 5 (1976) pp. 105–26.

Burns, R.I., (1986) 'The Crusade against al-Azraq: a thirteenth century Mudejar revolt in international perspective', paper read at *61st Annual Meeting of the Medieval Academy of America, University of New Mexico* (April 1986).

Burns, R.I., (2004) '100,000 crossbow bolts for the King of Aragon', *The Journal of Medieval Military History*, 2 (2004) pp. 159–64.

Burridge, P., 'The Castle of Vardounia and the defence of the Southern Mani', in P. Lock & G.D.R. Sanders (eds.), *The Archaeology of Medieval Greece* (Oxford 1996) pp. 19–28.

Buttin, F., (1965) 'La lance et l'arrêt de cuirasse', *Archeologia*, 99 (1965) pp. 77–178.

Byrne, E.H., (1920) 'Genoese trade with Syria in the twelfth century', *American Historical Review*, 25 (1920) pp. 191–219.

Byrne, E.H., (1928) 'The Genoese colonies in Syria', in L.J. Paetow (ed.), *The Crusades and Other Historical Essays Presented to Dana C. Monro by his Former Students* (New York 1928) pp. 139–82.

Cahen, C., (1934) 'La campagne de Mantzikert, d'après les sources Musulmanes', *Byzantion*, 9 (1934) pp. 613–42.

Cahen, C., (1940) *La Syrie du Nord au Temps ds Croisades* (Paris 1940).

Cahen, C., (1948) 'La première pénétration turque en Asie-Mineure (seconde moitié du XIe. s.)', *Byzantion*, 18 (1948) pp. 5–67.

Cahen, C., (1951) 'Seljukides de Rum, Byzantins et Francs d'après le Seljuknameh anonyme', *Annuaire de l'Institut de Philologie et d'Histoire Orientales et Slaves*, 11 (1951) pp. 97–106.

Cahen, C., (1983) *Orient et Occident au Temps des Croisades* (Paris 1983).

Canard, M., (1954) 'Un Vizir Chrétien à l'époque fatimide: l'Arménien Bahram', *Annales de l'Institut d'Etudes Orientales de la Faculté des Lettres d'Alger*, 12 (1954) pp. 84–113.

Canard, M., (1965b) 'La Campagne Arménienne du Sultan Salguqide Alp Arslan et la prise d'Ani en 1064', *Revue des Etudes Arméniennes*, 2 (1965) pp. 239–59.

Cathcart King, D.J., (1949) 'The taking of Le Krak des Chevaliers in 1271', *Antiquity*, 23 (1949) pp. 83–92.

Cathcart King, D.J., (1982) 'The Trebuchet and other siege engines', *Château Gaillard*, 9–10 (1982) pp. 457–69.

Chaladon, F., *Les Comnènes – Etudes sur l'Empire Byzantin* (Paris 1900–12).

Chambers, F.M., 'Three troubadour poems with historical overtones', *Speculum*, 54 (1979) pp. 44–54.

Cheetham, N., *Medieval Greece* (New Haven 1981).

Chehab, M.H., 'Tyr à l'époque des Croisades (vol. 2)', *Bulletin du Musée de Beyrouth*, 31 (1979) whole volume.

Chevedden, P.E., (1999) 'Fortifications and the development of defensive planning in the Latin East', in D. Kagay & L.J.A. Villalon (eds.), *The Circle of War in the Middle Ages* (Woodbridge 1999) pp. 33–43.

Christides, V., (1984) 'Naval warfare in the Eastern Mediterranean (6th–14th centuries): an Arabic translation of Leo's "Naumachica"', *Graeco-Arabica*, 3 (1984) pp. 137–43.

Christides, V., (1989) 'Some remarks on the Mediterranean and Red Sea ships in ancient and medieval times: a preliminary report', *Tropsis*, 1 (Piraeus 1989) pp. 75–82.

Christides, V., (1990a) Some remarks on the Mediterranean and Red Sea ships in ancient and medieval times, II: merchant-passenger vs. combat ships', *Tropsis*, 2 (Piraeus 1990) pp. 87–99.

Christides, V., (1994) 'New light on navigation and naval warfare in the Eastern Mediterranean, the Red Sea and the Indian Ocean (6th–14th centuries A.D.)', *Nubica*, 3 (1994) pp. 3–42.

Christides, V., (1997) 'Military intelligence and Arabo-Byzantine naval warfare', in K. Tsiknakis (ed.), *Byzantium at War (9th–12th C.)* (Athens 1997) pp. 269–81.

Ciggaar, K., 'Flemish mercenaries in Byzantium and their later history in an Old Norse miracle', *Byzantion*, 51 (1981) pp. 44–75.

Claverie, P-V., 'Le statut des templiers capturés en Orient durant les croisades', in G. Cipollone (ed.), *La liberazione dei 'Captivi' tra Cristianità e Islam: Oltre la Crociata e il Gihad: Tolleranza e Servizio Umanitario* (Vatican 2000) pp. 501–11.

Clavijo, Ruy Gonzales de, (Guy Le Strange tr.), *Clavijo, Embassy to Tamerlane, 1403–1406* (London 1928).

Clementi, D.R., 'Some unnoticed aspects of the Emperor Henry VI's conquest of the Norman Kingdom of Sicily', *Bulletin of the John Rylands Library, Manchester*, 36 (1953–4) pp. 328–59.

Clements, J., *Medieval Swordsmanship: Illustrated Methods and Techniques* (Boulder 1998).

Clifford, E.R., *A Knight of Great Renown. The Life and Times of Othon de Grandson* (Chicago 1961).

Coelho, E.T., 'Le armi di Campaldino', in (anon. ed.), *Il sabato di San Barnaba: La battaglia di Campaldino: II giugno 1289–1989* (Milan 1989) pp. 99–101.

Cohen, M., 'The fortification of the Fortress of Gybelin', in N. Faucherre (et al. eds.), *La Fortification au Temps des Croisades* (Rennes 2004) pp. 67–75.

Colardelle, M., (et al.), 'L'armament des chevaliers-paysans de Charavins au XIe siècle', in M. Letizia Heyer-Boscardin (ed.), *Wider das 'Finstere Mittelalter': Festschrift für Werner Meyer zun 65 Geburtstag: Schweitzer Beitrage zur Kulturgeschichte und Archäologie des Mittelalters, 29* (Basel 2002) pp. 107–16.

Colardelle, R. & M., 'L'habitat médiévale immergé de Colletière, à Charavines (Isère). Premier bilan des fouilles', *Archéologie Médiévale*, 10 (1980) pp. 167–269.

Collin, B., *The Riddle of a 13th Century Sword-Belt (Heraldry Society Monograph)* (East Knoyle 1955).

Comnena, Anna, (B. Leib ed. & tr.), *Annè Comnène, Alexiade* (Paris 1967).

Constable, G., 'The financing of the Crusades in the twelfth century', in B.Z. Kedar (et al. eds.), *Outremer: Studies in the History of the Crusading Kingdom of Jerusalem* (Jerusalem 1982) pp. 64–88.

Contamine, P., (1980) *La Guerre au Moyen Age* (Paris 1980).

Contamine, P., (1982) 'L'armée de Philippe Auguste', in R.-H. Bautier (ed.), *La France de Philippe Auguste – Les Temps des Mutations* (Paris 1982) pp. 577–94.

Cowdrey. H.E.J., 'The Mahdia Campaign of 1087', *The English Historical Review*, 362 (1977) pp. 1–29.

Credland, A.G., (1981) 'The blowpipe in Europe and the East', *Journal of the Arms and Armour Society*, 10 (1981) pp. 119–47.

Credland, A.G., (1994) 'The origins and development of the composite bow', *Journal of the Society of Archer Antiquaries*, 37 (1994) pp. 19–39.

Crouch, D., (1986) *The Beaumont Twins: The Roots and Branches of Power in the Twelfth Century* (Cambridge 1986).

Crouch, D., (1988) correspondence on the upbringing of the Beaumont twins (4 March 1988).

Cuoq, J., *Islamisation de la Nubie Chrétienne VIIe–XVIe Siècles* (Paris 1986).

Curtis, E., *Roger of Sicily* (London 1912).

Dachkévytch, 'Les Arméniens à Kiev (jusqu'en 1204)', *Revue des Etudes Arméniennes*, 10 (1973–4) pp. 305–56.

Dadoyan, S.B., *The Fatimid Armenians: Culture and Political Interaction in the Middle East* (Leiden 1997).

Dagron, G. and Mihaescu, H., *Le Traité sur la Guérille (De velitatione) de l'Empereur Nicéphore Phocas (963–969)* (Paris 1986).

Dain, A., *Histoire du Texte d'Elien le Tacticien: dès Origines à la fin du Moyen Age* (Paris 1946).

Darko, E., 'La tactique touranienne', *Byzantion*, 10 (1935) pp. 443–469, 12 (1937) pp. 119–47.

Dawkins, R.M., 'The later history of the Varangian Guard; some notes', *Journal of Roman Studies*, 37 (1947) pp. 39–46.

Dawson, T., 'Suntagma Hoplôn: the equipment of regular Byzantine troops, c.950 to c.1204', in D.C. Nicolle (ed.), *A Companion to Medieval Arms and Armour* (Woodbridge 2002) pp. 81–90.

De Foucault, J.-A., 'Douze chapitres inédits de la tactique de Nicéphore Ouranos', *Traveaux et Memoires*, 5 (1973) pp. 281–311.

De Hoffmeyer, A.B., (1972) *Arms and Armour in Spain, a short survey, vol. I* (Madrid 1972).

De Hoffmeyer, A.B., (1982) *Arms and Armour in Spain, a short survey, vol. II* (Madrid 1982).

De Joinville, (1921) (F. Marzials tr.), *Memoirs of the Crusades by Villehardouin and de Joinville* (London 1921) pp. 135–327.

De Joinville, (1952) (A. Pauphilet & E. Pognon eds.), 'Histoire de Saint Louis', in *Historiens et Chroniquers du Moyen Age* (Paris 1952) pp. 197–366.

De Mas Latrie, M.L., (ed.), *Chronique d'Ernoul et de Bernard le Trésorier* (Paris 1871).

De Oliveiro-Marques, A.H., *History of Portugal: vol. I, From Lusitania to Empire* (New York 1972).
De Poerck, G., 'L'artillerie à ressorts médiévale. Notes lexicologiques et étymologiques', *Bulletin du Cange*, 18 (1945) pp. 35–49.
De Riquer, M., (1948) *Resumen de Literatura Provenzal Trovadoresca* (Barcelona 1948).
De Riquer, M., (1969a) 'El armamento en el "Roman de Troie" y en la "Historia troyana"', *Boletín de la Real Acádemia Española*, 49 (1969) pp. 463–94
De Riquer, M., (1969b) 'La fecha del "Ronsvals" y de "Rollana Saragoss" según el armamento', *Boletín de la Real Acádemia Española*, 49 (1969) pp. 211–51.
De Riquer, M., (1980) 'Las armas en el "Amadis de Gaula"', *Boletín de la Real Acádemia Española*, 60 (1980) pp. 331–428.
De Vries, K., *Medieval Military Technology* (Peterborough Ontario 1992).
Dédéyan, G., 'Un émir arménien du Hawrân entre la principauté turque de Damas et le royaume latin de Jérusalem (1147)', in M. Balard (et al eds.), *Dei gesta per Francos* (Aldershot 2001) pp. 179–85.
Denkstein, V., 'Pavises of the Bohemian type, II; the origin and development of pavises in pre-Hussite Europe', *Sborník Národníko Muzea v Praze (Acta Musei Nationalis Praque), ser. A-Historia*, 18 (1964) pp. 149–194, pls. 1–39.
Dennis, G.T., (1981) 'Flies, mice and the Byzantine crossbow', *Byzantine and Modern Greek Studies*, 7 (1981) pp. 1–5.
Dennis, G.T., (1985) *Three Byzantine Military Treatises* (Washington 1985).
Der Nersessian, S., (1959) 'The Armenian Chronicle of the Constable Sempad or of the "Royal Historian"', *Dumbarton Oaks Papers*, 13 (1959) pp. 141–67.
Der Nersessian, S., (1969) 'The Kingdom of Cilician Armenia', in K.M. Setton (ed.), *A History of the Crusades, vol. II: The Later Crusades* (London 1969) pp. 599–659.
Diaconu, P., (1970) *Les Petchénègues au Bas-Danube* (Bucharest 1970).
Diaconu, P., (1978) *Les Coumans au Bas-Danube aux XIe et XIIe siècles* (Bucharest 1978).
Dieulafoy, M.M., 'La bataille du Muret', *Mémoires de l'Académie des Inscriptions et Belles Lettres*, 35 (1901) pp. 95–134.
Djanpoladian, R. and Kirpicnikov, A., 'Mittelalterlicher Säbel mit einer Armenischen inschrift, gefunden im subpolaren Ural', *Gladius*, 10 (1972) pp. 15–23.
Dobson, C., '"As tough as old boots"? A study of hardened leather armour: part 1: techniques of manufacture', in C. Dobson (ed.), *Art and Arms, Florence, City of the Medici* (Clare 2003) pp. 78–101.
Dodu, G., *Histoire des Institutions Monarchiques dans le Royaume Latin de Jérusalem 1099–1291* (reprint New York 1978).
Dotson, J.E., 'Jal's Nef X and Genoese naval architecture in the 13th century', *Mariner's Mirror*, 59 (1973) pp. 161–70.
Douglas, D.C., *The Norman Fate 1100–1154* (London 1976).
Dozy, R., *Recherches sur l'histoire et la littérature de l'Espagne* (Leiden 1881; reprinted Amsterdam 1965).
Duby, G., 'Au XIIe siècle: les "Jeunes" dans la société aristocratique', *Annales: Economies, Sociétés, Civilisations*, 19 (1964) pp. 835–46.
Ducellier, A., *La Façade Maritime de l'Albanie au Moyen Age: Durazzo et Valone du XIe au XVe siècle* (Thessaloniki 1981).
Dufourcq, C.-E., 'Rapports entre l'Afrique et l'Espagne au XIIIe siècle', *Medievalia*, 1 (1980) pp. 83–101.
Dunbabin, J., *Charles I of Anjou: Power, Kingship and State-Making in Thirteenth Century Europe* (London 1998).

Durand, R., 'Guerre et fortification de l'habitat au Portugal aux XIIe et XIIIe siècles', in A. Bazzana (ed.), *Castrum III* (Madrid 1988) pp. 179–86.

Ebersolt, J., *Monuments d'architecture Byzantin* (Paris 1934).

Edbury, P.W., *The Kingdom of Cyprus and the Crusades 1191–1374* (Cambridge 1991).

Edgington, S., (1994) 'Medical knowledge of the Crusading armies: the evidence of Albert of Aachen and others', in M. Barber (ed.), *The Military Orders: Fighting for the Faith and Caring for the Sick* (Aldershot 1994) pp. 320–6.

Edgington, S., (1996) 'The Doves of War: the part played by carrier pigeons in the crusades', in M. Balard (ed.), *Autour de la Première Croisade* (Paris 1996) pp. 167–75.

Edwards, J., 'Hostages and ransomers', *Medieval World*, 8 (January–February 1993) pp. 17–21.

Edwards, R.W., *The Fortifications of Armenian Cilicia* (Washington 1987).

El Bekri (Bakri, al-), (De Slane tr.), *Description de l'Afrique Septentrionale* (Paris 1913).

Ellenblum, R., (1996) 'Three generations of Frankish castle-building in the Latin Kingdom of Jerusalem', in M. Balard (ed.), *Autour de la Première Croisade* (Paris 1996) pp. 517–51.

Ellenblum, R., (2001) 'Frankish and Muslim siege warfare and the construction of Frankish concentric castles', in M. Balard (ed.), *Dei Gesta per Francos* (Aldershot 2001) pp. 187–98.

Ellenblum, R., (2003) 'Frontier activities: the transformation of a Muslim sacred site into the Frankish Castle of Vadum Iacob', *Crusades*, 2 (2003) pp. 83–97.

Ellis Davidson, H.R., 'The secret weapon of Byzantium', *Byzantinische Zeitschrift*, 66 (1973) pp. 61–74.

Epstein, S.A., *Genoa and the Genoese 959–1528* (Chapel Hill 1996).

Erdmann, C., *The Origin of the Idea of Crusade* (Princeton 1977).

Evans, M.R., (1996) '"A far from aristocratic affair": poor and non-combatant Crusaders from the Midlands, c.1160–1300', *Midland History*, 21 (1996) pp. 23–36.

Evans, M.R., (2000) 'The Ferrers Earls of Derby and the Crusades', *Nottingham Medieval Studies*, 44 (2000) pp. 69–81.

Eydoux, H.-P., 'L'architecture militaire des Francs en Orient', in J.P. Babelon (ed.), *Le Château en France* (Paris 1986) pp. 61–77.

Faucherre, N., 'Les campagnes byzantines du château de Saône (Syrie)', paper read at *Colloque International, La Fortification au Temps des Croisades, Parthenay* (26–28 September 2002).

Favreau-Lilie, M.-L., 'The Military Orders and the escape of the Christian population from the Holy Land in 1291', *Journal of Medieval History*, 19 (1993) pp. 201–27.

Fedden, R. and Thomson, J., *Crusader Castles* (London 1977).

Ferrard, C.G., 'The amount of Constantinopolitan booty in 1204', *Studi Veneziani*, 13 (1971) pp. 95–104.

Finó, J.-F., 'Le Feu et ses usages militaires', *Gladius*, 9 (1970) pp. 15–30.

Flori, J., 'Encore l'usage de la lance. La technique du combat chevaleresque vers l'an 1100', *Cahiers de Civilisation médiévale*, 31 (1988) pp. 213–40.

Flutre, L.F., 'Une arbaleste fait de cor, Cléomadés 2936', *Romania*, 95 (1974) pp. 309–17.

Foley, V. and Perry, K., 'In defence of LIBER IGNEUM: Arab alchemy, Roger Bacon and the introduction of gunpowder into the West', *Journal for the History of Arabic Science*, 3 (1979) pp. 200–18.

Forey, A., (1984) 'The militarisation of the Hospital of St. John', *Studia Monastica*, 26 (1984) pp. 75–89.

Forey, A., (1985) 'The emergence of the Military Order in the twelfth century', *Journal of Ecclesiastical History*, 36 (1985) pp. 175–97.

Forey, A., (1986) 'Recruitment to the Military Orders (twelfth to mid-fourteenth centuries)', *Viator*, 17 (1986) pp. 139–71.

Forey, A., (1991) 'The Military Orders and the ransoming of captives from Islam (twelfth to early fourteenth centuries)', *Studia Monastica*, 33 (1991) pp. 259–79.

Forey, A., (1992) *The Military Orders from the Twelfth to the Early Fourteenth Centuries* (London 1992).

Foss, C. and Winfield, D., *Byzantine Fortifications: An Introduction* (Pretoria 1986).

Foss, C., (1979a) 'Late Byzantine fortifications in Lydia', *Jahrbuch der Österreichischen Byzantinistik*, 28 (1979) pp. 297–320.

Foss, C., (1979b) *Ephesus after Antiquity: A Late Antique, Byzantine and Turkish City* (Cambridge 1979).

Foss, C., (1982) 'The defences of Asia Minor against the Turks', *Orthodox Theological Review*, 27 (1982) pp. 145–205.

Fotheringham, J.K., 'Genoa and the Fourth Crusade', *English Historical Review*, 25 (1910) pp. 26–57.

Fowler, G.H., 'Munitions in 1224', *Publications of the Bedfordshire Historical Record Society*, 5 (1920) pp. 117–32.

France, J., (1971) 'The departure of Tatikios from the Crusader Army', *Bulletin of the Institute of Historical Research*, 44 (1971) pp. 137–47.

France, J., (1996) 'Technology and the success of the First Crusade', in Y. Lev (ed.), *War and Society in the Eastern Mediterranean, 7th–15th centuries* (Leiden 1996) pp. 163–76.

Freeman, A.Z., 'Wall-breakers and river-bridgers: military engineers in the Scottish Wars of Edward I', *Journal of British Studies*, 10 (1971) pp. 1–16.

Frend, W.H.C., 'North Africa and Europe in the Early Middle Ages', *Transactions of the Royal Historical Society*. 5 ser. 5 (1955) pp. 61–80.

Friedman, Y., (1996) 'The ransom of captives in the Latin Kingdom of Jerusalem', in M. Balard (ed.), *Autour de la Première Croisade* (Paris 1996) pp. 177–89.

Friedman, Y., (2001) 'Did laws of war exist in the Crusader Kingdom of Jerusalem?', in Y. Hen (ed.), *De Sion exibit lex et verbum domini de Hierusalem: Essays in Medieval Law, Liturgy and Literature in Honour of Amnon Linder* (Brepols 2001) pp. 81–104.

Friedman, Y., (2002) *Encounter between Enemies: Captivity and Ransom in the Latin Kingdom of Jerusalem* (Leiden 2002).

Gabrieli, F., *Arab Historians of the Crusades* (London 1969).

Gaier, C., 'The lost shield of Baldwin of Flanders and Hainault: First Latin Emperor of Constantinople', in D. Nicolle (ed.), *A Companion to Medieval Arms and Armour* (Woodbridge 2002) pp. 91–96.

Galletti, A.I., 'La società comunale di fronte alla guerra nelle fonti perugine del 1282', *Bollettino della Deputazione di Storia Patria per l'Umbria*, 71 (1974) pp. 35–98.

García Fitz, F., (1990) 'Notas sobre la tenencia de Fortalezas: los Castillos del Concejo de Sevilla en la Baja Edad Media', *Historia, Instituciones, Documentos*, 17 (1990) pp. 55–81.

García Fitz, F., (1995) 'Las Huestes de Fernando III', in (anon. ed.), *Fernando III y su época. IV Jornadas Nacionales de Historia Militar* (Seville 1995) pp. 157–89.

García Fitz, F., (1996) 'La Batalla en su contexto estragégico: a propósito de Alarcos', in R.I. Benito & F.R. Gómez (eds.), *Alarcos 1195; al-Arak 592: Actas del Congreso Internacional Commenorativo del VIII Centenario de la Batalla de Alarcos (1995, Ciudad Real)* (Cuenca 1996) pp. 267–82.

García Fitz, F., (1997) 'Tecnología militar y guerra de asedios. La experiencia castellano-leonesa, siglos XI al XIII', in G. De Boe & F. Verhaeghe (eds.), *Military Studies in Medieval Europe – Papers of the 'Medieval Europe Brugge 1997' Conference, volume 11* (Zellik 1997) pp. 33–41.

García Fitz, F., (1998a) 'El Cerco de Sevilla: reflexiones sobre la guerra de Asedio en la Edad Media', in M. González Jiménez (ed.), *Sevilla 1248, Congreso Internacional Conmemorativo del 750 Aniversario de la Conquista de la Ciudad de Sevilla por Fernando III, Rey de Castilla y León* (Seville 1998) pp. 115–54.

García Fitz, F., (1998b) 'Fortificaciones, fronters y sistemas defensivos en al-Andalus, siglos XI al XIII', in (anon. ed.), *I Congreso Internacional Fortificaciones en al-Andalus (Algeciras, Noviembre–Diciembre 1996)* (Algeciras 1998) pp. 269–79.

García Fitz, F., (1999) 'La Conquista de Sevilla desde el punto de vista Militar "La Marina y la Guerra"', in (anon. ed.), *Santander y Cantabria en la Conquista de Sevilla, 750 Anniversario (Ciclo de Conferencias Cátedra de Menéndez Pelayo, Santander 1998)* (Santander 1999) pp. 11–28.

Garzella, G., 'L'arsenale medievale di Pisa; primi sondaggi sulle fonti scritte', in E. Concina (ed.), *Arsenali e città nell'Occidentale europeo* (Rome 1987) pp. 51–61.

Geanakoplos, D.J., (1953) 'Greco-Latin relations on the eve of the Byzantine Restoration: the Battle of Pelagonia – 1259', *Dumbarton Oaks Papers*, 7 (1953) pp. 99–141.

Geanakoplos, D.J., (1959) *Emperor Michael Palaeologus and the West* (Cambridge Massachusetts 1959).

Gertwagen, R., (1996) 'The Crusader port of Acre: layout and problems of maintenance', in M. Balard (ed.), *Autour de la Première Croisade* (Paris 1996) pp. 553–82.

Gertwagen, R., (2006) 'Harbours and facilities along the eastern Mediterranean sea lanes to Outremer', in J. Pryor (ed.), *Logistics of Warfare in the Age of the Crusades* (Aldershot 2006) pp. 95–118.

Giles, K.R., 'The Emperor Frederick II's Crusade, 1215–c.1231' (PhD thesis, Keele University 1987).

Gilet, J., 'L'armée du royaume arménien en Cilicie de 1187 à 1289' (MA thesis, Université Paul Valéry, Montpellier III, 2001).

Gillingham, J., (1978) *Richard the Lionheart* (London 1978).

Gillingham, J., (1984) 'Richard I and the science of war in the Middle Ages', in J. Gillingham & J.C. Holt (eds.), *War and Government in the Middle Ages: Essays in Honour of J.O. Prestwich* (Cambridge 1984) pp. 78–91.

Gillingham, J., (1989) 'War and chivalry in the History of William the Marshall', in P.R. Cross & S.D. Lloyd (eds.), *Thirteenth century England, 2. Proceedings of the Newcastle Conference 1987* (Woodbridge 1989) pp. 1–13.

Glaesener, H., 'L'Escalade de la Tour d'Antioche', *Revue de la Moyen Age Latin*, 2 (1946) pp. 139–48.

Glassl, H., 'Der deutsche Orden im Burgenland und in Kumanien (1211–1225)', *Ungarn Jahrbuch*, 3 (1971) pp. 23–49.

Glick, T.F., (1979) *Islamic and Christian Spain in the Early Middle Ages* (Princeton 1979).

Godfrey, J., 'The defeated Anglo-Saxons take service with the Eastern Emperor', *Battle Conference on Anglo-Norman Studies*, 1 (1978) pp. 63–74.

Goitein, S.D., (1952) 'Contemporary letters on the capture of Jerusalem by the Crusaders', *The Journal of Jewish Studies*, 3–4 (1952) pp. 162–77.

Goitein, S.D., (1956) 'Glimpses from the Cairo Geniza on naval warfare in the Mediterranean and on the Mongol invasion', in (anon. ed.), *Studi Orientalistici in Onore di Georgio Levi della Vida* (Rome 1956) pp. 393–408.

Goitein, S.D., (1967) *A Mediterranean Society: The Jewish Communities of the Arab World as Portrayed in the Documents of the Cairo Geniza, Vol. 1: Economic Foundations* (Berkeley 1967).

Goitein, S.D., (1970) 'Mediterranean trade in the eleventh century: some facts and problems', in M.A. Cook (ed.), *Studies in the Economic History of the Middle East* (London 1970) pp. 51–62.

Gorelik, M.V., (2002a) 'Arms and armour in south-eastern europe in the second half of the first millennium AD', in D.C. Nicolle (ed.), *A Companion to Medieval Arms and Armour* (Woodbridge 2002) pp. 127–47.

Graindor de Douai, (S. Duparc-Quic ed.), *Le Chanson d'Antioche* (Paris 1977–87).

Gravett, C., *Medieval Siege Warfare* (London 1990).

Greimas, A.J., *Dictionnaire de l'ancient Français jusqu'au milieu du XIVe siècle* (Paris 1980).

Guest, K., 'Too tired to fight?' *Military Illustrated, Past and Present*, 100 (September 1996) pp. 28–9.

Guillaume le Breton, 'Philippidos', in F. Delaborde (ed.), *Oeuvres de Rigord et de Guillaume le Breton, vol. II* (Paris 1885) whole volume.

Guillou, A., (1963) 'Inchiesta sulla populazione greca della Sicilia e della Calabria nel Medio Evo', *Rivista Storica Italiana*, 75 (1963) pp. 53–68.

Guillou, A., (1974) 'Italie méridionale byzantine ou Byzantins en Italie méridionale?' *Byzantion*, 44 (1974) pp. 152–90.

Haldane, D., 'The fire-ship of al-Salih Ayyub and Muslim use of "Greek Fire"', in D.J. Kagay & L.J.A. Villalon (eds.), *The Circle of War in the Middle Ages* (Woodbridge 1999) pp. 137–44.

Haldon, J.F., (1999) *Warfare, State and Society in the Byzantine World, 565–1204* (London 1999).

Haldon, J.F., (2001) *The Byzantine Wars: Battles and Campaigns of the Byzantine Era* (Stroud 2001).

Haldon, J.F. and Byrne, M., 'A possible solution to the problem of Greek Fire', *Byzantinische Zeitschrift*, 70 (1977) pp. 91–9.

Hallam, E.M., *Capetian France 987–1328* (London 1980).

Halphen, L., 'La conquête de la Méditerranée par les Européens aux XIe et XIIe siècles', in (anon. ed.), *Mélanges d'histoire offerts à Henri Pirenne, vol. 1* (Bruxelles 1926) pp. 175–80.

Hamilton, B., 'The Elephant of Christ: Reynald of Châtillon', in D. Blake (ed.), *Religious Motivation: Biographical and Sociological Problems for the Church Historian, Studies in Church History XV* (Oxford 1978) pp. 97–108.

Hanawalt, B.A., 'Violent death in fourteenth and early-fifteenth century England', *Comparative Studies in Society and History*, 18 (1976) pp. 297–320.

Hatto, A.T., 'Archery and chivalry: a noble prejudice', *The Modern Languages Review*, 25 (1940) pp. 40–45.

Hendrickx, B., 'Les Arméniens d'Asie Mineure et de Thrace au début de l'Empire Latin de Constantinople', *Revue des Etudes Arméniennes*, 22 (1991) pp. 217–23.

Hendrix, W.S., 'Military tactics in the poem of the Cid', *Modern Philology*, 20 (1922) pp. 45–48.

Herlihy, D., 'Some psychological and social roots of violence in the Tuscan cities', in L. Martines (ed.), *Violence and Civil Disorder in Italian Cities 1200–1500* (Los Angeles 1972) pp. 129–54.

Hiestand, R., 'Kingship and Crusade in twelfth-century Germany', in A. Haverkamp & H. Vollrath (eds.), *England and Germany in the High Middle Ages* (Oxford 1996) pp. 235–65.

Hill, D.R., (1973) 'Trebuchets', *Viator*, 4 (1973) pp. 99–114.

Hitti, P.K., 'The impact of the Crusades in Eastern Christianity', in S.A. Monroe (ed.), *Medieval and Middle Eastern Studies in Honor of Aziz Suryal Atiya* (Leiden 1972) pp. 211–17.

Hodgson, F.C., *Venice in the Thirteenth and Fourteenth Centuries* (London 1910).
Hollenback, G.M., 'A new reconstruction of the kestros or cestrosphendone', *Arms and Armour, Journal of the Royal Armouries*, 2 (2005) pp. 79–86.
Housley, N., *The Later Crusades, 1274–1580: From Lyons to Alcazar* (Oxford 1992).
Howard-Johnson, J.D., 'Studies in the Organization of the Byzantine Army in the Tenth and Eleventh Centuries' (PhD thesis, Oxford University 1971).
Hunt, T., *The Medieval Surgery* (Woodbridge 1992).
Hussey, J.M., 'The Later Macedonians, the Comneni and the Angeli 1025–1204', in J.M. Hussey (ed.), *The Cambridge Medieval History, Vol. IV: The Byzantine Empire part 1: Byzantium and its Neighbours* (Cambridge 1966) pp. 193–250.
Huuri, K., *Zur Geschichte des mittelalterliches Geschützwens, aus Orientalischen Quellen: Studia Orientalia* (Helsinki 1941).
Hyde, J.K., *Padua in the Age of Dante* (Manchester 1966).
Ibn al-Furat, (U. Lyons tr.), *Ayyubids, Memlukes and Crusaders. Selections from the Tarikh al-duwal wa'l-Muluk of Ibn al-Furat* (Cambridge 1971).
Ibn al-Qalanisi, (1908) (H.F. Amedroz ed.), *Bi Dhayl Tarikh Dimashq: History of Damascus* (Beirut 1908).
Ibn al-Qalanisi, (1932) (H.A.R. Gibb tr.), *The Damascus Chronicle of the Crusades* (London 1932).
Ibn Hauqal (1939) (Hawqal), (J.K. Kramers ed.), *Liber Imaginis Terrae, Kitab Surat al 'Ard* (Leiden 1939).
Ibn Hauqal (1964) (Hawqal), (J.K. Kramers & G. Wiet trs.), *Configuration de la Terre, Kitab Surat al 'Ard* (Beirut & Paris 1964).
Irwin, R., (1994) 'How many miles to Babylon? The *Devise des Chemins de Babilone* redated', in M. Barber (ed.), *The Military Orders: Fighting for the Faith, Caring for the Sick* (Aldershot 1994) pp. 57–63.
Jackson, P., (1980) 'The crisis of the Holy Land in 1260', *The English Historical Review*, 176 (1980) pp. 481–513.
Jackson, P., (1987) 'The Crusades of 1239–41 and their aftermath', *Bulletin of the School of Oriental and African Studies*, 50 (1987) pp. 32–60.
Jackson, P., (1991) 'The Crusade against the Mongols (1241)', *Journal of Ecclesiastical History*, 42 (1991) pp. 1–18.
Jackson, W.H., *Chivalry in Twelfth-Century Germany: The Works of Hartmann von Aue* (Woodbridge 1994).
Jacoby, D., (1967) 'Les Archontes grecs et la féodalité en Morée Franque', *Travaux et Mémoires*, 2 (1967) pp. 421–81.
Jacoby, D., (1973) 'The encounters of two societies: Western conquerors and Byzantines in the Peloponnesus after the Fourth Crusade', *American Historical Review*, 78 (1973) pp. 873–906.
Jacoby, D., (1976) 'Les états latins en Romanie: phénomènes sociaux et économiques (1204–1350 environ)', *XVe Congrès international d'études byzantines (Athens 1976). Rapports et co-rapports, I* (Athens 1976) pp. 1–51.
Jacoby, D., (1979) 'Crusader Acre in the thirteenth century: urban layout and topography', *Studi Medievali*, 3 ser. 20 (1979) pp. 1–45.
Jacoby, D., (1984) 'La littérature française dans les états latins de la Méditerranée orientale', in (anon. ed.), *Essor et fortune de la chanson de geste dans l'Europe et de l'Orient Latin, Actes du XIe Congrès International de la Société Rencesvales pour l'Etude des Epopées Romanes (Padoue-Venise 1982)* (Modena 1984) pp. 617–46.

Jacoby, D., (1986) 'Knightly values and class consciousness in the Crusader States in the Eastern Mediterranean', *Mediterranean Historical Review*, 1 (1986) pp. 158–86.

Jacoby, D., (1989) 'From Byzantium to Latin Romania: continuity and change', in B. Arbel (et al. eds.), *Latins and Greeks in the Eastern Mediterranean after 1204* (London 1989) pp. 1–44.

James, S., *Excavations at Dura-Europos 1928–1937: Final Report VII: The Arms and Armour and other Military Equipment* (London 2004).

Jamison, E., (1913) 'The Norman administration of Apulia and Capua', *Papers of the British School at Rome*, 6 (1913) pp. 211–481.

Jamison, E., (1957) *Admiral Eugenius of Sicily* (London 1957).

Janin, R., 'Les Francs au service des byzantins', *Echos d'orient*, 29 (1930) pp. 61–72.

Johns, J., (1987) 'Malik Ifriqiya: The Norman Kingdom of Africa and the Fatimids', *Libyan Studies*, 18 (1987) pp. 89–101.

Johns, J., (1993) 'The Norman Kings of Sicily and the Fatimid Caliphate', *Anglo-Norman Studies*, 15 (1993) pp. 133–59.

Jones, A.H.M. and Monro, E., *A History of Abyssinia* (Oxford 1935).

Jones, D., 'The Cappella Palatina in Palermo: problems of attribution', *Art and Archaeology Research Papers*, 1 (1972) pp. 41–7.

Jones, P.N., 'The metallography and relative effectiveness of arrowheads and armor during the middle ages', *Materials Characterization*, 29 (1992) pp. 111–17.

Jones, P.N. and Renn, D., 'The military effectiveness of arrow-loops: some experiments at White Castle', *Château Gaillard*, 9–10 (1982) pp. 445–56.

Kaegi, W.E., (1964) 'The contribution of archery to the Turkish conquest of Anatolia', *Speculum*, 39 (1964) pp. 96–108.

Kaegi, W.E., (1971) 'Patterns of political activity in the armies of the Byzantine Empire', in M. Janowitz & J. Van Doorn (eds.), *On Military Intervention* (Rotterdam 1971) pp. 4–35.

Kantorowixz, E., *Frederick the Second 1194–1250* (London 1931).

Kazhdan, A., (1984) 'Armenians in the Byzantine ruling class: predominantly in the ninth through twelfth centuries', in T.J. Samuelian & M.E. Stone (eds.), *Medieval Armenian Culture. University of Pennsylvania Armenian Texts and Studies 6* (Chicago 1984) pp. 439–51.

Kazhdan, A., (1997) 'Terminology of warfare in the History of Niketas Choniates: contingents and battle', in K. Tsiknakis (ed.), *Byzantium at War (9th–12th c.)* (Athens 1997) pp. 75–91.

Kedar, B.Z., (1972) 'The passenger list of a Crusader ship, 1250: towards the history of the popular element on the Seventh Crusade', *Studi Medievali*, 13 (1972) pp. 267–79.

Kedar, B.Z., (1979) 'Un projet de "passage particulier" proposé par l'Ordre de l'Hôpital, 1306–1307', *Bibliothèque de l'Ecole des Chartres*, 137 (1979) pp. 211–26.

Kedar, B.Z., (1982) 'The Patriarch Eraclius', in B.Z. Kedar (ed.), *Outremer: Studies in the History of the Crusading Kingdom of Jerusalem Presented to Joshua Prawer* (Jerusalem 1982) pp. 177–204.

Kedar, B.Z., (1990) 'The subjected Muslims of the Frankish Levant', in J.M. Powell (ed.), *Muslims under Latin Rule, 1100–1300* (Princeton 1990) pp. 135–74.

Kedar, B.Z., (1991) 'The Battle of Hattin revisited', in B.Z. Kedar (ed.), *The Horns of Hattin* (Jerusalem 1991) pp. 190–207.

Kedar, B.Z. and Pringle, D., 'La Fève: A Crusader castle in the Jezreel Valley', *Israel Exploration Journal*, 25 (1985) pp. 164–79.

Keen, M., (1968) 'The laws of war in the Late Middle Ages', in F.L. Cheyette (ed.), *Lordship and Community in Medieval Europe: Selected Readings* (New York 1968) pp. 210–16.

Keen, M., (1987) 'War, peace and chivalry', in B.P. McGuire (ed.), *War and Peace in the Middle Ages* (Copenhagen 1987) pp. 94–117.

Kelly, F.M., 'Zur Entstehung des Spangenharnischs', *Zeitschrift für Historisches Waffen- und Kostümkunde*, 4 (1933) pp. 105–6.

Kennedy, H., *Crusader Castles* (Cambridge 1994).

Kindi, Ya'qub Ibn Ishaq al-, (A.R. Zaki ed.), 'Al-Suyuf wa Ajnasuha', *Bulletin of the Faculty of Letters, Fuad I University*, 14 (1952) pp. 1–36.

Kindi, Ya'qub Ibn Ishaq al-, (R.G. Hoyland & B. Gilmour tr.), *Medieval Islamic Swords and Swordmaking: Kindi's Treatise 'On Swords and their Kinds'* (Oxford 2006).

King, E.J., (1931) *The Knights Hospitallers in the Holy Land* (London 1931).

King, E.J., (1934) *The Rule, Statutes and Customs of the Hospitallers 1099–1310* (London 1934).

Kinnamos, John, (C.M. Brand tr.), *Deeds of John and Manuel Comnenus by John Kinnamos* (New York 1976).

Kohlberg, E. and Kedar, B.Z., 'A Melkite physician in Frankish Jerusalem and Ayyubid Damascus: Muwaffaq al-Din Ya'qub b. Siqlab', *Asian and African Studies*, 22 (1988) pp. 113–26.

Kollias, T., (1980a) 'Ζαβα, ζαβαρετον, Ζαβαρειωτης', *Jahrbuch der Österreichischen Byzantinistik*, 29 (1980) pp. 27–35.

Kollias, T., (1980b) 'Die Schutzwaffen der Byzantinischen Armée' (Doctoral thesis, Vienna University 1980); see also Kollias, T., *Byzantinischen Waffen* (Vienna 1988).

Kollias, T., (1984) 'The Taktica of Leo VI the Wise and the Arabs', *Graeco-Arabica*, 33 (1984) pp. 129–35.

Kollias, T., (1988) *Byzantinische Waffen* (Vienna 1988).

Kosztolnyik, *Five Eleventh Century Hungarian Kings: Their Policies and their Relations with Rome* (New York 1981).

Kreutz, B.M., (1976) 'Ships, shipping and the implications of change in the early medieval Mediterranean', *Viator*, 7 (1976) pp. 79–109.

Kreutz, B.M., (1991) *Before the Normans: Southern Italy in the Ninth and Tenth Centuries* (Philadelphia 1991).

Krey, A.C., *The First Crusade: The Accounts of Eye-Witnesses and Participants* (Gloucester Massachusetts, 1958).

Krueger, H.C., 'Postwar collapse and rehabilitation in Genoa (1145–1162)', in (anon. ed.), *Studi in Onore di Gino Luzzatto* (Milan 1950) pp. 117–28.

Kyrris, C.P., 'Military colonies in Cyprus in the Byzantine period: their character, purpose and extent', *Byzantinoslavica*, 31 (1970) pp. 157–81.

La Monte, J.L., (1932) *Feudal Monarchy in the Latin Kingdom of Jerusalem* (Cambridge Massachusetts, 1932).

La Monte, J.L., (1937) 'John d'Ibelin, the Old Lord of Beirut 1177–1236', *Byzantion*, 12 (1937) pp. 417–58.

Lacarra, J.M., (1947) 'La Conquista de Zaragoza por Alfonso I', *Al Andalus*, 12 (1947) pp. 65–96.

Lacarra, J.M., (1963) 'Les villes-frontières dans l'Espagne des XIe et XIIe siècles', *Le Moyen Age*, 69 (1963) pp. 202–22.

Lacy, M.S., 'Coat of Plates to Brigandine: The Evolution of Cloth covered Armour 1250–1500' (MA thesis, Reading University 1992).

Lane, F.C., (1969) 'The crossbow in the Nautical Revolution of the Middle Ages', in (anon. ed.), *Essays in Honor of Robert L. Reynolds* (Kent Ohio 1969) pp. 161–71.

Lane, F.C., (1973a) 'Venetian seamen in the Nautical Revolution of the Middle Ages', in A. Pertusi (ed.), *Venezia e Levante fino al sec. XV, vol. 1* (Florence 1973) pp. 403–29.

Lane, F.C., (1973b) *Venice, a Maritime Republic* (London 1973).

Lang, D.M., *The Bulgarians from Pagan Times to the Ottoman Conquest* (London 1976).
Langlois, C.-V., *La Vie en France de la fin du XIIe au milieu du XIVe siècle: vol. II, D'aprés des Moralistes du Temps* (Paris 1925).
Lansing, C.L., 'Nobility in a Medieval Commune: The Florentine Magnates, 1260–1300' (PhD thesis, Michigan University 1984).
Latimer, J., 'But you must know they were deceived: naval war between Genoa and Venice in the thirteenth century', *Medieval History*, 14 (October 2004) pp. 40–7.
Laurent, J., (1913) *Byzance et les Turcs Seldjoucides dans l'Asie Occidentale jusqu'en 1081* (Nancy 1913).
Laurent, J., (1928) 'Byzance et Antioche sous de Curopalate Philarète', *Revue des Etudes Arméniennes*, 8 (1928) pp. 61–72.
Laurent, J., (1971) *Etudes d'Histoire Arménienne* (Louvain 1971).
Leaf, W. and Purcell, S., *Heraldic Symbols: Islamic Insignia and Western Heraldry* (London 1986).
Legge, M.D., 'The Lord Edward's Vegatius', *Scriptorium*, 7 (1953) pp. 262–65.
Leo VI (Emperor), (M. Joly de Maizeroi tr.), *Tactica* (Paris 1771).
Lev, Y., (1995) 'The Fatimids and Byzantium, 10th–12th centuries', *Graeco-Arabica*, 6 (1995) pp. 190–208.
Lev, Y., (2001) 'Prisoners of war during the Fatimid-Ayyubid wars with the Crusaders', in M. Gervers (ed.), *Tolerance and Intolerance* (Syracuse New York 2001) pp. 11–28.
Lewis, A.R., (1951) *Naval Power and Trade in the Mediterranean AD 500–1100* (Princeton 1951).
Lewis, A.R., (1964) 'La féodalité dans le Toulousain et la France méridionale (850–1050)', *Annales du Midi*, 76 (1964) pp. 247–59.
Lewis, A.R., (1985) 'James the Conqueror: Montpellier and Southern France', in R.I. Burns (ed.), *The Worlds of Alfonso the Learned and James the Conqueror* (Princeton 1985) pp. 130–49.
Liebel, J., (1980) 'Espringales et grandes arbalètes' (pre-publication draft 1990).
Liebel, J., (1998) *Springalds and Great Crossbows* (Leeds 1998).
Ligato, G., 'Saladino e i prigioneri di guerra', in G. Cipollone (ed.), *La liberazione dei 'captivi' tra Cristianita e Islam* (Vatican 2000) pp. 649–54.
Lilie, R.-J., 'Die Schlacht von Myriokephalon 1176: Auswitkungen auf das Byzantinische Reich im aus-gehended 12 Jahrhundert', *Revue des Etudes Byzantines*, 35 (1977) pp. 257–75.
Lindner, R.P., (1982) 'The impact of the West on Comnenian Anatolia', paper read at *XVI Internationaler Byzntinistenkongress, Acten* (Vienna 1982).
Little, D.P., 'The fall of 'Akka in 690/1291: the Muslim version', in M. Shalon (ed.), *Studies in Islamic History and Civilization in Honour of Professor David Ayalon* (Jerusalem 1986) pp. 159–81.
Livadas, G.K., 'Some questions of medieval nautical technology in Kameniates' 'Sack of Thessaloniki' (904 AD)', *Graeco-Arabica*, 6 (1995) pp. 145–51.
Lloyd, S., 'Gilbert de Clare, Richard of Cornwall and the Lord Edward's Crusade', *Nottingham Medieval Studies*, 29 (1985) pp. 46–63.
Lock, P.W., (1986) 'The Frankish towers of central Greece', *Annual of the British School at Athens*, 81 (1986) pp. 101–23.
Lock, P.W., (1989) 'The medieval towers of Greece: a problem of chronology and function', in B. Arbel (et al. eds.), *Latins and Greeks in the Eastern Mediterranean after 1204* (London 1989) pp. 129–45.
Lock, P.W., (1994) 'The Military Orders in mainland Greece', in M. Barber (ed.), *The Military Orders: Fighting for the Faith and Caring for the Sick* (Aldershot 1994) pp. 333–9.

Lock, P.W., (1998) 'Castles and seigneurial influence in Latin Greece', in A.V. Murray (ed.), *From Clermont to Jerusalem: The Crusades and Crusader Societies 1095–1500* (Turnhout 1998) pp. 173–86.

Lomax, D.W., *The Reconquest of Spain* (London 1978).

Lombard, M., *Les Métaux dans l'ancient Monde du Ve au XIe siècle* (Paris 1974).

Lonchambon, C. (ed.), *Nefs et Galères: Histoire Médiévale Hors Série No. 6* (Apt Mai-Juillet 2004).

Longworth, P., *The Rise and Fall of Venice* (London 1974).

Loud, G.A., (1981) 'How "Norman" was the Norman Conquest of Southern Italy?', *Nottingham Medieval Studies*, 25 (1981) pp. 13–34.

Loud, G.A., (1983) 'The church, warfare and military obligation in Norman Italy', *Studies in Church History*, 20 (1983) pp. 31–45.

Lourie, L., 'A society organized for war: medieval Spain', *Past and Present*, 35 (1966) pp. 54–76.

Luttrell, A.T., 'The Latins and life on the smaller Aegean islands, 1204–1453', in B. Arbel (et al. eds.), *Latins and Greeks in the Western Mediterranean after 1204* (London 1989) pp. 146–57.

Lyon, B.D., *From Fief to Indenture: The Transition from Feudal to Non-Feudal Contract in Western Europe* (Cambridge Massachussetts, 1957).

Lyons, M.C., 'The Land of War: Europe in the Arab hero cycles', in A.E. Aiou & P.R. Mottadeh (eds.), *The Crusades from the Perspective of Byzantium and the Muslim World* (Washington 2001) pp. 41–51.

Magdalino, P., (1976) 'The History of Thessaly, 1216–1393' (PhD thesis, Oxford University 1976).

Magdalino, P., (1989) 'Between Romaniae: Thessaly and Epirus in the Later Middle Ages', in B. Arbel (et al. eds.), *Latins and Greeks in the Eastern Mediterranean after 1204* (London 1989) pp. 87–110.

Makrypoulias, C.G., (1995) 'The navy in the works of Constantine Porphyrogenitus', *Graeco-Arabica*, 6 (1995) pp. 152–71.

Makrypoulias, C.G., (1997) 'Technological development in early Byzantine shipping', paper read at *First International Colloquium on Graeco-Oriental and African Studies, Neapoli* (24–27 July 1997).

Mann, J., 'Notes on the armour worn in Spain from the tenth to the fourteenth century', *Archaeologia*, 73 (1933) pp. 285–305.

Mantran, R. and De La Roncière, C., 'Africa opens up to the Old Worlds', in R. Fossier (ed.), *The Cambridge Illustrated History of the Middle Ages, vol. III: 1250–1520* (London 1986) pp. 356–96.

Marco Polo, (J. Masefield tr.), *The Travels of Marco Polo* (London 1908).

Marcombe, D., *Leper Knights: The Order of St. Lazarus of Jerusalem in England, c.1150–1544* (Woodbridge 2003).

Marino, L., (1997a) (ed.), *La fabrica dei castelli crociati in Terra Santa* (Florence 1997).

Marino, L., (1997b) 'The making of Crusader castles', in L. Marino (ed.), *La fabrica dei castelli crociati in Terra Santa* (Florence 1997) pp. 121–25.

Marshall, C.J., (1989) 'The French regiment in the Latin East, 1254–91', *Journal of Medieval History*, 15 (1989) pp. 301–7.

Marshall, C.J., (1990) 'The use of the charge in battle in the Latin East, 1192–1291', *Historical Research (Bulletin of the Institute of)*, 63 (1990) pp. 221–6.

Marvin, L.W., 'The non-knightly soldier in the Crusades of the twelfth century: his role and importance', paper read at the *29th International Congress of History, Kalamazoo* (6 May 1994).

Matheson, L.S.G., 'The Norman Principality of Capua (1058–1098) with particular reference to Richard I (1058–1078)' (D Phil thesis, Oxford University 1974).

Matveev, A., (1998a) 'A propos the causes of the success of the First Crusade: The Oriental point of view', unpublished article (1998).

Mayer, H.E., (1978) 'Latins, Muslims and Greeks in the Latin Kingdom of Jerusalem', *History*, 63 (1978) pp. 175–92.

Mayer, H.E., (1982) 'Carving up Crusaders: the Early Ibelins and Ramlas', in B.Z. Kedar (ed.), *Outremer: Studies in the History of the Crusader Kingdom of Jerusalem Presented to Joshua Prawer* (Jerusalem 1982) pp. 101–18.

Mayer, H.E., (1985) 'Le service militaire des vasseaux de Jérusalem á l'étranger et le financement des campagnes en Syrie du nord et en Egypte au XIIe siècle', *Mémoires de l'Académie des inscriptions et belles-lettres*, n.s. 5 (1985) pp. 93–161.

McGeer, E., (1991) 'Tradition and reality in the Taktika of Nikephoros Ouranos', *Dumbarton Oaks Papers*, 45 (1991) pp. 129–40.

McGeer, E., (1994) 'Byzantine siege warfare in theory and practice', in I.A. Corfis (ed.), *The Medieval City under Siege* (Woodbridge 1994) pp. 123–9.

Melville, M., *La Vie des Templiers* (2nd edition, Paris 1974).

Menache, S., 'The communication challenge of the earliest Crusades 1099–1187', in M. Balard (ed.), *Autour de la Prémiere Croisade* (Paris 1996) pp. 293–314.

Menéndez Pidal, R., *The Cid and his Spain* (London 1971).

Messier, R.A., 'The Christian community of Tunis at the time of St. Louis' Crusade, A.D. 1270', in V.P. Goss (et al. eds.), *The Meeting of Two Worlds: Cultural Exchange between East and West during the Period of the Crusades* (Kalamazoo 1986) pp. 241–55.

Miller, W., (1908) *The Latins in the Levant: A History of Frankish Greece (1204–1566)* (London 1908).

Miller, W., (1969) *Trebizond: The Last Greek Empire of the Byzantine Era 1204–1461* (reprinted Chicago 1969).

Minieri Riccio, C., 'Memorie della guerra di Sicili negli anni 1282, 1283, 1284 tratte da'registri angioni dell'Archivio di Stato di Napoli', *Archivio storico per la provincie napolitane*, 1 (1876) pp. 85–105, 282–315, 499–530.

Minnis, D. and Bader, Y., 'A comparative analysis of Belvoir (Kawkab al-Hawa) and Qal'at al-Rabad ('Ajlun Castle)', *Annual of the Department of Antiquities of Jordan*, 32 (1988) pp. 255–64.

Mitchell, P.D., (1999) 'The integration of the palaeopathology and medical history of the Crusades', *International Journal of Osteoarchaeology*, 11 (1999) pp. 333–43.

Mitchell, P.D., (2004a) correspondence on the study of wounds on the skeletons from Vadum Iacob (10 August 2004).

Mitchell, P.D., (2004b) *Medicine in the Crusades: Warfare, Wounds and the Medieval Surgeon* (Cambridge 2004).

Mitchell, P.D., Y. Nagar and R. Ellenblum, 'Weapon injuries in the 12th century Crusader garrison of Vadum Iacob Castle, Galilee', *International Journal of Osteoarchaeology*, 16 (2006) pp. 145–55.

Mitchell, R., correspondence on hardened leather armour and shields (13 August 2003).

Mitchison, R., *A History of Scotland* (London 1970).

Molin, B.K., 'The Role of Castles in the Political and Military History of the Crusader States and the Levant, 1187–1380' (PhD thesis, Leeds University 1996).

Mollat, M., 'Problème navale de l'histoire des croisades', *Cahiers de Civilisations médiévales*, 10 (1967) pp. 345–59.

Mollat du Jourdain, M., 'Philippe Auguste et la mer', in R.-H. Bautier (ed.), *La France du Philippe Auguste – Le Temps des Mutations* (Paris 1982) pp. 605–23.
Molmenti, P.G., *Venice, its individual growth from the earliest beginnings to the fall of the republic* (London 1906–8).
Moravcsik, G., *Byzantium and the Magyars* (Amsterdam 1970).
Morillo, S., (1999) 'The Age of Cavalry revisited', in D.J. Kagay & L.J.A. Villalon (eds.), *The Circle of War in the Middle Ages* (Woodbridge 1999) pp. 45–58.
Morillo, S., (2002) 'Battle seeking: the contexts and limitations of Vegatian strategy', *The Journal of Medieval Military History*, 1 (Woodbridge 2002) pp. 21–42.
Morris, J., (1961) 'Medieval Spanish Epic Style: its character and development and its influence on other forms of literature' (PhD thesis, Leeds University 1961).
Morris, J., (1980) *The Venetian Empire, a Sea Voyage* (London 1980).
Morris, W.S., 'A Crusader's Testament', *Speculum*, 27 (1952) pp. 197–8.
Mot, G.J., 'L'arsenal et le parc de matériel à la cité de Carcassonne en 1298', *Annales du Midi*, 68 (1956) pp. 409–18.
Mott, L.V., 'The Battle of Malta, 1283: prelude to a disaster', in D.J. Kagay & L.J.A. Villalon (eds.), *The Circle of War in the Middle Ages* (Woodbridge 1999) pp. 145–72.
Müller-Wiener, W, *Castles of the Crusaders* (London 1966).
Mullett, M., '1098 and all that; Theophylact, Bishop of Semnea and the Alexian reconquest of Anatolia', *Peritia*, 10 (1996) pp. 235–53.
Munro, D.C., 'The Western attitudes towards Islam during the Crusades', *Speculum*, 6 (1931) pp. 329–43.
Murray, A.V., 'The army of Godfrey of Bouillon: structure and dynamics of a contingent in the First Crusade', *Revue Belge de Philologie et d'Histoire*, 70 (1992) pp. 301–29.
Nelli, R. and Lavaud, R., *Les Troubadours, II, Le Trésor Poétique de l'Occitaine* (Paris 1966).
Nesbitt, J.W., 'The rate of marching of Crusading armies in Europe', *Traditio*, 19 (1963) pp. 167–81.
Nicholson, H., *Templars, Hospitallers and Teutonic Knights: Images of the Military Orders 1128–1291* (Leicester 1993).
Nicholson, R.L., (1940) *Tancred: A Study of his Career and Work* (Chicago 1940).
Nicholson, R.L., (1973) *Joscelyn III and the Fall of the Crusader States, 1134–1199* (Leiden 1973).
Nicol, D.M., (1972) *The Last Centuries of Byzantium, 1261–1453* (London 1972).
Nicol, D.M., (1979) *The End of the Byzantine Empire* (London 1979).
Nicol, D.M., (1984) *The Despotate of Epirus 1267–1479* (Cambridge 1984).
Nicolle, D.C., (1987) 'Armes et armures dans les Épopées des Croisades', in K.H. Bender (ed.), *Les Épopées des Croisades: Zeitschrift für französische Sprache und Literatur*, 11 (Trier 1987) pp. 17–34.
Nicolle, D.C., (1988) "Ain al Habis. The cave de Sueth' *Archéologie Médiévale*, 18 (1988) pp. 113–40.
Nicolle, D.C., (1989a) "Ain Habis,' in D. Homès-Fredericq & J.B. Hennessy (eds.), *Archaeology of Jordan. Akkadica, Supplementus VII* (Leuven 1989) pp. 141–9.
Nicolle, D.C., (1992) 'Byzantine and Islamic arms and armour; evidence for mutual influence,' *Graeco-Arabica*, 4 (1992) pp. 299–325.
Nicolle, D.C., (1993b) *Hattin 1187* (London 1993).
Nicolle, D.C., (1995) 'No way overland: evidence for Byzantine arms and armour on the 10th–11th century Taurus frontier,' *Graeco-Arabica*, 6 (1995) pp. 226–45.
Nicolle, D.C., (1999b) *Arms and Armour of the Crusading Era 1050–1350: Western Europe and the Crusader States* (London 1999).

Nicolle, D.C., (2002a) 'Jawshan, cuirie and coat-of-plates: an alternative line of development for hardened leather armour', in D.C. Nicolle (ed.), *A Companion to Medieval Arms and Armour* (Woodbridge 2002) pp. 179–221 & pls. XIII–1 to XIII–45.

Nicolle, D.C., (2002c) *Medieval Siege Weapons (2): Byzantium, the Islamic World and India AD 476–1562* (Oxford 2002).

Nicolle, D.C., (2004c) 'The vocabulary of medieval warfare: arms, armour and siege weaponry terminology in the Excidium Aconis', in Magister Thadeus, (R.B.C. Huygens ed.), *The Fall of Acre 1291. Corpus Christianorum, Continuatio Mediaeualis 202* (Turnhout 2004) pp. 165–87.

Nicolle, D.C., (2005a) *Carolingian Cavalryman AD 768–987* (Oxford 2005).

Nicolle, D.C., (2005b) *The Third Crusade 1191* (Oxford 2005).

Nikolova, J., 'La vie domestique et l'armament dans le Palais de Carevec d'après le matériel archéologique', in (Kr. Mijatev et al. eds.), *Carevrad Tarnov* (Sofia 1974) pp. 389–90.

Nishimura, D., 'Crossbows, arrow guides, and the Solenarion', *Byzantion*, 58 (1988) pp. 422–35.

Norman, A.V.B., 'An early representation of body armour', *Zeitschrift für Historische Waffen- und Kostümkunde*, 18 (1976) pp. 38–9.

Northrup, L.S., 'Muslim–Christian relations during the reign of the Mamluk Sultan al-Malik al-Mansur Qala'un (678/1279–689/1290)' (MA thesis, McGill University 1974).

Norwich, J.J., *Byzantium, The Decline and Fall* (London 1995).

Obolensky, D., (1974) 'The Byzantine frontier zones and cultural exchange', in (anon. ed.), *Actes du XIVe Congrès International des Etudes byzantines (Bucarest 1971), vol. I* (Bucharest 1974) pp. 303–13.

Obolensky, D., (1978) 'The Crimea and the North before 1204', in (anon. ed.), *Byzantine Black Sea (Symposium, Birmingham University, 18–20 March 1978)* (Athens 1978) pp. 123–33.

Oerter, H.L., 'Campaldino, 1289', *Speculum*, 33 (1968) pp. 429–50.

Oikonomides, N., (1964) 'Contribution à l'étude de la Pronoia au XIIIe siècle. Une formule d'attribution de parèques à un pronoiaire', *Revue des Etudes Byzantines*, 22 (1964) pp. 158–75.

Oikonomides, N., (1974) 'L'organisation de la frontière orientale de Byzance aux Xe–XIe siècles et le taktikon de l'Escorial', *Actes du XIVe Congrès International des Etudes Byzantines, Bucharest 1971* (Bucharest 1974) pp. 285–302.

Oikonomides, N., (1979) *Hommes d'Affaires Grecs et Latins à Constantinople (XIIIe–XVe siècles)* (Montreal & Paris 1979).

Pálóczi Horváth, A., *Pechenegs, Cumans, Iasians: Steppes Peoples in Medieval Hungary* (Budapest 1989).

Pamlényi, E., *A History of Hungary* (London 1975).

Partington, J.R., *A History of Greek Fire and Gunpowder* (Cambridge 1960).

Paterson, L.M., (1984) 'The concepts of knighthood in the XIIth-century Occitan lyric', in P. Noble & L. Paterson (eds.), *Chrétien de Troyes and the Troubadours: Essays in Memory of the Late Leslie Tospfield* (Cambridge 1984) pp. 112–32.

Paterson, L.M., (1986) 'The Occitan squire in the twelfth and thirteenth centuries', in C. Harper-Bill & R. Harvey (eds.), *The Ideals and Practice of Medieval Knighthood (papers from the first and second Strawberry Hill Conferences)* (Bury St. Edmunds 1986) pp. 133–49.

Paterson, L.M., (1988) 'Military surgery: knights, sergeants and Raimon of Avignon's version of the Chirurgia of Roger of Salerno (1180–1209)', in C. Harper-Bill (ed.), *The Ideals and Practice of Medieval Knighthood: Papers from the Third Strawberry Hill Conference, II* (Woodbridge 1988) pp. 117–46.

Paterson, W.F., (1983) correspondence on Nubian, Seljuk and Italian bows (29 January 1983).

Paterson, W.F., (1990) (A.G. Credland ed.), *A Guide to the Crossbow* (London 1990).

Peal, A., 'Olivier de Termes and the Occitan nobility in the thirteenth century', *Reading Medieval Studies*, 12 (1986) pp. 109–30.

Peel, C., 'Feudal institutions and vocabulary in the "Roman de Renart"' (M Phil thesis, Leeds University 1969).

Peirce, I., 'The knight, his arms and armour in the eleventh and twelfth centuries', in C. Harper-Bill & R. Harvey (eds.), *The Ideals and Practice of Medieval Knighthood (papers from the first and second Strawberry Hill Conferences)* (Bury St. Edmunds 1986) pp. 152–64.

Piel, C. and Bédat, I., 'La manche de saint Martin à Bussy-Saint-Martin (Seine-et-Marne), *Coré*, 2 (Mars 1997) pp. 38–43.

Pieri, P., (1953) 'I Saraceni di Lucera nella storia militare medievale', *Archivio Storico Pugliese*, 6 (1953) pp. 94–101.

Pieri, P., (1966) 'L'evoluzione delle Milizie Comunale Italiane', in P. Pieri, *Scritti Vari* (Turin 1966) pp. 31–90.

Piponnier, F., 'Une révolution dans le costume masculin au XIVe siècle', in M. Pastoureau (ed.), *Le vêtement: histoire, archéologie et symbolique vestimentaires au Moyen Age* (Paris 1989) pp. 225–42.

Pirie Gordon, C.H., 'The Reigning Princes of Galilee', *English Historical Review*, 28 (1912) pp. 445–61.

Pistarino, G., 'Genova medievale tra Oriente e Occidente', *Rivista Storica Italiana*, 81 (1969) pp. 44–73.

Pollo, S. and Puto, A., *The History of Albania from its Origins to the Present Day* (London 1981).

Powell, J.M., (1992) 'The role of women in the Fifth Crusade', in B.Z. Kedar (ed.), *The Horns of Hattin* (London & Jerusalem 1992) pp. 294–301.

Powell, J.M., (1999) 'Frederick II and the rebellion of the Muslims of Sicily 1200–1224', in (anon. ed.), *Ulusararasi Haçlı Seferleri Sempozyumu, 23–25 Harıran 1997, Istanbul* (Ankara 1999) pp. 13–22.

Powers, J.F., (1970) 'The origins and development of municipal military service in the Leonese and Castilian Reconquest 800–1250', *Traditio*, 26 (1970) pp. 91–111.

Powers, J.F., (1971) 'Towers and soldiers: the interaction of urban and military organization of the militias of medieval Castile', *Speculum*, 46 (1971) pp. 641–55.

Powers, J.F., (1985) 'Two warrior kings and their municipal militias: the townsman-soldier in law and life', in R.I. Burns (ed.), *The Worlds of Alfonso the Learned and James the Conqueror* (Princeton 1985) pp. 95–129.

Powers, J.F., (1994) 'Life on the cutting edge: the besieged town in the Luso-Hispanic frontier in the twelfth century', in I.A. Corfis (ed.), *The Medieval City under Siege* (Woodbridge 1994) pp. 17–34.

Prawer, J., (1952) 'The settlement of the Latins in Jerusalem', *Speculum*, 27 (1952) pp. 490–503.

Prawer, J., (1972) *The Crusaders' Kingdom* (New York 1972).

Prawer, J., (1977) 'Crusader cities', in H.A. Miskin (et al. eds.), *The Medieval City* (New Haven 1977) 179–199.

Prawer, J., (1980) *Crusader Institutions* (Oxford 1980).

Pringle, R.D., (1980) 'Crusader castles: the first generation', *Fortress*, 1 (1980) pp. 14–25.

Pringle, R.D., (1985) 'Reconstructing the Castle of Safad', *Palestine Exploration Quarterly*, 117 (1985) pp. 139–49.

Pringle, R.D., (1994a) 'Towers in Crusader Palestine', *Château Gaillard*, 16 (1994) pp. 335–70.

Pringle, R.D., (1994b) 'Town defences in the Crusader Kingdom of Jerusalem', in I. Corfis & M. Wolfe (eds.), *The Medieval City under Siege* (Woodbridge 1994) pp. 69–121.

Pringle, R.D., (1997) *Secular Buildings in the Crusader Kingdom of Jerusalem* (Cambridge 1997).

Pringle, R.D., (1998) 'A castle in the sand: mottes in the Crusader East', *Château Gaillard*, 18 (1998) pp. 187–91.

Prouteau, N., 'L'art de charpenterie et du génie militaire dans le contexte des Croisades, recrutement et fonctions des techniciens francs (XIIe–XIIIe siècles)', in N. Faucherre (et al. eds.), *La Fortification au Temps des Croisades* (Rennes 2004) pp. 279–86.

Pryor, J.H., (1982) 'Transportation of horses by sea during the era of the Crusades, eighth century to 1285 AD', *Mariner's Mirror*, 68 (1982) pp. 9–27, 103–26.

Pryor, J.H., (1983a) 'The naval architecture of crusader transport ships: a reconstruction of some archetypes for round-hulled sailing ships', *Mariner's Mirror*, 69 (1983) pp. 171–219, 275–92, 363–86.

Pryor, J.H., (1983b) 'The naval battles of Roger de Lauria', *Journal of Medieval History*, 9 (1983) pp. 179–216.

Pryor, J.H., (1988) *Geography, technology and war: studies in the maritime history of the Mediterranean 649–1571* (Cambridge 1988).

Pryor, J.H., (1990) 'The naval architecture of Crusader transport ships and horse transports revisited', *Mariner's Mirror*, 74 (1990) pp. 255–72.

Pryor, J.H., (1992) 'The Crusade of Emperor Frederick II: 1220–29: the implications of the maritime evidence', *American Nepture*, 52 (1992) pp. 113–31.

Pryor, J.H., (1993) 'The galleys of Charles I of Anjou, King of Sicily ca.1269–84', *Studies in Medieval and Renaissance History*, 14 (1993) pp. 33–103.

Pryor, J.H., (2001) 'Water, water everywhere, Nor any drop to drink; Water supplies for the fleets of the First Crusade', in M. Balard (ed.), *Dei Gesta per Francos* (Aldershot 2001) pp. 21–8.

Psellus, M., (E.R.A. Sewter tr.), *Fourteen Byzantine Rulers* (London 1966).

Rackham, D.J., 'Appendix: skeleta; evidence of medieval horses from London sites', in J. Clark (ed.), *The Medieval Horse and its Equipment, c.1150–c.1450: Medieval Finds from Excavations in London, 5* (London 1995) pp. 169–74.

Radulfus Niger, (L. Schmugge ed.), *Radulfus Niger: De Re Militari et Triplici via Peregrinationis Ierosolimitane (1187/88)* (Berlin 1977).

Rady, M., 'The Mongol invasion of Hungary', *Medieval World*, 3 (November–December 1991) pp. 39–46.

Rausing, E., *The Bow; Some Notes on its Origins and Development. Acta Archaeologica Lundensia, VI* (Lund 1967).

Raymond d'Aguilers, (J.H. Hill & L.L. Hill trs.), *Raymond d'Aguilers: Historia Francorum Qui Ceperunt Iherusalem* (Philadelphia 1968).

Renn, D.F., (1971) 'A bowstave from Berkhamsted Castle', *Hertfordshire Archaeology* (1971) pp. 72–4.

Renn, D.F., (2004) 'Master Jordan, who made the King's trebuchet', *Arms & Armour: Journal of the Royal Armouries*, 1 (2004) pp. 25–32.

Richard, J., (1945) *Le Comté de Tripoli sous la Dynastie Toulousaine* (Paris 1945).

Richard, J., (1960) 'Les premiers missionaires latins en Ethiopie (XIIe–XIVe siècles)', in (anon. ed.), *Atti del Convegno di Studi Etiopici* (Rome 1960) pp. 323–9.

Richard, J., (1979a) 'Le peuplement Latin et Syrien en Chypre au XIIIe siècle', *Byzantinische Forschungen*, VII (1979) pp. 157–73.

Richard, J., (1979b) 'Les causes des victoires Mongoles d'après les historiens occidentaux du XIIIe siècle', *Central Asiatic Journal*, 23 (1979) pp. 104–17.

Richard, J., (1979c) *The Latin Kingdom of Jerusalem* (Oxford 1979).

Richard, J., (1986) 'Les Turcopoles: Musulmans convertes ou Chrétiens Orientaux?', *Revue des Etudes Islamiques*, 54 (1986) pp. 259–70.

Richard, J., (1995) 'L'acheminement par mer des croisades du XIIe siècle', paper read at *Journée d'archéologie marine, Paris* (1995).

Richard, J., (1998a) 'Les prisonniers et leur rachat au cours des croisades', I (anon. ed.), *121e Congrès National des Sociétés Savants. Hist. Scient. Nice 1996, Histoire médiévales – Fondations* (Paris 1998) pp. 63–73.

Richard, J., (1998b) *La Papauté et les Missions d'Orient au Moyen Age (XIIIe–XVe siècles)* (Rome 1998).

Richter, H., correspondence on a medieval crossbow stave from Bernau (21 March 2001).

Riley-Smith, J., (1967) *The Knights of St. John in Jerusalem and Cyprus, c.1050–1310* (London 1967).

Riley-Smith, J., (1973) *The Feudal Nobility and the Kingdom of Jerusalem 1174–1277* (London 1973).

Riley-Smith, J., (1978) 'Peace never established: the case of the Kingdom of Jerusalem', *Transactions of the Royal Historical Society*, 28 (1978) pp. 87–102.

Riley-Smith, J., (1986) *The First Crusade and the Idea of Crusading* (London 1986).

Riley-Smith, J., (1999) 'An Army on Pilgrimage', paper read at *Second International Conference on the First Crusade, University of Zaragoza-Huesca* (1999).

Rist, R., 'Papal policy and the Albigensian Crusades: continuity or change?' *Crusades*, 2 (2003) pp. 99–108.

Rivallain, J., 'The horse, the status mount of Africa', in D. Alexander (ed.), *Furusiyya, vol. 1. The Horse in the Art of the Near East* (Riyadh 1996) pp. 216–21.

Robbert, L.B., (1969) 'A Venetian naval expedition of 1224', in D. Herlily (et al. eds.), *Economy, Society and Government in Medieval Italy: Essays in Memory of Robert L. Reynolds* (Kent Ohio 1969) pp. 141–51.

Robbert, L.B., (1994) 'Money and prices in thirteenth century Venice', *Journal of Medieval History*, 20 (1994) pp. 373–90.

Robert, E., 'Guerre et fortification dans la Philippide de Guillaume le Breton: approches archéologiques', in G. De Boe & F. Verhaeghe (eds.), *Military Studies in Medieval Europe – Papers of the 'Medieval Europe Brugge 1997' Conference, vol. 11* (Zellik 1997) pp. 7–19.

Robert de Clari, (A. Pauphilet & E. Pognon eds.), 'La conquête de Constantinople', in *Historiens et Chroniqueurs du Moyen Age* (Paris 1952) pp. 1–81.

Rocca, E.N., 'La lapide tombale del Marchese Guido Pallavicino a Fontevivo (d.1301), Contributo agli studi sull'Ordin Cistercense e sull'Ordine dei Templari', *Archivio Storico per le Province Parmensi*, 6 (1954) pp. 79–86.

Rogers, R., *Latin Siege Warfare in the Twelfth Century* (Oxford 1992).

Rose, R.B., 'The native Christians of Jerusalem, 1187–1260', in B.D. Kedar (ed.), *The Horns of Hattin* (Jerusalem & London 1992) pp. 238–49.

Ross, D.J.A., 'The prince answers back, "Les Enseignemens de Théodore Paliologue", in C. Harper-Bill & R. Harvey (eds.), *The Ideals and Practice of Medieval Knighthood (papers from the first and second Strawberry Hill Conferences)* (Bury St, Edmunds 1986) pp. 165–77.

Rosser, J., (1985) 'Excavations at Saranda Kolones, Paphos, Cyprus, 1981–83', *Dumbarton Oaks Papers*, 39 (1985) pp. 81–97.

Rosser, J., (1986) 'Crusader castles of Cyprus', *Archaeology*, 39 (1986) pp. 40–7.

Rule, M. and Monaghan, J., *A Gallo-Roman Trading Vessel from Guernsey: The Excavation and Recovery of a Third Century Shipwreck* (St. Peter Port, Guernsey 1993).

Russell, J.C., 'Demographic factors of the Crusades', in V.P. Goss (et al. eds.), *The Meeting of Two Worlds: Cultural Exchange between East and West during the Period of the Crusades* (Kalamazoo 1986) pp. 53–8.

Salch, C.L., J. Burnouf & J.F. Finó, *L'Atlas des Châteaux Forts en France* (Strasbourg 1980).

Salibi, K.S., (1957) 'The Maronites of Lebanon under Frankish and Mamluk rule', *Arabica*, 4 (1957) pp. 288–303.

Savvides, A.G.C., (2000a) 'Can we refer to concerted action amongst Rapsomates, Caryces and the Emir Tzachas between A.D. 1091 and 1093?' *Byzantion*, 70 (2000) pp. 122–34.

Savvides, A.G.C., (2000b) 'Kilij Arslan I of Rum, Byzantines, Crusaders and Danishmandids A.D. 1092–1107', *Byzantina*, 21 (2000) pp. 365–77.

Scalini, M., 'Protezione e segno di distinzione: l'equippaggiamento difensivo del Duecento', in (anon. ed.), *Il sabato di San Barnaba* (Milan 1989) pp. 80–9.

Schlumberger, G., 'Deux chefs normands des armées byzantins au XIe siècle', *Revue Historique*, 16 (1881) pp. 289–303.

Schneidman, J.L., *The Rise of the Aragonese-Catalan Empire 1200–1350* (London 1970).

Schwarzer, J.K., (1988) 'The eleventh century weapons from Serçe Limani', paper read at *Third International Congress on Greek-Arabic Studies, Athens* (17–20 July 1988).

Schwarzer, J.K., (1991) 'Arms from an eleventh century shipwreck', *Graeco-Arabica*, 4 (1991) pp. 327–50.

Sebestyén. K. Cs., 'Bogen und pfeil der Alten Ungarn', *Dolgozakot*, 8 (1932) pp. 227–55.

Serdon, V., *Armes du Diable: Arcs et Arbalètes au Moyen Age* (Rennes 2005).

Şesan, M., 'La flotte byzantine à l'époque des Comnènes et des Anges (1081–1204)', *Byzantinoslavica*, 21 (1960) pp. 48–53.

Settia, A.A., *Comuni in guerra, Armi ed eserciti nell'Italia della citta* (Bologna 1993).

Shepard, J., (1973) 'The English and Byzantium: a study of their role in the Byzantine army in the later eleventh century', *Traditio*, 29 (1973) pp. 53–92.

Shepard, J., (1993) 'The uses of the Franks in eleventh-century Byzantium', *Anglo-Norman Studies*, 15 (1993) pp. 275–305.

Shot'ha Rust'haveli, (M.S. Wardrop tr.), *The Man in the Panther's Skin* (London 1912).

Siberry, E., *Criticism of Crusading 1095–1274* (Oxford 1985).

Sinclair, T., 'Byzantine and Islamic fortifications in the Middle East – the photographic exhibition', in S. Mitchell (ed.), *Armies and Frontiers in Roman and Byzantine Anatolia. British Archaeological Reports, Int. Series 156* (Oxford 1983) pp. 305–30.

Sivan, E., *L'Islam et la Croisade: Idéologie et propagande dans les réactions musulmanes aux croisades* (Paris 1968).

Smail, R.C., (1956) *Crusading Warfare, 1097–1193* (Cambridge 1956).

Smail, R.C., (1982) 'The predicaments of Guy of Lusignan, 1183–87', in B.Z. Kedar (ed.), *Outremer, Studies in the History of the Crusading Kingdom of Jerusalem presented to Joshua Prawer* (Jerusalem 1982) pp. 159–76.

Smbat, (G. Dédéyan tr.), *La Chronique Attribué au Connétable Smbat* (Paris 1980).

Soler del Campo, A., (1986a) 'Aportacion al estudio de armamento medieval: un lote de piezas fechadas entre los siglos X–XIII', in (anon. ed.), *I Congreso de Arqueología Medieval Española (Huesca 1985)* (Zaragoza 1986) pp. 313–29.

Soler del Campo, A., (1986b) 'El armamento medieval hispano', *Cuadernos de Investigacion Medieval*, 3 (1986) pp. 1–51.

Soler del Campo, A., (1986c) 'Sistemas de combate en la iconografia mozárabe y andalusi altomedieval', *Boletín de la Asociación Española de Orientalistas*, 22 (1986) pp. 61–87.

Soler del Campo, A., (1993) *La evolucion del armamento medieval en el reino castellano-leonés y Al-Andalus* (Madrid 1993).

Sourdel-Thomine, J., 'Burdj: military architecture in the Islamic Middle East', in *Encyclopedia of Islam, volume 1*, 2nd edition (Leiden 1960) 1315–1318.

Spinei, V., (1974) 'Antichitatile nomazilor turanici din Molova în primul sfert al mileniului al II-lea', *Studii si cercetari do Istorie veche si Arheologi*, 25 (1974) pp. 389–415.

Spinei, V., (1986) *Moldavia in the 11th–14th centuries* (Bucharest 1986).

Ştefanescu, Ş., 'Considerations sur l'histoire militaire roumaine aux IIIe–XIVe siècles', in Al. Gh. Savu (ed.), *Pages de l'histoire de l'armée Roumaine* (Bucharest 1976) pp. 36–52.

Stern, S.M., 'An original document from the Fatimid Chancery concerning Italian merchants', in (anon. ed.), *Studi Orientalistici in Onore di Giorgio Levi della Vida* (Rome 1956) pp. 529–38.

Subotic, V., (ed.), *Guide, Military Museum* (Belgrade n.d.).

Subrenat, J., *Etude sur Gaydon: Chanson de Geste du XIIIe siècle* (Marseilles 1974).

Sullivan, D., 'Tenth century Byzantine offensive siege warfare: instructional prescriptions and historical practice', in K. Tsiknakis (ed.), *Byzantium at War (9th–12th c.)*, (Athens 1997) pp. 179–200.

Sumption, J., *The Abigensian Crusade* (London 1978).

Tabacco, G., 'Il regno italico nei secoli IX–XI', in (anon. ed.), *Ordinamenti militari in Occidente nell'alto medioevo. Settimane di Studio del Centro Italiano di Studi sull'alto Medioevo, XV/2* (Spoleto 1968) pp. 763–90.

Taviani-Carozzi, H., *La principauté lombarde de Salerne, IXe–XIe Siècle, Pouvoir et Société en Italie lombarde méridionale* (Rome 1991).

Taylor, A., (1974) 'Three early castle sites in Italy: Motta Camastra, Sperlinga and Petralia Soprana', *Château Gaillard*, 7 (1974) pp. 209–11.

Taylor, A., (1989) 'Master Bertram: Ingeniator Regis', in C. Harper-Bill (et al. eds.), *Studies in Medieval History presented to R. Allan-Brown* (Woodbridge 1989) pp. 289–304.

Tempany, T.W., 'The arbalest or crossbow', *Notes and Queries*, 10th ser., III (1904) pp. 443–4.

Thordeman, B., *Armour from the Battle of Wisby 1361* (Uppsala 1939).

Toumanoff, C., 'Armenia and Georgia', in J.M. Hussey (ed.), *The Cambridge Medieval History, vol. IV. The Byzantine Empire part I. Byzantium and its Neighbours* (Cambridge 1966) pp. 593–637.

Troso, M., *Le Armi in Asta delle Fanterie Europeen (1000–1500)* (Novara 1988).

Tucci, U., 'La navigazione Veneziana nel Duecento e nel primo Trecento a la sue evoluzione tecnica', in A. Pertusi (ed.), *Venezia e il Levante Fino al Secolo XV* (Florence 1973) pp. 821–41.

Tyerman, C., 'Who went on Crusades to the Holy Land?', in B.Z. Kedar (ed.), *The Horns of Hattin* (Jerusalem 1992) pp. 13–26.

Unger, R.W., *The Ship in the Mediterranean Economy 600–1600* (London 1980).

Usamah Ibn Munqidh, (1929) (P.K. Hitti tr.), *The Memoirs of an Arab-Syrian Gentleman* (Princeton 1929; reprint Beirut 1964).

Usamah Ibn Munqidh, (1930) (P.K. Hitti ed.), *Kitab al-I'tibar* (Princeton 1930).

Valdés Fernández, 'Ciudadela y fortificación urbana: el case de Badajoz', in A. Bazzana (ed.), *Castrum III* (Madrid 1988) pp. 143–52.

Vale, M.G.A., 'The Gascon nobility and the Anglo-French War, 1294–98', in J. Gillingham & J.C. Holt (eds.), *War and Government in the Middle Ages: Essays in Honour of J.O. Prestwich* (Cambridge 1984) pp. 134–46.

Vann, T.M., 'Twelfth Century castile and its frontier strategies', in D. Kagay & L.J.A. Villalon (eds.), *The Circle of War in the Middle Ages* (Woodbridge 1999) pp. 21–31.

Vasiliev, A.A., (1934–50) *Byzance et les Arabes* (Brussels 1934–1950).

Vasiliev, A.A., (1952) *A History of the Byzantine Empire* (London 1952).

Verbruggen, J.F., (1947) 'La tactique militaire des armées de chevaliers', *Revue du Nord*, 29 (1947) pp. 161–80.

Verbruggen, J.F., (1977a) 'De Goedendag', *Militaria Belgica*, 3 (1977) pp. 65–70.

Verbruggen, J.F., (1977b) *The Art of Warfare in Western Europe during the Middle Ages* (Oxford 1977).

Verbruggen, J.F., (2005) (K. De Vries tr.), 'The role of cavalry in medieval warfare', *Journal of Medieval Military History*, 3 (2005) pp. 46–71.

Villehardouin, (1921) (F. Marzials tr.), *Memoirs of the Crusades by Villehardouin and de Joinville* (London 1921) pp. 1–133.

Villehardouin, (1952) 'La conquête de Constantinople', (A. Pauphilet & E. Pognon eds.), in *Historiens et Chroniquers du Moyen Age* (Paris 1952) pp. 89–194

Voisin, J-C., 'Le Moyen-Orient des fortifications: espace d'échanges entre Byzantins, Arabo-musulmans et Occidentaux du Moyen Age', in N. Faucherre (et al. eds.), *La Fortification au Temps des Croisades* (Rennes 2004) pp. 313–29.

Vryonis, S., (1967) *Byzantium and Europe* (London 1967).

Vryonis, S., (1971) *The Decline of Medieval Hellenism in Asia Minor and the Process of Islamization from the Eleventh through the Fifteenth Century* (Berkeley 1971).

Vryonis, S., (1975) 'Byzantine and Turkish societies and their sources of manpower', in V.J. Parry & M.E. Yapp (eds.), *War, Technology and Society in the Middle East* (London 1975) pp. 125–52.

Waley, D.P., (1954) 'Combined operations in Sicily, AD 1060–78', *Papers of the British School at Rome*, 22 (1954) pp. 118–25.

Waley, D.P., (1975) 'Condotte and condottieri in the thirteenth century', *Proceedings of the British Academy* (1975) pp. 337–71.

Walker, J.M., 'The Saracens in the Thirteenth-Century Chansons de Geste and Romances' (MA thesis, London University 1961).

Walker, R.F., 'The Anglo-Welsh Wars, 1217–1267: with special reference to English Military Developments' (D Phil thesis, Oxford University 1954).

Walter the Chancellor (Asbridge, T.S. and Edgington, S.B. (tr.), *Walter the Chancellor's The Antiochene Wars* (Aldershot 1999).

Welsby, D.A., 'Recent work at Soba East in Central Sudan', *Azania*, 18 (1983) pp. 165–80.

Whitney, E., 'The Mechanical Arts in the Context of Twelfth and Thirteenth Century Thought' (PhD thesis, City University of New York 1985).

Whittow, M., 'How the East was lost: the background to the Komnenian Reconquista', in M. Mullett (ed.), *Alexios I Komnenos. Belfast Byzantine Texts and Translations 4* (Belfast 1996) pp. 56–67.

Wiet, G., 'Les relations égypto-abyssines sous les sultans Mamlouks', *Bulletin de la Société d'archéologie copte*, 4 (1938) pp. 115–40.

William of Rubruck, (1900) (W.W. Rockhill tr.), 'The Journey of William of Rubruck', in W.W. Rockhill (ed.), *The Journey of William of Rubruck to the Eastern Parts of the World 1253–55, as narrated by himself, with two accounts of the earlier journey by John of Pian de Carpine* (London 1900) pp. 40–283.

William of Rubruck, (1955) (C. Dawson tr.), 'The Journey of William of Rubruck', in C. Dawson (ed.), *The Mongol Mission* (London 1955).

William of Rubruck, (1990) (P. Jackson tr.), *The Mission of Friar William of Rubruck: His Journey to the Court of the Great Khan Möngke 1253–1255* (London 1990).

Williams, J., 'The making of a Crusade: the Genoese anti-Muslim attacks in Spain, 1146–8', *Journal of Medieval History*, 23 (1997) pp. 29–53.

Wolff, P., *Regards sur le Midi médiéval* (Toulouse 1978).

Wozniak, F.E., 'Tmutarakan: Khanate of', in J.R. Strayer (ed.), *Dictionary of the Middle Ages, vol. 12* (New York 1989) p. 66.

Yarnley, C.J., 'Byzantine Relations with the Armenians in the Eleventh Century, with special reference to Cilicia' (B Litt thesis, Oxford University 1972).

Yarrison, J.L., 'Force as an Instrument of Policy: European Military Incursions and Trade in the Maghrib, 1000–1355' (PhD thesis, Princeton University 1982).

Zakythinos, D.A., *Le Despotat grec de Morée: Vie et institutions* (London 1975).

Zozaya, J., (1988) 'Evolocíón de un yacimiento: el castillo de Gormaz (Soria)', in A. Bazzana (ed.), *Guerre, Fortification et Habitat dans le Monde Méditerranéen au Moyen Age, Actes du colloque Guerre, habitat et fortification au Moyen Age (Madrid 1985), Castrum III* (Madrid 1988) pp. 173–8.

Index